Exceptionally Queer

Exceptionally Queer

Mormon Peculiarity and U.S. Nationalism

K. MOHRMAN

UNIVERSITY OF MINNESOTA PRESS

MINNEAPOLIS • LONDON

The University of Minnesota Press gratefully acknowledges the financial assistance provided for the publication of this book by the University of Colorado Denver.

Published by the University of Minnesota Press
111 Third Avenue South, Suite 290
Minneapolis, MN 55401-2520
http://www.upress.umn.edu

ISBN 978-1-5179-1128-7 (hc)
ISBN 978-1-5179-1129-4 (pb)

A Cataloging-in-Publication record for this book is available from the Library of Congress.

Printed in the United States of America on acid-free paper

The University of Minnesota is an equal-opportunity educator and employer.

31 30 29 28 27 26 25 24 23 22   10 9 8 7 6 5 4 3 2 1

Contents

Introduction

Peculiar, Exceptional, Queer

But ye are a chosen generation, a royal priesthood, an holy nation, a peculiar people.

    —1 Peter 2:9 (KJV)

No doubt [Mormonism] was and is a unique faith, but it is also uniquely American. It was born at a peculiar moment in the history of the United States, and it bears the marks of that birth.

    —Gordon Wood, "Evangelical America and
       Early Mormonism"

Queerness has its own exceptionalist desires: exceptionalism is a founding impulse, indeed the very core of a queerness that claims itself as an anti-, trans-, or unidentity. . . . We have less understanding of queerness as a biopolitical project, one that both parallels and intersects with that of multiculturalism [and] the ascendancy of whiteness. . . . Queerness as transgression . . . relies on a normative notion of deviance, always defined in relation to normativity, often universalizing. Thus deviance, despite its claims to freedom and individuality, is ironically cohered to and by regulatory regimes of queerness—through, not despite, any claims to transgression.

    —Jasbir Puar, *Terrorist Assemblages*

Illuminated by a single spotlight, Elder Price belts out "I Believe," one of several hit songs from the record-breaking musical *The Book of Mormon*. The audience begins to laugh first nervously and then hysterically as he breaks into the chorus: "I believe that ancient Jews built boats and sailed to America! / . . . I believe [God's] plan involves me getting my own planet! / . . .

I

I believe that in 1978 God changed his mind about Black people! / . . . I believe that God lives on a planet called Kolob! / . . . I believe that the Garden of Eden was in Jackson County, Missouri!"¹ Regardless of whether the audience understands the specific historical or theological references made in these lyrics—from the ancient history recounted in the Book of Mormon, to the power of revelation to change The Church of Jesus Christ of Latter-day Saints' racist policies, to beliefs regarding divinity, preexistence, and U.S. exceptionalism—their humor is not lost on listeners.² Elder Price's statements are a select, but revealing, sample of the beliefs that non-Mormons have questioned and ridiculed for almost two centuries. Like *The Book of Mormon,* most contemporary texts that engage Mormonism, such as *South Park*'s "All about Mormons" episode, Tony Kushner's acclaimed play *Angels in America,* and hit television shows like HBO's fictional *Big Love,* TLC's *Sister Wives,* and Bravo's *The Real Housewives of Salt Lake City,* invoke a notion of Mormons and Mormonism as enigmatically peculiar, whether it be for comic effect, as a foil, or simply for high ratings.³ But emphasis on the strangeness of Mormons and Mormonism is not just a contemporary phenomenon. In fact, Mormonism has been contested in U.S. popular culture and politics ever since the founding of the Latter-day Saint tradition in the early nineteenth century, a history that is recounted in the following chapters. *The Book of Mormon* is merely one of the most recent and visible in a long line of cultural texts that trades on an enduring but, until now, unnamed discourse, which I call Mormon peculiarity.

Mormon peculiarity is a performative discourse that does not merely describe but constructs Mormonism as its object, characterizing that object as inherently odd, unique, or strange. Saints and non-Mormons, scholars and lay people alike have accepted and reiterated the idea of Mormon peculiarity over the course of Mormonism's almost two-hundred-year history, even as the substance and meaning of that peculiarity has changed over time. The concept emerged alongside the birth of the Latter-day Saint tradition in the 1830s, when the term *Mormonite* was coined by anti-Mormon writers wary of the new belief system, a term that soon evolved into the more familiar expression *Mormon.*⁴ Originally used as pejorative, and at first rejected by the Saints as ignorant and misguided, *Mormon* soon took hold on a much wider scale. By 1831, if not before, Mormonites or Mormons were regularly described as "ignorant," "dupes," "silly sheep," "fanatical," and "degraded," but above all, "strange."⁵

While the early development and usage of these terms by anti-Mormons was meant to signal a distinctly negative difference, the Saints were quick to counter such descriptions with their own religious, and more positive, explanation for outsiders' perception of Mormonism as peculiar—a perception that the Saints, not incidentally, shared with non-Mormons. Over the first four decades of Mormonism's growth (in an early foreshadowing of the remarkably successful twenty-first-century "I'm a Mormon" marketing campaign),[6] leaders used the popular descriptors *Mormon* and *Mormonism* as entry points for educating the masses about the Latter-day Saint faith, often placing the terms in scare quotes to indicate their vernacular and derogatory origins.[7] Brigham Young, the second president of The Church of Jesus Christ of Latter-day Saints, along with other Church leaders, regularly expounded on the faith's "peculiar" reputation. He explained that "the people called 'Mormons' by the world have a peculiarity about them that is understood by very few" and pointed to the Saints' beliefs in "the Gospel of salvation—the Priesthood of the Son of God . . . [and the] principles of eternal existence by which the worlds are and were" to explain their purported peculiarity.[8]

As Young's explanation indicates, the Saints have proudly presented themselves as peculiar in a truly religious sense: *peculiar* in Mormon theology does not denote otherness or oddness but singles out its subject as unique or special.[9] In their own estimation, what makes the Saints peculiar is the fact that they are God's chosen people, that He revealed and restored to them, through Joseph Smith and the Book of Mormon, the priesthood, the nature of existence, and the path to divine exaltation, making them seem strange to nonbelievers. For followers of the Latter-day Saint tradition, then, biblical references to God's chosen or peculiar people—such as Peter's declaration that "ye are a chosen generation, a royal priesthood, an holy nation, a peculiar people" and Moses's pronouncement in Deuteronomy that "the Lord hath chosen thee to be a peculiar people unto himself, above all the nations that are upon the earth"—do not refer to either Jews or Christians generally or metaphorically but are instead taken as explicit references to the Saints' special status as direct descendants of the Tribes of Israel and therefore as the rightful custodians of the original Christian Church as revealed by Jesus Christ.[10]

Since the 1830s, Church leaders have spun the derogatory identification of the Saints as Mormons into an opportunity to promote the theological

distinctiveness of their faith, even interpreting anti-Mormon persecution
as evidence that, like the Jews of the Old Testament, they are God's elect
people. But while early Church leaders argued that the Saints' peculiarity
sprung from divine mandate, which directly guided their efforts to build
up the Kingdom of God on Earth, nineteenth-century anti-Mormons simultaneously represented Mormons first as heretical, fanatical, and delusional
and then, even more potently, as despotic patriarchs whose licentious and
depraved desires produced a degenerative and barbarous racial stock. In
contrast, twentieth-century articulations of Mormon peculiarity—by both
the Saints themselves and non-Mormon commentators—shifted drastically to resignify Mormonism as a benign, religious oddity and a legitimate
faith that was admirable for its promotion of normative sexual, gendered,
and economic practices and even exceptional in the high percentage of
Saints who adhered to those norms. More recently, in the wake of the
national LGBTQ civil rights movement, Mormon peculiarity discourse
has framed Mormonism as a hopelessly homophobic and backward religion, situating the Church as a foil against which the U.S. nation-state is
represented as accepting and tolerant of sexual diversity in contrast. This
book explores these varying, and often contradictory, articulations of Mormon peculiarity to expose Mormonism as a potent and productive assemblage and not as an inherent aspect of Latter-day Saint religion, culture, or
history.

The popular conception that Mormonism is innately peculiar has been
paralleled in Mormon studies, American studies, and U.S. history scholarship, helping to ensure that the discourse has gone perennially unnoticed
as a discourse. Analyses of Mormonism's place in U.S. history and culture have relied on what might be called "the peculiarity thesis" to interpret and explain its emergence, development, and relationship to broader
social and political patterns. The peculiarity thesis has been variously used
to argue that Mormonism is simply different or distinctive from other religious traditions or cultures in the nation; that it is unique or even anom-
alous in the recorded patterns of U.S. (religious) history; or that it is
so exceptionally enigmatic that it eludes proper historical explanation.
This work often takes one of two tacks, arguing either that intrinsic differences have always existed between Mormons and other Americans or
that Mormons are typical, even model Americans. The problem with this
approach is not only that it disproportionately emphasizes differences over
similarities to the exclusion of other interpretive possibilities but that it

reifies "Mormon" and "American" as distinct and stable social and political categories with definite and identifiable attributes. If, as this book asserts, Mormon peculiarity is a historically significant and persistent discursive construction with material effects, then uncritically promoting that discourse does not merely describe but (re)produces the very effects that such scholarship seeks to explain. Thus, this project's driving questions ask when and why Mormonism, Mormons, and the beliefs and practices associated with them have been represented and accepted as inherently peculiar, how this peculiarity has become naturalized as an essential characteristic of Mormonism, and most importantly, what the effects of this naturalization process are.

A typical expression of the peculiarity thesis is prominent Mormon studies scholar Jan Shipps's description of Mormonism as a "peculiarly American minority faith" that is "distinctive, even unique" in U.S. (religious) history.[11] Similar are rhetorician Brett Lunceford's contention that "unlike most other religious practices in the United States, Mormonism is a distinctly American religion" and historian Gordon Wood's claim that there is "no doubt [Mormonism] was and is a unique faith, but [that] it is also uniquely American . . . born at a peculiar moment in the history of the United States, . . . bear[ing] the mark of that birth."[12] As characteristic expressions of the peculiarity thesis, it is notable that Shipps's, Lunceford's, and Wood's statements all tie Mormonism's so-called peculiarity to its national origins, suggesting that the religion's uniqueness—whether it is seen as a faith or as an ethnic group—is derived from its heritage in the nineteenth-century United States. This use of peculiarity as an interpretive and explicatory framework for analyzing Mormon history mimics, and is in fact part and parcel of, the exceptionalist paradigm in the study of U.S. history and culture.[13] While many scholarly examinations of U.S. history have touted the nation's religious dimensions as particularly notable, even suggesting that they are at the core of the nation's "exceptional" character, explaining Mormonism's peculiarity as a result of its U.S. birth flips that thinking on its head, framing the religion's apparent uniqueness as a product of being born in and from an exceptional nation.[14] The classification of Mormonism as both essentially peculiar and peculiarly American is paradoxical, though perhaps not unsurprising, in the context of a tradition that views U.S. history as "'essentially the history of one long millenarian movement'" in which Americans have considered themselves "'God's chosen [people], leading the world to perfection.'"[15]

U.S. exceptionalism does not merely describe its subject but actively produces it, presenting the U.S. nation-state and its citizens as unique, exemplary, and, increasingly since World War I, specially and justifiably exempt from certain international standards and regulations. While the form, meaning, and usages of U.S. exceptionalism have changed over time, its foundations in Puritan Massachusetts, by way of Tudor England, shed important light not only on the emergence of the Latter-day Saint tradition itself but also on Mormon peculiarity as a particularly potent version of U.S. exceptionalism. As Deborah L. Madsen chronicles, the exceptionalist logic of the Massachusetts Bay Puritan colonists, led by John Winthrop, included many of the defining elements of U.S. exceptionalist discourse recognizable today. The popularly held "belief that England was God's elect nation and Elizabeth [I] His appointed servant to transform the nation into a new Israel" was transported to North America by the Puritan colonists, fundamentally influencing their own assertions that their "errand into the wilderness" was divinely sanctioned.[16] Specifically, they believed that they had been chosen by God as a community to reestablish the true Church in the so-called New World, thereby serving as a model for the world's salvation—a model so excellent that it would even facilitate Christ's Second Coming. The Puritans believed that as a model church theirs would be a beacon of hope to other Christians worldwide, inspiring a global return to the original Christian Church. These beliefs resonate deeply with contemporary claims that the establishment of the United States was divinely inspired, that it is a model for other nations, and that it serves as an inspiration for, even a savior of, other peoples worldwide.

The Puritan certainty that theirs was an exceptional mission undertaken as an elect community—so famously articulated by Winthrop as "a city upon a hill" and later embellished by Ronald Reagan as a "shining city upon a hill"—is one that was transmuted and adopted by the emergent U.S. nation-state.[17] Over the course of the eighteenth century, Puritan notions of exceptionalism continued to dominate the colonial mindset but were subtly altered to reflect the economic and political values of what became a new country. Republican government, and not just religious community, was increasingly spoken of as a divinely mandated organization that would facilitate the deliverance of God's chosen people.[18] Central figures to the founding of the nation, such as Benjamin Franklin, argued that Providence, a Puritan concept denoting God's intervention in human affairs, had dictated the creation of a secular republic "purified of the corruption of European politics and a social structure based on inherited title" that would become an example for the rest of the world.[19]

A successor of the Puritan tradition, Mormonism shares many of the same ideas and ideals that the original colonists propounded, including a belief in the divine inspiration for the Puritans' immigration, the (re)establishment of the pure and uncorrupted Christian Church on the North American continent, and its facilitation of Christ's return. Essentially, the Saints identify themselves, like the Puritans, "as latter-day Israelites occupying the New Canaan by divine decree."[20] Importantly, this sense of themselves as a divinely elected people, advancing the original Church of Christ, is also deeply grounded in their own religious explanations for U.S. exceptionalism. Unlike U.S. Protestantism, Mormon views about the nation's so-called exceptional qualities arise from Mormon scripture and theology, which identify the "American continent" as the site for the New Jerusalem and interpret the creation of the nation, specifically a representative government that ensures religious liberty, as the necessary condition for the establishment of a new Zion.[21] Thus, the Saints' exceptionalist views about the nation are intertwined with their own knowledge of themselves as a "peculiar" or "chosen" people.

As a potent articulation of U.S. exceptionalism, Mormon peculiarity has frequently been central to shaping notions of Americanness—particularly, although certainly not exclusively, through the production of sexual and racial normativity—that have motivated and justified the biased, exclusionary, and colonialist policies and practices of the U.S. nation-state. Put another way, *Exceptionally Queer* examines how both political and cultural representations and affective experiences of Mormonism's purported peculiarity—from nineteenth-century battles over polygamy and its alleged effects on racial development, to accounts of the Church's emphases on "individual responsibility" and "family values" as laudatory examples of racial citizenship, to the recent legal and cultural contestation over same-sex and plural marriage—have often been central to, and in fact are indicative of, the processes of othering through which "Americanness" has been defined as white, Protestant, capitalist, and heteronormative, thereby entrenching racial nationalism in the service of U.S. empire. In so doing, the book highlights how Mormonism, which often appears as an outlier or anomaly on the U.S. historical and cultural landscape, has actually played a pivotal, and in some cases ongoing, role in determining debates over religious freedom, the regularization of capitalism as the inevitable and most

ethical economic system, the naturalization of gender binarism, the institutionalization of heteronormativity, and processes of racial formation,
colonialist practice, and imperial policy.

Over the last twenty years, a gradual but steadily growing body of Mormon studies scholarship attentive to the discursive construction of Mormonism has emerged.[22] Unsurprisingly, this scholarship has focused largely
on what nineteenth-century discourse about Mormonism reveals about
the nation's claims to religious liberty, particularly interrogating the validity of assertions that the United States has made good on its guarantee of
the free exercise of religion. These studies, like Kathleen Flake's *The Politics of American Religious Identity* and Peter Coviello's *Make Yourselves Gods*,
highlight popular cultural constructions of Mormons as others in order to
expose the implicitly "Protestant shape" of the United States' constitutional
order, as well as the disciplinary power of biopolitical secularism, which
forced the Church to alter its system of "bad belief" in order to survive, let
alone gain the privileged protections of "religious freedom."[23] Many, if not
most, of these studies focus on the controversy over nineteenth-century
Mormon plural marriage and its place in defining national identity, as well
as U.S. citizenship and law. For example, Sarah Barringer Gordon's work
examines how legal battles over Mormon polygamy were key to the institutionalization of a distinctly Protestant notion of disestablishment and
freedom of religion through constitutional jurisprudence, while Christine
Talbot convincingly argues that polygamy was a challenge not simply to
the sexual and marital mores of the Victorian-era United States but more
broadly to the gendered public/private divide that was becoming essential
to notions of Americanness at that time.[24]

Despite the predominately racial nature of popular representations of
Mormonism during this period, only two major works primarily tackle the
racial dimensions of nineteenth-century discourse about it. Both W. Paul
Reeve's *Religion of a Different Color* and Max Perry Mueller's *Race and the
Making of the Mormon People* demonstrate that "rather than being an anomaly in frontier history, the Mormons helped to define America's racial and
religious identity."[25] However, very few scholars have addressed Mormonism's racial dynamics in the twentieth and twenty-first centuries, reflecting
a general pattern of substantially less attention paid to twentieth-century
Mormonism. Important exceptions to this pattern are J. B. Haws's *The
Mormon Image in the American Mind,* which bookends his examination of
the "process through which the meaning of 'Mormon' has taken shape"

with the political campaigns of George Romney in the 1960s and those of his son Mitt Romney fifty years later, as well as Brenda R. Weber's *Latter-day Screens*, which provides a thorough overview of mediated Mormonism in the late twentieth and early twenty-first centuries.[26]

But despite interest in analyzing how and why Mormonism has been represented and discussed, many, if not all, of these studies nonetheless retain an attachment to the notion of Mormon peculiarity as a fundamental essence rather than a discursive formation. For example, standing in contrast to his argument that the meaning of *Mormon* has shifted over time, Haws insists that "the challenge before [the Saints] has been to navigate the American mainstream as a 'peculiar,' but not 'pariah' people."[27] In the same vein, Terryl Givens's statement that it is a "mistaken impression that categories like 'Christian' or 'American,' and the identities they imply, are objective realities, outside of negotiation or manipulation, rather than the products of political conflict and ideological construction" sharply contrasts with his assertion that there is "'something peculiar to Mormonism'" and that "that something *does* bring the church [*sic*] out of the religious sphere."[28] This attachment to Mormon peculiarity is also reflected in more critical scholarship on Mormonism, most obviously in Coviello's argument that early Mormons were peculiar in their "deviant carnality," making them "queer," a "queerness" that he claims "adheres to [Mormons] even now."[29]

Both building off and amending this work, this study provides a more comprehensive picture through a consideration of "peculiarity" as a historically consistent organizing framework that continues to define interpretations, representations, and experiences of Mormonism today. Rather than focus exclusively on Mormonism in the nineteenth century, which gives the mistaken impression that Mormon peculiarity is a purely historical discourse that disappeared after the Church formally renounced the notoriously "peculiar" practice of plural marriage in 1890, the book also scrutinizes instantiations of Mormonism-as-peculiar in the twentieth and twenty-first centuries. Although Mormon peculiarity discourse is most obviously identified in the nineteenth-century conflict between the Saints and anti-Mormons, it has continued to articulate and define Mormonism in relation to Americanness well after 1890, evidenced by its consistent reappearance at the center of U.S. popular and political culture. Just take these few examples: between the 1930s and the 1950s, both federal officials and the national press praised the Church's new welfare program and its

commitment to family as an exceptional model for the nation; during the
1960s, 1970s, and early 1980s, press coverage of the Church's restrictions
on Black people's and women's membership was, paradoxically, used to
undercut calls for social and political change related to race and gender;
fervor over the Church's influence in gay marriage referenda in the 1990s
and the early 2000s was portrayed as an example of Mormonism's exces-
sively strong influence over both its adherents and political processes; both
of Mitt Romney's presidential campaigns elicited renewed interest in the
supposed strangeness of Mormonism; and, most recently, popular reality
TV series, such as *Sister Wives* on TLC and *Escaping Polygamy* on A&E, portray Mormon polygamy as an entertaining curiosity.[30] These examples illustrate the malleable ways that Mormonism has been portrayed as peculiar,
as well as the centrality of not only religion but race, sexuality, gender, and
class to those representations.

Unfortunately, most scholarly studies of Mormonism have attempted
to segregate religious, racial, sexual, gendered, and classed representations
and experiences of Mormonism from one another. Such one-dimensional
(and occasionally two-dimensional) analyses have resulted in a picture of
Mormon history and culture that is not only flat but also incomplete. The
problem with scholarly frameworks that approach social categories as set,
discrete, or immutable is that they not only dismiss the material effects of
discourse but obscure how those categories are elaborated in and through
relationship to one another. To give just one example, depictions of Mormons as "Oriental" in the nineteenth century were not solely racial. Such
representations communicated their racial significance, in part, through
references to gendered relations and sexual practices, among others. In
one typical account, respected academic and anti-Mormon commentator
Francis Lieber argues that "'wedlock, or monogamic [*sic*] marriage'" as
the ideal gendered and sexual relation between men and women "'is one
of the elementary distinctions . . . between [the] European and Asiatic'"
races.[31] Lieber's contention that one's choice of marital practice is in fact a
racial signifier is a pointed example of how social formations—especially
race, sexuality, and gender—cohere and attain meaning through their relationship to one another. Indeed, during the early period of anti-Mormonism
when Lieber's comments were made, the linkages drawn between racial
identity, sexual practices, and religious belief were intimately tied to the
state's commitment to a racial, colonialist nationalism. Another example
can be found in an 1855 *Putnam's Monthly* article about Mormonism that

declares monogamy "one of the preexisting conditions of our existence as civilized white men. . . . Strike it out, and you destroy our very being, and when we say *our* we mean our race—a race which has its great and broad destiny, a solemn aim in the great career of civilization."[32]

Accordingly, this study uses queer of color critique, based as it is in women of color feminisms, alongside critical ethnic and Native studies frameworks and various strains of anticolonial critique—such as comparative racialization, critical race theory, and postcolonial and decolonial theories of the colonial relation to power—in order to scrutinize various social formations at "the intersections of race, gender, sexuality, and class" *as well as* religion "with particular interest in how those formations correspond with and diverge from nationalist ideals and practices."[33] Because Mormonism's apparent strangeness has been consistently linked to sets of interrelated practices that touch on religion, race, sex, gender, family, economy, and governance (sometimes one practice encompasses all these components, such as polygamy), the book emphasizes and analyzes how the articulations of Mormon peculiarity have operated as a critical method of racialization in the service of biopolitical nationalism and empire in the United States.[34] Most frequently, although certainly not exclusively, these articulations come in the form of gender and sexual exceptionalism. American, feminist, postcolonial, and sexuality studies scholars have identified gender and sexual exceptionalism as important strains of U.S. exceptionalist discourse that assert a nation's or group's superior racial status through claims to advanced knowledge about, or engagement in, evolved gendered and sexual roles, relationships, and practices.[35]

For the most part, analyses of gender and sexual exceptionalism have almost exclusively focused on the post-9/11 United States and Europe.[36] Postcolonial and transnational feminist scholarship, for example, has critiqued mainstream feminist narratives of "saving" Muslim women from Muslim men specifically, and Islamic religion and culture more generally (very often articulated as a critique of veiling practices), as a modern illustration of gender exceptionalism discourse. While gender exceptionalism's colonialist history has helped scholars to expose its more recent neocolonial and modern imperial instantiations, sexual exceptionalism has been represented as, or has at least been assumed to be, a relatively recent discursive construction with the rise of what Jasbir Puar coined "homonationalism."[37] Puar defines U.S. sexual exceptionalism as a contemporary nationalist discourse that temporarily acknowledges and embraces certain queer subjects for the purpose of framing the United States as a tolerant, progressive, and therefore potentially liberating society.[38] She argues that the seeming progressiveness of tolerance or acceptance of same-sex sexuality in the United States, for example, has been used to distinguish the nation-state as sexually, and by extension racially and religiously, exceptional in contrast to Islamic nations that are presumed to be inherently homophobic—a distinction that has been subsequently used to rationalize, alongside other justifications, military intervention in Southwest Asia. While Puar's conceptualization of sexual exceptionalism has been taken up in analyses of the war on terror in U.S. and European contexts, almost no scholarship has examined its history or potential genealogies. One important exception is Hiram Pérez's examination of the "tacit, if complex, participation of gay modernity in U.S. imperialist expansion."[39] Pérez argues that the modern gay male subject has been central, not peripheral, to U.S. and European national projects of war and colonialism since the late Victorian era, specifically as an incidental agent of imperialism through leisure, consumerism, and travel.

While Pérez's work moves beyond the twenty-first-century focus of U.S. sexual exceptionalism scholarship, it maintains an exclusive emphasis on the contingent inclusion of certain homosexual subjects. This emphasis is shifted somewhat in Coviello's consideration of early Mormon theology and practice where he concludes that nineteenth-century "Mormons are America's own exemplars of a sort of protohomonationalism . . . in inchoate form and moving toward solidarity in tandem with the becoming-hegemonic of a new style of political liberalism." In other words, Coviello argues that "homonationalism has a history as long as, and longer than, homosexuality—and the Mormons are that history."[40] Indeed, I, like Coviello, argue that Mormon history does reveal quite a bit about the (racial) history of sexuality in the United States, especially how earlier hegemonic binaries predated and helped to form later ones (specifically, monogamy versus polygamy's relationship to heterosexuality versus homosexuality). Examining earlier versions of sexual exceptionalism discourse, specifically in this case in relation to Mormonism, is incredibly helpful for understanding and explaining later versions of the discourse, homonationalism in particular. However, unlike Coviello, I stop short of taking (early) Mormonism as queer because doing so runs a paradoxical, yet real, risk of reifying rather than critically disassembling not only the heterosexual/homosexual binary, which has characterized queer theory's Western centricity, but also U.S. exceptionalism.[41]

Thus, as my definitions of gender and sexual exceptionalism attest, this project takes a necessarily broader view of both discourses to encompass multiple knowledges, formations, and assemblages of sex and gender. Put another way, while homosexual subjects and same-sex sexuality more generally have certainly been lightning rods around which modern societies have come to define sexual normativity, other forms of sexual subjectivity, modes of sexual practice, and knowledges of sex and sexuality have been and continue to be central in creating and maintaining hierarchical relations between and within racialized nation-states. Therefore, the following chapters highlight gender and sexual exceptionalism not as solely modern expressions of U.S. exceptionalism but as ones that have existed since well before the 1850s, when anti-Mormon disdain for plural marriage, coupled with a corresponding self-righteousness about monogamy as supposedly more civilized, was used to help justify federal intervention in Utah and bolster a growing sense of obligation to colonize so-called savage or barbaric peoples around the world. Consequently, *Exceptionally Queer* explicitly identifies gender and sexual exceptionalism as vehicles that have driven racial articulations of Americanness as early as the nineteenth century.

Bringing feminist theory, queer of color critique, and critical ethnic studies to bear on the study of Mormonism addresses the unfortunate limitations critical sexuality and queer studies scholarship have reserved for questions of religion. As Melissa Wilcox observes, these areas of study have most often only been able to account for religion "as a stultifying, oppressive institution of a [homophobic], sexist social order," an assessment reflecting what Puar calls "the queer liberal imaginary . . . resolutely secular [and] unforgiving in its understanding of (irrational, illogical, senseless) religion, faith, or spirituality as the downfall of any rational politics."[42] Indicative of how thoroughly the secularity thesis has been imbibed, the dismissal of religion as merely "oppressive," "irrational," "illogical," or "senseless" also neglects the complex role that various religious movements and institutions have played and continue to play in the nation's cultural and political landscape, particularly the ways that religion has come to stand in for race, often through reference to sexual and gendered practice and identity.

Breaking Wilcox's observed pattern and purposefully reveling in references to Mormonism's peculiarity, Coviello proclaims early Mormonism as queer.[43] Critically attuned to the racial history of sexuality, he deploys an interdisciplinary analytical framework that allows him to proffer a masterful breakdown of secularism as a biopolitical project. Yet, consequently, although paradoxically and certainly unintentionally, Coviello's argument does propagate certain exceptionalist notions of Mormonism that are deeply connected to ideas about its national origin. Thus, as referenced earlier, the few studies that have taken up questions of Mormonism and queerness tend to perpetuate Mormon peculiarity discourse. One of the other few queer theorists to engage Mormonism, Michael Cobb also regurgitates the discourse claiming that Mormonism "is marked by its devotion to families. . . . A devotion that seems peculiar, even in a nation enthralled by its almost unquestionable devotion to making families."[44] Like much of the twentieth- and twenty-first-century Mormon peculiarity discourse that I examine in chapters 4 and 5, Cobb uses the notion of Mormon hypernormativity to underwrite his argument that "perhaps what makes Utah families so troubling and so terrorizing for so many is not always the polygamous difference."[45]

In contrast to these arguments, this project does not take up the notion of Mormon peculiarity to characterize Mormonism, or its famous association with polygamy, as queer. While these are incredibly attractive moves to make and can be quite useful, as Coviello demonstrates, especially given the underlying associations between queerness and peculiarity (Siobhan Somerville reminds us that from 1700 until "the mid-twentieth century, 'queer' tended to refer to anything 'strange,' 'odd,' or 'peculiar,' with additional negative connotations that suggested something 'bad,' 'worthless,' or even 'counterfeit'"), doing so not only continues to leave unexamined the discursive construction of Mormon peculiarity, but it can and does reify interpretations of Mormonism grounded in U.S. exceptionalism.[46] Lauding a specific religious tradition or sexual practice as queer by virtue of (some of) its (early) transgressive or nonnormative qualities problematically defines queerness as a prescriptive ideal that assumes a stagnant and universalizing relationship between normativity and deviance. Instead, this project considers how regulatory queer ideals are propagated through, and productive of, Mormon peculiarity as a version of U.S. exceptionalism.

Consequently, I do not hail Mormonism or any of the practices associated with it, polygamy included, as either strange (peculiar), unique (exceptional), or transgressive (queer). Rather, the book uses feminist, queer of color, and critical and comparative theories of race, colonialism, and religion to frame its examination of Mormonism as an assemblage, helping to elucidate the ways that queerness sometimes functions as a biopolitical project that advances "ascendant white American nationalist formations."[47] Defined as "continuously shifting relational totalities comprised of spasmodic networks between different entities (content) and their articulation within 'acts and statements' (expression)," assemblages allow for a necessary rethinking of the study of history and culture that does not assume the discrete ontological essence of any social categories but still acknowledges their performative and material effects.[48] Therefore, this book approaches Mormonism not as a religion or an ethnic group but as a racialized assemblage produced in and through Mormon peculiarity discourse that has been used to forward and reaffirm a national project of white supremacy that marks certain populations as expendable under the colonial relation of power.[49]

Advocating for a conceptualization of race that accounts for its relationship to colonialism, rather than phenotype or biology, Sylvester A. Johnson explains that "religion can be racialized in order to constitute part of the assemblage of differential essences that ground the exercise of governing through the colonial relation of power."[50] In this vein, I consider exactly how Mormonism as a racialized assemblage has been used to advance and revalidate this project in the United States in various ways. Not only do I examine how Mormons and Mormonism were racialized as degraded and/or nonwhite in the nineteenth century, which justified their treatment as a "political unit whose relationship to the political community of the ruling state [wa]s denied pristine status" such that they were viewed as "aliens . . . because by their very nature (i.e., according to the coda of their racialization), they [were] people of a fundamentally different type (this is 'differential essence')" who were "*in* the society but not *of* it, even if they have been born in that society," but I also examine how Mormon peculiarity discourse in the twentieth and twenty-first centuries has produced Mormonism, paradoxically, as hypernormative, allowing it to function as both conduit and foil against which white supremacy is reasserted and settler colonialism is made invisible and normalized as liberal, multicultural democracy.[51]

In order to provide a historical overview of Mormon peculiarity discourse, its numerous elaborations, and the multitude of uses to which it has been put, this project examines a variety of sources from several analytical vantages. The book relies primarily on archival material about

Mormonism—including newspaper and magazine articles, religious study guides, medical reports, novels, court cases, graphic images, sermons, phrenological charts, travel narratives, congressional debates, exposés, diary entries, television episodes, local and national statutes, letters, popular advice literature, political platforms and speeches, sacred texts, and news reports—to elucidate both the complicated processes through which the concept has been discursively, affectively, and materially formed and the ways that Mormon peculiarity discourse has been used to assert U.S. exceptionalism by defining Americanness as white, Protestant, capitalist, and heteronormative. While this is not a traditionally comparative study, evaluating a broad range of primary sources helps to contextualize Mormonism within U.S. history not as substantially different from but rather as a representative example of the ways that religious, racial, gendered, and sexual othering has been fundamental, not incidental, to the nation's perpetuation. Coupling historical analysis with critical discourse analysis, as well as close visual and textual evaluation, uncovers the enduring (historically consistent), yet flexible (context specific) features of Mormon peculiarity discourse. While a multitude of sources and analytical tools permit me to provide a macro-level portrait of Mormon peculiarity discourse in historical context, this project is not meant to be a comprehensive review of all the formulations and elaborations of Mormon peculiarity. Instead, the book provides a chronological outline of Mormonism's importance to justifying the imperial project of U.S. exceptionalism.

Part I, "Making Mormonism Peculiar," examines the emergence of Mormon peculiarity discourse and its earliest instantiations in the nineteenth century. The first chapter, "Becoming Peculiar, 1830–1852," details the concurrent emergence of the Latter-day Saint faith and Mormon peculiarity discourse in the context of the Jacksonian era debates over what it meant to be American. Anti-Mormons used Mormon peculiarity to discredit Joseph Smith and the Book of Mormon, while the Saints used it to champion and implement their restorationist beliefs, both through recourse to logics of exceptionalism. Exposing these logics, the chapter analyzes both the development and widespread criticism of the nascent faith in the context of broader social, cultural, and political conflicts of the 1830s and 1840s. While other scholars focus on the context of the widespread religious revival of which Mormonism was a part, this chapter highlights the economic, spatial, and gendered transformations of settler colonialism and industrial capitalism, including the state's forced removal of Native peoples, debates over slavery, and women's rights.[52] Despite their differing goals, this chapter elucidates both the similarities and differences between the Saints and non-Mormons to show how Mormon peculiarity discourse functioned to solidify a patriarchal, white supremacist, and expansionist notion of national identity and culture in the antebellum era.

Chapter 2, "A Peculiar Race with Peculiar Institutions, 1847–1874," begins with the Saints' arrival in the present-day Salt Lake Valley and traces the increasingly hostile culture of anti-Mormonism that emerged after The Church of Jesus Christ of Latter-day Saints publicly announced the practice of plural marriage in 1852. It illustrates how Mormon peculiarity discourse functioned to construct Mormons as not only sexually but economically and politically backward, resulting, it was assumed, in their racial degradation and consequently in anti-Mormons labeling them alien, foreign, and even anti-American. By emphasizing the racial dimensions of nineteenth-century Mormon peculiarity discourse, which have often been ignored at the expense of scholarly fascination with objections to polygamy as a religious or marital practice, this chapter argues that anti-Mormon articulations of Mormon peculiarity represent some of the key conceptual antecedents of late nineteenth- and early twentieth-century notions of gender binarism, sexual identity, and eugenics by emphasizing the fluidity between cultural, scientific, and governmental articulations of the discourse.

The third chapter, "The Problems of (Mormon) Empire, 1874–1896," highlights what became known as the "Mormon problem" or "Mormon question" after the Civil War. Already considered a religiously, culturally, politically, economically, and therefore racially un-American threat to the nation's identity, culture, and government, Mormonism, in conjunction with other racialized "problems"—such as the Chinese and Indian "problems"—was used to motivate a reinvestment in a national culture of white supremacy in the thirty years before the nation's open embrace of overseas imperialism. Between the 1870s and the 1890s, Mormonism was produced vis-à-vis Mormon peculiarity discourse as a threat so dangerous that it was used to rationalize the federal government's experimentation with various tactics of colonialist-style governance in Utah Territory. In turn, the so-called Mormon problem, this chapter asserts, helped to pave the way for the nation-state's acceptance, justification, and implementation of global imperial governance in the twentieth century. In particular, this chapter identifies assertions of gender and sexual exceptionalism—that "Americans" were (racially) superior to Mormons because of their advanced knowledge and exercise of gendered and sexual roles, relationships, and practices—as key discursive tactics used to justify particular strategies of paternalistic governance.

Part II, "Exceptionally Normal," shifts to an examination of how Mormonism was constructed in significantly different ways in the twentieth century. Many have noted but few have attempted to explain the abrupt change in how Mormonism was regarded in the short period between 1890 and World War II. Chapter 4, "Resignifying Mormon Peculiarity, 1890–1945," examines this change in light of the underlying ideological affinities between Mormons and other (white) Americans in the first chapter. These shared views of, and attachments to, whiteness and white supremacy (which have been obscured by late twentieth-century versions of Mormon peculiarity discourse), this chapter argues, account for the rapid and extreme change in perceptions of Mormonism during the new century. As a result of the forced reinterpretation of many of the institution's fundamental teachings during this period, the Church began to express new commitments to heteronormativity and capitalism, embarking on theological and practical campaigns that encouraged followers to adhere to binary gender roles, marry monogamously and young, have as many children as possible, and participate in the two-party political system and capitalist economy. As a result, Mormons were no longer dismissed as sexually deviant and racially degraded; instead, twentieth-century representations of Mormons tended to praise the Saints for their commitment to "responsible individualism" as exceptionally American. Promoting responsible individualism, a key part of the prevailing discourse of Americanness—exemplified in virtues such as self-control, self-cultivation, and hard work—helped to communicate, at first explicitly but increasingly implicitly, the Church's underlying investment in U.S. nationalism as a fundamentally white supremacist enterprise, therefore endorsing and advancing the state's biopolitical agenda.

The period between the mid-1930s and the early 1980s witnessed major social and political changes related to not just economics and politics but race, gender, and sexuality. Thus, chapters 5 and 6, "A Thoroughly American Institution, 1936–1962" and "Making Mormon Peculiarity Colorblind, 1960–1982," both reflect on the role of Mormon peculiarity discourse in the endurance of white supremacy as the central feature of U.S. nationalism during the Cold War, both despite and because of these major changes. Chapter 5 weaves together the stories of the Church's racist limitations on

Black membership and its increasingly proactive attention to both homosexuality and Native assimilation as important for stabilizing the integrity
of the heteronormative family unit, in the context of mainstream press
coverage that continued to portray Mormonism and the Saints as hypernormative. During the early Cold War, Mormon hypernormativity came
to verify the supposed truth of both U.S. exceptionalism and the American
dream and therefore functioned to insulate the Church from criticism
of its white supremacist and anti-Black racism. Chapter 6 examines how
Mormon peculiarity helped to affect the transition away from articulating
the nation-state's investment in white supremacy through explicit commitments to segregation and toward a narrative of colorblindness, often
communicated through appeals to what were assumed to be traditional
family values, by looking at the controversies surrounding Black student-
athlete protests of Brigham Young University (BYU) and the Church's involvement in activism against the Equal Rights Amendment. In other words,
both chapters identify the Church's changing views on race, gender, and
sexuality in the larger political context as not in and of themselves overly
bigoted (although they certainly were racist, sexist, and homophobic) but
rather as part and parcel of a national redistribution of social and cultural knowledge in which processes of racialization change but continue
to articulate heteropatriarchy as natural and preferable in the service of
racial nationalism and U.S. imperial interests.

Shifting to more contemporary articulations of the discourse, Part III,
"Regulatory Queer Varieties of Mormon Peculiarity," examines Mormonism's role in twenty-first-century U.S. culture and politics. Chapter 7,
"Polygamy, or The Racial Politics of Marriage as Freedom," features contemporary legal articulations of Mormon peculiarity discourse in the context of the national debate over same-sex marriage. Based on an analysis
of two federal court cases—*Kitchen v. Herbert* (2013), the case that legalized
gay marriage in Utah, and *Brown v. Buhman* (2013), a case that temporarily
and partially reversed Utah's antipolygamy statute—this chapter argues
that contemporary Mormon peculiarity discourse reinforces claims of U.S.
exceptionalism that are leveraged to justify, among many other rationalizations, the nation's ongoing settler colonial and (neo-)imperialist agendas.[53]
The tendency to view these cases as examples of the complete acceptance of sexual nonnormativity in the United States, especially so because they occurred in Mormon-dominated Utah, is itself an assessment
grounded in the false logic of Mormon peculiarity. Instead, the chapter

contextualizes them in the landscape of marriage case law—recalling the
often overlooked importance of *Reynolds v. United States* (1879), which I
first discuss in chapter 3, as the first Supreme Court decision to interpret
the U.S. Constitution's guarantee of the free exercise of religion and that
helped to define the racist parameters of (sexual/religious) belonging in
the United States—to demonstrate that they entrench a narrow definition
of sexual freedom as marriage, disguising the state's interests in heteronormativity and whiteness.[54] Identifying the elaboration of Mormon peculiarity discourse in *Kitchen* and *Brown* exposes how the legal concepts of sexual
and religious freedom rely on a willful denial of both the nation's racial
history and the continued effects of that legacy.

Finally, the book's Coda, "What Mormonism Can Tell Us about Critical
Theory," reflects on the potential lessons of bringing critical theory to bear
on Mormonism, and Mormonism as assemblage to bear on critical theory. What does an examination of Mormonism through the lens of critical
theory—especially queer theory, queer of color critique, and critical and
comparative studies of race, ethnicity, religion, and colonialism—tell us
about the racialization of religion, as well as about both the dominant
epistemologies and ontology of race? How does viewing Mormonism as a
racializing civilizational assemblage provide a valuable perspective on the
politics of religion, race, gender, sex, class, and nationality in the United
States? How might Mormonism help us rethink deployments of queerness
in scholarly work? I propose preliminary answers to these questions while
advocating for a serious and sustained engagement with racial-religious
formations, including Mormonism, by critical theorists.

PART I

Making Mormonism
Peculiar

1 Becoming Peculiar, 1830–1852

There is something about this people that is truly peculiar.

—Brigham Young, "The Saints a Peculiar People,"
Journal of Discourses

You can read it in [the federal government's] own report[:] . . .
"When we go [*sic*] there, we found that the people were all
Mormons"; as if we were horses, or elephants, or Cyclops.

—George A. Smith, "Liberty and Persecution,"
Journal of Discourses

It is well known, if not always considered central to U.S. history, that for the better part of the nineteenth century, a major conflict raged between The Church of Jesus Christ of Latter-day Saints and its anti-Mormon opponents. Since the Church's founding in 1830, the Saints suffered religious persecution and as a result moved first from New York to Ohio, onto Missouri, and then Illinois, and finally to Utah in 1847. Anti-Mormon fervor began to climb during the 1850s after the Church announced publicly that polygamy was one of its key doctrinal practices, confirming rumors that had been circulating since at least the early 1840s. The persecution of the Saints reached a fever pitch during the late 1870s and 1880s, when federal legislation sought to break Mormon resistance to the imposition of prevailing social, political, and economic values in the United States. During the forty-year cold war between the Church and anti-Mormons, the single issue that both sides could agree on was that the Saints were a peculiar people. But any consensus ended where it had begun; the meaning and measure of the peculiarity in question was the most essential and fundamental battle of the contest. While Church leaders insisted that the Saints'

peculiarity was a sign of divine favor—just as the nation's supposedly exceptional character was—anti-Mormons insisted ever more fervently that Mormons were distinctly un-American. The chasm between anti-Mormon and
Mormon uses of Mormon peculiarity discourse illuminates the contest
over Mormonism as a focal point around which notions of national identity, culture, and expansion were developed, deployed, and challenged.

   The attempt on the part of the Saints to establish Zion in present-
day Utah, Nevada, Idaho, Arizona, California, New Mexico, and northern
Mexico included experimentation with social and political institutions that
shocked many non-Mormons. Advocating plural marriage, establishing
communal and cooperative economic systems, consenting to theocratic
governance, and implementing an ecclesiastical court structure were all
practices that chafed against the values and norms that had come to define
citizenship, governance, and belonging in the antebellum United States.
Novelists, preachers, legislators, doctors, feminists, judges, abolitionists,
journalists, freed people, and presidential candidates alike (albeit for differing reasons and to different ends) reviled the Saints' choices and participated in a campaign of harassment to end their unconventional way
of life. This campaign resulted in the capitulation of The Church of Jesus
Christ of Latter-day Saints to federal pressure and its ultimate conformity
to mainstream norms between 1890 and 1907. While scholarship has often
marginalized the significance of this struggle in the greater course and
context of U.S. history, Mormon studies has argued for its centrality to key
developments in the nineteenth-century United States.[1] Yet a comprehensive understanding of this conflict and its significance is not possible without
a broader examination of the emergence and development of Mormonism
in mainstream U.S. culture and politics during the 1830s and 1840s.

   Peter Coviello argues that much scholarship on early Mormonism has
inaccurately represented it as *"already* in step with the presumptions of
liberal personhood, the dictates of liberal rationality, and the (it is always
assumed) finally beneficent norms of liberal polity and sociality," and he
instead asserts that the Mormons "were not wholly assimilable to such
iterations of liberalism."[2] Coviello's interest in the theological possibilities
that early Mormonism engendered but ultimately surrendered is based
on his identification of the "carnal extravagance" of its early history—an
extravagance that was used to firmly situate Mormonism as "bad" rather
than "good belief" during the 1830s and 1840s. However, what this position
disregards is the extent to which social and political mores were in extreme

flux during these decades and that what constituted "good belief" was not yet solidified. In fact, cultural conflict about Mormonism—and other new churches during the Second Great Awakening—was what helped to solidify normative, liberal standards of "good belief." Although the Saints certainly did challenge some prevailing mores and institutions throughout the nineteenth century, they also maintained several ideological and practical similarities with the rest of U.S. society.[3] These similarities are significant not only because they underwrote much of the racial confusion caused by the Saints' nonnormative beliefs and practices but also because they ensured the Saints' ability to avoid many of the violent and lethal forms of colonialism and racism enacted against other marginalized racial and religious groups in the nineteenth century. These similarities also allowed the Saints to assimilate into whiteness, and therefore Americanness, with notable speed in the early twentieth century, a process discussed in chapter 4.[4]

By exposing and describing both the differences and the similarities the Saints shared with non-Mormons around U.S. exceptionalism, racial hierarchy and relations, gender roles and sex and marriage, political economy, and settler colonialism, this chapter charts the emergence and development of Mormon peculiarity discourse as an important tool for defining and solidifying the concept of Americanness over the course of the nineteenth century.[5] Instead of accepting "Mormonism" as a self-evident and self-contained category, this chapter highlights the mutable ways that it was represented and discussed in order to argue that Mormon peculiarity discourse did not merely describe, criticize, or applaud Mormonism but actively produced it as an object of concern. In other words, this chapter analyzes Mormonism, particularly its reputation as fundamentally different or peculiar, as a discursive formation that emerged alongside and in relation to the Latter-day Saint movement, as well as how that formation played a central role in consolidating a mainstream notion of Americanness. What follows, then, is an overview of the historical period in which the birth of a new religious tradition simultaneously produced a new discursive construction.

DUELING EXCEPTIONALISMS

U.S. society in the Jacksonian era underwent an intense religious revival largely in response to the first wave of the Industrial Revolution that was transforming not just the United States but also the global economy. The pressures that nascent industrialization produced, especially for agrarian and rural workers, resulted in a hardship that was answered by what Charles Sellers calls the "free religious market" of the Northeast United States.[6] With the rate of church affiliation doubling since 1800 as a result of the Second Great Awakening, Joseph Smith's new church was anything but unique. When Smith founded the Church of Christ in the "burnt-over district" of 1830 upstate New York, the United States was still an adolescent nation struggling over the parameters of what it meant to be American not only religiously but economically and culturally.[7] A product of its period, Smith's church reflected many of the trends that characterized the antebellum United States.

Compared to other contemporary burgeoning religious movements, Smith's new church adhered relatively closely to the values and norms of early nineteenth-century U.S. society. Not only did the early Saints share non-Mormons' fundamental views on white racial superiority, men's and women's roles, and reserved sexual expression for procreation within marriage, but they also, perhaps most significantly, shared a belief in the unique nature of U.S. government and the divinity of the Constitution. Mormon conviction in the righteousness of the nation's republican form of government went beyond simple patriotism to form an axiom of their system of belief. The Articles of Faith, which outline the basic principles and teachings of the Church, hint at the intensity of the Latter-day Saint tradition's investment in the nation-state and its form of governance.[8] According to the tenth article, the Saints believe "in the literal gathering of Israel and in the restoration of the Ten Tribes; that Zion will be built upon the [North] American continent." This belief in the United States as the New Jerusalem is taken literally in all three sacred Latter-day Saint scriptures.[9] Not only is the North American continent identified as the site of Zion and future dealings with God, but it is also described as the place where Jesus Christ reappeared to spread the gospel immediately after his crucifixion. Moreover, the Saints believe that "the founding of the United States is merely one step in a chain of events that were necessary to bring forth the true church [sic]. The discovery of the American continent by Columbus and the later arrival of the Pilgrims" and the founding fathers themselves are all thought to be a part of that process.[10] For the early Saints, the nation was exceptional not because of its lauding of representative government but because that government provided the necessary condition—religious freedom—for the restoration of the true Church on the North American continent. The Saints saw the Constitution and the nation itself as merely a stepping-stone, albeit a vital one, in "the restoration of all things," a phrase that would come to denote what D. Michael Quinn fittingly calls a complex theology and radical worldview.[11]

Herein lies one of the most vital disagreements between the Saints and anti-Mormons: the meaning and place of U.S. exceptionalism. The Saints understood themselves to be superior to their fellow citizens in the sense that they had received and accepted God's commandment to restore the original and true form of Christianity. Thus, for them, what might be called "Mormon exceptionalism" transcended U.S. exceptionalism—a stance that anti-Mormons simply could not stomach. The battle that ensued over Mormonism and its peculiar reputation went directly to the ideological root of Americanness. Smith's was not the first, or even the most radical, religion to appear in the young nation, but as it became one of the most centralized and politically powerful U.S. religions, it presented a compelling and threatening alternative to an as yet unfixed understanding of what it meant to be American.[12]

This friction between Mormon and U.S. exceptionalism can help to account for anti-Mormons' early attempts to smear Joseph Smith and his church's reputation. Critics were quick to label Smith, paradoxically, both an "imposter" and a "fanatic" and stamped the new church as a "fake," "counterfeit" religion that "deluded" and "deceived" its "misguided" followers.[13] In just the first few years of the Church's existence, scores of articles published in newspapers in New York, Massachusetts, Vermont, Ohio, and Missouri decried Mormonites, Mormons, and Mormonism on these terms, claiming to "expose," "unveil," or "unmask" the "so-called religion" and its prophet.[14] By 1834, only four years after the Church's founding, at least two major anti-Mormon tracts had been published, including Alexander Campbell's *Delusions: An Analysis of the Book of Mormon* (1832) and Eber D. Howe's more famous *Mormonism Unvailed* (1834). As these examples attest, from almost the moment of the Latter-day Saint tradition's birth, anti-Mormons constructed Mormonism in a negative light.

At the same time that the Church took root and achieved an exponential growth in membership during the 1830s and 1840s, Manifest Destiny—a term that was coined in 1845 by New York journalist John Louis O'Sullivan in order to rationalize the annexation of Texas—became an increasingly attractive and popular interpretation of national expansion as inevitable, compulsory, and divinely inspired. Territorial expansion was understood to be a unique mission entrusted by God to white Protestants, specifically that Anglo-Saxon Americans had been endowed to bring the North American continent together under the auspices of the also divinely inspired U.S. Constitution, a philosophy that was paralleled in early Mormon belief and doctrine.[15] The Saints' sense of their own exceptionalism, which agreed with and repeated the religious tenets that underpinned Manifest Destiny, stemmed directly from their belief in a divine mandate to build up the Kingdom of God on Earth. But the Saints' open and forceful assertion that Zion would eventually supersede and overtake the U.S. government provoked the considerable ire of anti-Mormons.

COMPETING COLONIAL IMPERATIVES AND THE RACIALIZATION OF MORMONISM

In an era characterized by religious innovation and proliferation, the Saints' explicit policy of (global) colonization and aggressive proselytization for Mormon exceptionalism grated its nails against the mainstream Protestant chalkboard. Even before their final exodus from Nauvoo, Illinois, in the late 1840s to the Great Basin—what later would be dubbed the Salt Lake Valley—the Saints had sent missionaries to convert Indigenous peoples across what became the midwestern United States and had established missions on the Eastern Seaboard (1839), in Britain (1837), and in French Polynesia (1844). Moreover, during the Saints' tenure in Nauvoo between 1839 and 1847 they established a government virtually independent from its parent state of Illinois. Rumors of the Saints' military might mingled with charges of sexual impropriety on the part of Smith and his followers. Although the Saints forcefully and repeatedly pledged their allegiance to the U.S. government in the 1830s and 1840s and actively participated in U.S. settler colonialism, anti-Mormons saw them as threatening for two key reasons: first, the Saints' divergent understanding of racial hierarchy and relations (specifically their views of Native peoples) clashed with the accepted racial underpinnings of removal policy, ongoing genocide, and Manifest Destiny; and second, their social and political unity, as well as their governmental independence, was regarded as a material manifestation of their claim that Mormon governance would one day replace the U.S. nation-state.

As practices of the violent expansion of U.S. borders, both removal policy specifically and Manifest Destiny generally reflected and were undergirded by various theories of race, both "scientific" and popular. The early nineteenth century witnessed a rough transition from one major explication of racial-religious origins to another, monogenesis and polygenesis, occasioning competing theories to circulate in society as if they were compatible, even complementary. By the time Smith moved his followers to Nauvoo, ideas of white racial superiority were flourishing throughout the nation. Southern white people's racial justifications for slavery and settler colonialism had become increasingly explicit during the 1830s, bolstered in part through the newly developed disciplines of phrenology and physiognomy. Phrenology, a so-called science developed in the 1790s and popularized by the 1820s, advocated the inherent racial inferiority of nonwhite peoples, particularly Black and Indigenous people.[16] Various measurements of the head were thought to hold the key to explaining individual and racial differences (brain size was thought to correspond positively with intelligence, for example). Phrenological researchers studied what they believed to be the division of the brain into different faculties or sections, each corresponding with different emotional or rational abilities. Utilizing techniques such as observation and physical examination of the contours of a subject's head, phrenologists claimed to be able to assess the innate abilities of individuals, communities, and even entire races. Both European and United States–based phrenologists maintained that those races with a basically sound brain structure (i.e., Anglo-Saxon white people) could use the insights of phrenology to help develop their affective and intellectual capabilities, but those who were considered of poorer stock were incapable of improving their status.[17]

Treated seriously in the scientific community until the early 1840s, phrenology retained a formative influence on the general population's views of racial determination and personal development well into the last quarter of the century. The most dominant phrenological thinker of the period, George Combe, stressed a genetic explanation for racial difference, forwarding the widely held belief that "Anglo-Saxons had the most perfect cerebral organization, an organization that placed them above other Caucasians as well as far above the non-Caucasians of the world." Combe also explained away the attempted extermination of Native peoples using typical phrenological thinking: "'The existing races of native American Indians show skulls inferior in their moral and intellectual development to those of the Anglo-Saxon race, and that, morally and intellectually, these Indians are inferior to their Anglo-Saxon invaders, and have receded before them.'"[18] This kind of racial theorizing had two main functions. First, it (re)produced notions of white supremacy, specifically Anglo-Saxon whiteness, as a fundamental quality of Americanness. In other words, not only were Americans divinely endowed with the responsibility of Manifest Destiny, but they were racially qualified and destined to do so according to this line of thinking. Second, such theorizing introduced a modern, supposedly scientific foundation for the explicitly racial justifications that had been used to fuel European and U.S. colonialism in the Americas since the late fifteenth century.[19]

Relatedly, several religious theories about the whereabouts of God's chosen people also emerged during this period, not coincidentally aligning with the popular theories of Anglo-Saxon, white racial superiority. In the case of the Saints, they believed themselves to be direct blood descendants of one of the tribes of ancient Israel who, as the chosen people, had been selected to prepare the earth and its inhabitants for Christ's return.[20] This belief dovetailed nicely with contemporary, widely held racial-religious beliefs in Anglo-Saxonism and British Israelism.[21] The latter was a scholarly theory that posited the British Isles were populated by the ancestors of the lost Israelites and that England was to be one of the gathering places for the ten lost tribes. According to early nineteenth-century scientific and religious explanations, blood and lineage, rather than environment, were responsible for the reputed greatness of Anglo-Saxon Christians.

The Saints' claimed that their Israelite blood, by way of their Anglo-Saxon origins, tied them directly to what those in power saw as the most prized racial stock. Over the course of the 1830s, 1840s, and early 1850s, the Saints attempted to cement the relationship between what they saw as their birthright and the national investment in Anglo-Saxonism. While British Israelism was used to account for the Saints' missionary success in England—the chosen people were thought to be especially susceptible to the word of God as extended by Mormon disciples—phrenology was used to buttress their claims of divinely sanctioned Anglo-Saxon triumphalism. Held in high regard both within and outside of the Church, phrenology was used to demonstrate the superior quality of the Church's leadership, adherents, and, particularly, converts from England and Scandinavia. Many Saints, including major figures in the Church's leadership, relied on phrenology to prove their Anglo-Saxonism and, therefore, their rightful place in the divinely sanctioned nation. However, they also used phrenology to reinforce their claims of superiority over and above other white settlers—a tactic that did not ingratiate them to their neighbors.

Davis Bitton and Gary Bunker's survey of phrenology's popularity among the Saints demonstrates its importance in establishing Mormon exceptionalist claims to Anglo-Saxon whiteness and, thus, Americanness.[22] During the Nauvoo period, several Church leaders—including two future Church presidents, Brigham Young and Wilford Woodruff, as well as other influential figures, such as Hyrum Smith (Joseph Smith's brother), Willard Richards, and James J. Strang—underwent phrenological examinations, often publicizing the results of their assessments. Joseph Smith himself underwent three different examinations, the results of which at least one, a phrenological diagram depicting the measurements of the prophet's personal attributes based on an analysis of his skull, was published in Mormon newspapers and magazines in the early 1840s.[23] While Smith displayed only a moderate personal interest in the new discipline, the fact that he assented to three separate examinations and the fact that numerous Saints invested their time, energy, and money in their own readings are reflective of the widespread popularity and influence of phrenology during the nineteenth century generally and in the Mormon community specifically. In fact, phrenology achieved its ideological stature as a mode of justification and explanation for Manifest Destiny in part through its entrance into mainstream U.S. culture as a fashionable pastime.

For the Saints, their interest in phrenology was threefold. First, their theological investment in individual progress and self-perfection was reflected in phrenologists' insistence that Anglo-Saxons could use its insights to attain personal development and betterment. Second, in many ways phrenological thinking dovetailed with the Saints' own hierarchical thinking about race, specifically the correlation they saw between personal choice (morality, behavior, etc.), physical attributes (skin color, hair texture, etc.), and abilities (mental and physical). For example, in keeping with ideas popular to nineteenth-century Christianity, the Saints would develop a belief that dark skin was a curse reflecting individuals' poor morality.[24] Finally, in phrenology the Saints recognized a method of defense that might help insulate them against charges of racial difference that anti-Mormons had begun to circulate. For the Saints, phrenological charts were not just a popular pastime, they also served as proof of their Anglo-Saxon origins, their whiteness, and, therefore, their Americanness at a time when critics were challenging their loyalty to the nation through accusations of religious-racial treason and degeneration.

While Mormon theology clearly retained and reflected the racial attitudes of the period out of which it was born, it promoted a somewhat different approach to dealing with Native peoples than those advocated by
both the federal government and non-Mormon settlers. Historically, the
U.S. government and its citizens engaged in a program of missionizing to
Indigenous peoples, displacing Native people and settling Native land, and
genocidal warfare against various tribes. In the 1830s and 1840s, the early
Saints largely forewent genocide for displacement, settlement, and proselytization.[25] Just as the Saints were identified as relatives of the Israelites
in the Book of Mormon, so too were Indigenous peoples, a not uncommon idea that various religious scholars and popular thinkers promoted in
the late eighteenth- and early nineteenth-century United States.[26] According to the Book of Mormon, a family of Israelites traveled from Jerusalem
to North America around 600 BC but, over time, split into two warring
factions, the "white, and exceedingly fair and delightsome" Nephites and
the dark-skinned Lamanites, who are commonly regarded by the Saints as
ancestors of Native peoples.[27] The sacred account of racial origins in the
Book of Mormon aligned with and challenged developing ideas and policies toward Indigenous peoples, evident in both the romanticism and violence with which they are depicted in the text.[28] While the Indian Removal
Act, signed into law by President Andrew Jackson in 1830, represented the
continuation and formalization of policies of extreme violence against
Indigenous peoples, the Saints saw it as their duty to convert and "save"
their long-lost relatives.[29] Thus, although the Saints shared an investment in
white supremacy with non-Mormons, because of their vision of what Max
Perry Mueller calls a "white universal gospel" they treated Native peoples
as potentially valuable converts who themselves could later become (literally) white-skinned, influencing the hostile attitudes of anti-Mormon white
settlers in Ohio, Missouri, and Illinois.

The Saints' policy of conversion chafed against the realities of U.S. colonialism and hardening attitudes toward so-called hostile Indians. As the
Saints moved from state to state, local settlers found the Saints' desire to
incorporate Native peoples into their religion, and by extension their communities, both disconcerting and in open conflict with their own policy of
blanket hatred, forced removal, and violent suppression. For example, the
Saints' formal missionary policy was one among several reasons Missourians
objected to Mormon settlement in the western part of the state between
1831 and 1838. In response to their more open and patronizing racist attitudes

toward and beliefs about Indigenous peoples (among other issues), anti-Mormons racialized the Saints variously as degraded or nonwhite people. Racializing them as inferior was an extremely effective strategy that was key for denying the Saints equal rights to property, enfranchisement, and the protection of state governments, as well as justifying (extralegal) violence against them.[30]

W. Paul Reeve argues that discursive constructions of Mormons had become explicitly racial as early as the first few years of the 1830s, transforming the Saints' peculiarity from religious duplicity into racial difference. In the early period of polygenic racial taxonomy, and in an increasingly nativist national context, non-Mormons began to conceptualize the Saints as a new, distinct race evident in the way the terms Mormonite and Mormon were used not just as religious descriptors but simultaneously as racial designations. By 1831, "Mormonites" were described as "'vagrants,'" "'strange people,'" "'fanatical and deluded beings' who 'degraded themselves,'" and, only ten years later, as "'savages,'" echoing racist descriptions of other groups, particularly Native peoples, during this period.[31] Religious objections to fanaticism or delusion, for example, melded with dehumanizing language to racialize Mormons and thereby justify their differential treatment. Importantly, Mormonism was racialized within preexisting epistemological frameworks of racial-religious difference that characterized Euro-American representations of Islam and Judaism. Immediately upon the founding of the new church, critics compared Joseph Smith with the Prophet Muhammad, and the Saints were consistently likened to Muslims in popular media. Early nineteenth-century U.S. citizens' "knowledge of Islam was informed by exposure to African Muslims through either the slave trade or naval conflict off the North African coast," a knowledge that would have been inevitably inflected with contemporary racial attitudes toward Black people and long-standing histories of Christian prejudice against Islam and Islamic cultures more generally.[32] The fact that the Saints were racialized as Mormons through coconstitutive racial and religious registers should come as no surprise, given the history of racial-religious justifications used for the colonization of the Americas and the Atlantic slave trade.[33] These early descriptions of Mormonites and Mormons quickly gave way to a commonly accepted distinction between (Anglo-Saxon) white Americans and Mormons.[34]

By the 1850s, "a growing sense that Mormons were degraded whites bound together by a shifting set of degenerate traits or that they were

'foreigners' or 'aliens'" characterized anti-Mormons' growing animosity toward the Saints and would later inform the national response to
their nonnormative practices, polygamy especially.[35] The condemnation
of Mormons simultaneously through accusations of religious fraud (religious othering), racial regression (scientific racism), and declarations of
foreignness (the colonial relation of power) is significant, given that in
the early nineteenth century race was understood to denote more than
a purely biological designation; indeed, race was understood to communicate religious and national origin and belonging. As an influx of immigration from Europe resulted in an upswing of nativist sentiment during
midcentury, Mormons were conceptualized in much the same way as Irish,
Catholic, and Jewish immigrants, whose status as white was contested during the second half of the nineteenth century.[36] While most historians of
whiteness have focused on how European immigration put pressure on
the broad category of "free white persons" enshrined in pre–twentieth
century U.S. naturalization law, resulting in the creation of internal hierarchies within whiteness (hierarchies that distinguished "those of the Anglo-
Saxon 'old stock'" from "Celts," "Slavs," "Hebrews," "Mediterraneans,"
"Teutons," "Nordics," etc.), the history of Mormonism reveals a more
complicated picture in which those with white skin and non-Protestant
religious identities could be and were subject to processes of racialization
that attempted to excommunicate them from the category of whiteness
altogether.[37]

Mormon speeches from this period evidence the Saints' irritation that
they were viewed as racially degraded or nonwhite people. Reflecting on
the government's unwillingness to acknowledge and support the Saints'
settler colonial occupation of the Great Basin as it had other territories,
Mormon leader George A. Smith concluded that non-Mormons saw the
Saints "as if we were horses, or elephants, or Cyclops. [Federal officials
come to Utah and exclaim] 'Oh! we will run home again, because when we
got there, we found the people all Mormons.'"[38] Smith's incredulity that
the federal government would pay for "Indian wars" in Oregon, California, New Mexico, or Minnesota but not in Utah because it was occupied
by Mormons evidences not only that the Saints were popularly portrayed
as strange and animalistic—as religiously and racially other—but that they
were aware of and indignant at such portrayals. The Saints' indignation,
expressed in Smith's sermon celebrating the Saints' entry into the Salt Lake
Valley five years earlier, was a result of their own perception of themselves

as Anglo-Saxon white Americans who had been specially chosen by God to reinstitute the true Church on the North American continent—a project Smith believed that the federal government should support by extending its suppression of Native resistance to settler colonialism in Utah. Numerous homilies from the 1850s, 1860s, and 1870s self-consciously employed the terms *Mormon* and *Mormonism* as the accepted terminology with which to refer to the Church and its members but did so to challenge negative perceptions of the religion and its practices. In other words, the Saints were fully aware that *Mormonism* was not merely a descriptor but rather a concept whose meaning was being actively contested. Fighting a hard but ultimately losing battle over its meaning, nineteenth-century Church leaders preached sermon after sermon maintaining that the "strange" or "peculiar" qualities of the Mormons were a result of their religion's divine endorsement, not a result of racial degeneration.[39]

During the Saints' tenure in Missouri, Church leaders had also entered the national fray over slavery. Early in its history, the Church had several Black members, many of whom rose to prominence in the Church's lay priesthood structure; but the Church also welcomed white Southern converts who brought enslaved people with them when they migrated to western Mormon settlements in Ohio and Missouri.[40] Joseph Smith and other Church leaders held racial views about interracial marriage, abolition, and emancipation that reflected the conservative outlook of many Northerners. While maintaining a stance against the so-called amalgamation between white and Black people, Smith articulated a vision of gradual and controlled emancipation during his 1844 bid for the presidency of the United States. However, like most politicians during this period, including Abraham Lincoln, emancipation connoted a vision of white paternalism, in which white people were still solidly placed above and in control of Black people. Overall, the first two decades of Church policy concerning Black people evinced an ambivalent and oscillating attitude about race and slavery, but by 1847, with Brigham Young as second president of the Church, the hierarchy had begun to solidify an explicitly racist policy of denying the priesthood to Black men.[41] But even as the vast majority of Saints aligned with widespread views of the inferiority of Black people—reflected in formal policies toward Black members and the Church's firm support of the prohibition of interracial sex and marriage—the Saints fell prey to charges of racial "mixing," implicating them in a "Mormon-black conspiracy" in Missouri.[42]

GENDER AND SEXUAL NORMS AMONG THE SAINTS

Mormon association by contiguity with other new religious movements that promoted free love, such as the Owenites, helped to fuel concerns about interracial sex and marriage among the Saints. Boiling tensions between the Saints and anti-Mormons in Missouri and Illinois were certainly promoted by a wellspring of religious bigotry, but accusations of crossing racial boundaries were used to cement the Saints' place on the wrong side of the racial divide just as the color line was solidifying. Rumors about marriages between Black and white Saints in Ohio and a scandal involving a column promoting Mormon missionizing to Black people printed in a July 1833 edition of the Mormon newspaper the *Evening and the Morning Star* prompted an outbreak of outrage on the part of local anti-Mormon residents. The column enflamed the already tense situation in western Missouri, and residents "accused Mormons of conspiring to incite a slave rebellion and ultimately to promote a racial assault on white women," with one resident proclaiming that the Saints had achieved the racial "'condition of the black population'" and were "'little above the condition of our blacks either in regard to property or education.'"[43] Thus, the Saints were racialized through accusations of "race treason," propelling the construction of "Mormons" as a new racial category distinct from white non-Mormon Americans.[44]

As concerns over racial mixing indicate, racial ideas about the Saints, like other groups, were formed largely in and through ideas about gender and sex. As feminist, queer (of color), and critical ethnic studies scholarship demonstrates, racial formation is a process that often advances through the elaboration of normative gender roles and sexual practices.[45] By tying the Saints' purportedly nonnormative sexual and marital behavior to their racial categorization, anti-Mormons promoted the Saints' peculiar outsider status as degraded or nonwhite people. In the reigning, yet contradictory, logic of nineteenth-century scientific and popular thought, (sexual and gendered) behavior could define racial status, while one's (designated or perceived) race could simultaneously determine the behaviors that an individual (supposedly) exhibited. In other words, procreation between those of different races—taboo behavior (at least for some) in the 1830s United States—could actually produce racial degeneracy, while having a racially inferior status such as "mulatto," for example, was thought to ensure inappropriate and promiscuous behavior like interracial and out-of-wedlock sex. For those struggling to stake a claim to whiteness, and therefore Americanness, like the Saints, this logic worked against them while it also functioned to reinforce the oppression of those groups that were unable to even attempt such a claim, particularly Black people.

However, the Saints' racially suspect status was complicated by their participation in the normative gender and sexual cultures of the era.[46] Predominant thinking regarding Anglo-Saxon, white racial superiority underlying the call to Manifest Destiny was entangled with shifting notions of sex, gender, and marriage during this period. The synchronized concept of the cult of domesticity, which dictated popular thinking regarding white middle- and upper-class women in the early to mid-1800s, promoted piety, purity, domesticity, and submissiveness as values these women should ideally embody. But as many feminist scholars have shown, the cult accomplished much more than this. It implicitly relied on racialized and classed notions of femininity that privileged well-to-do white women and enforced an ideological separation between public and private as distinct spheres that gendered and racialized wage-earning and formal politics in opposition to home life and child-rearing.[47] Of course, this opposition also served to make sense of and reinforce the changes resulting from the development of industrial capitalism, insulating the home as an escape from the distressing consequences of expanding market forces. The Latter-day Saint movement was born just as the ideology of domesticity began to alter expectations regarding women's economic roles and during a period when women were entirely subject to their husbands' legal authority. The Saints unquestioningly absorbed these new attitudes about women's roles.

Although it is commonly assumed that the practice of plural marriage is evidence of a dramatic dissimilarity between the highly prized gendered and sexual norms of the Victorian-era United States and those of nineteenth-century Mormonism, the opposite is in fact true. Polygamy was not formally introduced into the faith until 1843 and the Saints did not openly or widely practice plural marriage until 1852. Before 1852, plural marriage was mostly practiced by select, high-ranking officials in the Church's hierarchy and was not always or even usually accompanied by sexual relationships between spouses.[48] Like their non-Mormon counterparts, the Saints accepted and integrated the cult of true womanhood into their worldview and daily lives. As the "most heavily male-dominated" religious communal experiment to emerge out of the Second Great Awakening, the Church held patriarchal views about gender, and women's roles in particular, that

were the "closest to the attitudes of the outer society," compared to other
religious experiments.[49] Women's participation in the priesthood, for example, was only possible indirectly through marriage, and their status was
exalted directly through childbearing and child-rearing. As B. Carmon Hardy
and Dan Erickson point out, even after the Saints began to openly advocate
polygamy, they did so by drawing on popular scientific theories of gender
and sexuality, theories that aligned and intersected with rapidly developing racial theories, to argue that the supremacy and divinity of polygamy
best maintained and enriched the purportedly inherent sex/gender differences between men and women.[50] Early Church history shows that the
attitudes of Mormon leaders reflected those of non-Mormons when it
came to the accepted and expected relations between men and women,
husband and wife.

The Doctrine and Covenants, which contains the revelations received
by Church leaders from God, provides invaluable insight into the similarities and differences between the Saints and non-Mormons during the early
years of the religion's development.[51] In particular, Section 132—famously
expressing God's commandment for the Saints to practice plural marriage—
evinces that Mormon attitudes regarding the nature of, and appropriate
roles for, men and women aligned quite well with contemporary non-
Mormon ideals and norms. Through the invocation of the Old Testament
relationship between Abraham, his wife Sarah, and his concubine Hagar,
the revelation commands women's (particularly wives') submission to men;
in the specific case of the revelation, the submission of Joseph Smith's wife
Emma to her husband:

> God commanded Abraham, and Sarah gave Hagar to Abraham to wife. And
> why did she do it? Because this was the law; and from Hagar sprang many
> people. . . . A commandment I give unto mine handmaid, Emma Smith,
> your wife, whom I have given unto you, that she stay herself and partake not
> of that which I commanded you to offer unto her; for I did it, saith the Lord,
> to prove you all, as I did Abraham, and that I might require an offering at
> your hand, by covenant and sacrifice. And I command mine handmaid, Emma
> Smith, to abide and cleave unto my servant Joseph, and to none else. But if she
> will not abide this commandment she shall be destroyed, saith the Lord.[52]

Emma Smith is instructed to submit to both God's and her husband's
authority in all things temporal and divine. Of course, many have disputed

the truth of Joseph Smith's revelation. It is often described as simply a ruse to coerce his wife into accepting his other marriages and to silence her stream of objections to plural marriage:

> If any man espouse a virgin, and desire to espouse another, and the first give her consent, and if he espouse the second, and they are virgins, and have vowed to no other man, then is he justified . . . for they are given unto him to multiply and replenish the earth, according to my commandment. . . . If any man have a wife, who holds the keys of this power, and he teaches unto her the law of my priesthood, as pertaining to these things, then shall she believe and administer unto him, or she shall be destroyed.[53]

However, questions about the sincerity and divinity of the revelation distract from the more interesting fact that the Church, including its leaders and lay membership alike, accepted and promoted notions of female subordination through the ideology of domesticity even as, over the course of the nineteenth century, white women were, paradoxically, afforded "extremely varied and flexible economic roles" in Mormon society and oftentimes participated more fully than their non-Mormon counterparts in the traditional political realm.[54] Moreover, the fact remains that after Smith's death and the exodus to Utah, Mormon women maintained a seemingly paradoxical submissiveness under the doctrine of plural marriage; they actively fought against the federal government's repeated attempts to destroy polygamy, a patriarchal institution, at the same time that they argued for and achieved suffrage in Utah.[55]

Couched in the language of religious sacrifice and dutiful obedience to God, the revelation mirrors common attitudes that regarded wives as their husbands' property and women as naturally submissive. Unsurprisingly, the revelation uses this sexist logic to explain plural marriage as not only a divinely sanctioned but also as a required practice. In order to move beyond the overly simplistic interpretation of this revelation as proof of Joseph Smith's apparently licentious and manipulative nature, the text in its entirety must be approached as a historical document replete with examples of the ideals, values, and norms of early nineteenth-century U.S. and Mormon culture. Importantly, the revelation also explains the concept of eternal marriage as essential for the restoration of the true Church and the salvation of humankind.[56] The concept of eternal marriage, in which the marital union lasts beyond the temporal realm, into the eternity of the afterlife, illustrates the extent to which the Saints prized and privileged the marriage relation as fundamental to exaltation after death:

> I reveal unto you a new and an everlasting covenant; and if ye abide not that covenant, then are ye damned; for no one can reject this covenant and be permitted to enter into my glory. . . . All covenants, . . . that are not made and entered into and sealed by the Holy Spirit of promise, of him who is anointed, both as well for time and for all eternity, . . . are of no efficacy, virtue, or force in and after the resurrection from the dead; for all contracts that are not made unto this end have an end when men are dead. . . . Therefore, if a man marry him a wife in the world, and he marry her not by me nor by my word, . . . their covenant and marriage are not of force when they are dead. . . . Therefore, when they are out of the world they neither marry nor are given in marriage; but are appointed angels in heaven; which angels are ministering servants, to minister for those who are worthy of a far more, and an exceeding, and an eternal weight of glory. For these angels did not abide my law; therefore, they cannot be enlarged, but remain separately and singly, without exaltations, in their saved condition, to all eternity.[57]

Just as the Saints took seriously U.S. exceptionalism as evidence of divine intervention, so too did they prize the Mormon marriage contract as a heavenly relationship that extended beyond the confines of mere mortality and enabled their own attainment of godhood.[58]

Valued above all other relationships in the nineteenth-century United States, the marriage contract made a woman into "a feme convert, and a husband possessed a dependent wife. Without marriage, none of this existed. Without marriage, sex was fornication; with marriage, it became duty and right."[59] For the Saints, the marriage contract went beyond the earthly implications of these values, attaching an individual's ability to achieve the highest level of glory in the afterlife to marriage and procreation. Both eternal and plural marriage were considered essential religious customs for practitioners because they ensured heavenly adulation and provided the quickest route for bringing about the millennium. In other words, without a marriage performed, sanctioned, and sealed by a priesthood holder, a man could not achieve godhood and a woman could not become a Mother in Heaven; both would be merely angels "without exaltations" after death for all eternity.[60] For women, marriage and childbearing were the only ways to achieve a godlike status, in addition to a more protected and privileged position on Earth.

As an in-depth reading of Section 132 makes clear, the Saints were more similar than they were different from non-Mormons when it came to gender norms. But it is equally clear that their adherence to such norms and standards in the 1830s and 1840s did not prevent their detractors from effectively racializing them as degraded or nonwhite people, a trend that gained increasing traction after their move to Utah and their open acknowledgment of plural marriage in 1852. As with other historical examples, the Saints' compliance to gendered norms, expectations, and practices was an essential prerequisite for being read as Anglo-Saxon white people, but it alone did not determine their racial status. In fact, in the nineteenth-century United States deviation from those standards could be used to ensure one's exclusion from the privileged construction of whiteness and, therefore, Americanness. Furthermore, the supposedly natural relationship that was understood to exist between gender norms and sexual practices was tenuous to the point of fragility, ensuring that the slightest inconsistency could destroy an individual's or group's claim, as in the case of the Saints.

Such divergences between the nineteenth-century Saints' views of racialized gender and sexuality, which they shared with non-Mormons, and their practical application of those views demonstrate this tenuous state of affairs. These divergences emerged at the intersection between industrial capitalism and changing notions of marriage, family, gender roles, love, and sex. The shift from a purely patriarchal notion of marriage to one of companionship between the 1790s and 1830s did not align with plural marriage's increasingly important place in the Mormon system of belief and practice after the 1850s, which required the suppression of emotions that were promoted in the nineteenth-century culture of sentimentality. What Shirley Samuels calls the "national project" of sentimentality promoted a state of exclusivity between a husband and wife that the structure of plural marriage simply could not sustain.[61] In the 1830s and 1840s, women, particularly white and middle- and upper-class women, derived increased "status, standing, and power through the medium of affection and self-expression in their relationships with men," in turn strengthening hierarchal gendered distinctions that appeared to clearly separate the public and private spheres of work and home.[62] As Barbara Epstein notes in her study of women's experiences of religion and temperance in the nineteenth-century United

States, "domesticity represented a weakening of women's power in relation to men, but in an immediate sense, it represented the best of all available alternatives; and by providing women with a role that was clearly
defined and widely venerated, it offered them an arena for self-development
and a base from which to press their claims."[63] Thus, even as middle- and
upper-class white women were losing power through the diminishment
of their influence in the nuclear family as an economic unit, the 1840s
witnessed an upshot in women's political activism, exemplified in Black
women's abolitionism and the 1848 Seneca Falls Convention. Many of these
norms, dictated by white, middle-class northeasterners, became less important for the Saints as the significance of plural marriage increased once they
established their western colonies in 1847.

EARLY MORMON POLITICAL ECONOMY

Mormon women, like their husbands, engaged in physically demanding
work that contributed to the economic development of both the household and the community. Additionally, the increasing value that was placed
on individual achievement under industrial capitalism was countered by
early socialistic experiments conducted by the Saints. Although the faith
came of age during a time when money and earthly goods were thought
to reflect a man's work ethic and success, Smith's implementation of the
Law of Consecration and Stewardship challenged these still solidifying
standards. As early as 1831, the Saints attempted to live in communal harmony under a structure called the United Order. This system of "economic equality, socialization of surplus incomes, freedom of enterprise,
and group economic self-sufficiency" was based upon the notion that all
the earth and everything on it belonged to the Lord and not to individual
property owners.[64] Under the fledgling system, Saints would consecrate
or deed their property to the Church and in return receive a stewardship.
This system allowed Church leaders to allocate based on want and need
and to care for impoverished converts, of whom there were many joining
the Church. By implementing these communal economic practices in Ohio
and Missouri, the Saints not only challenged the notion of separate spheres,
they also questioned the individualistic order of industrial capitalism that
was coming to characterize, but did not yet define, national identity, citizenship, and ideology.

Because these economic-religious attempts to set themselves apart
coincided with their less physically violent but still racist treatment of

Indigenous peoples, the Saints' ostracism was virtually ensured. Their early economic experimentations appreciably affected their peculiar reputation, only adding to the surety of anti-Mormons that the Saints stood in stark contrast to what it meant to be American, religiously, racially, sexually, and economically. The large influx of Mormon settlers, their early economic experimentation, differing attitudes toward Native peoples, and rumors about their proselytizing to Black people incited anti-Mormons to drive them out of both Ohio and Missouri. Violent mobs forced the Saints to put their economic experiments on hold as they fled from the borderlands of Missouri into the temporary safety of Nauvoo, Illinois, in 1839.

Although the Saints managed to attain an unprecedented level of autonomy in the early 1840s, they continued to face increasing levels of prejudice during their residence in Illinois. Throughout their tenure there, they achieved all but political independence—from both state and federal governance—first as a result of an unprecedentedly generous city charter and subsequently because of the sheer numbers that made bloc voting a mainstay of Mormon political power in the state. Not only did Nauvoo virtually function as a state within a state, but it boasted a large and well-trained militia and the second largest population in Illinois, after Chicago, with ten thousand residents. But beneath the prosperous surface, Nauvoo was built on a precarious economic foundation, like many other western settlements. Moreover, key theological developments were rapidly transforming the Church in ways that would have implications far beyond the 1840s.[65]

It was in Nauvoo that Smith introduced plural marriage to his most trusted advisers, and the practice spread horizontally among the leadership. Unfortunately for him, the introduction of polygamy coincided with and precipitated the defection of several high-level leaders. John C. Bennett, who had served as a close confidant of Smith and the mayor of Nauvoo, published a highly embarrassing, sensationalized, and extremely erroneous exposé of the Church and its leadership. In it, he revealed the practice of polygamy, exaggerating and even inventing details about the practice among the Saints. He also accused leaders, especially Smith, of other types of sexual misconduct.[66] Bennett went so far as to declare: "Joe Smith meditates the *total overthrow, not only of our government and of our social fabric,* but of all creeds and religions that are not in perfect accordance with his own bloody and stupid imposture [Mormonism]."[67] Here Bennett explicitly linked the well-being of the state to the norms and practices of society, charging Mormonism with blurring the distinction between the public and

private spheres that had begun to cohere under the joint auspices of industrial capitalism and the cult of true womanhood. He also employed accusations of religious bigotry against the Saints—rendering invisible the real
and violent religious intolerance they had experienced—to paint a portrait of Mormons as not just un-American but anti-American in both their
attempts to establish a theocratic state and in their religious and cultural
differences. While in retrospect many of his claims are highly suspect and
plainly inflammatory, they nonetheless reflected and helped to construct
Mormonism as un-American, and sometimes anti-American, between the
1830s and the 1850s.

Bennett's accusations of religious persecution were especially ironic
given that anti-Mormons used Mormon peculiarity as a foil against which
to establish Protestantism as the unspoken national religious tradition, all
the while lauding religious freedom.[68] Such accusations pushed an already
simmering anti-Mormonism to the boiling point, confirming and height-
ening the fears of non-Mormons in the Midwest. Bennett fed into fears of
both race treason and political sedition, accusing the Saints of planning to
"exterminate" all non-Mormons if they would not convert, obscuring the
realities of violent anti-Mormon suppression of Mormon settlements.[69]

SOLIDIFYING MORMON PECULIARITY

By the spring of 1844, events were congealing that would result in Joseph
Smith's martyrdom that summer. Lingering resentments on the part of
Missourians and growing concern over the Saints' political power in Illinois found their outlet when more top leaders began to defect from the
Church. The secrecy with which Smith had disseminated the practice of
plural marriage within the upper echelons of the Church resulted in confusion and schism. Disaffected leaders began to print indictments of Smith
as a fallen prophet in local newspapers. The city council of Nauvoo, led by
Smith, responded by declaring one press apostate and a civic nuisance, order-
ing it destroyed. Too late did Smith realize that destroying the press gave
his enemies the perfect excuse to come after him with the legal force of the
state. After an arrest warrant was issued by Governor Ford of Illinois, Smith
and his brother Hyrum surrendered themselves and were held in the Car-
thage Jail for trial. On June 27, 1844, a mob made up primarily of the Warsaw,
Illinois, militia, stormed the jail and killed Smith and his brother Hyrum.
Smith's martyrdom, even more than previous persecution they had suffered,
cemented the Saints' sense of themselves as a distinct ethnic group.[70]

Following Smith's death, the Saints were forced to reevaluate their position in Nauvoo as violent anti-Mormonism once again began to manifest. They soon decided to leave the state and settle in a territory outside the reach of anti-Mormon violence and U.S. governmental interference. Brigham Young, the Church's new leader, led a massive exodus from Nauvoo to the Mexican territory of the Great Basin, present-day Salt Lake City, arriving in July 1847. During the Saints' yearlong migration, the United States declared war against Mexico. By the time the Saints arrived in the Salt Lake Valley, it was contested territory. Despite continued persecution and multiple failed attempts to elicit help from the federal government during their time in Illinois, Young dispatched troops to fight in the Mexican–American War as a sign of allegiance to the U.S. government.

The Saints commenced a concerted project of colonial settlement immediately upon their arrival in the Great Basin, yet their support of the U.S. government in the war did nothing to improve their reputation. Reginald Horsman argues that while tribal resistance to the appropriation of their lands was used to characterize Native Americans as "subhuman savages" and helped to support an understanding of white superiority, the more significant "catalyst in the overt adoption of a racial Anglo-Saxonism was the meeting of Americans and Mexicans in the Southwest, the Texas Revolution, and the war with Mexico."[71] Just as the Saints had been racialized as degraded or nonwhite people through claims of race treason and miscegenation in Ohio and Missouri, Mexicans were vilified during the war as dangerous because of their purportedly mixed-race status. Not only were Mexicans considered to be mixed, in and of itself considered a problematic status, but they had also infused what was considered to be the least desirable ancestry into their racial makeup by white Americans—African and Native blood—through interracial sexual unions.[72] Debates among elected officials during the war reveal that anxiety about the annexation of Mexican land circulated around the implied annexation of Mexican bodies that came with the territory.

It is not unreasonable to assume that officials' concern around the integration of Mexican bodies into U.S. society extended to the bodies of Mormons; Mormon bodies, in the eyes of nineteenth-century state officials, like Mexican bodies, would have represented a dangerous collision of religious difference, racial impurity, and sexual impropriety. Already discursively distinguished from Anglo-Saxons—despite their best efforts—the Saints' residence in a disputed territory assumed to be populated with so-called undesirable Mexicans combined with increasingly prevalent rumors about plural marriages to further other the Saints. By the time Orson Pratt, a member of the Quorum of the Twelve Apostles, the second highest body in the Church, announced plural marriage as a calling and obligation of faithful Saints in August 1852 at the behest of Young, publicly confirming over ten years of rumors, anti-Mormons had already been racializing the Saints through reference to their supposed sexual and marital practices. Long before sexology co-opted comparative anatomy and embraced eugenics, both methods of late nineteenth-century racial science, to produce sexualities—homosexuality in particular—race was being constructed in and through discourses of sex.[73] This ready-made and seasoned strategy would prove incredibly useful in the coming conflict over what would become known as the "Mormon question"; it became a central strategy for justifying federal intervention in Utah's governance over the next four decades.

The colonial, racial, religious, gendered, sexual, and political-economic dimensions of early and mid-nineteenth-century U.S. society detailed above are all essential for contextualizing both mushrooming anti-Mormon sentiment and activity at midcentury and, particularly, the popularization of Mormon peculiarity discourse. Even in the early decades of the Church's history, anti-Mormons' nascent articulations of Mormon peculiarity—that characterized Mormonism as a strange, deluded, racially suspect cult—helped to determine what was considered unacceptable, peculiar, and deviant and, by extension, what was understood to be expected, normal, and natural. As I explain in the following two chapters, the peculiarizing of Mormonism was part and parcel of the racializing colonial process that forwarded U.S. empire via notions of gender and sexual exceptionalism, gaining extensive traction as the century progressed. As the Saints themselves found, but could not understand, their adherence to even a majority of the cultural, economic, and political norms in U.S. society was not enough to ensure them inclusion within the political community of the nation-state and thus what Johnson calls "the right to have rights."[74]

2 A Peculiar Race with Peculiar Institutions, 1847–1874

> The remarks of Surgeon Barthelow [*sic*] respecting the identity
> of facial expression, and other peculiarities, chiefly physical,
> afford an illustration . . . of the tendency of peculiar institu-
> tions . . . to produce permanent *varieties* of [a] particular race.
>
> —C. G. Forshey commenting on Roberts
> Bartholow's "Hereditary Descent"

> There is a feeling throughout the earth that there is something
> remarkable connected with [the Latter-day Saints], that we are
> not as other people are. . . . What is it that distinguishes us from
> the average American, Englishman, Scandinavian, German,
> Swiss, Italian, or Frenchman, or from the average Asiatic?
> There is something; they feel it and we feel it.
>
> —George Q. Cannon, "Stirring Times,"
> *Journal of Discourses*

In her study of the ways religious freedom was invoked and articulated
in the nineteenth- and early twentieth-century United States, Tisa Wenger
demonstrates that "religious freedom talk" was critical to both the maintenance and the navigation of biopolitical governance. Used by those
already classified as Anglo-Saxon white people to reaffirm their civilizational superiority, religious freedom talk was also deployed by those racialized as nonwhite to refute their categorization as civilizationally inferior.
Overall, Wenger explains, religious freedom talk functioned to "delineate
what counted as religion" (i.e., Protestantism), primarily through the construction of various racializing civilizational assemblages.[1] What she defines

as "the complex interplay of ideological and institutional processes that work together to define who and what counts as civilized and thus as fully human—and by contrast, who and what does not," these assemblages were both the topic and the product of religious freedom talk.[2]

Wenger's history helps to illustrate how under the structure of colonialism, as the "essential matrix of racialization," race has been produced in the United States as biopolitical governance through reference to religion.[3] More specifically, her work helps to demonstrate how race is often manufactured through religious freedom talk as the primary product of the colonial relation of power, a "form of political order through which a polity . . . rules a population by treating its members as political aliens." Put another way, within systems of settler and extractive colonialism, which have characterized the modern history of the Americas, race functions as a governing strategy that continuously includes some and excludes others from "the political community through which the constitution of the state is conceived."[4] Race and processes of racialization are thereby used not only to justify differential treatment of various groups by and within the U.S. nation-state but also to elide the ongoing nature of U.S. colonialization of Indigenous land and sovereignty. These "concomitant global systems" of colonization and racialization, which "secure white dominance through time, property, and notions of self," are made evident, and their relationship further elucidated, I argue, in the history of Mormonism.[5]

While chapter 1 detailed how Mormon peculiarity discourse had framed Mormonism as un-American not just religiously but culturally, economically, and politically well before The Church of Jesus Christ of Latter-day Saints announced the official practice of plural marriage in 1852, this chapter details how after that 1852 declaration Mormonism moved from a sporadic regional preoccupation to a consistent national obsession. While scholarly attention has concentrated on polygamy as ground zero for the mid- to late nineteenth-century conflict over Mormonism, this attention has often neglected to sufficiently assess the ways that Mormon plural marriage—as a multidimensional practice that embodied religious belief, kinship structure, sexual and gender roles and relations, and economic and political organization—was actively racialized with far-reaching biopolitical effects. This chapter and the next highlight conflict over nineteenth-century Mormonism as a particularly potent illustration of how racial formation functioned in and through the delineation of what practices counted as civilized not just in terms of "appropriate" or "good" religious belief and practice but also in terms of normative cultural, economic, and political values and practices. As such, these chapters highlight Mormonism as a racializing civilizational assemblage that, in constitutive relation to other civilizational assemblages of the period, ultimately helped to engrain Protestant Anglo-Saxon whiteness as Americanness. Specifically, it analyzes how the mid-nineteenth-century construction of Mormons as racially degraded or nonwhite people was not grounded in objections to lineage or skin color but rather to a variety of perceived values and practices related to religion, marriage, sex, gender, labor, and citizenship that were assumed to both reveal and produce biological racial inferiority.

As work at the intersections of Native studies, U.S. religious history, and feminist and queer theory has amply documented, both the racialized proscription and prescription of normative culture has long been central to the projects of European and U.S. colonialism in North America.[6] Because neither African nor Indigenous cultures recognized or practiced the specific relations between gender, sex, marriage, and property that were considered fundamental to European and U.S. settler cultures, they were dubbed "savage" and "barbaric" in order to justify expulsion, enslavement, and genocide.[7] In much the same way, anti-Mormons styled the Saints' practices—polygamy, theocracy, and cooperative economics, in particular—as "peculiar," "barbaric," and "foreign," consequently constructing them as racially and civilizationally inferior, regardless of their somatic presentation and their cultural, national, and geographic ancestry.

Even as scholarship has begun to engage the question of how and why Mormonism was racialized, researchers—like nineteenth-century Mormons themselves—have puzzled at what they characterize as white Protestant Americans' denial or obfuscation of Mormons' supposedly obvious whiteness. For example, in his important and thorough study of how nineteenth-century Mormons were racialized, W. Paul Reeve conceptualizes whiteness as obviously definable, sometimes as lineage and sometimes as phenotype (skin color especially), reflecting a broader trend in somatic-centered theories of race.[8] Such conceptualizations are both incomplete and restrictive for several reasons. First, even as they chart the socially constructed nature of race, they simultaneously and paradoxically adhere to a kind of pseudobiological framework that insists race is always embedded within or visible upon the body. Second, and relatedly, they cannot fully account for processes of racialization that do not rely primarily on the body for their point of reference. And third, they often examine race outside of the larger political system from which it is produced—in this case, U.S. colonialism.

Therefore, in order to help promote a divestment from somatic-centered theories of race, this chapter elucidates Johnson's observation that "the simple fact that religion can be racialized . . . renders analytically mute any phenotypic paradigm of race, as religion is not a phenotypic formation," through an examination of Mormon peculiarity discourse's role in the elaboration of whiteness as the dominant political category of belonging in the U.S. nation-state.[9] More specifically, it focuses on how the racialization of Mormons as degraded or nonwhite people was achieved through reference to the gendered and sexual norms of both the state's colonial governance and capitalism's expansionist imperatives in order to illustrate "how 'race' even in [the] late nineteenth century . . . was deployed in excess of the corporeal, having multiple references of association (e.g., territory, climate, history, culture, [and] religion), suggesting that the body was less the ubiquitous metaphor of 'race' than its privileged metonym."[10]

Thus, this chapter and the next seek to elucidate the biopolitics of racializing Mormonism during the mid- to late nineteenth century. Scholarship on this period of Mormon history has concentrated primarily, although certainly not exclusively, on two foci: the significance and impact of anti-Mormon literary representations and Mormonism's importance to the history of religious freedom in the United States. Although these trends are shifting somewhat, these emphases remain understandably central. To provide a more comprehensive picture, this chapter focuses on the Saints' marital, economic, and political practices, representations of those practices, and anti-Mormon responses to both. Examining Mormon peculiarity discourse between the 1850s and the 1870s helps to illuminate the constitutive relations between scientific, popular, and political discourses about race, sex, gender, economics, and governance as part and parcel of U.S. colonialism.

WHITE FOLKS?

Entering the Salt Lake Valley for the first time in July 1847, Brigham Young boldly declared, "This is the right place."[11] His abbreviated statement—"This is the place"—has become a famous affirmation of the site's material and divine significance to his church's colonial project. In hindsight, his declaration might also be regarded as a harbinger of Utah Territory's important role as a site where the constitutive work of U.S. empire was undertaken. When the Great Basin region was ceded by Mexico to the United States under the Treaty of Guadalupe Hidalgo in 1848, the Saints formally reentered the country after less than a year outside of it. As early as 1849, the Saints sent a formal petition to Congress asking them to grant statehood to an area that encompassed present-day Utah and major portions of Nevada, California, Arizona, Idaho, Wyoming, Colorado, and New Mexico. Refusing to recognize the extensive and theocratically controlled State of Deseret, Congress only granted territorial status to a much smaller region under the Compromise of 1850, renaming the jurisdiction "Utah."[12] Despite the federal government's icy reception of petitions for statehood, upon their arrival the Saints immediately set about building Zion. A provisional government was formed by Church leadership that functioned as the de facto administration long after the Saints' first statehood petition was denied. After Congress appointed Young as Utah's governor in 1851, the Church administration continued to function as a shadow government well into the 1870s.[13]

Reflecting similar accusations during the Saints' time in Illinois, charges of autocratic theocracy arose almost before they had established themselves in the valley and only increased once outsiders saw that lay members unanimously endorsed Church directives with the ballot. Although most scholarship has focused on anti-Mormon assaults against polygamy, such attacks were almost always accompanied by accusations of theocracy. The ecclesiastical court system that had accompanied the (de facto, if not de jure) establishment of the State of Deseret would remain the primary legal structure in Utah Territory until Congress passed the anti-Mormon Poland Act in 1874.[14] Utah's court system was one of the most offensive institutions to anti-Mormons and one of the most effective insulations against federal control of the territory.[15] The Church also established the Perpetual Emigrating Fund—a self-replenishing account—that fostered the emigration of converts from across the globe, but mainly from Britain and Scandinavia. The systematically organized gathering of all followers in Zion, and the global immigration that it promoted, resulted in the settlement of over eighty-five thousand people to the Great Basin area by 1887.[16]

In addition to establishing political and governmental control, colonial parties were sent out to survey and claim land, slowly but systematically working to convert and expel Indigenous inhabitants. The Church's attitude toward and approach to interacting with local tribes ebbed and flowed. Like their non-Mormon counterparts, the Saints experimented with killing, forcibly removing, enslaving, trading with, marrying, and converting Native peoples, tactics that were all ultimately subsumed under a policy of "civilizing" based on widespread white supremacist notions of Anglo-Saxon "civilization" and the "barbarism" of nonwhite people.[17] Despite the Mormon belief that Indigenous peoples were descendants of the ancient Lamanites of the Book of Mormon, the Church's treatment of them was guided by the attitude expressed by Young that "we are located in the midst of savage tribes who for generations untold have been taught to rob[,] plunder[,] and kill. . . . They are moreover ignorant and degraded[,] living in the lowest degree of filthiness[,] practicing extreme barbarity."[18] With an attitude frequently indistinguishable from non-Mormons, the Saints "asserted their role as agents of civilization and progress," simultaneously using that role to argue for their religious superiority and for what they saw as their rightful place as executors of U.S. imperial rule.[19] As with other marginalized groups staking a claim to whiteness and Americanness, the Saints asserted their claims through settler colonial occupation and the denigration and violent suppression of Indigenous groups who had already been firmly established as culturally and racially inferior.

Widespread debates about the incorporation of Native, Mexican, Irish, and Chinese people into the nation during the 1850s coincided with the Saints' ambitious proselytizing efforts and their attempts to establish economic and political self-sufficiency across the Southwest. By 1850, the Saints had also established missions on the Hawaiian Islands, in Scandinavia, France, Italy, and Switzerland. Over the next two years, they set up delegations in Australia, East India, Germany, and South Africa. While the Latter-day Saints were serious about bringing their faith not just to North America but to everywhere else as well, they did so within a complex colonialist framework that assumed and promoted racial hierarchy. This vast missionary undertaking clashed with the solidification of "Americanness," which had congealed by 1850, as fundamentally Protestant Anglo-Saxonism. While Protestant missionizing was encouraged as an important tactic of U.S. colonialism, Mormon missionizing, which strongly advocated converts migrate to Utah and furthered the Church's own settler colonial project, utterly exacerbated nativist alarm about the integration of immigrants—particularly those who were not Protestant or Anglo-Saxon—into the U.S. nation-state.

Opinions about the assimilation of non-Protestants and nonwhite people varied in the United States: some considered it the destiny and responsibility of Anglo-Saxon Protestant Americans to govern and civilize supposedly lowlier peoples, others thought that the United States had a divine right to usurp territory and expel its former inhabitants. But while opinions about integration varied, notions of Anglo-Saxon Protestant supremacy did not. As the first chapter detailed, well before the early 1850s Mormons were designated racially other, a designation that was created largely, but not exclusively, through vehement religious persecution. Since the time of contact, the process of what Moustafa Bayoumi calls "racing religion" has played a fundamental role in the creation of a racial caste system in North America.[20] Its maintenance as a central strategy of U.S. colonialism is evident in the nineteenth-century consternation over Mormonism. This conflict is a particularly potent example of the racialization of religion and, specifically, the central role that delineating nonnormative gendered, familial, and political-economic practices played in that process. Native, Mexican, Irish, and Chinese peoples, as well as the Saints themselves, were all racialized as degraded or nonwhite people with reference to their religiocultural practices.

In the early 1850s, the Saints' geographic proximity to and their interactions with populations deemed racially inferior to Anglo-Saxon white people—Indigenous and Mexican peoples in particular—combined with the fact of their nonnormative religious practices to place them even further outside the ideal notions of whiteness and, therefore, outside what Barbara Welke calls "the borders of belonging" that constituted personhood and citizenship in the United States.[21] For example, federal Indian agents repeatedly used the fact that Native peoples in Utah distinguished between "Americans" and "Mormons" as evidence of the Saints' racial, and therefore political, treason.[22] Reports that "'the Mormons'" had fostered this distinction at the peril of federal troops circulated in Washington, D.C., throughout the 1850s, specifically charging that Young had gone to "'great pains and considerable expense to procure and retain the friendship of the Indian tribes. He has made them valuable presents, has invited them to his settlements, has educated their children, and loaded them with every favor which it was in his power to bestow.'"[23] While the Saints saw themselves as proselytizing to the ancestors of the Lamanites in fulfillment of God's plan, helpfully forwarding the intertwined projects of Manifest Destiny and Zion, anti-Mormons saw their actions as a treasonous threat to U.S. empire.

Responding to reports of the Saints' nonwhiteness, high-ranking Church leader Heber C. Kimball directly challenged accusations of Mormon racial treason:

We are white folks; a good portion of us were born in the United States, and a great many in Old England; and they are our brethren and sisters. My father came from there, and fought for this country, and sustained it; if he did not my grandfather did, it is along in that train somewhere. We have all come from the old countries, and come into a new country, into the States; and from that we have emigrated into still newer countries.[24]

Kimball's proclamation makes clear not only that race was commonly thought to be equivalent to phenotype and ancestry but also that whiteness was commonly understood to be an essential characteristic of U.S. citizenship and nationalism. Narrating the entrance of U.S. troops into the Salt Lake Valley that winter, Kimball claimed that the soldiers "rejoice[d] to dwell in the midst of white people. They never thought for a moment we were *white* men and women; but when they came, they found out, to their astonishment, that the people in Utah were quite white, and right from their own country," reflecting the importance of perception and phenotype in processes of racialization.[25] In addition to his declaration of Mormons' white skin and Anglo-Saxon ancestry, he also emphasized their commitment to the project of Manifest Destiny. "We have all come from the old countries, and come into a new country, into the States," Kimball implored, advancing the exceptionalist narrative of immigration and benevolent, religious settler colonialism as the historical basis of the nation's past.

Yet, Kimball's emphasis on the visible, phenotypical similarities between the Saints and other U.S. citizens, the English ancestry of many Saints, and his framing of the Church's colonial projects as exemplary of U.S. colonialism did not convince anti-Mormon critics. Despite Kimball's assertions that some non-Mormons were relieved to find the Saints were actually *"white men and women,"* the Saints would be increasingly racialized through Mormon peculiarity discourse as nonwhite during the 1850s and 1860s as a result of their failure to conform to mainstream marital, economic, and political practices. Or, as Coviello explains, the Saints failed to realize that "settler-colonial whiteness was . . . a matter larger than both phenotype and a willingness to indulge in racist disidentification and violence. Whiteness entailed, too, specific ways of living in relation to gender, to sex, and to secularity, not all of which were easily claimed by devoted Mormons."[26]

The platform of the Republican National Party, announced at their first convention in 1856, demonstrates just how far outside the boundaries of acceptability the Saints had wandered both culturally and politically, and therefore racially. Mormon studies scholars have repeatedly pointed to the Republicans' call for the elimination of polygamy and slavery as the "twin relics of barbarism" as an especially significant sign of Mormonism's place in U.S. history. The platform signaled an important shift in popular understandings of Mormon peculiarity that would characterize the rest of the century. The rhetoric of barbarism was an explicitly racial, and therefore imperial, language that anti-Mormons argued constituted Mormonism. If by the mid-1850s an understanding of Mormons as a separate race was still budding, then by the middle of the next decade it had ripened into a fine fruit. "Barbarism" was a label that signaled the Saints' inferior racial status through reference to their deviant cultural, economic, and political practices. This inferior status subsequently justified the federal government's increasingly strict regulation of the Saints in the mid-1870s, which I explore in the following chapter.

By the mid-1850s, public knowledge that the Saints practiced plural marriage had encouraged the development of a burgeoning anti-Mormon industry: travel writers, journalists, novelists, and cultural critics all put pen to page in an effort to define Mormon polygamy as an un-American danger; in doing so, these writers ensured the continued relevance of Mormonism to the biopolitics of the imperial nation-state. The importance of sentimental antipolygamy fiction has, in particular, been well established by scholars who have focused on the forms, messages, and effects of such writing on the general public's perception of Mormonism, an especially persuasive example of Kyla Schuller's thesis that "sentimentalism, in the midst of its feminized ethic of emotional identification, operates as a fundamental mechanism of biopower."[27] Immensely popular sentimental novels such as Maria Ward's *Female Life among the Mormons* (1855), Alfreda Eva Bell's *Boadicea; The Mormon Wife: Life-Scenes in Utah* (1855), and Orvilla S. Belisle's *The Prophets: Or, Mormonism Unveiled* (1855) did not encourage a resurgent interest in Mormonism's strangeness, rather they actively constructed Mormonism as peculiar. Because numerous analyses have already well documented the breadth and importance of antipolygamy fiction's role in suturing gendered notions of public and private, domesticity, and monogamy to the project of Manifest Destiny, below I focus on the visual representation of Mormonism in conjunction with other types of anti-Mormon discourse to scrutinize how the concept was actively produced as a racial peculiarity that, in contrast, produced Americanness as white.

BREASTWORKS, CRINOLINE CAMPS, AND MOVEABLE HAREMS

Both visual and written representations of the Saints deployed entangled logics of sex and gender to construct Mormonism as racially peculiar in the mid-nineteenth-century popular imagination. While sexuality was only an embryonic concept—it would formally enter both popular and professional lexicons in the United States by the end of the century as an especially important tool for identifying and representing "inferior," "barbaric," and "foreign" peoples as threatening to the domestic space of the nation—what can be identified as its progenitors or precursors were already functioning to define racial status for biopolitical purposes.[28] As Siobhan Somerville's work so expertly illustrates in *Queering the Color Line,* sexuality and race were not distinct, unrelated, or merely parallel concepts; rather, the invention of homosexuality as an identity was intertwined with dominant notions of a Black/white color line. Specifically, as Somerville's analysis of the relationship between scientific racism and sexology implies, and as Kyla Schuller's work on the emergence of biopower within nineteenth-century sentimentalism establishes, conceptions of both sexual practice and sex were predicated upon racialized understandings of bodies. Along these lines, an in-depth examination of visual representations of Mormonism during midcentury, along with other articulations of Mormon peculiarity discourse, demonstrates that polygamy and monogamy were not peripheral but central categories used to determine racial-religious-national belonging when scientific racism was at its height but well before sexology emerged as a dominant scientific discourse.[29] Thus, as conceptual antecedents to homo- and heterosexuality (as well as the theories that explained those identities and desires, such as sexual inversion), polygamy and monogamy were central categories in biopolitical rationalizations for U.S. colonialism.

As with burgeoning notions of sexual identity at the end of the century, gender presentation and behavior played a central role in defining certain sexual practices as deviant at midcentury. Similar to early sexological theorizations of homosexuality as gender inversion, many depictions of Mormon polygamy between the 1850s and the 1870s focused on the ways that those who practiced plural marriage supposedly experienced the reversal of normative gender presentation and roles.[30] Predating the formal announcement of polygamy by Church leaders by almost five months, a comic image printed in the April 1852 edition of the *Old Soldier* played on the reversal of normative gender roles to criticize the Saints. The federal government's attempts to install federal officials in territorial posts in Utah resulted in sour relations between the Church and the public officials dispatched to Utah Territory. Several officials abandoned their posts, traveled back to Washington, and reported on the unwillingness of the Saints to cooperate with the appointees, some describing them as disloyal and treasonous. Such reports included stories of plural marriage that quickly made it into the popular press. Playing on the military term for a temporary defensive fortification, *Mormon Breastworks and U.S. Troops* (Figure 1) depicts wives confronting fleeing U.S. troops, wielding exaggerated features of their femininity—their large breasts and screaming infants in arms—as weapons against the enemy, while Mormon men squat behind them with guns at the ready. The reversal of normative gender roles in graphic images such as this subtly communicated the links that were assumed to exist between gender roles and racial status. Women fighting on the front lines defending men not only maligned Mormon men's masculinity as cowardly

MORMON BREASTWORKS AND U. S. TROOPS.

Officer U.S.A. *(Trumpeter! Sound the retreat! we never can carry that Battery in the world, Cesar himself would be defeated before such Breastworks.)*

FIGURE 1. *Mormon Breastworks and U.S. Troops.* "Officer U.S.A.: 'Trumpeter! Sound the retreat! we never can carry that Battery in the world, Cesar himself would be defeated before such Breastworks.'" Reprinted from *Old Soldier*, April 1, 1852. American Antiquarian Society, Worcester, Massachusetts.

but also indirectly suggested that Mormonism produced gender inversion among phenotypically white people. This image anticipated the tropes of anti-Mormon illustration that were employed time and again against the Saints during the Utah War of 1857–58, but it also served as a forerunner to the ways other biopolitical knowledges, such as eugenics, would come to link gender and sexuality with the processes of racial othering that fueled U.S. imperialism at the turn of the century.[31]

Mid-nineteenth-century visual culture built upon the spate of sentimental antipolygamy novels published in the early 1850s, which generally portrayed evil polygamous patriarchs as deceptively and treacherously luring young white women into what was described as the worst form of slavery—polygamy—subsequently destroying their innocence, virtue, and, eventually, their lives. While antipolygamy literature surged in the first few years after the Church's 1852 announcement (by the end of the century, over eighty such novels would be published), visual anti-Mormonism exploded with fervor during the Utah War between 1857 and 1858.[32] Based on the sensationalized and much exaggerated accounts of the so-called runaway federal officials, who had abandoned their posts in Utah after butting heads with the Saints, and hoping to score some easy political points, President James Buchanan sent federal troops to Utah in early 1857 in order to suppress what was cast as "Mormon rebellion."[33] As soon as Young heard that Buchanan had dispatched troops, he organized a complete evacuation of northern Utah, created alliances with local tribal leaders, and implemented effective strategies to waylay the coming army. Buchanan's decision to send federal troops to the territory revealed both the inaccuracy of many of the charges made against the Saints by federal officials and the loyalty and organization of the Saints under Young's command, reinforcing fears of Mormon authoritarianism. Even though the Utah War never included any formal battles, it did result in the Mountain Meadows Massacre, in which a group of Saints and Paiutes attacked and killed members of the Baker-Fancher wagon train. War hysteria, combined with a general fear of non-Mormon outsiders based on past experiences of religious persecution, is thought to account for the slaughter of the traveling settlers; however, the incident remains one of the most well-known and cited events of Mormon history and was touted extensively during the second half of the nineteenth century as evidence of both Mormon treason and the Saints' supposed barbarism.

Cartoonists employed the tropes of inverted gender roles and presentation throughout the Utah War, denigrating Mormon masculinity (especially

Brigham Young's courage), mocking the practice of plural marriage, and presenting Mormonism as a threat to the cult of domesticity. *Brigham Young from Behind His Breastworks Charging the United States Troops* (Figure 2), an image from late 1857, highlights the portrayal of inverted gender roles and presentation.

Young sits astride the shoulders of a robust woman trumpeter as he leads a host of elderly women into battle. At first glance, the image merely repeats the previous breastworks theme from the 1852 image, mocking the notion of women as soldiers, as well as Young's cowardice; upon further inspection, however, the lithograph contains subtle, yet telling, details about how anti-Mormons deployed concepts of sex and gender. For example, one of the Mormon soldiers stands slightly in front of the rest, placed in the left forefront of the picture, outfitted in a dress and a high, frilled bonnet. The figure wields an extremely large and dangerous looking pair of scissors, which appear to have just been pulled from the sewing bag hanging from their shoulder. Despite feminine accoutrement and weaponry, the figure betrays a distinctly masculine countenance, with a hooked nose, bushy eyebrows, a goatee, and even men's pants and shoes visible underneath a dress. The contrast between feminine garb and masculine

BRIGHAM YOUNG FROM BEHIND HIS BREASTWORKS CHARGING THE UNITED STATES TROOPS

FIGURE 2. *Brigham Young from Behind His Breastworks Charging the United States Troops*. Lithograph for sale at 217 Walnut Street, Philadelphia, circa 1857–58. American Antiquarian Society, Worcester, Massachusetts.

physical features is evident in the entire crowd of Mormon soldiers standing behind Young, who are variously carrying brooms and brushes as weapons instead of guns or swords.

The artist uses the tools of domestic maintenance—brooms, scissors, and dusters—to mock both the threat of Mormon resistance to federal pressure and President Buchanan's blunder in sending troops to Utah in the first place. But the choice to replace weapons with domestic utilities does more than simply ridicule the sex/gender imbalance that polygamy was thought to produce. While on the surface an army populated by women was laughable to nineteenth-century audiences, the image subtly communicates the ways that state institutions relied on practices of domestication and, in particular, the labor of women to maintain and reproduce itself as a settler colonial enterprise.[34] The Mormon system was therefore understood to be, and was consequently portrayed as, a threat to that delicate balance because of the challenge it posed to normative ideals of femininity, domesticity, and the public/private binary.[35]

The funny but alarming threat of Mormonism is made clear by focusing on the group of young women and children placed at the center of the picture, between the oncoming Mormon multitude and the escaping federal troops. Young and his trumpeter are about to trample over several screaming women and babies, some tearing out their hair at the prospect of being overtaken. It is easy to assume that these figures represent the innocents of the nation who were portrayed as the most likely to be taken in and hurt by Mormon polygamy—vulnerable women and children—which was a consistent trope of anti-Mormonism generally and antipolygamy writing specifically, but it is equally likely that these figures were meant to represent the Mountain Meadows Massacre. This explanation seems probable, considering that in the upper right-hand corner of the lithograph a wagon train is burning.

These apparently clear references, however, must be tempered by a closer look at the women and children standing directly behind those being trampled. At first glance, they appear to be part of the group being crushed, fearful and attempting to flee. But the expressions of some of the women still standing and holding their children in outstretched arms at the back of the image are gleeful rather than fearful. They seem to be holding out their crying children in order to scare the federal troops away. Another interpretation of this group of women and children, then, is that they themselves are the "breastworks"—they represent the young wives and mothers of

Mormonism put on the front lines of the battle by Young. These women contrast with the figures behind Young, who he refers to as "Grannydears," and could either represent the excess detritus of polygamy, widows and grandmothers, or devious Mormon men dressed as women in an effort to hide their cowardice at standing behind young mothers and children. Thus, the image depicts polygamy as doubly threatening—first, in Mormonism's apparent devaluing of young white women and children who can be trampled without a second thought (there are always more wives and children to be had), and second, in polygamy's gradual destruction of appropriate racialized gender roles and presentation evident in the elderly Mormon women whose sense of patriotism and propriety is represented as having been so depleted under plural marriage that they are willing to take up the roles of men to defend their prophet, or in Mormon men who dress in women's clothes in order to deceive the enemy.

Several images that appeared in *Frank Leslie's Illustrated Newspaper* and *Harper's Weekly* between 1857 and 1858 depicted plural wives as deceptive or fickle soldiers under the command of Brigham Young (Figure 3). Portrayal of Mormon women as soldiers allowed for the reinforcement of stereotypes about women—particularly that they were naturally weak, capricious, and cowardly, therefore making a poor choice for soldiers—and that the inversion of gender roles and presentation was threatening to white women's natural purity, obedience, piety, and domesticity. For example, several images portrayed these women as wild, disloyal, deceptive, and man-crazy (Figures 3 and 4). In one image from a serial cartoon published in December 1857 (Figure 3), the Mormon women soldiers rush toward the enemy with arms outstretched and coattails and hair flying behind them. Looking crazed and disorganized, their long hair contrasts with their uniform pants and morning coats to emphasize their inverted gender roles and presentation as the caption proclaims, "B.Y. . . . gives orders for a charge, which is executed with astonishing alacrity and enthusiasm." In the next and final image, the women, still in their uniforms and with undone hair, dance blithely with the invading federal troops as Young pulls at their coattails. The final image portrays the women not only as indecent, suggested in both their public state of undress and willingness to interact so intimately with men they do not know when they are presumably married (even if polygamously), but also as failing in both obedience and piety to their husbands, Brigham Young, and their so-called religion. These kinds of failures would not be insubstantial during a period when the cult of domesticity

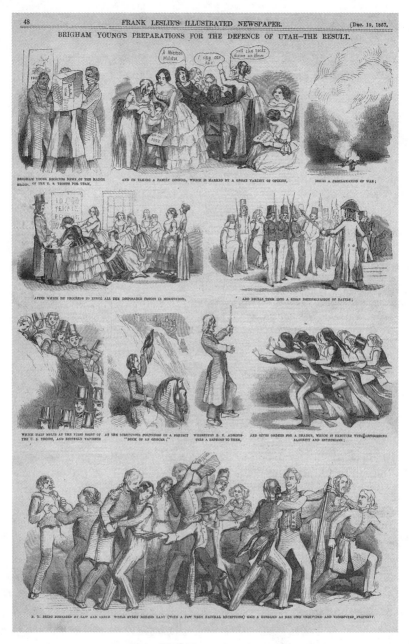

FIGURE 3. *Brigham Young's Preparations for the Defence of Utah—The Result.* Reprinted from *Frank Leslie's Illustrated Newspaper,* December 19, 1857, 48. L. Tom Perry Special Collections, Harold B. Lee Library, Brigham Young University, Provo, Utah.

was prized above all for white, Christian, middle- and upper-class women but rather would indicate the complete failure of Mormonism to function as a true Christian (i.e., Protestant) religion. This theme is repeated in another image from May 1858 in which federal soldiers are showered with physical attention from multiple Mormon women (Figure 4). The double entendre of the image's title, *Frightful Scene of Carnage and Desolation at the Sack of Salt Lake City by the United States Troops,* suggests both that the Saints' claims of persecution were overblown and that the "frightful scene of carnage and desolation" was the women's overly familiar behavior with the federal soldiers as they drink to their victory over the Mormon patriarchs tied up in the corner. The scene looks more like one from a midcentury brothel than from a military campaign, playing into the commonly repeated equation of polygamy with prostitution.[36]

Many anti-Mormon illustrations lampooned Mormon polygamy with scenes such as those of "crinoline camp[s]," the "parasol guard," and an "artillery, prepared with . . . fire irons" (Figure 6), but in addition to portraying inverted gender roles and presentation, many of these images

FRIGHTFUL SCENE OF CARNAGE AND DESOLATION AT THE SACK OF SALT LAKE CITY BY THE UNITED STATES TROOPS. (By our own Special Electric Designer.)

FIGURE 4. *Frightful Scene of Carnage and Desolation at the Sack of Salt Lake City by the United States Troops.* Reprinted from *Harper's Weekly,* May 22, 1858. L. Tom Perry Special Collections, Harold B. Lee Library, Brigham Young University, Provo, Utah.

simultaneously employed explicitly racialized tropes that nineteenth-century readers in the United States would have associated with what were assumed to be the gendered and sexual practices inherent to Indigenous, southern and western Asian, North African, and Islamic cultures. For instance, one cartoon in *Frank Leslie's* mocked Brigham Young as a coward running away from federal troops with his "moveable harems" (Figure 5), drawing on long-standing associations made between supposed Mormon and Islamic barbarism, while in another image from the December 1857 serial cartoon, captioned "[Young] issues a proclamation of war," a smoking campfire elicited popular assumptions about Native American war rituals, again playing on popular ideas about the so-called savage racial affinities between Native peoples and the Saints (Figure 3). This cursory linkage was

THE MORMONS CONVERT THEIR CARTS INTO MOVEABLE HAREMS, AND GO ON THEIR WAY REJOICING.

FIGURE 5. *The Mormons Convert Their Carts into Moveable Harems, and Go on Their Way Rejoicing.* Reprinted from *Frank Leslie's Illustrated Newspaper,* June 5, 1858, 16. Courtesy of Library of Congress.

FIGURE 6. *The Mormon War.* Reprinted from *Nick Nax*, June 1858. L. Tom Perry Special Collections, Harold B. Lee Library, Brigham Young University, Provo, Utah.

not the first time the Saints were compared to another group deemed "savage" or "wild"—considered as such in part because of their gendered and sexual practices—and in need of domestication. Nor, by any means, would it be the last. This is apparent in a February 1860 edition of *Vanity Fair* in which a report claimed that "territories are less savage when abandoned to their primitive bears and indigenous buffaloes than when subjected to the half-civilized influence of such a socialism as the Mormon megatherium."[37] In one frame from another serial illustration, printed in *Nick Nax* in June 1858, the Saints were represented by a typically racist caricature of a Black man, complete with exaggerated facial features and dull expression; the caption reads: "The Mormon fighting. Great cry and little wool." Playing on the association between southern and western Asian, North African, and Islamic cultures and polygamy, the serial's last image showed a figure, complete with top hat and umbrella shielding against the rays of

Yᵉ Popular Idea of Brigham Young and his Followers,

FIGURE 7. *Ye Popular Idea of Brigham Young and His Followers.* Reprinted from *Yankee Notions*, April 1858.

a bright sun, on the back of a running camel as it crosses the desert, followed by the caption "Express with News from Utah." Other images, such as *Ye Popular Idea of Brigham Young and His Followers* (Figure 7), printed in the April 1858 edition of *Yankee Notions,* and *The Veiled Prophet of Polygamutah,* published in the February 11, 1860, edition of *Vanity Fair,* recycled racist caricatures of Jewish people to represent the Saints as animalistic and evil (Figure 8). *Yankee Notions* portrayed Young as a horned, hooved, and bearded goat tipping his hat to his bowing followers, who are also adorned with horns, while *Vanity Fair* represented Young as half man, half

THE VEILED PROPHET OF POLYGAMUTAH.

FIGURE 8. *The Veiled Prophet of Polygamutah.* Reprinted from *Vanity Fair,* February 11, 1860, 100. Making of America Journal Articles, University of Michigan Digital Library Text Collections, University of Michigan Library, University of Michigan.

goat, blindfolded, and carrying a musical pipe labeled "Polygamy" as he points to a warning sign declaring that all non-Mormons "shall be SHOT." Such examples of early visual representations of Mormonism, its followers, and the practice of polygamy demonstrate how gendered, sexualized, and racialized logics coalesced to demean the Saints and to reinforce already established stereotypes against other marginalized groups in the nineteenth-century United States.

THE PHYSIOLOGICAL ASPECTS OF MORMONISM

Graphic images, along with antipolygamy fiction, travel narratives, sensationalistic news reporting, and federal officials' own dramatized accounts of their time in Utah, functioned to solidify a perception of the Saints as racially other, and therefore, un-American. Such mediated and political representations of Mormonism were bolstered by, and reinforced, the popular racial sciences of phrenology and physiognomy. Just as federally appointed officials had come and gone in Utah Territory, either shocked by their superfluous status or disgusted by their lack of power in the Mormon-controlled territory, other anti-Mormons who had visited Utah used their professional expertise and storytelling skills to construct the Saints as racially peculiar. For example, Roberts Bartholow, who had accompanied the troops dispatched by President Buchanan during the Utah War (the same troops Church leader Heber C. Kimball had said were shocked to find that the Saints were white men and women), wrote a report on the "physiological aspects of Mormonism."[38] On his first major assignment as an army doctor, Bartholow parlayed his observations of the Saints during summer 1858 into a fantastically popular perspective that argued polygamy had actually produced a new and degenerate race: "Mormons."

Originally published in the 1860 Surgeon General's Statistical Report, Bartholow's account was influenced by and reinforced already circulating reports of disease, degeneracy, and death in the Mormon population such as *Harper's Weekly*'s claim that "Mormon children . . . appear like a neglected uncared-for set, generally dirty and ill-clad. The majority of them are girls. . . . These children are suffered to grow up in ignorance and vice. Without the hallowed influence of home to restrain them, they are vicious, profane and obscene."[39] Reports like this one played off similar accounts of the living conditions and habits of Indigenous peoples. As overland travel to the Pacific coast increased, so too did travel narratives, both popular and "scientific." Claiming to describe Mormon life and practice in

Utah, but largely inventing colorful fictions about it, these accounts served as equally popular companions to antipolygamy novels.[40] Terryl Givens explains that fictional writing about Mormonism was easily and frequently confused with nonfiction writing on the topic, such that novels, exposés, travel writing, and newspaper articles were read interchangeably as reliable sources of fact by nineteenth-century readers. Moreover, because standards of accuracy, fact, and citation were significantly lower and even nonexistent during this period, nonfiction writing about Mormonism that was based on inaccuracies, hyperbole, and invention was frequently accepted as accurate and trustworthy. Such accounts were even used to support federal anti-Mormon legislation. "That [anti-Mormon authors] w[ere] taken at their word," Givens explains, "is evident from the fact that such important debate as that surrounding the Cummins Bill [legislation designed to strip the Utah Territory of self-governance] was largely informed by 'facts' garnered from 'reliable sources' that turn out, on inspection, to be novels and 'exposés.'"[41]

Looking to distinguish between Mormons and Anglo-Saxon white Americans, anti-Mormon commentators increasingly admonished the Saints for producing a biologically different race. Bartholow's report fell firmly in this camp, explaining that polygamy and the Saints' isolated existence had produced in them "a physical and mental condition, in a few years of growth, such as densely-populated communities in the older parts of the world, hereditary victims of all the vices of civilization, have been ages in reaching."[42] Subtly aligning the Saints with "older" and "densely-populated" civilizations was understood by readers to denote Asian, African, and Islamic cultures that practiced polygamy. The parallels drawn between Mormon, Asian, African, and Islamic religion and cultures were reinforced in his report and elsewhere with references to "harems," "sexual desires stimulated to an unnatural degree," and "eastern life, where [polygamy] has been a recognized domestic institution for ages."[43] Bartholow connected new ideas about racial development with popular stereotypes of those who were thought to be in need of colonial control in Africa and Asia, stereotypes that were perpetuated in the media. Bartholow's report was reproduced in several prominent scientific and popular journals in the 1860s, including the *Medical Times and Gazette* of London, the southern periodical *DeBow's Review,* the *San Francisco Medical Press,* the *Cincinnati Lancet and Observer,* the *Boston Medical and Surgical Journal,* the *British Medical Journal,* and the *American Medical Times,* among others.

According to Bartholow, the Saints' inferior status was evident in "the preponderance of female births, by the mortality in infantine life, by the large proportion of the albuminous and gelatinous types of constitution, and by striking uniformity in facial expression and in physical conformation of the younger proportion of the community." Moreover, "one of the most deplorable effects" of Mormon polygamy was "the genital weakness of the boys and young men, the progeny of the 'peculiar institution.'"[44] Much like the images discussed above, scientific descriptions such as this one connected sex and gender, sexual practice, and racial status in order to construct Mormons as completely outside of and threatening to the nation. An overabundance of female births and a substandard masculinity (equally undesirable by nineteenth-century standards) were directly attributed to the sexual practices of racially inferior populations. The circular logic of this type of racial science maintained that certain sexual practices could actually produce new, inferior races but also that only the most racially inferior people practiced such a marital system to begin with. Discourses of Mormon peculiarity ripened, through accounts such as Bartholow's, by deriving racial meanings from religious, cultural, sexual, and gendered nonnormative practices.

Bartholow's physical descriptions leave little doubt as to both the scientific and the popular perception of Mormons only a decade after the Saints had moved to Utah and a year before the Civil War began:

> Compounded of sensuality, cunning, suspicion, and a smirking self-conceit. The yellow, sunken, cadaverous visage; the greenish-colored eyes; the thick, protuberant lips; the low forehead; the light, yellowish hair; and the lank, angular person, constitute an appearance so characteristic of the new race, the production of polygamy, as to distinguish them at a glance.[45]

His portrayal leaves one to wonder exactly how any individual could possess such juxtaposing characteristics. Yet, having utilized many of the stereotypes employed against Black and Indigenous people, as well as Irish, Catholic, and Jewish immigrants, Bartholow's supposedly scientific representation of the Saints—written by a member of the U.S. military and a doctor—serves as a particularly accurate barometer of the state's investment in whiteness and how that investment was reinforced through the construction of Mormons as a distinctly un-American (i.e., degraded or nonwhite) race through

Mormon peculiarity discourse. Bartholow's description of the Saints would be almost comical in its insincerity, if not for the fact that his report was taken so seriously by the medical and scientific communities of the time.

His contentions caused enough sensation to be debated at the 1860 meeting of the New Orleans Academy of Science. After his report was read aloud by the association's secretary, several members discussed the accuracy of the report's claims. While there was certainly disagreement as to the plausibility of a new race being produced in such a short span— thirty years or less—those who disagreed with his thesis admitted that "the remarks of Surgeon Barthelow [sic] respecting the identity of facial expression, and other peculiarities, chiefly physical, afford an illustration, rarely offered in so brief a period, of the tendency of peculiar institutions, and of isolation, to produce permanent *varieties* of the particular race, such as the Saxon, the Celt, the Slave, and the Briton."[46] In other words, these medical professionals saw a difference between the production of separate races and the production of multiple varieties within a single race. But the distinction between races and varieties did not matter insomuch as all scientists agreed "peculiar institutions" could result in degraded, infe-rior, and, in fact, "peculiar" people. Thus, for scientists and the public alike, Mormonism was a peculiarity that produced racial degeneracy, if not a new race altogether, through polygamy.

Bartholow's critics' comments clarify why Mormonism was understood to be such a threat and can help explain why anti-Mormons worked so hard to control the Church. According to one medical professional at the conference:

The intercommerce of these varieties, when established by no violation of natural law such as degrades the Mormon type, is, doubtless, beneficial to the progeny, while the violation of the natural law, which all men read in the instinctive aversion of *different* races, degrades the offspring and com-mences the process of a certain extinction. The *mulatto*, a reproduct [sic] of the European and negro races; the *mestizo*; a product of Saracenic . . . and Indo-American races—all these are mongrel or hybrid, and have the seeds of decadence and extinction in their constitution. While the offspring or reproduct [sic] of Celtish, Saxon, and British varieties, as illustrated in the American citizen, presents the highest type of physical and mental health that has adorned the history of the master race or mankind.[47]

While variety within the Anglo-Saxon race could be beneficial in its ability to encourage intelligence and strength (and ultimately a "master race" of Americans), the intermixing of various races would produce a deficient product—one that was destined for extinction. But what is illuminating about this critic's commentary is not the stance against amalgamation—that had been more than established as commonplace in the mid-nineteenth-century United States—but rather that he equated the exercise of certain sexual practices, polygamy especially, with amalgamation. In other words, if individuals of one racial stock utilized the sexual practices of another racial stock—in this case, Mormons with presumably Anglo-Saxon origins practicing an "Oriental" sexual system—then they were thought to produce inferior racial descendants, just as amalgamation would. Anxiety over maintaining white racial dominance functioned to erect normative sexual practice in the mid-nineteenth-century United States. As a discourse, Mormon peculiarity constructed the Saints not just as a religious threat but as a racial threat to the white, Protestant nation, thereby helping to establish certain practices, sexual and otherwise, as inherently white and American.

Unsurprisingly, the Saints vehemently insisted their ancestry made them white, using contemporary scientific theories of race. Evident in their own descriptions of themselves, Mormon leaders argued that they were racially distinct, but as supposedly improved white people rather than degraded ones. Church leader George Q. Cannon was quick to note:

> Men from afar cannot cross the continent without coming to visit the Latter-day Saints. Why is this? It is because there is a feeling throughout the earth that there is something remarkable connected with us, that we are not as other people are. What is it that distinguishes us from our fellows? What is it that distinguishes us from the average American, Englishman, Scandinavian, German, Swiss, Italian, or Frenchman, or from the average Asiatic? There is something; they feel it and we feel it.[48]

Cannon reinforced the idea that the Saints were different from other races, but he did so through God's selection of the Saints as His chosen people.[49] For Cannon and other Mormon leaders, what made the Saints unique was their knowledge of the true Church. "'A strange people' is a peculiar expression, as though we were different from others!" Brigham Young asserted. Yet the Saints were different, he maintained, because God "has planted within each of us the germ of the same intelligence, power, glory and exaltation that He enjoys Himself. This proves that we are a peculiar race."[50] The Saints understood themselves to be of Anglo-Saxon, white ancestry, but they also knew themselves to be the chosen people, special in their lineage and in their responsibility to spread the knowledge of the one true Church. In the minds of the Saints, the fact that God had selected them proved their superiority but also explained non-Mormons' need to debase them. By the end of the Civil War, both non-Mormons and the Saints were actively constructing Mormonism as peculiar, yet they disagreed on the source and nature of that peculiarity.

THE STRUGGLE TO CONTROL (ECONOMIC) CIVILIZATION

While the Utah War never resulted in any major battles, it did enflame tensions. Although the conflict was resolved through diplomatic means in 1858, the federal government's actions had significantly sharpened the Saints' sense of urgency to fortify themselves against the federal government and non-Mormon culture generally—a task that was mainly implemented by Young's institution of both old and new programs for economic self-sufficiency during the 1860s. As for anti-Mormons, the incident increased interest in and pressure to assume control over the Saints as racially inferior others. Young pushed hard to revitalize the Church's efforts to build a completely independent, self-sustaining community in Utah. Persisting in their own religiously guided settler colonial project, the Saints took on an invigorated program of segregation that diverged from the economic ideology that was becoming increasingly associated with U.S. exceptionalism. Previous efforts at isolation in the 1850s were encouraged by the Church hierarchy's close management of Utah's economic, legal, and political systems, but the reality of slow overland travel made that control less critical than it became in the 1860s. Unfortunately for the Saints, the stationing of federal troops at Camp Floyd, one result of the deal brokered to end the Utah War, brought a significant change to an extremely isolated and tightly managed territorial economy.

Like polygamy, the Saints' economic practices deeply disturbed anti-Mormons. Since their time in Nauvoo, the Saints had been subject to a strict policy of tithing. Members donated 10 percent of their total income, with the majority of Saints tithing in kind, giving of their time and goods due to the scarcity of cash. Individual members were expected to work on group enterprises (for example, providing labor for community building) every tenth day, while families gave livestock, dry goods, and other homemade products. In contrast to the prevailing individualistic attitude of most non-Mormons, the Saints believed that all property belonged to God; individuals only held property in His stead and its use was subject to the direction of God's prophet on Earth, the president of the Church. The Saints' views of property and work, as well as their precarious economic situation upon arrival in Utah, encouraged the development of a cooperative economic system that idealized the equitable distribution of resources among all Church members. As a result, most major natural resources and certain essential industries were publicly owned and directed by the Church's administration, helping to ensure group survival and cohesion.

Following several years of bad harvests, in 1854 Young had attempted to restore Joseph Smith's policy of consecration and stewardship, a religiously regulated form of communal property ownership first attempted in Kirtland, Ohio, in 1831. Members were asked and expected to give all of their property to the Church; this meant individual Saints were expected to deed everything they owned, receiving an inheritance according to their needs in return. While not completely successful, partial participation in the consecration movement still allowed the Church to control spending on community works and religious programs, helping to facilitate the distribution of resources to the needy (many of whom were poor converts arriving from Europe), and ensured Church regulation of the local economy. The Church focused on developing foodstuff and textile industries in an effort to remain self-sufficient and discouraged outside interest in Utah's natural resources.

The Female Relief Society, the women's organization of the Church, first formed in Nauvoo in 1842 but disbanded during the succession crisis following Smith's death, was one organization that not only helped the Saints maintain economic independence but forwarded the Church's colonialist missionizing to Indigenous peoples. As early as 1852, the Female Relief Society had been reinstated informally by its former members, mostly polygamous wives of high-level Church leaders, in order to "'clothe the Lamanite children and women.'"[51] Indeed, in early 1852 what would be reinstated by Young as the Female Relief Society was originally referred to by its organizers as the Indian Relief Society. These women, like their Protestant counterparts, adhered to the strictures of the cult of domesticity but utilized their gendered position to independently promote the goals and health of their church: the conversion of Paiutes and the building up of Zion. By 1854, individual ward Relief Societies were making clothing and other essentials for the Mormon poor, many of them immigrants.[52] Middle-class white women engaging in charitable work for the poor was a common enough activity in the midcentury United States, but these Mormon organizations were viewed with suspicion by outsiders as supplements to Church proselytizing, colonization, and communalism.

To outsiders, the Saints' communal economics "extended the private sphere into the public, creating a family and a marketplace that encompassed the whole community of Zion."[53] As such, their practices were additional fodder for anti-Mormon charges of the Saints' uncivilized status. As Matthew Frye Jacobson argues, civilization was at its core an economic concept; individual property rights, among other characteristics, represented the very essence of a civilized nation in the nineteenth-century United States.[54] In the eyes of anti-Mormons, the Church leadership's ability to control, even annul, an individual's property rights amounted to a form of autocracy that paralleled anti-Semitic criticisms of Jewish people as greedy and Indigenous people as barbarous in their communal approach to land and resources. Anti-Mormon images during the Utah War utilized racist, anti-Semitic stereotypes about Jews (Figure 7), for example, depicting Young as a ram-like figure with horns, surrounded by followers kneeling prostrate before him as they lay large bags of money at his feet.

A growing non-Mormon presence in Utah presented valuable sources of trade and other forms of economic exchange that ran against the official policy of economic consecration and isolation. The gold rush of 1849 made Salt Lake City the only major waylay point for travelers between the Rocky Mountains and California. The presence of U.S. troops and the slowly but steadily rising non-Mormon population meant that the Saints found it harder and harder to maintain economic independence. The year 1861 brought not only the beginning of the Civil War but also the completion of the transcontinental telegraph. Despite the fact that President Lincoln and Brigham Young had agreed on a policy of mutual disregard, in 1862 Congress passed the Morrill Anti-Bigamy Act (distinct from the Morrill Land-Grant Act of 1862), which outlawed bigamy in the territories, annulled the legal incorporation of the Church, and prohibited any religious organization from owning real estate worth more than $50,000.[55]

It is significant that this first federal anti-Mormon legislation passed just as the U.S. economy was beginning to shift into the era of big business. As industry became corporatized, bureaucracy came to define the process of production on a much larger scale, and a new rendition of laissez-faire capitalism cemented itself as a major component of U.S. exceptionalism. Glenn Porter explains that "although individualism has always been a powerful force in the United States, there were also strong long-standing notions of the importance of community. . . . [Yet] that older America, largely republican and dominated by the ideal individual as producer, was swept away during the years that brought big business."[56] Of course the dominance of consumer capitalism, specifically the placement of individual consumption over and above individual production, which came to replace this older form of economic communalism, was predicated upon a reinforcement of gendered ideals that promoted a racialized and classed sense of public and private. Just as industrialization in the early part of the century had major impacts on labor, geography, and kinship, specifically restricting idealized notions of women's roles, so did the era of big business and consumer culture entrench these roles along racial and class lines. The gendered and racialized entrenchment of a public/private binary during this era ensured not only that much work went unpaid and unacknowledged as work but also that essential social functions of past communal and familial economies were rearticulated as properly private, disregarding the ways industrial capitalism exacerbated the needs and plights of those not privileged enough to own property, those not able to acquire or complete wage labor, or those whose labor was under- and devalued.[57]

Chafing against this rise of secular corporate capitalism, the female consumer, and wage labor, the Saints' midcentury recommitments to resisting the development of Utah's natural resources, home industry, and a publicly organized economy only reinforced non-Mormon perceptions of Mormons as peculiar. Christine Talbot argues that "polygamy destabilized" the public/private binary, but it is also apparent that the sense of polygamy's challenge to a distinct public/private divide was linked to anti-Mormons' distaste for Mormon economic practices, especially what were perceived to be paradoxically socialistic characteristics with an authoritarian foundation. As a result, "anti-Mormons argued that Mormonism rendered its subjects incapable of free conscience and of participating as free agents in marital or social contracts."[58] Now not only was polygamy seen as producing biological racial inferiority by virtue of a gendered imbalance, but the Saints' implementation of communal and cooperative economic practices was cited as further evidence of their supposedly uncivilized and racially regressive status in its challenge to the gendered division of public and private labor.

The ties between perceptions of a new Mormon race and the Church's economic practices are evident in Representative Justin Smith Morrill's oft-cited February 1857 speech. His comparison of the Mormons with "Turks"—"it is natural that the Mormons should sympathize more with Turks than with Christians. . . . They do rank them higher in the scale of civilization, repeat their slanders, and assimilate their domestic institutions"—evoked already prevalent notions of Mormon racial-religious peculiarity through references to nonnormative martial practice and familial organization as a justification for federal oversight of the territory.[59] But Morrill also identified the Saints' political and economic nonnormativity as signs of their racial-religious similarity with "Turks." His position was not only against polygamy as "a Mohammedan barbarism revolting to the civilized world" but also against Mormon policies of tithing, religious control of property and resources, and Mormon theocracy.[60] As an important contribution to the intensifying din of Mormon peculiarity discourse, he argued that multiple Mormon beliefs and practices were strange and, therefore, un-American. With the passage of the Morrill Anti-Bigamy Act, Congress took direct action to diminish the financial resources of the Church, striking at its power to control the economic conditions of the territory at the same time that Young was instituting new measures to maintain that control.[61]

As economic and political pressures increased with the Morrill Anti-Bigamy Act, Young's new economic policies sought to insulate against non-Mormon business interests:

> We do not intend to have any trade or commerce with the gentile world, for so long as we buy of them we are in a degree dependent upon them. The Kingdom of God cannot rise independent of the gentile nations until we produce, manufacture, and make every article of use, convenience, or necessity among our own people. . . . I am determined to cut every thread of this kind and live free and independent, untrammeled by any of their detestable customs and practices.[62]

In particular, Young promoted independence from eastern manufacturers, discouraging consumption of outside goods. While the Saints understood their prophet's economic policies to be in direct accordance with God's wishes, anti-Mormons characterized these new policies as just another example of Young's despotic control of the Utah Territory. As the Saints continued to colonize, displacing Indigenous peoples in order to found 150 new towns across the Southwest between 1857 and 1867, they also introduced and dutifully pursued a boycott of non-Mormon businesses. The Church hierarchy also reinstituted two major organizations in 1868, the School of the Prophets and the Relief Society, to direct economic planning across the Mormon cultural region. As Leonard J. Arrington describes it, the School of the Prophets was an "economic planning conference" that worked to meet the challenges posed by the coming completion of the transcontinental railroad. The group was also the main coordinator of cooperative enterprises intended to "make the community less dependent on imports from the East."[63] The cooperative movement was one of the main economic strategies deployed to protect against non-Mormon economic incursion, with enterprises producing everything from wool to agricultural machinery. Lasting from 1868 until 1884, the movement included the establishment of cooperative retail stores and factories in almost every Church settlement between Utah and California. While these cooperatives were simply "joint-stock corporations, organized under the sponsorship of the Church, with a broad basis of public ownership," they were designed to ensure community welfare and were not primarily motivated by profit.[64] Cooperatives made it easier to patronize only Mormon businesses and to avoid engagement with the national economy. Just as large industries like the railroads and manufacturing were bureaucratizing, and ownership and management were divided, the Church was trying to bring production, consumption, and ownership closer together.

Reinvigorated by Young in 1867 after its neglect since 1857 at the beginning of the Utah War, the Female Relief Society was headed by Eliza R. Snow, a plural wife of Joseph Smith and Brigham Young and leading Mormon feminist. Like the School of the Prophets, the Female Relief Society was implemented at Young's insistence to ensure the local manufacture and consumption of goods. While the stated objective of the society was to help the poor, the key motivation in re-forming the organization was to encourage retrenchment among women Saints. It was Young's belief—one that he articulated often and loudly in his preaching—that women needed to suppress their worldly desires for fashions and other unnecessary consumer goods to help insulate the Saints from outside economic forces. Sermons on such subjects as "home manufacture," "domestic economy," and the Word of Wisdom (a religious health code that prescribed abstinence from tea, coffee, tobacco, and alcohol, among other products) were plentiful just before and after the completion of the transcontinental railroad in Utah.[65] These homilies instructed Saints to produce all goods at home, only shop at Church cooperatives, and completely refrain from, or at least reduce, one's consumption of tea and coffee. The Relief Society was, in effect, organized to emphasize the messages of these lectures, specifically encouraging women to dress modestly and plainly in home-styled garments, to refrain from consuming hot drinks, and to teach their children to work hard in the effort to build Zion.

While not intended, the establishment of the Relief Society resulted in a ready-made women's rights organization, one that advocated for white women's suffrage over the next two years. The Relief Society provided a forum through which Mormon women could organize around a variety of issues. Stirred by the anti-Mormon Cullom Bill two years after the society's founding, members used their platform to publicly protest the bill and its sentiments.[66] Their surprisingly effective political organizing morphed into a push for women's enfranchisement in Utah, achieved in 1870, a mere two months after Wyoming became the first state to give some women the franchise.[67] The reality of women's suffrage in Utah came as a surprise to anti-Mormons who assumed it would help eradicate polygamy; to their utter amazement, Mormon women did not vote away the practice. Shifting tactics, anti-Mormons used the logic of patronizing paternalism to argue that Mormon women had failed to use the vote in a way that properly "exercised the purposes that should be accomplished by Government."[68] In failing to criminalize polygamy, Mormon women were thought to have proven incapable of properly governing themselves, a situation that affected popular opinion about the merits of women's suffrage nationally.

While the Saints had been given a brief respite from congressional assaults during the Civil War, an anti-Mormon legislative campaign began in earnest after 1865. The Wade Bill (1866), Cragin Bills (1867 and 1869), Julian Bill (1869), Ashley Bill (1869), Cullom Bill (1870), Voorhees Bill (1872), Logan Bill (1873), and the finally successful Poland Act (1874) were vigorously debated and each sought to break, in differing ways and to differing degrees, the Church's economic and political control in Utah.[69] Politicians' vehement disapproval of the Church's influence in all matters public and private has been well established by other scholars, but the extreme level of anti-Mormon abhorrence can only be fully understood in the context of the Saints' self-righteous insistence on the exceptionalism of their own religious project.[70] When the House debated the Poland Act in June of 1874, Representative Ward from Illinois declared:

> "I espouse no particular form of religion [and] I would not in any way impose unnecessary or improper burdens on that people or any other; but," he continued, "when they stand up in the light of this age and tell me that their religion is better than mine, that their faith is better than mine, that their civilization is better than mine, that their institutions are entitled to protection beyond what our institutions are entitled to, I say 'Hands off; I will not oppress you, but there must be fair play.'"[71]

His comments illuminate just how much anti-Mormons resented the Saints' claim that theirs was a religion whose exceptional status transcended even that of the United States itself. This was a claim that could not be tolerated, especially at a time when the nation was beginning to deploy U.S. exceptionalism to justify imperialism outside North America.

Another representative's resolve that consumer capitalism was sure to end the Saints' resistance demonstrates the extent to which political elites were beginning to frame free market capitalism as an inevitable aspect of the civilizing process. Representative Potter from New York insisted that "it could not be long in any event before these people would have to move on; that the railways coming into the country would introduce into it not only new people but new Ideas." According to this popular line of thinking, the railroad, like the settlers before it, would rightfully change the "old" and "backwards" ways of an "uncivilized" people because with "the railroad came new ideas and new wants." He jested to his colleagues:

> Think of a man with twenty wives going out of a morning to buy back-hair and crinoline and silk dresses. Nothing could meet the cost of supporting their families in such style, and it therefore seems to me as if these changes will have a certain and growing effect in breaking up this system, so at variance with our race and time. Indeed it seems to me these influences will have more effect in destroying and rooting out polygamy than any legislation we can adopt.[72]

In other words, consumer capitalism would inexorably and rightly undermine what was thought to be Mormonism's problematic practice of polygamy, a practice so at odds with modernity's elevation of the United States as a white, Protestant nation that it had produced another race altogether.

While Representative Potter's imagery of twenty wives buying silk dresses was a tactic of comic exaggeration, it also subtly expressed an assumption about the proper relationship between the family and the economy. In the nineteenth-century mind, polygamy and capitalism could not exist in tandem. One cultural commentator, Hepworth Dixon, jokingly opined about the sale of *Harper's Bazaar* in Salt Lake City that "'whatever might have been possible in an isolated community, where women dressed in calico and sun-bonnets, plural marriage could not exist in company with fashion journals which set wives dressing against each other,'" reflecting the sentiments of one contemporary cartoon (Figure 9).[73] Politicians and cultural critics alike banked on the fact that just "as middle-class Americans increasingly relied on heads of household for economic support and attempted to isolate the home from the competitive capitalist market," polygamous families "necessitated precisely the opposite, a kind of consecrated economic cooperation involving all family members," a state of affairs that would soon be destroyed by the transcontinental railroad.[74] Monogamy, not polygamy, was therefore assumed to be the only way to

FIGURE 9. Hal Coffin, *The Only Solution of the Mormon Problem.* 1871. Courtesy of the Library of Congress.

ensure free market capitalist principles were put into effect at both the micro and macro levels. Thus, it was not just that polygamy was thought to be a relic of past, distant, or racially and religiously inferior cultures but that it was uncivilized precisely because it challenged free market capitalism's unhampered march across the continent. More specifically, because plural marriage contested the gendered separation of public and private, it was thought to also challenge the foundation of the nation's dominant economic system.

Potter's and Dixon's predictions that the railroad would spell the end of the Mormon system were only partially correct. The railroad did bring more than manufactured goods from the east, introducing "an emerging national bourgeois sensibility" upon which the Saints began to draw in order to make sense of their world and themselves.[75] Although the Saints had worked to gain immunity from the developments of the national and global economies, they were nonetheless subject to the cultural forces that accompanied those developments, especially given that their own culture was a product of the early nineteenth-century national ethos. Thus, the introduction of consumer culture was a much more complex invasion than simply the tempting availability of fashions from the east. Advocating "home manufacture" encouraged individuals to refrain from entangling themselves in the evils of an individualistic, free market capitalism, but it did not stop the more subtle infiltration of national culture and the new processes of meaning making that came with it.

Despite their attempts at isolation, the Panic of 1873 severely affected Utah's economy. Recognizing the need for more extreme measures, Young called for the creation of United Orders throughout Mormon settlements across the Southwest during the winter of 1873–74. Drawing on Joseph Smith's early articulations of a more perfect economic order, Young preached that the current system of consecration was "only a stepping stone to . . . the Order of Enoch, which is in reality the order of Heaven."[76] Pointing to the Brigham City Cooperative as an example, a northern settlement that remained virtually untouched by the national crisis, he claimed that the United Order was the only way to successfully separate Mormon interests from the sinister grip of free market capitalism. The United Order, as it was conceptualized and practiced, was a kind of self-supporting, insulated, cooperative community with varying socialistic components. Four different types of orders emerged, reflecting hierarchical levels of communal commitment.

The first type of order was an extension of the Brigham City model in which community ownership and operation of cooperative enterprises was increased. Under this model, individuals were not required to consecrate their property or labor to the United Order but benefited from the prosperity of the cooperative network already in place. The second type was also an extension of the Brigham City model but was modified to function at the level of wards in larger cities where high proportions of non-Mormon residents made it impossible to attempt complete economic reorganization. These orders were focused on one cooperative enterprise—for example, the Eighth Ward in Salt Lake City operated a hat factory, while the Eleventh Ward ran a tailor's shop. The third type was an expansion, rather than an extension, of the cooperative movement. In St. George, Utah, community members gave all of their property to the United Order and in return received wages and dividends that reflected their contributed labor and property. Finally, the fourth kind was the most communal in nature. Members contributed all their property and labor to the system following the Gospel Plan. There was no private property, everyone shared equally in the common products, and all lived and ate together as a large family.

The majority of United Order enterprises failed to drastically change the fabric of local economies; however, those orders that followed a more socialist model were much more successful in becoming self-sufficient and lasted several years. Orderville, Utah, for example, was founded for the specific purpose of forming a United Order community and followed the Gospel Plan. Members ate, prayed, and worked together while the Board of Management regulated the labor and production of the order. Like other Gospel Plan Orders, including those in Price City, Springdale, and Kingston, Utah, as well as Bunkerville, Nevada, and several Arizona orders, Orderville lasted for many years until the federal government's legislative incursion made it impossible for them to maintain operation. A compelling economic alternative, the United Orders are one historical example that challenges the narrative of capitalism's inevitability as is still preached under the auspices of U.S. exceptionalism. Because the United Order system represented the Saints' most extreme divergence from the norms of the national economy, Mormonism was dubbed a dangerous threat.

INTO THE ERA OF EMPIRE

In 1871, when federal appointee Judge James B. McKean described the Church as an "imperium in imperio,"—an empire within an empire—he precisely described the power struggle between the Church and the U.S. government.[77] Both sides were engaged in intertwined settler colonial endeavors claiming divine sanction and both were convinced that one would eventually succumb to the other. Unfortunately for the Saints, the federal government's recourse to state of exception legislation, explored in the next chapter, easily outweighed the Saints' attempts at isolation. After several bills were debated and rejected by Congress, the Poland Act emerged as the triumphant legal remedy to the ineffective Morrill Anti-Bigamy Act. The act facilitated prosecutions of polygamy by transferring power from the Mormon-controlled probate courts to the non-Mormon federal courts. The ecclesiastical probate courts in Utah had served as the primary court system taking on civil and criminal matters since the Saints' arrival in 1847. This meant that federal officials had been left without any practical recourse for prosecuting polygamy. Among other measures, the act also drastically altered the jury selection processes in favor of the non-Mormon minority, virtually excluding all Mormon jurors. The Poland Act represented a very real danger to the stability of the Saints' way of life. By redrawing the lines of legislative and judicial control in Utah Territory, the federal government wrested enough power away from both local politicians and the Church hierarchy—virtually one and the same—to begin the prosecution of polygamists. No longer able to retain full control of the political and legal structure of the territory, the Church's strategies for resistance were substantially undermined. The final quarter of the nineteenth century witnessed an increasingly explicit and hostile discourse of Mormon peculiarity that was used to justify explicitly acknowledged forms of U.S. imperialism.

3 The Problems of (Mormon) Empire, 1874–1896

> Polygamy leads to the patriarchal principle, and which, when applied to large communities, fetters the people in stationary despotism, while that principle cannot long exist in connection with monogamy.
>
> —*Reynolds v. United States*

> I pursue these connections between the broad-scale dynamics of colonial rule and the intimate sites of implementation . . . because domains of the intimate figured so prominently in the perceptions and policies of those who ruled.
>
> —Ann Laura Stoler, *Carnal Knowledge and Imperial Power*

Matthew Frye Jacobson identifies the years between 1876 and 1917 as a turning point in the geography, style, and execution of U.S. imperialism. Three major developments defined this new imperial epoch: first, the end of Reconstruction; second, the so-called closure of the frontier; and third, a new phase of industrialization that pushed the nation-state onto the global stage. Up to this point, U.S. empire had been mainly (although not exclusively) characterized by violent forms of settler colonialism and slavery in North America. As the nation-state pushed its way west, producers exploited the land's natural resources to fuel the growth of the capitalist economy. But as the close of the nineteenth century approached, "politicians and manufacturers feared that the engines of industry could not be slowed without undermining the nation's stability, but also that, at its accustomed pace of production, the nation risked outstripping its own capacities to absorb its goods.["1] A turn toward overseas imperialism in the 1890s addressed this problem by providing new markets, augmenting the nation's workforce, and appropriating new terrain for producers to exploit.

It was during this period, not coincidentally, that Mormon peculiarity discourse became characterized by the rhetoric of "national problems" or "questions." This rhetorical shift reflected a broader modification to the ways that biopolitical governance in the United States was reasoned and enacted as a result of the addition of the Thirteenth, Fourteenth, and Fifteenth Amendments to the U.S. Constitution. Racializing civilizational assemblages, Mormonism included, were no longer solely used to solidify the boundaries between white and nonwhite, Christian and non-Christian, secular and religious, public and private, domestic and foreign. Instead, as Reconstruction came to a close, with white northerners abandoning projects of racial justice and white southerners seeking to regain political power in the postbellum period, the so-called Mormon problem, alongside and concomitant with other supposed problems like the Indian problem and Chinese problem, became central to a reinvestment in the national culture of white supremacy just as U.S. empire was expanding globally.[2] More specifically, during the last three decades of the nineteenth century, the Mormon problem functioned in two ways: first, to help rationalize ongoing modifications to the ways that race was deployed as a form of biopolitical governance, ensuring that certain populations continued to be designated politically alien, and second, to help justify the nation-state's experimentations with various tactics of colonial governance, adapted for the new imperial epoch.

The historical record demonstrates that alongside the continued expulsion and genocide of Native peoples, the rise of Jim Crow segregation, and the enforcement of racist immigration, alien land, and marriage laws, the state tested a variety of paternalistic, imperialist-style legal tactics—largely on a trial-and-error basis—in Utah Territory. This chapter examines how this experimentation was directly related to the processes of racialization that presented Mormonism as a warning against the dangers of racial mixing, both in terms of the reproductive results of interracial sex and in terms of the engagement by members of a supposedly superior racial group in the practices deemed the provenance of inferior groups. Such portrayals communicated that any racially inferior (i.e., uncivilized) practices were direct threats to the ascendency of U.S. culture and empire. In constructing Mormonism as an uncivilized racial problem, then, Mormon peculiarity

discourse was used not only to maintain but to extend the rigid racial hierarchy that had been established in the United States as a divinely and naturally
sanctioned political structure critical to achieving the status of global empire.
Building off the plethora of scholarly analyses of nineteenth-century antipolygamy fiction, I analyze graphic images, newspaper articles, sermons,
political pamphlets, legislative debates, statutes, and Supreme Court decisions in order to map the connections between mediated articulations of
Mormon peculiarity and some of the legal tactics of colonial governance
with which the federal government was experimenting in the late nineteenth century.[3]

Throughout (but increasing in the last decades of) the nineteenth century, Mormon peculiarity discourse, whether leveraged by anti-Mormons
or the Saints themselves, was often used to express gender and sexual exceptionalism, notions of civilizational superiority that were based on what
were proffered to be a group's advanced gendered and sexual practices
or knowledge. In the modern era, gender and sexual exceptionalism have
historically been deployed to strengthen claims of racial hierarchy and
Euro-American (i.e., white) superiority and thereby justify colonial rule.
Reflecting this pattern, these discourses were used in the context of Mormonism to bolster claims of U.S. exceptionalism that rationalized federal
intervention in the management of Utah Territory's governance, just as
these discourses were used to help discredit the sovereign claims of Native
groups. However, gender and sexual exceptionalism were also used by the
Saints to maintain their own sense of religious supremacy and program
of racially hierarchized settler colonialism. Part and parcel of racializing
civilizational assemblages, gender and sexual exceptionalism depend upon
the assumed existence of a linear, progressive development of civilization
in which the most developed guide the least. Of course, what gender and
sexual norms are considered advanced or backward have shifted across
time, as have the knowledges that are used to substantiate them. Therefore, I define *gender exceptionalism* as a discourse that asserts a nation's or
group's advanced status based on superior knowledge about sex and gender and the subsequent maintenance of ostensibly natural sex and gender
relations, while *sexual exceptionalism* describes a related but distinct discourse that asserts a nation's or group's civilized status through claims to
advanced sexual knowledge and practice.

My focus on the racialization of Mormonism as an uncivilized, barbarous, foreign threat used to justify the suppression and the denial of political

rights to Mormons as part and parcel of the colonial relation of power characteristic of U.S. democracy departs from previous histories of nineteenth-century anti-Mormonism. Scholars such as Christine Talbot caution against "misconstruing anti-Mormonism as a colonialist discourse and the [Saints] as colonized subjects."[4] While the Saints were (and are) not colonized subjects as Native peoples are, dismissing the relationship between anti-Mormonism and U.S. colonialism downplays several historical realities. First, it discounts the significance of the federal government's strategic interventions in the governance of Utah Territory and its purposeful subjugation of the Saints. Not only did the state implement legislation that inhibited and fundamentally altered—in some cases destroying—the Saints' religious and cultural practices, but it revoked many of the Saints' constitutional rights, such as the right to vote, to serve on juries, and to run for and hold political office. Second, it misses the critical and direct ways that Mormon peculiarity discourse served to help rationalize the colonization of Native people and land, as well as how it helped to racialize other groups as non-white in order to justify their treatment as political aliens who, to paraphrase Sylvester Johnson, are denied the right to have rights.[5] Lasty, it underestimates the role Mormon peculiarity discourse played in preparing the way for the nation-state's future imperial endeavors outside North America, most obviously through the Supreme Court's 1879 decision *Reynolds v. United States.*[6]

To be clear, my argument does not and is not meant to equate the Saints' experiences with other colonized and racially marginalized groups. Rather, by seeking to better understand what Nancy Bentley calls the Saints' "ambiguous relation to [other] imperial subjects," it is possible to tease out the uneven applications, improvisational maneuvers, and underexplored nuances of U.S. colonialism.[7] Like Ann Laura Stoler's work on the intimate dimensions of European colonial rule, this chapter contends that it would be a mistake to take the "politically constructed dichotomy of colonizer and colonized as a given rather than as a historically shifting pair of social categories that needs to be explained."[8] Rather than asserting that the Saints were solely "agents of the colonization of the American West," a claim I suggest that is not born out by the evidence, this chapter considers the complex ways that the colonial relation of power dictated the Saints' ability to act as agents, and serve as targets, of a variety of devices of racial and colonial-style management.[9] The Saints of course have been themselves complicit in the U.S. nation-state's violent colonial projects and also engaged in their own such projects. It is beyond dispute that their religiously determined program of settler colonialism contributes to a national culture of white supremacy that has been maintained throughout the twentieth and into the twenty-first centuries, a history I take up in chapters 5 and 6. Yet, the Mormon problem, as it was articulated through nineteenth-century Mormon peculiarity discourse, affords an important opportunity to better understand the relationship between colonization and racialization and thereby to more fully comprehend how the U.S. nation-state, as a democratic empire, has continuously reformulated its biopolitical (i.e., racial) governance so critical for disguising the ongoing structure of settler colonialism on which it relies.

NATIONAL PROBLEMS

Between 1874 and 1877, the federal government passed xenophobic, racist immigration laws, amplified its violent suppression of Indigenous groups, formally ended Reconstruction, and officially announced its entrance onto the global stage at the Centennial Exposition in Philadelphia, the first World's Fair to be held in the United States. Reflecting these events, the rhetoric of national questions had begun to saturate the popular press, exemplified in widespread graphic images that reflected and fueled anxiety about the racial dynamics of U.S. society as it walked onto that stage. Like Chinese immigration, freed slaves, and Native resistance, Mormonism was represented as a national problem that illustrated the need for imperialist-style regulation. The words and images that shaped this version of Mormon peculiarity discourse reflected a contradictory attitude toward Mormonism as a foreign yet paradoxically domestic problem.

A product of the Jacksonian era northeast, it was difficult for anti-Mormons to deny the U.S. cultural origins of the religion and the Anglo-European ancestry of the majority of its followers. In order to preserve the predominant logic of racial hierarchy as a biological rather than political categorization, anti-Mormons constructed the Saints as racially other, the supposedly inevitable result of polygamous marriage and reproduction. However, scholarship has tended to exceptionalize the Mormon problem as "peculiarly American" because the Saints shared phenotypical similarities with those firmly classified as white in the late nineteenth century.[10] Exceptionalizing the Mormon problem in this way not only reinforces visibly determinable notions of race, but it also ignores the nineteenth-century media's own elaboration of multiple national problems, all of which were used to reinforce Americanness in opposition to not just nonwhite skin color but particular practices and customs as racially other. The Mormon question, the Indian question, and the Chinese question, among others, were all leveraged alongside and against one another in the production of Americanness versus non-Americanness as fundamentally racial categories.

Two years after the Centennial Exposition in Philadelphia, an illustration in *Puck* magazine parodied many of the nation's so-called problems. Satirizing the country's contributions to the 1878 World's Fair in Paris, Joseph Keppler illustrated a mock "American Exhibit" that symbolized these problems as agricultural products (Figure 10). The assembled goods represented everything from questions of labor to issues of race and class. The "Dead 'Beets'" in the central foreground of the cartoon, as well as the "'Boss' Squash Head" and "'Champion' Cabbage Head" on the left and right, alluded to various political scandals captivating the nation, while to the left and right, packaged products symbolized various class, racial, and religious issues.[11] Small, typically racist caricatures of Black heads fill a jar labeled "Black-Berry Jam," which sits next to a "Best Boot Blacking" tin and a package of "Stove Polish"; resting above these lies a box of "Pickled Tramps," with the image of a drunken, lazy, and unkempt man; on the left-hand side is another jar depicting an old, ugly "Spiritualist" woman divining a skull; and above her is a container of "Dried Hoodlums," donning the image of a hanged man. On the right are similar products, including a can of "White Trash" showing a lanky, downtrodden figure and "Micks in Irish Whiskey," rendered as a drunk, dancing Irishman with a shillelagh between his teeth.

Each of these stuffs evoked contemporary stereotypes used to disparage various marginalized groups, including Black people, poor white people, Spiritualists, and Irish immigrants. Keppler's choice to represent national issues with agricultural products such as jams, jellies, and vegetables played on multifaceted concerns about rapid changes to the U.S. economy and the effects of those changes, each product linking uneasiness over labor and consumption to growing tensions over the nation's racial makeup. Because "immigration and expansion constituted two sides of the same coin . . . public discussion of problematic aliens at home . . . [and] debate[s] over the 'fitness for self-government' of problematic peoples abroad" became inevitable results of industrialization.[12] The products in the cartoon were depicted as the worrisome side effects of industrialization, yet these so-called problems were also necessary for defining the nation-state as a global leader whose job it was to foster democracy among those considered less civilized.

Perhaps most tellingly, the *Puck* cartoon expressed an underlying, if disavowed, anxiety that the nation-state had cultivated its own problems from within, problems that warned of racial threats requiring federal intervention. Although the image was drawn to coincide with the 1878 World's Fair, the plant at the center of the image recalled the nation's centennial celebration in Philadelphia two years previous. That fair had marked the one hundredth anniversary of the signing of the Declaration of Independence, represented by the "Century Plant" at the center of the image. All the products surround the Century Plant, which is flanked by two others, the rosebush of Mormon polygamy and another representing preacher Henry Ward Beecher's adulterous affair. Mormonism, whose largest bloom is the head of John Taylor, then president of The Church of Jesus Christ of Latter-day Saints, is surrounded by eleven tiny blooms—his wives.

Mormon polygamy and the Beecher scandal are portrayed as two of the most pressing and dangerous problems of the day. Not only do these plants most closely resemble the Century Plant, but placed on either side they lean in to stifle its further development. Unlike the other packaged and harvested products, "Mormonism" and "Beecherism" were especially concerning because their digressions struck at the heart of claims that the United States' citizenry represented the pinnacle of civilization by virtue of its moral and sexual standards and, therefore, racial development. Beecher's affair enthralled a nation who knew the clergyman for his views on abolition, temperance, women's suffrage, and sexual morality. Mormon polygamy, like Beecher's hypocritical affair, challenged contemporary standards of women's morality and sexual propriety. In other words, Beecher's affair and the Saints' plural marriages were both thought to undercut assertions of U.S. sexual and gender exceptionalism because they were considered evidence of a racial threat to white Anglo-Saxon Protestant American civilization.

In another illustration, which appeared in *The Wasp*, Mormonism is again depicted as one of several national problems (Figure 11). In a school filled with unruly children, Uncle Sam presides as a teacher desperately, but unsuccessfully, trying to maintain order. At the front of the image, the Democratic Party, drawn as an apelike Irish child—a typical racist depiction used to symbolize the Democratic Party's courting of Irish American votes—fights with another student, the Republican Party. Uncle Sam

FIGURE 10. J. Keppler, *A Truly Representative American Exhibit, Arranged by Puck for the Paris Exhibition*. Reprinted from *Puck*, May 15, 1878. Courtesy of HathiTrust.

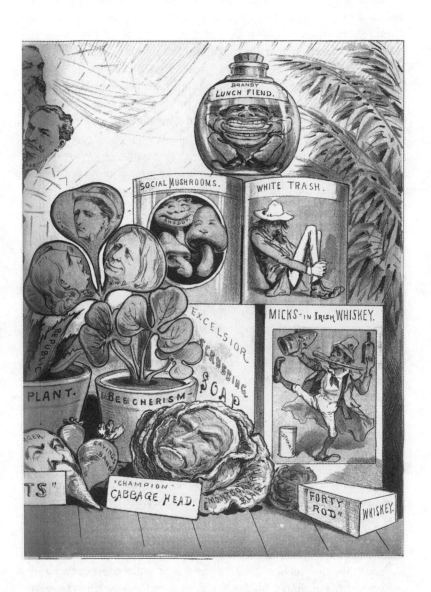

reaches frantically over his desk to grab the coat of "Mormon," who already
has his clutches around three young girls, while two stereotypically rendered "Sioux" covertly attach dynamite to their teacher's coattails, and
"Geronimo" creeps across the classroom with a knife behind his back.
Yet another scuffle between "Labor" and "Capital" ensues, while "California" shuts the door on a sinister-looking Chinese student at the back of
the classroom. While each problem is represented as serious, Uncle Sam
chooses first to deal with the problem of Mormonism, represented as a
child-sized Brigham Young. Reflecting notions of white civilization as firmly
rooted in the paternalistic treatment of white women, Uncle Sam's decision to first deal with Mormonism reflected the government's unrelenting
campaign against the Church, which reached its peak only a year after this
image was published.

While Figures 10 and 11 highlight Mormonism as one of several national
problems, including concerns over class, religion, race, production, consumption, labor, and immigration, they merely allude to its racial significance. Figures 12 and 13 are typical examples of how Mormonism was
increasingly constructed as an explicitly racial problem in the last quarter
of the century—a threat on par with immigration, Indigenous resistance,
and the supervision and management of freed populations. In Figure 12,
an annoyed Uncle Sam contends with five "troublesome bed fellows"—
racist caricatures of Mormon, Chinese, Indigenous, African American, and
Irish people. Clearly aggravated, Uncle Sam is unceremoniously kicking the
Chinese man out of the national bed, having already ejected an unhappy
Brigham Young, identifiable by a scroll he carries labeled "Polygamy" (illus-
trating that Uncle Sam, as in Figure 11, has chosen to deal with the problem
of Mormonism first). Still laying in the bed are a Native man, sticking his
finger into Uncle Sam's ear; an apparently contented Black man, rendered
in a typically racist fashion, who seems confident of his inclusion in the
national bed; and an Irish man who sleeps undisturbed by the commotion,
next to a bottle of whiskey. Each child-sized figure represents a so-called
problematic group that was thought to require an exclusionary or repressive solution. As these images suggest, continued federal suppression of
Indigenous resistance, flaring nativist sentiment, and waning commitment
to Reconstruction all coincided with and informed anti-Mormon responses
to the Saints in Utah.

Similarly, Figure 13 depicts the "China Question," "Mormon Question,"
and "Indian Question" as children of mother Columbia, while their father,

FIGURE 11. *Uncle Sam's Troublesome School.* Reprinted from the *Wasp*, June 5, 1886. Courtesy of California State Library via Internet Archive.

Uncle Sam, is too distracted reading about "Politics," and "$$$$" in his news-paper to witness the children tormenting their mother. Uncle Sam's whip, labeled "Law," with which he is presumably supposed to discipline the children, lies limp at the back of his chair. The "China Question" and the "Mormon Question" (the latter once again represented by Young) sit comfortably in their mother's lap as they harass her—pulling her hair and spitting in her face, respectively—while the "Indian Question" sits on the floor destroying toy U.S. soldiers with his tomahawk. In both images, all the questions are represented as equally problematic and all as children in need of a father's discipline. Of course, depicting national problems as children, as each of these images does, played on the popular gendered (and heteronormative) colonial trope of civilized nations as parents who must consciously and consistently discipline, watch over, and teach inferior others, a trope that continually reappeared in debates over Mormonism between 1860 and 1890.

Perhaps more than other national problems, the Mormon and Chinese questions often appeared together in popular debate (Figures 14 and 15). Decades of racialization had produced Mormonism as "Oriental," mainly

UNCLE SAM'S TROUBLESOME BED FELLOWS

FIGURE 12. *Uncle Sam's Troublesome Bed Fellows.* Reprinted from the *Wasp,* February 8, 1879. Courtesy of the Library of Congress.

THE THREE TROUBLESOME CHILDREN.

FIGURE 13. Keller, *The Three Troublesome Children*. Reprinted from the *Wasp* 7, no. 281, December 16, 1881. Courtesy of the Bancroft Library, University of California, Berkeley.

through claims that polygamy was an inherently Islamic, Asian, and African practice. As W. Paul Reeve points out, as early as 1830 the Saints had been compared to Muslims "and [Mormonism] was labeled the 'Islam of America,'" a construction that withstood the test of time.[13] Stereotypical depictions of Muslims, "Turks" in particular, as overly sexual were easily applied to the polygamous Saints, whose marital practices were used as evidence in a chain of circular logic that reinforced common stereotypes against both groups. The very location of Church headquarters in the western desert seemed to support perceptions of Mormons as "Oriental"—the hot, desert landscape was dubbed the "domestic orient" and Salt Lake City was likened to places such as Palestine, Mecca, Jerusalem, "Canaan," "Tadmor," and Damascus.[14] Racist assumptions that certain cultures, especially Islamic ones, were inherently despotic and theocratic were used to racialize Mormonism, inflecting perceptions and representations of the Saints' marital, economic, and political practices.

Given these comparisons, it should be no surprise that racist responses to the Chinese question mirrored those to the Mormon question, both of

UNCLE SAM'S NIGHTMARE.

FIGURE 14. Keller, *Uncle Sam's Nightmare*. Reprinted from the *Wasp*, March 24, 1882. Courtesy of the Bancroft Library, University of California, Berkeley.

which evoked prostitution and slavery as animating issues. The 1875 passage of the Page Act responded to the increasingly fervent anti-Chinese sentiment in California by restricting so-called undesirable immigrants from emigrating under forced labor contracts and virtually prohibiting the entrance of all Chinese women on the faulty assumption that they were prostitutes.[15] In the same way that the assumptions about Chinese women immigrants as prostitutes served to represent all Chinese immigrants as undesirable, so too did assumptions about polygamy's allegedly real purpose signify the perceived foreignness of the Saints. One Senate report that declared women "are bought and sold like slaves at the will of their masters," brought to the United States for the purposes of prostitution, could easily have been drawn from either the anti-Chinese or anti-Mormon discourse of the period.[16] Denunciations of plural marriage as a religiously sanctioned form of prostitution functioned to demean Mormon women, denying them the privileged status of white womanhood in the national sphere, and indicted Mormon men, especially Church leaders, as lecherous patriarchs.[17] Both the anti-Mormon and the anti-Chinese movements charged that the prostitution they saw as inherent to each problem was forced; it was assumed that women immigrants in both groups were brought to the United States under coercion and were enslaved once they arrived. Moreover, just as Chinese immigration was used to heighten white racial anxiety, so too was the Church's active encouragement and facilitation of the immigration of thousands of converts to Utah exploited to enflame national concern.

In his September 1880 sermons on Chinese immigration and Mormonism delivered to his Brooklyn congregation, Reverend Thomas De Witt Talmage argued that Chinese immigrants, but not the Mormons, should be integrated in the nation. In his September 19 sermon, Talmage praised the industry of Chinese immigrants and promoted tolerance and acceptance on their behalf, while on the very next Sunday he described the absolute degeneracy of the Mormons and advocated the religion's complete destruction "by the guns of the United States Government."[18] Although he was mocked by the press for his unusual position (Figure 15), Talmage's logic was more similar to than different from those who advocated the expulsion of Chinese immigrants and suppression but not extradition of the Saints.

His seemingly opposing characterizations of the two groups are instructive for thinking through the ways the late nineteenth-century United

"The Chinese may stay, but the Mormons must go."—DeWitt Talmage.

FIGURE 15. Hamilton, *"The Chinese May Stay, but the Mormons Must Go."—DeWitt Talmage.* Reprinted from the *Judge*, October 27, 1883. Digital Collections, University Libraries, Ohio State University.

States was taking on an increasingly explicit imperial vision of the nation's global position. While Talmage framed Chinese immigrants as in need of tolerance and paternalistic oversight, he aggressively attacked the Saints as sinners—people who were capable of self-governance but who had chosen to become the worst kind of malefactors: degenerate racial traitors. He characterized Chinese immigrants as naturally "industrious," "genial," "harmless," and "obliging"—descriptive choices that reveal the condescending, racist-imperialist logics underlying his position.[19] His recognition that the country needed cheap labor for its rapidly developing industrial economy is buttressed by his feminization of Chinese immigrants and vision of them as an entry point into the Chinese market. Talmage's open acknowledgment and repetition of racist tropes about Chinese people helped him to argue that they could easily be controlled and should be tolerated for the sake of economic prosperity.

Unlike his attitude toward Chinese immigrants, Talmage's concerns about the Saints derived from what he described as their sacrilegious nonnormativity. Comparing Salt Lake City to the doomed biblical city of Sodom, he detailed Mormon offenses: refusals to aid immigrant wagon trains; the Mountain Meadows Massacre; deceptive missionizing that tricked poor, uneducated immigrants into coming to Utah; swindling the poor with tithing and cooperative systems; religious blasphemy against "true" Christianity; sedition and treason against the U.S. government; and finally, as well as most egregiously, polygamy. Proclaiming Mormonism to be "one great surge of licentiousness . . . THE SERAGLIO OF THE REPUBLIC," Talmage emphasized Mormonism as racially treasonous by virtue of its sexual deviance and, therefore, in need of destruction like Sodom before it.[20]

Of all the crimes laid at the Saints' door, to Talmage nothing was worse or required such swift and uncompromising action as the crimes against "WOMANHOOD IN UTAH." In hindsight, Talmage's rhetorical query "If a gang of thieves should squat on a territory and make thievery a religion, how long would the United States Government stand that?" is only slightly more ironic than his answer: "Yet a community founded on theft would not be so bad as a community founded on the grave of desolated, destroyed, and embruited womanhood."[21] In his formulation—one that conveniently ignored the thievery of Indigenous land and lives—Talmage reframed the Saints as foreigners squatting on U.S. land, who had regressed to what his contemporaries called, "the patriarchal principle," a common phrase used to refer to polygamy. The assumed exploitation of women, which was thought to inevitably accompany polygamy, became the ultimate symbol of a civilization's retrogression. In other words, Talmage's was a nineteenth-century articulation of gender and sexual exceptionalism in which "the patriarchal principle" was evidence of a culture's barbarity, while a woman's ability to consent to heterosexual, monogamous marriage, and by extension her husband's authority, was proof of a civilization at its height.

Talmage's assumptions about what constituted racially, religiously, and politically civilized gendered and sexual relations, and his claim that the degradation of womanhood in Utah was more serious than the past crime of "negro slavery" were shared by his fellow anti-Mormons. "Come, now," Talmage chided federal politicians, "instead of exhuming the wrapped-up and entombed mummy of negro slavery, and tossing it about in these Presidential elections, have *one live question*—Mormonism, the white slavery of to-day."[22] As Republicans, abolitionists, feminists, and Protestant leaders like

Talmage shifted their focus away from the situation of Black people in the South, their focus came to settle on white women, especially around the issues of suffrage, temperance, and prostitution.[23] The potentially radical project of racial justice was replaced by a reinforcement of white supremacist patriarchy. Politicians, activists, and religious leaders actively worked to dismantle slavery's associations with the liberation of Black people and sutured it to the imagined menace of white women's exploitation, Mormonism emerging as the perfect culprit on which to blame the situation.[24] While the issue of white slavery would not peak until the 1910s and 1920s, social purity crusaders' ideological foundation was laid in the late nineteenth century through debates over white slavery in the context of Chinese immigration and Mormon polygamy.

More specifically, throughout the 1870s and 1880s, activist concern about prostitution, referred to euphemistically as "white slavery," was brought to the public's attention largely through the vehicle of Mormon peculiarity discourse.[25] Readers were flooded with fictional exposés, which often masqueraded as nonfiction accounts, that sensationalized the plight of vulnerable white women who had been duped into polygamy by evil Mormon men beginning in the 1850s and steadily through the 1910s.[26] Novels such as Alfreda Eva Bell's *Boadicea* (1855), Captain Mayne Reid's *The Wild Huntress* (1861), Charles Bertrand Lewis's *Bessie Baine* (1876), A. Jennie Bartlett's *Elder Northfield's Home* (1882), and Rosetta Luce Gilchrist's *Apples of Sodom* (1883) all told stories of young white women, victimized and corrupted by polygamy; lured into Mormonism, these women's experiences as plural wives pushed them to engage in jealous, evil, and even murderous behavior.[27] Concerns over white slavery were also evident in numerous anti-Mormon caricatures, often depicting elderly Mormon patriarchs enticing gullible young women into their licentious clutches. Figures 16, 18, 19, 20, 21, 24, 25, 26, and 29 exemplify the widespread perception of polygamy as a threat to white women's innocence by making them prostitutes and slaves.

In these images, women are depicted not only as sexual slaves but as domestic and agricultural workers imported to labor for their husband/master. For example, in Figure 16 women immigrants wear placards that designate the role they would fulfill for the waiting "Mr. Polygamist" in addition to being his wives/concubines. Here the title's sarcasm, *Pure White "Mormon Immigration,"* plays on multiple national anxieties, alluding to representations of the Saints' degraded racial status, the assumed racial peril

CHAMBER MAID

COOK.

NURSE

WAITRESS

SEAMSTRESS

LAUNDRESS

PURE WHITE "MORMON IMMIGRATION" ON THE ATLANTIC COAST..
More *cheap* "help-mates" for Mr. Polygamist.

FIGURE 16. Thomas Nast, *Pure White "Mormon Immigration" on the Atlantic Coast.*
"More *cheap* 'help-mates' for Mr. Polygamist." Reprinted from *Harper's Weekly*,
March 25, 1882, 191. Courtesy of dilibri Rheinland-Pfalz (www.dilibri.de).

of immigration, and concerns about the consequences of exponentially increasing industrial production. Just as Chinese men were depicted as sexual threats to white women's purity—and, by extension, the nation's—in anti-Chinese images of the period, Mormon men were depicted as tricking white women into prostitution and slavery, practices that were thought to degrade their womanhood, as well as the nation's racial superiority. Three of the nine images explicitly reference "cheap labor," suggesting that the immigration of Mormon converts was tied to broader concerns about labor, immigration, and markets.

The racial threat of Mormon immigration is represented in another typical cartoon from the *Wasp* (Figure 17). In *Mormon Fishing in Foreign Lands*, the artist played up fears of miscegenation by depicting a Mormon man literally fishing for new wives in Europe and Asia. Sitting astride a symbolic eagle, the Mormon's decision to bring what were thought to be racially inferior wives into the United States is represented as poor repayment to a nation that has ensured his freedom of religion. Tellingly, the elder casts his lines not only into France, Holland, and Sweden but also into Italy, Russia, and Turkey, countries whose populations were considered inferior compared to the purity of Anglo-Saxon white Protestants. Thus, the image connects the Mormon problem to larger concerns about immigration from places like eastern and southern Europe and western Asia.

Nativist concerns expressed over contract labor and slavery in both the anti-Chinese and anti-Mormon movements were tied to the nation's recent battle over slavery. Figures 16 and 18 both allude to slavery through visual suggestions of a slave market. In Figure 16, as the women file down the gangplank, advertising their function as a "waitress," "cook," or "laundress," a male figure at the top of the platform waves his hand over the heads of the descending women, seemingly offering them up for sale, while in Figure 18 the women have disembarked, looking exhausted and weary. Several older Mormon men circulate among them, while one of them leans in and reaches up to the face of one scared young woman, as if to inspect her, subtly referencing the violent bodily inspection of enslaved Black people in antebellum slave markets.[28]

Figure 19 explicitly indicts the Mormons for engaging in white slavery. In the upper right-hand corner of the page, the inset image shows a Mormon man pointing to the "Promise of a Happy Home Out West," distracting three women immigrants from the bear-style trap of "Degradation" and "Polygamy" that surrounds it. In the main image, a patriarch sits idly

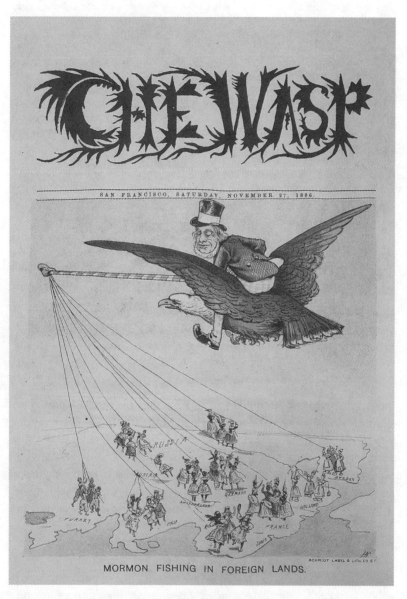

FIGURE 17. *Mormon Fishing in Foreign Lands.* Reprinted from the *Wasp*, November 27, 1886. Courtesy of the California History Room, California State Library, Sacramento.

FIGURE 18. *"The Twin Relic of Barbarism."—The Wolves and the Lambs—Arrival of Scandinavian Converts, in Charge of Mormon Missionaries, at Castle Garden, En Route for Salt Lake City.* Reprinted from *Frank Leslie's Illustrated Newspaper,* December 15, 1883, 264–65.

holding the whip of "Intimidation" as he counts the profits made by enslaving the women who toil in the field in front of him. These women are fettered by the chains of "Ignorance" and "Sealed," a reference to the Mormon marriage ritual, as they dig, carry, and plant. The expressions and physical bearing of the women themselves are meant to elicit indignation and concern from a Victorian audience that valued a fragile white femininity. One wife at the center of the frame looks up, as if contemplating her bondage, while another's muscled arm emphasizes the physical labor she has been forced to undertake.

Of special significance is the Black man holding a scroll labeled "Emancipation 1862, Lincoln," who stands looking on at the women unconcernedly. Contrasted with these women, his presence serves two functions. First, to a white audience his detached observation of the women toiling in the fields would have represented a troubling lack of empathy for one who had recently experienced slavery and a lack of sympathy from a man

FIGURE 19. *Woman's Bondage in Utah. The Mormon Solution of the "Cheap Labor" Question.* Reprinted from *Frank Leslie's Illustrated Newspaper* 54, no. 1,381, March 11, 1882. Church History Library, The Church of Jesus Christ of Latter-day Saints.

witnessing the exploitation of women who, to the minds of nineteenth-century audiences, should have been protected. Not only does this figure reinforce the evil of the Mormon slave driver, but he also reinforces already prevalent notions of Black people's inhumanity and, in particular, Black men's failure to properly perform masculinity. Second, his nonchalance references the paternalistic sentiment among white people that Black people did not "appreciate" their emancipation and that they now presented yet another national problem, tied as ever to concerns of labor and race.

In their preaching, and communicated through their political representatives in Congress, Church leaders sought to counter claims that Mormonism was an example of white racial degradation caused by the practice of plural marriage. On the contrary, they argued polygamy was the superior marital practice of white civilization, which was why it had been commanded by God through the revelation to Joseph Smith. Between the 1850s and the 1880s, various Church representatives drew on contemporary scientific research and popular advice literature about race and sex to support such claims. B. Carmon Hardy and Dan Erickson detail how Church leaders drew on this type of literature to argue that polygamy was neither a form of prostitution nor white slavery but, on the contrary, protected against such evils by giving righteous white women security from a lack of righteous men, offering them safe and comfortable homes and providing the chance to fulfill their gendered purpose as wives and mothers.[29] Yet, this line of argumentation, while deftly trafficking in the racialized language of nineteenth-century U.S. culture and reinforcing Church leaders' own white supremacist racism, did not convince anti-Mormons.

As Bruce Burgett and W. Paul Reeve reason, the equation of Mormon polygamy with prostitution and slavery, both actual chattel slavery and supposed white slavery, served to reinforce white supremacy throughout the nineteenth century.[30] But the fact that both Northerners and Southerners found common cause in the supposed enslavement of white women under Mormonism during the second half of the century was a major indication of the failure of Reconstruction and the consequent reprivileging of whiteness far and above Blackness after the Civil War. This reconsolidation of white Anglo-Saxon Protestant superiority as the basis for U.S. exceptionalism occurred just as the nation-state sought to extend its empire overseas. The Mormon question, among other national problems helped to "conflat[e] whiteness, American nationalism, [and] Protestant Christianity" in the service of new forms of U.S. imperialism.[31] The shift in focus from Reconstruction and the immorality of chattel slavery to the "white slavery" of Mormon polygamy was paralleled in a shift from the situation in the south to what Sarah Barringer Gordon calls a "second reconstruction in the West."[32]

NEW MODES OF COLONIAL MANAGEMENT

When the Republicans announced their platform at the party's introductory convention in 1856, they stressed the hegemony of the federal government over its territorial acquisitions:

> The Constitution confers upon Congress sovereign powers over the Territories of the United States for their government; and that in the exercise of this power, it is both the right and the imperative duty of Congress to prohibit in the Territories those twin relics of barbarism—Polygamy, and Slavery.[33]

In this oft-cited selection from the Republicans' original manifesto, the absolute power given to Congress is articulated as a power of colonial-style rule.[34] Condemning both polygamy and slavery as "twin relics of barbarism," the Republicans defined the nation-state as simultaneously the defender and duty-bound proprietor of civilization whose benevolent yet firm guidance would end the vestiges of savagery: polygamy and slavery. By invoking Article IV, Section 3 of the Constitution, they figuratively waved the banner of U.S. democracy (i.e., U.S. imperialism) in order to simultaneously validate and mask the colonial relation of power exercised by Congress. Although terms like *barbarism* and *civilization* are often more commonly associated with European colonialism, an effect of the discourse of U.S. exceptionalism, this language has been used to justify the appropriation of land as well as slavery since before the founding of the U.S. nation-state. Evident in the present-day mythology of U.S. nationalism, this language is still used to claim that white Europeans were the first to cultivate, tame, and, in a word, settle North America's "virgin" landscape.[35] While numerous scholars in a variety of disciplines—most especially Native studies, American studies, history, and anthropology—have debunked this myth, it remains stubbornly persistent.[36] The ideological hegemony of U.S. exceptionalism, which denies the nation-state's imperial nature frequently through Mormon peculiarity discourse, alongside the predominance of somatic-centered conceptualizations of race helps to account for the fact that scholars have been reluctant, or at least not fully able, to analyze the federal government's treatment of Mormons in the context of U.S. colonialism and imperialism.

Yet, the paternalist language of both is evident in almost every congressional debate over anti-Mormon legislation between the mid-1850s and the 1880s. In one early example, Massachusetts representative Daniel W. Gooch promoted a bill that would have harshly criminalized adultery, polygamy, cohabitation, and fornication in Utah.[37] The debate the bill engendered exemplifies the paternalistic attitude that the federal government—like cultural critics—took toward the Saints and how that attitude was used to justify federal intervention in Utah's governance between the 1860s and 1890. While discussion about the bill mainly revolved around the reach of the proposed legislation, specifically the implications it would have concerning the issue of territorial slavery, neither side of the aisle objected to the bill on the grounds of religious freedom or colonialism, the latter a practice that U.S. politicians emphatically (but erroneously) dismissed as in conflict with the nation's commitment to democracy and freedom.[38] Indeed, there was no debate as to the immorality of polygamy—it was considered a practice of less civilized, nonwhite, and non-Christian peoples. Or, as Representative Gooch explained, "It seems to be conceded on all sides of the House that polygamy . . . is a crime, or, rather, is an evil, which should be made a crime, and be punished by law. . . . An evil which strikes at the very foundations of society [and that] corrupts the morals of the community, pollutes the blood, and confounds all title to property."[39] The bill's opponents never questioned Gooch's contentions about the racial and political-economic nature of this so-called evil, or the need to legislate against it, but instead asked again and again about the implications for slavery: "I understand the gentleman from Massachusetts to take the position that Congress has the power to exclude polygamy in the Territories of the United States. Now, I desire to know if he finds power, under the same clause of the Constitution, to exclude slavery from the Territories?"[40] Slavery was, of course, a more complicated question, in part because it was a practice that was thought to involve the regulation of both so-called barbaric and civilized peoples.[41]

Determined not to let slavery overshadow the need to legislate against polygamy, Gooch argued that territories could govern themselves on the condition that "you shall govern yourselves properly; that you shall exercise the power which we give to you in such a manner as it should be exercised for the accomplishment of the purposes that should be accomplished by

Government; and when you fail to do that, we reserve to ourselves the right to take back the power that we have given you."[42] Employing the implicitly coded racial-colonial language of classical liberalism, Gooch did not feel it was necessary to explicate what fell under the rubric of "proper" governance or what a government "should" accomplish.[43] In fact, his remarks perfectly reflect the workings of what Barnor Hesse identifies as the epistemological and governmental forms of racialization that adjudicate and valorize "Europeanness and . . . debase[] and appropriate non-Europeanness" through the exercise of regulatory, administrative power "but without explanatory reference to the impact of coloniality."[44] The protracted debate over whether slavery was acceptable makes clear that although civilization and racial progress were thought to be self-evident concepts, they were in fact discursive constructions that Gooch and his contemporaries fought hard to define. Yet even if Congress could not agree on the morality of enslaving Black people, they could definitively agree that polygamy constituted an egregious, immoral breach of acceptable social relations in the mid-nineteenth-century United States. Thus, polygamy fell well outside the bounds of tolerability because it was thought to pose a threat to Anglo-Saxon Protestant whiteness, while slavery's threat was understood to be a stain on exceptionalist claims that the United States was the altruistic custodian of racially "inferior" peoples.[45]

The pitiful condition of the Saints, Gooch maintained, was evident in their choice to practice polygamy. Accordingly, he argued that the federal government was and should act as a parent to Utah because the Saints were understood to be incapable of governing themselves "properly." This meant that the federal government not only had the right but was obligated to intervene in Utah's governance: "the Constitution of the United States authorizes us to punish polygamy in the Territory of Utah, and that . . . exigency demands such legislation."[46] The call for federal action in Utah actively employed the paternalistic language of European and U.S. colonialism citing polygamy as evidence of lack of "proper" self-governance— language that had been levied against both Native and Black peoples since the sixteenth century.[47] Federal officials pinpointed plural marriage as the most compelling evidence of the Saints' so-called barbarity, tying racial concerns ("pollutes the blood" and "corrupts the morals of the community") neatly together with political-economic ones ("confounds all title to property"). Just as white people had "expressed horror at the practice[] of polygamy . . . among Indian tribes," claiming that the practice "demeaned women," so too were those claims about Mormons leveraged to justify intervention in Utah's governance.[48]

Indicative of the power of U.S. exceptionalism, Gooch was careful to avoid any accusations that the government's "fostering and protecting" of the Saints in any way resembled European colonialism.[49] "When they have reached a stage of maturity in which they are capable of instituting certain acts of legislation for themselves," Gooch declared in his argument for the bill, "it is good policy—and experience has taught us so—to authorize them to act for themselves."[50] Preemptively clarifying his position, Gooch argued that the relationship between the central government and its territories was definitively anti-colonial. Categorically rejecting any characterization of the federal-territorial relationship as such, he argued, "we do not propose to hold any region or country as a colony, or to retain it in that position." Instead, he insisted, "we propose to assist it in its own government until it shall reach the first stage of manhood, when we will admit it as a State upon an equality with all the other States of the Union."[51] What Gooch's gendered analogy failed to articulate was the racial bedrock upon which any statehood decision rested: it belied the real and absolute control that the nineteenth-century federal government held in the biopolitical management of its territories and decisions about statehood.

Despite his insistence that the federal government was not a colonial agent and that the Saints would eventually be allowed to self-govern, his parent–child analogy revealed what would become the federal government's typical approach toward territorial acquisitions by the turn of the century. In a parallel logic that was applied to Black citizens after the Civil War, Gooch outlined an eternal parent–child dynamic in which the child never comes of age:

> When they fail to govern themselves as they should, I believe we should adopt the same policy that a judicious parent pursues with reference to his child. He permits that child to regulate and govern his own conduct so long as he applies wholesome and salutary rules to himself; but when he fails to do that, the parent again resumes the exercise of control over his own offspring.[52]

In this formulation—enshrined in the Constitution—the control of populations or territories (children) is ceded to the perpetual care of the federal government (parent) as a condition of U.S. democracy. Moreover, Gooch makes clear that Utah could not and would not advance its status from territory to state until it was ensured that the Saints would apply "wholesome and salutary rules" to themselves; in other words, until they could govern themselves by adherence to Protestant norms and morals.[53]

In the 1870s, as several of the images above show, Indigenous resistance to centuries of violent displacement and genocide—further facilitated in the second half of the nineteenth century by the Morrill Land Grant Act of 1862—was also represented as a persistent national problem that required the judicious hand of a parental governing body (Figures 11, 12, and 13), reflecting Jodi Byrd's argument that Native sovereignty was and continues to be rejected and erased, thereby eliding the very nature of U.S. settler colonialism through the process of racializing the "Indian," in this case as a troublesome internal, national problem.[54] The settler state's established strategies of displacement and genocide of Indigenous groups were increasingly focused during this period on assimilationist tactics.[55] This mirrored the federal government's decision to utilize similar assimilationist tactics in its management of Utah Territory and its attempts to quash Mormon difference, inaugurated with the Morrill Anti-Bigamy Act of 1862.[56] As with the earlier 1860 bill promoted by Gooch, debate over the Morrill Anti-Bigamy Act was replete with the language and logic of colonial governance. The act itself, enacted in 1862, criminalized bigamy in the territories, rescinded the Church's incorporation by Utah's territorial legislature, and made it unlawful for any religious organization to hold any real estate valuing more than $50,000.[57] The law struck at the three main objections anti-Mormons levied against the Saints: polygamy, theocracy, and economic communalism. But in a tacit agreement between Brigham Young and Abraham Lincoln, the U.S. president agreed not to enforce the new law, buying the allegiance of the Saints during the Civil War. Yet the fervent insistence that the Mormons constituted a religious, racial, political, and economic problem was now enshrined in the law.

Immediately after the war, legislators once again picked up the gauntlet against the Church in Utah, debating at least eight anti-Mormon bills between 1865 and 1874, many of which displayed much of the same imperialist logic as had the bill promoted so fervently by Representative Gooch in 1860 and the Morrill Anti-Bigamy Act of 1862.[58] The 1874 Poland Act used the federal government's constitutionally mandated powers of control over its territories to manipulate Utah's judicial system in order to facilitate prosecutions of polygamists under the Morrill Anti-Bigamy Act.[59] Essentially, the Poland Act shifted power from local probate judges to the U.S. district courts, taking authority away from local Mormon judges and giving it to federal non-Mormon judges. Moreover, the act gave the duty of selecting jury pools to the U.S. marshal, whisking it cleanly out of Mormon hands. By granting itself almost complete power over Utah's legal system, the federal government effectively endowed anti-Mormons, mostly federally appointed officials and non-Mormon territorial residents, with governing authority in Utah. The Poland Act's legal implications did not remain unquestioned; they were hotly debated in Congress. As with many of the more extreme bills proposed before the passage of the Poland Act, questions arose about the constitutional rights of Utah's Mormon inhabitants.

Representative Crounse of Nebraska, for example, was quick to point out the hypocrisy of a government that claimed to be representative when the federal government legislated against the clear wishes of its people: "You are taxing men without representation, you are demanding obedience to laws which they have no voice in making, and you foist upon them officers to execute the laws under no responsibility to the people governed." To Crounse, sidestepping the laws and procedures established by the territorial government amounted to the type of colonial management England had employed against the first thirteen colonies. He further argued that "when a people in a Territory cannot be accorded the right to enact their own laws . . . as long as they do not conflict with the Constitution of the United States, and if they cannot select their own officers to execute those laws, then I say you are striking down the very first principles of American liberty."[60] Despite his impassioned arguments to the contrary, Congress passed the Poland Act, seeing it not as the Saints did—as "an oppression of [a] peculiar people with a peculiar religion, worshipping a peculiar god"—but as a justified application of federal power over a people who had racially degraded themselves.[61]

Thus, the Poland Act's significance lay not just in its facilitation of prosecutions under the Morrill Anti-Bigamy Act but in its instantiation of a colonial-style administration of Utah's judicial system. Now not only had the federal government taken territorial governance out of the hands of the population's elected leaders—after the war of 1857–58, for instance, only non-Mormons were appointed in posts such as territorial governor and other key positions—but it had ensured that the legal system now became an instrument of anti-Mormon dominance. Sarah Barringer Gordon argues that statutory intervention in Utah constituted "a second reconstruction in the West," in which anti-Mormon legislation was adapted from Reconstruction legislation imposed on the South.[62] It is apparent not only from the laws themselves but also from debates over anti-Mormon legislation that Republicans did impose their will on Utah's population in ways similar to those used to transform the states of the former Confederacy. However, anti-Mormon legislation did not simply recycle Reconstruction law and policy; rather, drawing directly from Mormon peculiarity discourse, it adapted those precedents to the requirements of governing a territorial possession—something that radical Reconstructionists had attempted and failed to do in the case of the South.

Although "Utah did not become, at least immediately, an economic province whose chief function was to supply raw materials to the industrial East," after the completion of the transcontinental railroad in 1869 as anti-Mormon legislators had predicted, the erosion of Mormon control of the legal and political operations of the territory took its toll in and beyond the economic realm.[63] As the federal government implemented regulations that limited the Saints' legal rights and stifled their access to and participation in representative government, Congress instituted other laws that squeezed the life out of Mormon religious and cultural practices and overrode the Saints' constitutional rights. These methods of legal and administrative control were not exceptions but mimicked and adapted tactics of colonialist governance used against Indigenous people, strategies that would be further adapted once the nation-state extended its empire overseas in places like Hawai'i, Cuba, Puerto Rico, Guam, and the Philippines. In 1876, for example, the Utah legislature, now under the control of anti-Mormon territorial residents and federal deputies, was compelled by the presidentially appointed non-Mormon governor, George W. Emery, to adopt California's penal code. In addition to incorporating antibigamy and antipolygamy laws, a notable component of the new code was that Utah gained its first statute against "the crime against nature," a sexual practice that had remained outside the purview of the Mormon-controlled legislature. Non-Mormon officials decried the deplorable state of Utah's criminal statutes, apparently evident in this type of omission, and considered it yet another sign of Mormon barbarism.

The imposition of this external criminal code in Utah especially sought to regulate sexual practice, kinship formation, and gender relations among the Saints, key sites needed for the policing of racial status. On the local level, the new penal code criminalized a host of activities in an effort to administer and supposedly civilize the local population—producing and regulating subjects—while on the macro level, its imposition represented a new regime of biopolitical management that formally linked sexual practice, gender relations, and racial status. Historians of European colonialism have highlighted these constitutive links between "intimate" control, gendered management, and racial formation.[64] Ann Stoler argues that "the very categories of 'colonizer' and 'colonized' were secured through forms of sexual and kinship control that defined the domestic arrangements of Europeans" and were central to establishing what were assumed to be the distinct "boundaries of race."[65] Federal attempts to control the marital practices of the Saints were meant to halt, and even reverse, what were thought to be the biological racial effects of polygamy and had entrenched the discursive distinction between Mormons and Americans.

While forms of sexual and, by extension, gender exceptionalism that criticized polygamy as demeaning to women had been used to help justify the ongoing genocide and dispossession of Native peoples, in the case of the Saints the United States recycled those discourses to establish legal and administrative apparatuses of control. More specifically, in Utah the federal government used claims of sexual and gender exceptionalism to force the implementation of laws that formally established monogamy and the gendered separation of public and private spheres as reflective of the moral and sexual standards of U.S. civilization.[66] And although they rode the wave of antipolygamy sentiment sweeping the country, administrative control of sexual and domestic intimacy in Utah was not the primary target for politicians. On the contrary, federal officials targeted the intimate spaces of family, sex, marriage, and religious practice because they were understood to undergird the structure of U.S. political dominance and the engines of industrial capitalism. Mormonism, while offering an at times strikingly similar yet alternative vision to U.S. exceptionalism, had to be crushed because it was thought to represent a real threat to those alignments. Thus, the tactics of assimilatory control worked to suppress resistance to a unified vision of U.S. nationalism and empire. What intervention in Utah Territory's governance helps to demonstrate is that, in tandem with other processes of racialization and tactics of colonialization, the federal government was testing approaches to imperialist management and rule before the United States openly entered the race for empire at the fin de siècle. The nation-state's turn-of-the-century colonial systems and imperial policies were not simply copying European colonialism but were tested and carefully molded over the course of the nineteenth century, in part through the regulation of the Mormons in Utah Territory.

NAMING U.S. EMPIRE IN AND BEYOND
REYNOLDS V. UNITED STATES

Unlikely cooperation between the Church and federal officials character-ized the events that led to George Reynolds's indictment for polygamy under the Morrill Anti-Bigamy Act in October 1874. Reynolds, Brigham Young's private secretary and the husband of two wives, was called by Young to serve as the test case that would determine the constitutionality of the anti-Mormon laws. The Saints' cooperation was essential for the prosecution. Proof of polygamous marriages was all but impossible for prosecutors to acquire because Mormon marriage records were privately held by the Church and individual Saints "withdrew behind a wall of silence" when questioned about plural marriages in their community.[67] Both the Saints and anti-Mormons were sure of their eventual vindication by the Supreme Court. This hubris ensured the Saints' participation in the early prosecutorial process, a choice they soon regretted. Although the Church attempted to revoke its willing participation in the conviction of Reynolds, the damage was done. By 1876 Reynolds's test case conviction had been appealed all the way to the Supreme Court. The court's decision, penned by Chief Justice Morrison Waite, formalized the popular conception of the Saints as "Oriental foreigners" who were squatting in U.S. territory and in need of federally dispensed discipline.

Early comparisons between Mormonism and Islam that likened Joseph Smith and Brigham Young to the "false prophet" Muhammad and the Book of Mormon to the Qur'an as a religious record of "dubious" origin paved the way for the more intensive racialization of Mormonism in the late nine-teenth century.[68] The prevailing comparative portrayals that were circu-lated in the media produced Mormonism as shorthand for a conglomerate religious/racial/sexual other in need of colonial regulation. For example, one anti-Mormon critic wrote that polygamy "belongs now to the indolent and opium-eating Turks and Asiatics, the miserable Africans, the North American savages, and the latter-day saints [sic]," while another maintained that "the teachings of Christianity had been supplanted by an attempt to imitate the barbarism of Oriental nations in a long past age."[69] Such descrip-tions coincided with and reinforced pseudoscientific reports like Army Surgeon Roberts Bartholow's and numerous travelogues that maintained

Mormon polygamy was producing a new, degenerate race. Prominent physician George Naphey concluded that if left to their own devices, the Mormons "would soon sink into a state of Asiatic effeminacy," while a congressional official confidently proclaimed, "Point me to a nation where polygamy is practiced, and I will point you to heathens and barbarians. It seriously affects the prosperity of the States, it retards civilization, it uproots Christianity."[70] Well before Supreme Court Chief Justice Waite penned the *Reynolds* decision in 1878, anti-Mormons had reached the conclusion that the Saints required the guiding hand of federal management or they risked the widespread deterioration of the nation.[71]

Much to the delight of anti-Mormons, a few disaffected Mormon women published exposés about their experiences in polygamy during the mid-1870s.[72] These autobiographies helped fuel fears about Mormon theocracy, white slavery, and racial degeneracy. Doing particular damage to the Church's reputation was Ann Eliza Young, former wife of Brigham Young, whose autobiography, *Wife No. 19,* and public lecture tour condemned both Mormonism and polygamy. Billed unmistakably as "The Rebel of the Harem," her descriptions of women's experiences in polygamy both thrilled and offended audiences already primed to imagine "Scenes from an American Harem."[73] Popular concern about white slavery generally, and women's oppression under polygamy specifically, were coalescing at exactly the moment when the federal government was finally able to convict a Mormon man for practicing polygamy.

Many scholars have pointed out that "*Reynolds* immediately and irrevocably raised the pitch of antipolygamy activism," but they often neglect to link the heightened interest in suppressing Mormon practices to the larger racial-political context.[74] This obscures that *Reynolds* was not just a tipping point in Mormon history but that it also signaled the nation-state's self-acceptance and even promotion of itself as an imperial actor. Nathan B. Oman convincingly argues that the Supreme Court's decisions relating to the Church between 1879 and 1890 provided the legal foundation upon which U.S. imperialism proceeded during and after the Spanish–American War.[75] In these decisions, polygamy was officially labeled a barbaric practice, comparing it to the practice of suttee and equating Indians and Mormons as racially inferior populations in need of civilizing, as well as Britain and the United States as the two nations destined to provide such guidance.

While interpretations of *Reynolds* vary, it is unanimously regarded as important because it was the first Supreme Court case to determine the meaning and scope of the Free Exercise Clause of the First Amendment. Sarah Barringer Gordon analyzes the decision for the insights it provides about federalism, arguing that it extended the constitutional debates generated by slavery into the postbellum period.[76] Most important for my argument here, however, is Oman's assertion that *Reynolds* set the stage for the constitutional contestations over U.S. imperialism represented in the *Insular Cases*.[77] The *Insular Cases,* which refers to a group of Supreme Court decisions from the first years of the twentieth century dealing with the United States' acquisition of territories as a result of the Spanish–American War, held that full constitutional rights did not necessarily extend to the inhabitants of U.S. colonies.[78] Even a cursory review of *Reynolds* demonstrates that Waite's opinion and the court's finding displayed a clear reliance on European imperial analogies, which were used to strengthen the case for federal rule in Utah and soon reappeared in the logic of the *Insular* opinions.

The major subject addressed in Waite's decision was the question of George Reynolds's freedom to pursue his religious duty (i.e., his right to engage in plural marriage at the direction of his religious superiors), despite the criminal nature of his activities. In other words, the court had to determine whether by banning bigamy in the territories, the Morrill Anti-Bigamy Act had violated the Free Exercise Clause of the First Amendment, which guarantees "Congress shall make no law respecting an establishment of religion, or prohibiting the free exercise thereof." Waite based his verdict on what has come to be known as the belief–action distinction, a principle that distinguishes between the prohibition of laws that restrict individuals' rights to their own religious opinions but leaves free Congress's ability to legislate against actions "which [are] in violation of social duties or subversive of good order."[79] It should be no surprise that nineteenth-century officials designated polygamy an activity that violated social duty and subverted good order, given the prevailing assumptions about polygamy's subjugation of women, its connection to political authoritarianism, and, ultimately, its threat to white civilization.

Waite sidestepped the arguments of Reynolds's attorneys, George Biddle and Benjamin Sheeks, who maintained that only crimes that were malum in se, crimes in and of themselves, and not crimes that were malum prohibitum, crimes considered wrong because they were legislated against, were subject to congressional restriction under the Free Exercise Clause. Significantly, the defense also put forward a claim that the Morrill Anti-Bigamy

Act was unconstitutional because it violated Article IV, Section 3 of the Constitution—the very same clause that had been invoked by the Republicans in their call to prohibit the "twin relics of barbarism" in 1856. While Biddle and Sheeks did not deny that the Constitution gave Congress the authority to regulate its territories, they emphasized that Congress only had the "power to dispose of and make all needful rules and regulations respecting the territor[ies]" of the United States.[80] Reynolds's defense team argued that Congress had no substantive reason for legislating marriage in Utah and that therefore the Morrill Anti-Bigamy Act had not been "needful." Tellingly, in his brief to the court, Biddle maintained that "the power to create a territory did not confer upon the federal government the power to rule the inhabitants as 'mere colonists, dependent upon the will' of the center."[81] Biddle's statement reveals the extent to which the Saints, as well as sympathetic politicians, saw federal intervention as the activities of an empire working to maintain control over its colonial possession.

The decision itself reflects that the Church and its attorneys were not the only ones approaching the issue in the register of imperialism. Waite's proclamation, that "polygamy has always been odious among the northern and western nations of Europe, and until the establishment of the Mormon Church, was almost exclusively a feature of the life of Asiatic and of African people," implicitly negated Reynolds's claim that polygamy was merely malum prohibitum.[82] Drawing a clear line between the "northern and western nations of Europe" and the people of Asia and Africa, his statement also annulled any argument that Congress's regulation of polygamy was not a "needful" rule or regulation. His distinction between European *nations* and Asian and African *peoples* reinforced assumptions of linear progression in which European peoples and their descendants had achieved civilization, while Asian and African peoples merely wallowed in their so-called barbarity. Thus, polygamy emerged in the decision as proof of the Saints non-Europeanness (and by extension non-Americanness) and was used to call for, even beseech, the federal government to exercise complete authority in Utah.

Waite's distinction flowed easily from Attorney General Charles Devens's sensational oral argument that had virtually ignored any constitutional questions and claimed that polygamy would open a Pandora's box of religious evils: "'Hindu widows [would] hurl themselves on the funeral pyres of their husbands, Easter Islanders . . . expose their newborn babes, Thugs . . . commit gruesome murders,' all in the 'name of religion.'"[83] These types of fantastic comparisons were repeated in the decision as examples of the necessity and logic of the belief–action distinction: "Suppose one believed that human sacrifices were a necessary part of religious worship, would it be seriously contended that the civil government under which he lived could not interfere to prevent a sacrifice? Or," Waite continued incredulously, "if a wife religiously believed it was her duty to burn herself upon the funeral pile of her dead husband, would it be beyond the power of the civil government to prevent her carrying her belief into practice?"[84] Comparing suttee, the ritual suicide of a Hindu widow, to Mormon plural marriage was nothing new. This comparison had been deployed again and again by popular critics, academics, and federal officials during the mid-1800s, including vice president Schuyler Colfax's framing of the "federal government as an agent of civilization against barbarism, akin to the civilizing British imperialism under Macaulay in India."[85] Thus, in his decision Waite affirmed decades of anti-Mormon sentiment, formally pronouncing Mormons a foreign race analogous "to the inhabitants of the Indian subcontinent" and encouraging "federal rule in territorial Utah," equating it with "the British Raj in India . . . bringing civilization through law to the benighted masses over whom it ruled."[86]

Justifying this new willingness to identify the United States as an imperial actor by virtue of its exceptionally civilized nature, the court drew upon respected political philosopher Francis Lieber to explain why polygamy warranted federal intervention. Lieber wrote academically and popularly about the Mormon question as early as 1855, arguing:

"Monogamic marriage, . . . is one of the elementary distinctions—historical and actual—between European and Asiatic humanity. . . . Strike it out and you destroy our very being; and when we say *our,* we mean our race—a race which has its great and broad destiny, a solemn aim in the great career or civilization, with which no one of us has any right to trifle."[87]

Connecting sexual practice to racial status and equating racial status with nationality, Lieber used his prominent position to argue that polygamy would lead directly to a civilization's decline. His argument rhetorically linked U.S. exceptionalist ideas of the nation's divine destiny to the latest "scientific" thinking on race—in particular, the superiority of Anglo-Saxon whiteness. Waite pinpointed Lieber's argument that "polygamy leads to the patriarchal principle, and which, when applied to large communities,

AN UNSIGHTLY OBJECT—WHO WILL TAKE THE AXE AND HEW IT DOWN?

FIGURE 20. *An Unsightly Object—Who Will Take the Axe and Hew It Down?*
Reprinted from the *Judge*, January 28, 1882. Courtesy of the Library of Congress.

fetters the people in stationary despotism," to expound what were considered the extreme dangers of allowing such a practice in a U.S.-controlled territory.[88]

Lieber's logic played heavily on charges of gender and sexual exceptionalism to make the case that Mormonism was a threat to "American civilization." Invoking the "evil consequences that were supposed to flow from plural marriages," both Leiber and the *Reynolds* decision underscored the connections that were assumed to exist between gendered behaviors, practices, and relations to racial status.[89] Specifically, they drew on contemporary debates over women's roles and rights to argue that U.S. society was exceptional in its treatment of women, affording them the right to consent to monogamous marriage, a position that would provide them not only with protection but also with respect. The Saints, however, were considered retrograde in their treatment of the so-called weaker sex because it was assumed women were forced into polygamous relationships, which by virtue of their very plurality degraded women's femininity (see Figures 19, 20, 21, 24, 25, 26, 27, and 29). "In anti-Mormon imaginations," then, "part of what united the backward cultures of the Orient with Mormonism was a shared belief in the inferiority of women."[90] In other words, the supposedly regressive attitudes toward women that Mormons were assumed to hold were used as unimpeachable evidence of their racial inferiority, justifying the state's biopolitical management of Utah and its inhabitants.

That Mormon gender relations were considered not only backward but also threatening to U.S. racial purity is evident in the numerous images depicting women's oppression under Mormonism during the 1880s. Many of these images rehearsed and mixed the tropes of women's oppression and white slavery. For instance, Figures 19, 20, 21, 24, 25, and 26 show wives in chains or tied with rope, forced to obey their abusive husbands. All of these images also criticize ineffective governmental efforts to help the oppressed women. Relatedly, Figure 22 represents Mormonism as a skull, symbolizing the death of the innocent white, European immigrant women being consumed by the Mormon hierarchy in Utah. These images served, as did many images that tackled the issue of white slavery, not simply to condemn the plural marriages of Mormon men as barbaric but also to reinforce sexist ideas about women's weakness and need for protection from both men and the state. Even as anti-Mormons charged the Church's leadership with "patriarchal despotism," they used those same assertions to reinforce the patriarchal power of monogamous marriage.

FIGURE 21. *The Mormon Question. What Is Uncle Sam Going to Do about It?*
Reprinted from the *Daily Graphic*, October 22, 1883. Courtesy of the Library of Congress.

In addition to these sexist tropes, numerous caricatures utilized the figure of the "Mormon Bluebeard," to cement popular associations between Mormon plural marriage, white women's supposed enslavement, and stereotypes of Asian cultures and peoples (see Figures 23, 24, 25, 26, and 27). Widespread references to a Mormon "Sultanate" in Salt Lake City were reinforced by images that depicted "a mythic Arab brute who abused captive

FIGURE 22. *Mormonism in Utah—The Cave of Despair.* Reprinted from *Frank Leslie's Illustrated Newspaper*, February 4, 1882. L. Tom Perry Special Collections, Harold B. Lee Library, Brigham Young University, Provo, Utah.

women."[91] Although originally a French folktale, by the mid-nineteenth century Orientalism had transformed the bluebeard story into a legend of "Oriental," most often Turkish, origin. Accordingly, Mormon bluebeards were frequently depicted by the press as nonwhite, Islamic, or Asian figures. Graphic images played on Orientalist stereotypes of Muslim and Asian men as barbaric in their treatment of women. For example, in the *Judge's Hit 'Em Again* (Figure 23), D. Mac drew a Mormon bluebeard with dark skin and a large nose and ears and dressed him in a turban, vest, and striped, billowy pants. The link between his racial status and his treatment of women is confirmed in the dangerous-looking spiked club he holds, labeled "Polygamy." Even more frequently, illustrators gave Mormon bluebeards features associated with other non-Christian or nonwhite groups, such as Jews or Indigenous people, including pointy ears, horns, and almond-shaped eyes (Figures 24, 25, 26, and 27). In these cases, the Mormon bluebeard is often shown dragging women by their hair or tied by their hair to his belt, images that would have evoked sensational stories in the press about scalping during the 1870s and 1880s. The association drawn between stereotypes of Native people scalping white settlers and Mormon bluebeards collecting trophy wives hanging from their belts would only have been heightened by the appearance of feathers in the Mormon bluebeard's hat brim.

Finding no contradiction in women's lack of political and economic rights across the nation, and instead identifying a superior organization of gender in U.S. society, commentators argued that Mormon women in Utah suffered from extreme exploitation and oppression, far worse than any suffered by formerly enslaved Black people. Claims to superior gender relations were propounded not only by politicians but by feminists and suffragists as well. For example, celebrated suffragist Frances Willard tellingly declared of Mormonism, "Turkey is in our midst. . . . Modern Mohammedanism has its Mecca in Salt Lake City, where Prophet Heber C. Kimball speaks of his wives as 'cows.'"[92] Statements from famous activists such as Willard helped to lend credence to a political project that relied upon the reassertion of a racial hierarchy both within and outside the United States.

Another image from *Puck* magazine (Figure 28) depicted the so-called "Oriental nature" of white women's supposed slavery under Mormon polygamy as a Turkish harem in which the hookah-smoking patriarch is catered to by no less than nine women. Embodying anxieties about gender and sexual exceptionalism, these wives were conjured up by dramatic media

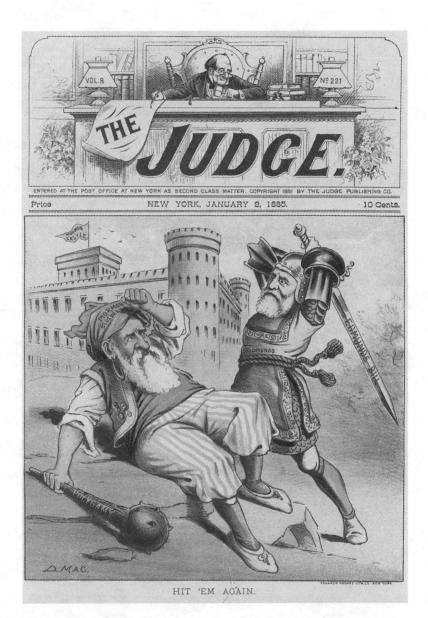

FIGURE 23. D. Mac. *Hit 'Em Again*. Reprinted from the *Judge* 9, no. 221, January 9, 1885. Courtesy of the Library of Congress.

FIGURE 24. *The Modern Blue Beard.* Reprinted from the *Daily Graphic,* August 21, 1883, 1. Courtesy of the Library of Congress.

FIGURE 25. *The Remaining Twin.* "Uncle Sam—'I Don't Know Exactly What to Do with That Fellow. I Must Decide Before He Decides What to Do with Me.'" Reprinted from the *Daily Graphic* 32, no. 3,279, October 15, 1883. Courtesy of the Library of Congress.

FIGURE 26. *Shall Not That Sword Be Drawn?* Reprinted from the *Daily Graphic* 32, no. 3,288, October 25, 1883. Courtesy of the Library of Congress.

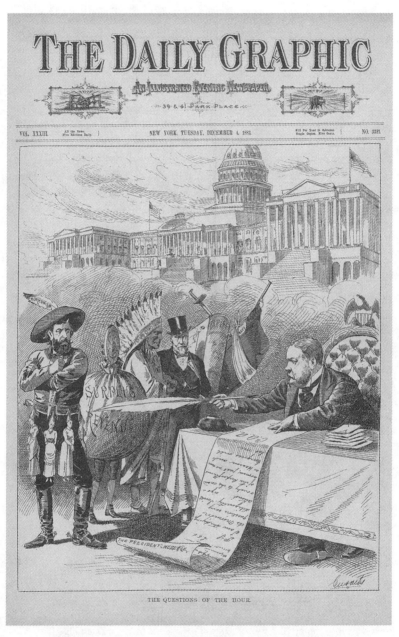

FIGURE 27. *The Questions of the Hour.* Reprinted from the *Daily Graphic* 32, no. 3,321, December 4, 1883. Courtesy of the Library of Congress.

coverage of Mormon plural marriage as white slavery. Some wives present platters of food and wine to their husband, others fan or sing for him. One wife dances provocatively with an exposed stomach as she plays the tambourine, an image that would have aroused fears of sexual excess and deviance for a nineteenth-century, middle-class audience. The presumed exploitation of white women under Mormonism that concerned both the media and the government was inextricably connected to concerns over the sexual peculiarity of the Saints. Anxieties about Mormon sexual peculiarity were perhaps best exemplified by yet another wife standing on the right side of the image whose brown skin would have invoked suspicions of interracial sex and the supposed accompanying racial decline thought to occur as a result of polygamous unions. Miscegenation was an issue of broader social concern that was regarded as threatening to the purity and supremacy of Anglo-Saxon Protestant whiteness. The end of slavery, the continued acquisition of territories, and increased immigration, in addition to Mormon plural marriage, all excited fears about racial mixing. Only four years after *Reynolds* was decided, the Supreme Court upheld the criminalization of interracial sexual relations, marriage, and cohabitation in *Pace v. Alabama* (1883).[93]

FIGURE 28. Keppler, *A Desperate Attempt to Solve the Mormon Question.* "I imagine it must be a perfect Paradise." Reprinted from *Puck,* February 13, 1884. Courtesy of the Library of Congress.

Claims that the Saints had reverted to less developed or racially inferior gender and sexual relations infused typical representations of the Mormon problem in the media and subsequently seeped into the juridical logic of *Reynolds*. Claims of U.S. gender and sexual exceptionalism continued to escalate after *Reynolds* was decided in 1879, apparent in the reasoning that was used to justify new legislation targeting the Church in the 1880s. Having established Congress's right to legislate against polygamy as a religious activity that violated "good social order," Waite's decision dealt a severe blow to the Saints' hopes for freedom of religious practice. The decision legally affirmed the racial-religious distinctions between Anglo-Saxon white Protestant Americans and Mormons, thereby revalidating federal control of Utah, but also establishing a significant precedent for imperial expansion that U.S. politicians had, thus far, attempted to deny. Waite's classification of "the peculiar character of [polygamy]" merely formalized what was already a potent civilizational assemblage.[94]

Before *Reynolds*, politicians had vigorously refuted attempts to name or acknowledge the nation's colonial nature, exemplified in the debate over the 1860 anti-Mormon bill Gooch so fervently promoted. Post-*Reynolds*, the nation found itself willing to claim an imperial identity. Between 1882 and 1887, the rhetoric of national problems produced congressional responses that reaffirmed the nation's commitment to regulating its "troublesome children," both at home and abroad, using tactics of colonial administration. For example, two years after Talmage gave his sermons calling for the inclusion of Chinese immigrants and the exclusion of the Saints, Congress passed the Edmunds and Chinese Exclusion Acts.[95] Passed only two months before the Chinese Exclusion Act, which prohibited the immigration of all Chinese laborers and virtually excluded all Chinese immigrants from entering the United States, the Edmunds Act targeted the Saints far beyond any previous federal legislation had before. Named after George Edmunds, a senator from Vermont, the law sought to strengthen the government's ability to more effectively prosecute Mormon men for practicing polygamy.

Unlike previous legislation criminalizing bigamy, the Edmunds Act proscribed "cohabitation," making it a misdemeanor punishable by up to six months in prison and a $300 fine. Outlawing cohabitation, which the law defined as living concurrently with more than one woman and holding them out publicly as one's wives, released the state from having to prove that actual marriage ceremonies had taken place, making it substantially easier for prosecutors to indict and prosecute polygamist patriarchs. But the Edmunds Act went much further. It disenfranchised all polygamists, excluding anyone who practiced, or even believed in, polygamy from serving on juries or holding political office. The consequences of these restrictions were vast and ultimately fatal for the Saints' resistance. George Q. Cannon, a member of the Quorum of the Twelve Apostles who had long served as Utah's territorial delegate to Congress, was disqualified from service, resulting in the loss of what had been one of the Church's most effective representatives in Washington. All of Utah's political offices were declared vacant, and a five-man commission was appointed to supervise future elections to enforce the proscription against polygamists voting or running for office.

Even before the act was passed, several senators had expressed concern over the constitutionality of the bill. During the debate over the Edmunds Bill, Senator George H. Pendleton of Ohio pointed out that withholding the right to vote and to hold office were means of punishing individual Saints before they were even convicted of an offense, a clear violation of constitutional protections against bills of attainder.[96] Similarly, Senator Wilkinson Call of Florida objected that excluding those who believed in polygamy from serving on juries was tantamount to "impos[ing] a religious test upon jurors which is in violation of that cardinal provision of the Constitution of the United States" and also clashed with the belief–action distinction Waite had established in *Reynolds*.[97] But "even those who attacked the Edmunds Bill," Oman points out, "did so using imperial analogies."[98] Even though Senator Brown of Georgia was against federal regulation of polygamy, he supported his position by analogizing federal intervention in Utah to British rule in India, arguing that when England "assumed dominion of India she found polygamy there. . . . [And] the English people did not attempt to crush it out by law, but the British Parliament and the British courts recognized it in India on assuming control and recognize it to-day."[99] But because the Supreme Court had already disposed of many (but not all) of the constitutional roadblocks inherent to the Edmunds Act in *Reynolds,* anti-Mormon legislation effectively situated Mormonism "in a global narrative of racial superiority that accommodated the rising force of Jim Crow by exoticizing" the Saints as non-European and non-American and therefore in need of "suppression as part of the onward march of the 'northern and western nations of Europe.'"[100] While the style of suppression was debated by Congress, the need for it was not.

The Edmunds Act's immediate effect on the daily life of the Saints was extremely disruptive. What little national influence they had was immediately checked with the loss of Cannon in Washington. The local political dominance the Church had enjoyed was radically lessened with the evacuation of local political offices and the rapid indictment of polygamists. The Raid, as the Saints referred to the federal assault against them, redirected their efforts away from effective forms of resistance and insulation toward avoiding and undermining the federal government's attempts to prosecute the prominent heads of polygamous families who were often Church leaders. Realizing that their best possible defense was avoidance and obfuscation, the Church leadership quickly went underground, hiding from marshals attempting to arrest, prosecute, and imprison them. Those who remained aboveground, wives and children, were targeted by officials in the hunt for polygamous patriarchs. Wives continued to utilize the strategy of forgetfulness to prevent prosecution. When questioned about their marriages and husbands' whereabouts, wives would suddenly "forget" the specifics of their marital status and their family's makeup, while those who performed marriage ceremonies would "forget" whether they had done so. Because wives' obfuscation helped to thwart federal prosecution, federal sympathy for polygamy's presumed victims began to evaporate. While hiding was an effective way to frustrate anti-Mormon officials, it had several drawbacks; these disadvantages ultimately spelled the doom for the Saints' other nonnormative practices. Perhaps most important, the realities of hiding made it extremely difficult for the faith's leaders to execute normal management of the Church's affairs. Not only did Church leaders, who were daily shuffled from hiding place to hiding place, find it almost impossible to keep up with their regular administration duties, but their success at outrunning the law meant that federal officials decided to go after all polygamist practitioners, not just high-ranking ones. As Sarah Barringer Gordon points out, unexpectedly this exposed the less mobile and less financially stable polygamists and their families to the hardships of federal prosecution.[101]

By 1884, the remaining anticapitalist resistance strategies that had been put in place by Young and his successor John Taylor were rendered unsustainable under the weight of the Edmunds Act. The majority of the remaining United Order towns, cooperative and socialistic economic experiments, failed; the economic boycott of Gentile enterprises was ended; private enterprise was once again sanctioned by Church leaders; and the

Zion's Board of Trade, which had been organized to ensure collective, cooperative economic exchange among the Saints, died.[102] These failures coincided with the continued penetration of the national economy into Utah's borders through the railroad and, increasingly, non-Mormon business interests. But perhaps most essential, the disintegration of economic resistance strategies also coincided with what is typically referred to as the "closure of the frontier." Eastern firms, which had been thus far kept at bay, began to buy controlling interests in Utah's industries, especially mining.

The integration of local and regional economies, such as Utah's, into the national economy also coincided with the latter's absorption into the world economic system. Yet even as penetration of U.S. producers into foreign markets and the influx of immigrants into the United States fulfilled the demands of the country's increasingly rapid industrialization, those factors stirred the anxiety of a population that viewed "industry as the highest incarnation of civilization."[103] Paradoxically, capitalism, which was thought to mark the ultimate embodiment of civilization, was also believed to be threatening the very purity of Anglo-Saxon Protestant whiteness that underlay that status. Steadily increasing levels of immigration were polluting the nation's racial purity, elites argued, while the effects of industrial capitalism were thought to both promote the confusion of proper gender roles and contribute to dangerously decreasing birth rates among white people.

Although the nativist and social scientific responses to immigration during this period have been well-documented as a process of racial formation, especially between 1880 and 1920, less attention has been paid to the ways that these racial ideas were deeply rooted in notions of civilization and development as economic concepts. As Jacobson argues:

> The very idea of "civilization" implacably ranked diverse peoples' ways of life according to a hierarchy of evolutionary economic stages . . . [and] these assessments themselves had tremendous economic consequences, as the value judgments embedded within the notion of "civilization" at once suggested and justified any number of interventions into "savage" society on the part of "civilized" nations, ranging from total extermination on one end of the spectrum to paternalistic assimilation on the other.[104]

The economic logic underlying the discourse of civilization is evident upon inspection of the policies of removal and assimilation that were implemented against Indigenous peoples during the last quarter of the nineteenth century. For example, federal officials would often cite the supposedly primitive economic arrangements of Indigenous groups as proof that they were less developed than "Americans." Civilizing missions often took the form of educational campaigns that emphasized notions of private property, wage earning, and heteronormative family units.[105] Like the Chinese Exclusion and Edmunds Acts, the Dawes Act of 1887 was passed as a solution to the so-called Indian problem.[106] The act utilized new strategies of assimilation that purposefully disrupted tribal organization, encouraged investment in private property, and promoted the formation of nuclear familial units.[107]

The Saints held the same views of Indigenous peoples as anti-Mormons. Painting themselves as more enlightened than other peoples, the Saints saw it as their obligation to help Native peoples by "civilizing" them. For example, Young exhorted the Saints to "feed and clothe . . . [and to] teach [Indians] the arts of husbandry," arguing that "independent of the question of exercising humanity towards so degraded and ignorant a people, it was manifestly more economical and less expensive, to feed and clothe, than to fight them."[108] Putting aside the rather callous attitude of Young, his comments reveal the extent to which the Saints viewed themselves as superior to Indigenous people—religiously, racially, and economically—just as non-Mormon white people saw themselves as superior to the Saints. The difference was that the Saints believed Mormon exceptionalism, and not U.S. exceptionalism, endowed them with a divinely sanctioned obligation to civilize Indigenous people. Thus, although they too engaged in differing cultural, economic, and political practices from non-Mormons, the Saints did not see Native practices as viably different but as in need of significant change. Even as the Saints themselves were subjected to the racializing assessments that ranked their social, political, and economic practices as supposedly savage, they too advanced assimilatory civilizing missions that sought to bring Indigenous peoples into more supposedly developed ways of life.

ENTRENCHING U.S. EXCEPTIONALISM

After the passage of the Edmunds Act effectively undercut Mormon resistance, Congress began to look for ways to target the Saints' economic communalism more explicitly. In 1886, Representative John Randolph Tucker, a Democrat from Virginia, contended:

The Mormon system is directly antagonistic to all ideas of European and American civilization. A family springing from the marital relation of one man to many wives seems to make a home of unity, harmony, and hearty co-operation impossible. Its elements are heterogeneous, alien, and must in most cases be hostile. If the Biblical origin of our race be admitted, one man and one woman—the dual unity—constituted the Divine appointment for the family. Affection concentrated not divided; care and protection by the man for the woman, and natural assistance and sympathy, which are found in a wedded pair rearing a common offspring in a home from which none stray . . . and the twin become one and indivisible in life, labor, and interest.[109]

Tucker outlined a divinely ordained progressive trajectory for Euro-American civilization in which the success of capitalism depends upon the (fragile) stability of the white, monogamous, heteronormative family unit. More specifically, his argument maintained that the "one man and one woman" pairing, sustained by patriarchal obligation, fostered the racially responsible procreation of a self-contained economic unit that sustained capitalist growth. On the flip side, he cast the "Mormon system" as "alien," as well as "antagonistic" and "hostile" to the "natural" progression of white, Protestant, capitalist—in a word, American—civilization.[110]

But even as free market capitalism had achieved mainstream ideological dominance, the growing disparities that arose out of nineteenth-century industrialism were fueling a politicized resistance to that economic system. By the 1880s, labor had developed a strong response to the exploitative and dangerous working conditions in factories. While industrialists were amassing enormous fortunes and big business became a defining feature of U.S. capital, numerous depressions during the last quarter of the century were also producing low wages, unemployment, starvation, and horrid living conditions for many. Strikes and protests, as well as the violent responses to them, became common fodder for a sensationalizing press.[111] While politicians concerned themselves with legislating against monopolies, trusts, and corruption in an effort to promote "true" free market capitalism, popular animus was directed at those who challenged the very morality of a capitalist economy. Labor unions, socialists, and anarchists were commonly criticized by popular religious and political figures as un-American.

In perhaps the most well-known example, clergyman and author Josiah Strong argued in his influential tome *Our Country* that "the despotism of the few and the wretchedness of the many" were two equally dangerous perils to the future of the U.S. nation-state, one helping to promote the other.[112] Published in 1885, Strong's book diagnosed what he saw as the most pressing threats to the white nation, including immigration, Catholicism, intemperance, wealth, the evils of urban living spurred by industrialization, and Mormonism. In diagnosing these threats, Strong's text advocated white supremacy as reason and imperative for imperialist, missionary intervention both at home and abroad. Scholars have pointed to Strong's wildly popular text, which was outsold only by the Bible in the postbellum period, as an example of the ways white Protestantism came to disregard the problems facing freed people after the failure of Reconstruction and instead sacrificed racial justice "at the altar of white reunion."[113] In other words, Strong's manifesto exchanged the Reconstruction-era project of racial justice for a religiously authorized capitalist-imperialist agenda firmly rooted in white supremacy.

Like Representative Tucker, Reverend Strong saw Mormonism as a threat to the intertwined agendas of industrial capitalism, white supremacy, and U.S. empire. He argued that Mormonism's danger did not lie in polygamy per se but in the anticapitalist immigrants he claimed the religion was importing:

> Immigration furnishes most of the victims of Mormonism; and there is a Mormon vote. Immigration is the strength of the Catholic church; and there is a Catholic vote. Immigration is the mother and nurse of American socialism; and there is to be a socialist vote.[114]

Rolling the national problems of Mormonism, Catholicism, socialism, and immigration into one, his argument focused on the threat that so-called despotic religions posed to the economic and racial well-being of the United States. Only a year after his book was published, the Haymarket Affair rocked the country, fueling the fears Strong articulated about immigration, labor activism, and racial degeneracy. One of the most famous events in U.S. labor history, the bombing of a May 4, 1886, labor demonstration calling for an eight-hour workday and the subsequent trials of eight anarchists for the bombing intensified nativist sentiment and linked racial inferiority to labor and anticapitalist activism. Strong insisted that "Mormonism is doing a . . . preparatory work. It is gathering together great numbers of ill-balanced men, who are duped for a time by Mormon mummery" and who "becoming disgusted, leave the church . . . skeptical, soured, cranky"

and become "excellent socialistic material." Such a claim was inflammatory for readers already primed by Mormon peculiarity discourse.[115]

Strong's concern was not wholly unsupported, but not in the way he
assumed. For example, prominent anarchist, labor activist, and left-wing
intellectual Dyer Daniel Lum, who had written extensively about the trials
of the accused Haymarket bombers, published a pamphlet titled "The Mormon Question in Its Economic Aspects." In his pamphlet, Lum reasoned
that "we need not waste words on polygamy, though the Utah system
is well worth study. *That is not the issue!* That is but the gaudily-colored
bait to catch the inexperienced denizens of economic waters."[116] Instead,
he argued, the Edmunds Act, as part of a wider federal campaign to regulate Utah, was an attempt to suppress the principles of cooperation and
arbitration that were at the heart of the Mormon economic system; "necessarily," he concluded, "in the eyes of monopoly-restricted competition,
this is a foe."[117] Lum even went so far as to declare, incorrectly, that the
abolishment of the wage system was "a problem the Mormon has alone
solved," pointing to their "passive resistance to oppression" as a model for
"the American workingman."[118]

Lum's pamphlet was not nearly as widely circulated as Strong's *Our
Country*, yet the Saints' economic practices were still cause for concern
among politicians and businessmen. Instead of representing the Saints as
socialists as both Strong and Lum had done, albeit in support of opposite
agendas, most anti-Mormons successfully represented Mormonism as a
monopolistic enterprise and thus the enemy of the workingman. Sarah
Barringer Gordon shows how anti-Mormon politicians borrowed popular concerns about corporate power, trusts, and corruption to paint the
Church as a large corporation with amoral executives.[119] While the Church
leadership did exercise great control over economic activity in Utah, anti-
Mormons had to work actively to paint the Church as an evil corporation
and its leadership as amoral fortune hunters. Deftly manipulating reality,
anti-Mormons transformed fears about Mormon economic difference into
fears of monopoly.

Circumventing any sympathy that could be afforded to a religious institution that might have similarities with the working class, anti-Mormon
politicians equated the exploitation of factory workers with the Church's
requirement that all Saints tithe 10 percent of their income. With this rhetorical sleight of hand, the Church's economic program was transformed
from one of economic cooperation with socialistic characteristics to one of

exploitative monopoly. An 1886 House Report on the proposed Edmunds–Tucker bill, for example, declared that "the enormous power of the [Mormon] corporation to increase its means and influence in the infant State" was evidence of Church leaders' corruption.[120] Another official argued that "the man with four wives must have the means of supporting them; he must *monopolize* power, property, and privilege," while "the man not permitted to marry one wife is deprived of other rights and reduced to an inferior position."[121] In these statements, the Church was transformed into a monopoly that completely dominated both production and consumption in the interest of a religious elite (rather than an entire religious community), while the monogamist ("the man not permitted to marry one wife") and not the polygamist became subject to governmental oppression.

Lum's diagnosis of the government's procapitalist motivations for legislating against the Church's financial stability was reflected in one of the final pieces of anti-Mormon legislation. Passed in early 1887, the breadth and depth of the Edmunds–Tucker Act demonstrates the extent to which gender roles and marital structure were thought to inform the operation of economics.[122] In the eyes of anti-Mormons, "polygamy created a host of economic consequences, all of them irretrievably at odds with liberty, democracy, competition—in short with capitalism. The habits of home life, the argument went, determined the political economy of the territory."[123] Anti-Mormon politicians used these assumptions about the inherent connections between gender, marriage, and economy to produce policies that enforced a normative vision of the "proper" relationship between all three.[124] To do this, the 1887 Edmunds–Tucker Act, signed into law only a month after the Dawes Act, supplemented the earlier Edmunds Act in several ways. Although the earlier law had disenfranchised all practicing polygamists, the Saints still dominated the electorate. Taking a dual tack, the new act further eroded the Saints' political rights and worked to dismantle the Church itself. It revoked women's suffrage in Utah and further regularized marriage law, easing the burdens of prosecutors in proving polygamous marriages. But most significantly, the act disincorporated the Church, confiscated its property in excess of $50,000, and dissolved the Perpetual Emigration Fund Company, a church organization that had brought thousands of converts to Utah.

Rescinding women's suffrage in Utah was a direct response to Mormon women's unwillingness to criminalize polygamy with the vote. Often overlooked in historical scholarship, suffrage in Utah was considered a test case for national women's suffrage—its success or failure was gauged by the fate of polygamy.[125] Federal politicians cited Mormon women's failure to use their newfound voting power to eradicate polygamy as evidence that women in general could not be trusted to govern themselves properly and therefore should not be granted the right to vote nationally. This logic paralleled narratives of white slavery that insisted women need to be pro- tected and shielded rather than be engaged and independent citizens. Un- surprisingly, the press continued to portray federal legislators as saviors in their efforts to crush the Church's power. One cover of *Puck* magazine (Figure 29), for example, memorialized Senator Edmunds, the sponsor of both the Edmunds and the Edmunds–Tucker Acts, as the savior of Mor- mon women (also see Figure 23). The image promotes the idea of white slavery by depicting a lazy, polygamous patriarch who is suddenly shaken from reading the Book of Mormon by Senator Edmunds's towering appa- rition. Edmunds's figure floats in the clouds above a field where the hus- band's eight wives are laboring in the hot sun, ready to be freed from their bondage. While this image is a racial one, it is also an image that shows the links that were assumed to exist between gender relations, marital struc- ture, and economic practice that the Edmunds–Tucker Act attacked (also see Figures 9, 16, 18, and 19). For anti-Mormon politicians, monogamy was thought to promote competition, with a husband and wife supporting one another in their own independent economic unit, while polygamy was blamed for the growth of monopolistic and anticompetitive behavior.

After 1887, federal officials were in complete control of Utah's gover- nance and were close to achieving the complete capitulation of the Church. Each successive piece of anti-Mormon legislation had implemented new and more effective measures that struck at the heart of Mormon life. The constitutionality of many of these anti-Mormon laws was, and continues to be, challenged. Edwin Brown Firmage and Richard Collin Mangrum, for example, argue that "under even the most generous standards of legis- lative latitude, the Edmunds–Tucker Act skirted the boundaries of consti- tutionality" by blatantly "attacking a religious institution and impos[ing] civil punishments on an entire group of people solely for their religious beliefs."[126] Regardless of the constitutionality of these laws and the Supreme Court decisions that upheld them, nineteenth-century anti-Mormon legis- lation, like other federal policies and regulations, fundamentally reflected forms of biopolitical governance. These statutes sought to wrestle politi- cal control from the hands of the Church and enforce federal jurisdiction,

VOL. XXI.—No. 525.   NEW YORK, MARCH 30, 1887.   PRICE, TEN CENTS.

KEPPLER & SCHWARZMANN, Publishers.   PUCK BUILDING, Cor. Houston & Mulberry Sts.

ENTERED AT THE POST OFFICE AT NEW YORK, AND ADMITTED FOR TRANSMISSION THROUGH THE MAILS AT SECOND CLASS RATES.

AN INTERRUPTED IDYLL.
Danger Impending to the System of Woman-Slavery in Utah.

FIGURE 29. *An Interrupted Idyll.* "Danger Impending to the System of Woman-Slavery in Utah." Reprinted from *Puck* 21, no. 525, March 30, 1887. Courtesy of HathiTrust.

citing the Saints' barbarism as sufficient justification for doing so. By proclaiming Mormons and their practices racially backward, the state was able
to induce social, economic, and political control, enabling the exploitation
of Utah's natural landscape and forcing the eventual assimilation of the
Saints to national norms.

Between 1887 and 1890, the weight of federal pressure and a series of
unlucky events coincided to ensure that the Saints would no longer be able
to sustain the kind of open resistance they once had. Only five days before
the U.S. district attorney began escheatment proceedings to confiscate the
Church's property required by the Edmunds–Tucker Act in 1887, Church
President John Taylor died while in hiding. With the Church's highest office
vacant, the entire Church hierarchy on the run, and prosecutors indicting
and convicting every polygamous man they could arrest, the Saints last
major strategy of defense was to challenge the Edmunds–Tucker Act in
court. The Supreme Court's decision in *Late Corporation of The Church of
Jesus Christ of Latter-day Saints v. United States* was announced in May 1890,
not incidentally the same year the Sherman Antitrust Act was passed by
Congress.[127] Like the Sherman Act, which banned trusts and regulated
business activities that were considered anticompetitive, the Edmunds–
Tucker Act sought to end the Church's economic dominance in Utah by
redistributing its funds to what were considered more civilized enterprises
than polygamy. The Church's attorney, James Overton Broadhead, argued
against the federal government's right to disestablish the Church's incorporation on the grounds that Congress did not have the power to negate
an executed contract, the Church's charter. More persuasive to the court,
if not actually factual, was U.S. Attorney General Augustus Hill Garland's
argument that the early territorial legislation creating the church corporation was void because it had endowed a religious organization with the right
to make laws.[128]

In *Late Corp.* the court reaffirmed Congress's constitutionally mandated
capacity to govern absolutely in its territories, although the decision was
less than unanimous. One dissenter asserted that it was not within the
authority of Congress to "seize and confiscate the property of persons, individuals, or corporations . . . because they may have been guilty of criminal
practices."[129] However, the logic of *Reynolds* remained strong enough to
ensure an opinion in favor of the federal government. In the decision, Justice
Joseph P. Bradley reiterated polygamy's "uncivilized" nature, calling it a
"barbarous practice," and rehearsed, almost exactly, the comparison Chief

Justice Waite had made between British imperialism over India and federal control over Utah in *Reynolds,* once again equating polygamy to "the right of assassination [in] religious belief," "suttee," and "human sacrifice."[130]

Key to Bradley's decision was his contention that the United States was an essentially Christian nation.[131] Citing the religious basis of U.S. exceptionalism, Bradley disavowed the Saints' own understanding of theirs as a Christian faith and, according to late nineteenth-century sensibility, argued that as a non-Christian faith the Church could not undertake a charitable cause under the banner of a corporate charter. "The principles of the law of charities are not confined to a particular people or nation, but prevail in all civilized countries pervaded by the spirit of Christianity," he opined.[132] This reasoning reflected the increased importance of Protestant missionizing to U.S. imperialism between the 1880s and the 1890s and firmly differentiated between U.S. and Mormon colonization projects.[133] The charitable and philanthropic activities of white Protestant religious groups promoted what was understood to be the divinely ordained white supremacist, capitalist domination of foreign peoples by the United States. But while the Saints were engaging in their own version of colonial dominance, the teachings of the Church clashed too fundamentally with mainstream notions of U.S. exceptionalism—as articulated by Senator Tucker, "the Mormon system is directly antagonistic to all ideas of European and American civilization"—to be defined as Christian by the Supreme Court. The fact that the Church's funds were "intended to . . . promote[] the inculcation and spread of . . . polygamy,—a crime against the laws, and abhorrent to the sentiments and feelings of the civilized world," excluded the Church from official participation in the U.S. imperial project.[134] Simply put, religious charity was only Christian and American if it promoted monogamy and capitalism.

Late Corp. was the last major blow to Mormon resistance. It affirmed the financial disassembling of the Church and placed the Saints in an unsustainable position. By September 1890, Wilford Woodruff, who had succeeded John Taylor as president of the Church, announced the capitulation of the Saints to federal pressure. In a document that has become known as "the Manifesto," Woodruff pledged obedience to U.S. law and declared that Church leaders were no longer "teaching polygamy or plural marriage, nor permitting any person to enter into its practice."[135] History has framed the Manifesto as the ultimate symbol of the Church's capitulation, but it was not dissimilar to other public declarations leaders had made in an attempt to appease federal opponents.[136] Anti-Mormons doubted the sincerity of the Manifesto with good reason, charging the Saints with the continued, but now covert, practice of polygamy. Not only were anti-Mormons weary of the leadership's continued hold over individual Saints, but experience had taught them that the Saints would not give in on issues fundamental to their faith. Historians have chronicled the confusion that the Manifesto produced among Church leaders and the consequent contradictory policies concerning plural marriage advocated by various leaders between 1890 and 1904.[137] The continued, albeit inconsistent, practice of polygamy ensured that anti-Mormonism remained an animating but declining feature of U.S. popular and political culture until the 1920s.

Thus, anti-Mormon sentiment did not disappear overnight. Rather, the Saints continued to be relationally racialized with and against other groups well into the beginning of the twentieth century. For example, in December 1890 when, only a few months after the Manifesto was released, the massacre at Wounded Knee took place, both the popular press and federal agents partially blamed the massacre on the Saints. Long-standing irritation on the part of U.S. Indian agents about Mormon "interference" with Native peoples and public anxiety about the Saints' missionizing among them fueled speculation that Mormon teachings had inspired the so-called Messiah craze, more accurately known as the Ghost Dance religious movement. This movement motivated U.S. military action against Great Basin and Plains tribes whose religious dances were interpreted as violent threats to white settlers.[138] Implicitly blaming the Saints for the atrocities committed at Wounded Knee, popular perception of Mormons as race traitors reiterated prevalent anxieties about what were wrongly assumed to be the completely opposite goals of Mormon and U.S. exceptionalism. These dynamics were anticipated in an 1882 *Harper's Weekly* image that showcased notions of Mormon sedition (Figure 30). Not only did the image play on fears of supposed senseless Native savagery, represented by the discarded sabers and a gun lying at the feet of a dead U.S. solider just visible on the lower left-hand side of the image, but it reasserted the racial links between the Native figure and the Mormon "Polygamous Barbarian," who sought to incite even more violence for his own gain. Presumably his barbarism was a result of his marital status and his racial treason; not only did his sexual practices threaten racial purity, but his self-made alliance with "savage" Indians was a direct attack on the nation.

These kinds of representation ensured that the Church remained a target of both the federal government and the popular press. On a lesser scale,

"WHEN THE SPRING-TIME COMES, GENTLE"—INDIAN!

POLYGAMOUS BARBARIAN. "Much guns, much ammunition, much whiskey, and much kill pale-face."

FIGURE 30. Thomas Nast, *"When the Spring-time Comes, Gentle"—Indian!* "Polygamous Barbarian. 'Much guns, much ammunition, much whiskey, and much kill pale-face.'" Reprinted from *Harper's Weekly*, February 18, 1882, 109. Courtesy of the Library of Congress.

Mormonism continued to be portrayed as a national problem after 1890, retaining a status as an embarrassing but controllable reality. After nearly fifty years of petitioning, Congress admitted Utah to the Union as a state in 1896, but statehood was only granted on the condition that Utah's constitution would include a ban on polygamy. The 1894 Enabling Act, guaranteeing statehood to Utah, explained "that perfect toleration of religious sentiment shall be secured, and that no inhabitant of said State shall ever be molested in person or property on account of his or her mode of religious worship; provided, that polygamous or plural marriages are forever prohibited."[139] Thus, Utah's statehood was predicated on the exclusion of a practice that was deemed racially degrading and therefore at odds with the nation's commitment to white supremacy.

During the debates over Utah's constitution, the Saints learned to accept and advance U.S. exceptionalism without boasting Mormon exceptionalism above and beyond loyalty to the nation. In *Utah Magazine,* editor E. L. T. Harrison and his associate Edward W. Tullidge advocated for including women's suffrage in Utah's new constitution, arguing that "'the nation which does not assign to women a very high part to play not only in the home circle but also in all the vital concerns of humanity, is barbaric in its notions and estate,'" an indication that "'true civilization had not yet'" been achieved.[140] Using the logic of gender exceptionalism that had so often been deployed against them, some Saints advocated for women's rights on the basis that it proved that the United States—and by extension Utah— was civilized. The debate that ensued over women's suffrage was not like past polarizations with Mormon insistence on the morality of polygamy and anti-Mormon assertions of the practice's brutality. Instead, it mirrored larger national debates about what women's roles should be in what many regarded as the most civilized nation in the world.[141]

By 1896, "most of the goals of the pioneer church . . . the gathering, the Mormon village, unique property institutions, economic independence, the theocratic Kingdom," and plural marriage "were abandoned, or well on their way toward abandonment."[142] By exceptionalizing the Mormon question as a singularly peculiar racial-colonial problem, anti-Mormons had effectively advocated an imperial-style solution to that problem. The measures instituted against the Saints in Utah, alongside the genocidal, segregationist, and assimilationist policies applied to Native and Black peoples, helped to inaugurate new forms of colonial administration, management, and regulation that proved useful for U.S. imperial interests overseas at the turn of the century. In this way, federal control in Utah was part and parcel of the ongoing project of U.S. imperialism. But of the lasting geographic, political, economic, and cultural effects the anti-Mormon campaign had produced, nothing would follow the Saints more doggedly than "Mormonism" itself. As an enduring, yet flexible, racializing civilizational assemblage, it would continue to influence the production of cultural, economic, and political normativity, helping to maintain white supremacist racial hierarchy and render invisible colonization as the fundamental structure of the U.S. nation-state.

PART II

Exceptionally Normal

4 Resignifying Mormon Peculiarity, 1890–1945

"Mormonism" makes for good citizenship, don't you see?
. . . There is no hyphen with "Mormonism." We have in this
Church no Scotch-Americans or Danish-Americans, or
German-Americans, not one; we are all *Americans*.

—Charles W. Nibley, "'Mormonism'
Makes for Good Citizenship"

In looks, clothes, language, education, business pursuits, and
the ordinary social practices, Mormons are like other people.
When the term "peculiar" is applied to us, reference is made
to our religious beliefs, and our practices based upon those
beliefs—matters which we differ from other Christian creeds
and churches. These differences are vital, and cannot be
denied. They will make us a peculiar people until the world
comes to a unity of faith. We do not flaunt our differences
before our friends of other faiths[, but n]either do we try to
hide them.

—John A. Widtsoe, "Evidences and Reconciliations"

Many of the roots of heteronormativity are in white supremacist ideologies which sought (and continue) to use the state and
its regulation of sexuality, in particular through the institution
of heterosexual marriage, to designate which individuals were
truly "fit" for full rights and privileges of citizenship.

—Cathy J. Cohen, "Punks, Bulldaggers,
and Welfare Queens"

Six years after the Church formally abandoned plural marriage in the
Woodruff Manifesto and a year and a half after Utah achieved statehood,

Tip Top Weekly, a serial magazine popular for its Frank Merriwell series, featured a story in which its title character, an exceptional Yale athlete who solved mysteries and tackled moral dilemmas with the ethical compass of early twentieth-century Progressivism, saved a young Mormon woman from the clutches of an evil polygamous Mormon patriarch. But the story did not end as most nineteenth-century anti-Mormon tales had, with a harrowing rescue of the innocent woman who was enlightened to the barbarity of, and deliverance from, Mormonism. Instead, the series creator, Gilbert Patten, introduced a new kind of Mormon figure: Tom Whitcomb.[1] Gary L. Bunker and Davis Bitton assert that in contrasting the monogamous Whitcomb with the story's polygamous patriarch, Elder Asaph Holdfast, Patten forwarded a new interpretation of Mormonism as a modern, thoroughly American religion.[2] Holdfast's old-fashioned name, advanced age, antiquated speech, religious and cultural views—he recoils at the sight of Merriwell's bicycle as an "invention of Satan"—and especially his possessive and disrespectful attitude toward women all stand in telling juxtaposition to the more modern Whitcomb, the young woman's suitor of choice.

Merriwell is so struck by the difference between Holdfast and Whitcomb that he is at pains to explain it to his companion Jack:

> "[Whitcomb] seems to be a white man and all right even if he is a Mormon. Do you know, I am getting a different opinion of the Mormons than I once had. . . . The Mormons I have seen seem like other people. I believe some of the wild stories told about their religion, and their ways are a mess of lies. The Mormons are not what they were, Jack. They have changed in recent years, and the younger Mormons are all right. They still hold to their religion, but they have cast aside polygamy, and I believe no man has a right to say how another shall worship God."[3]

Merriwell's comments are significant for two reasons. First, they demonstrate the sea change in how Mormonism was discursively constructed between the nineteenth and twentieth centuries. Indeed, by the 1930s Mormons would no longer be considered sexually deviant and therefore racially degenerate; instead they were first provisionally and then fully accepted as white, despite what were now considered their peculiar but tolerable religious beliefs. Second, and most importantly, Merriwell's description serves to highlight that Mormon assimilation into mainstream U.S. society was an essentially racialized process embedded in the logic of heteronormativity

and narratives of religious freedom. Sharply contrasting with the racialization of Mormons over the previous fifty years, Merriwell's assertions
that Whitcomb "seems to be a white man" and that "Mormons . . . seem
like other people" were fundamentally connected to the abandonment
of polygamy and younger Mormons' engagement in the accepted rituals
of romance, courtship, marriage, and procreation. Like preceding representations, "Frank Merriwell among the Mormons or the Lost Tribe of
Israel" links racial status to sexual practice but does so in a way that realigns
Mormonism with whiteness through claims to monogamous heterosexuality. Tellingly, by the end of the story, Merriwell and his friend Jack
not only have rescued the young woman from Elder Holdfast, leaving
her to freely select Whitcomb as her beau, but they openly declare their
friendship for this younger, modern Mormon man, exclaiming, "'we have
pledged ourselves to Tom Whitcomb, and we'll stand by him through thick
and thin.'"[4]

Why and how did this new portrayal, exemplified by Patten's story, sup-
plant the ubiquitously deleterious representations of Mormonism from
the nineteenth century? The early twentieth-century assimilation of the
Saints into U.S. society and the concurrent resignification of Mormonism
as an expression of benign but often praiseworthy religious eccentricity
were predicated upon three distinct but deeply interdependent factors.
First, Mormon assimilation did not materialize overnight after the Manifesto
announcing the Church's abandonment of plural marriage was released.
Rather, Church leaders had long been engaged in various rhetorical and
political efforts to convince non-Mormons of the affinities between white
Protestant and Mormon culture. These efforts, alongside significant conces-
sions to non-Mormon pressure in the late nineteenth century, would prove
vital to the Saints' swift racial assimilation in the early twentieth century.

Second, although Taylor G. Petrey contends that "modern Mormon
views of gender and sexuality were products of the mid-twentieth century," this chapter illustrates that the Church reformulated its views on
sex and gender much earlier, specifically articulating new commitments
to heterosexuality and heteronormativity between 1900 and 1920, laying
a critical foundation for Church leaders' renewed interest in regulating
gender and sexual practices at midcentury.[5] These distinctly modern commitments to heterosexuality and heteronormativity were characterized
by a divinely preordained system of sexed difference, naturalized gender
roles, and opposite-sex desire that could only appropriately be expressed

within marriage. Moreover, these new commitments were accompanied by an increasingly rigorous surveillance and management of sexual activity. Corresponding with the explosion in cultural, medical, scientific, and legal interest in the relationship between race, gender, and sex at the turn of the century, the Church's evolving teachings related to gender and sex functioned to legitimize their claims to national inclusion by serving as an endorsement and fundamental advancement—at first explicitly but increasingly tacitly—of white supremacist nationalism.

Third, during this same period, the Church fiercely embraced and promoted free market capitalism in both its own financial dealings and in its teachings and advice to members. Contrasting with Church leaders' openness to creative, communal, cooperative, and socialistic economic practices and teachings in the nineteenth century, beginning in the 1890s leaders made a concerted effort to align Mormon economic practices, alongside political ones, with the national mainstream. This meant not only the leadership's withdrawal from economic planning in Utah and other Mormon-dominated areas but also a vast rhetorical campaign from the pulpit and in Church publications. Between the mid-1880s and World War II, this campaign was characterized by three key tactics: an open and hostile opposition to reformist and anticapitalist economic and political ideologies, especially unionism, socialism, and communism; an infusion of capitalistic rhetoric in discussions of Church theology; and a reinterpretation of the Church's economic history as definitively capitalist.

The Church's post-1890 emphasis on responsible individualism—exemplified in its promotion of such virtues as self-control, self-cultivation, and hard work, especially in relation to marriage, reproduction, leisure, and labor—signaled the Church's investment in and commitment to a rapidly coalescing "master narrative of national whiteness at the core of twentieth-century American modernity."[6] Because the qualities associated with responsible individualism already had long-standing associations with widely held beliefs about civilization, Anglo-Saxonism, and Americanness, and because they had long been used to rationalize apartheid in the United States, their deployment in official Mormon discourse communicated the Saints' racial qualifications for citizenship through the Church's promotion of heteronormativity and capitalism. Thus, examining the ways that Mormons and Mormonism were recoded as white is helpful both for explaining how race continued to remain central to definitions of Americanness in the twentieth century, even as explicitly racial discourse began to be eschewed, and for demonstrating the centrality of Mormon peculiarity discourse in establishing and retaining capitalism and heteronormativity as requirements for full and unfettered participation in the nation-state.

It was no accident that by the mid-1930s non-Mormons were praising the Saints for two specific aspects of their religion—their commitment to families (with all the attendant connotations about gender roles, sexual relationships, and parenting) and the Church Welfare Program, a program developed in response to the Great Depression—as evidence of both their whiteness and their Americanness. By the end of World War II, Mormonism was no longer represented as a threat to claims of U.S. exceptionalism but had become an unconventional, sometimes comical, but ultimately tolerable and often estimable form of religious difference whose peculiarity was now derived from its exceptional normality.

PREREQUISITES TO ASSIMILATION

Many scholars have marveled at the speed with which the Church was able to achieve acceptance in U.S. society, as well as the remarkably anemic effects of anti-Mormonism in the post-1890 period given its previous vehemence. However, the pace of assimilation and the fading impact of anti-Mormonism can only be characterized as extraordinary or unexplainable if these events are examined through the lens of Mormon peculiarity itself. Generally, Mormon assimilation is identified as beginning with the 1890 Manifesto, the granting of Utah's statehood in 1896, or with the debates over whether to seat B. H. Roberts in 1898 and Reed Smoot between 1903 and 1907, both of whom had been elected to Congress in Utah.[7] But such periodization not only ignores the long-standing similarities between white Mormon and white non-Mormon U.S. society and culture, it also problematically overlooks major adaptations that the Church undertook in the pre-Manifesto era.

As set forth in the first chapter, the Saints shared and the Church promoted values that were far more alike than they were different from white Protestants, reflected in shared views about white racial superiority; settler colonialism justified by Manifest Destiny and, later, imperial intervention abroad; gender roles, relationships, and regulations; reserved sexual expression for procreation within marriage; and the unique nature of the government and divinity of the Constitution. Despite the heated contestations over Mormonism in the nineteenth century, these similarities continued to underwrite the relationship between Mormons and white non-Mormons in the United States.[8] The Saints did not ignore these similarities but emphasized them—interpreting their affinities with white Protestants in such a way that set the stage for their assimilation in the twentieth century.

For example, while Church leaders argued for polygamy's superiority as a familial, marital, and sexual practice before 1890—a position that clashed mightily with non-Mormon elites—their use of popular advice literature, research on physiology and race, and fashionable medical theories on gender and sex signaled their fundamental agreement with those same elites about the supposedly scientifically established superiority of the Anglo-Saxon race, the supposedly fundamental inferiority of nonwhite people, and the gendered ideas upon which those racial claims to civilizational ascendency were based.[9] These agreements were evident not just in Church leaders' use of mainstream theories to support their own theological positions but also in the Church's attitudes and policies concerning specific racial groups. Indeed, the Church, and the vast majority of its membership, participated in the renewed national culture of white supremacy that gained momentum and power between the 1880s and the 1920s. As did Protestant leaders across the country, Mormon leaders encouraged their followers "to view peoples of color—both within the United States and in other parts of the world . . . as unsuited for full inclusion in the nation" and incapable of self-government, helping to reestablish "a multitiered understanding of American nationalism, one that positioned peoples of color as subordinate citizens."[10] Most notably, between the 1870s and 1920s, Church leaders solidified the religion's racist views and policies regarding Black people especially, but also toward other nonwhite people, as "fundamentally inferior."

In Utah's 1852 legislative session, territorial representatives—all Mormons and at the behest of Brigham Young—had legalized Black servitude, what they deemed a more "humane" form of slavery, after Southern slaveholding converts had approached the Church's leader about legalizing slavery in the new territory. The law also included a ban on interracial sex, but not marriage, between white and Black people.[11] At that same legislative session, Young had also instituted the Church's infamous ban on Black men's priesthood ordination; however, the reality that Joseph Smith had ordained a Black man, Elijah Abel, into the priesthood, and that Abel held the priesthood until his death in 1884, meant that the Church's practices around Black membership were not solidified until the early 1900s. In 1879, Church President John Taylor had launched an investigation into the status of Black people, prompted by Abel's own request for full participation in temple ordinances.[12] The investigation ultimately hardened restrictions on Black members' access to temples, but it was not until 1908 that President Joseph F. Smith reversed his own previous testimony given in both 1879 and 1885, which recounted Joseph Smith's ordination of Abel and refuted others' testimony that the original prophet had later renounced Abel's ordination.[13] In reversing his testimony, Joseph F. Smith legitimized false justifications for the bans and introduced a formal policy of not prosely-tizing to Black people (both inside and outside the United States), which were both upheld well into the 1970s.[14]

False Mormon explanations of the "inferiority" and enslavement of Black people followed the national pattern. Both the Curse of Cain and the Curse of Canaan (or Curse of Ham) were cited by Church leaders as explana-tions for Black people's "inherent inferiority" and were used as justifiable limitations on Black people's membership in the Church.[15] Additionally, a uniquely Mormon explanation for racial hierarchy and Black people's exclusion from Church ordinances gained traction around the turn of the twentieth century. This explanation, completely unsupported by any scrip-ture, asserted that a person's race reflected the actions of their spirit in pre-existence, with Blackness reflecting cowardice and disloyalty to God and whiteness reflecting faithfulness and devotion. By 1907, this explanation was held "quite generally" among the Saints, according to Joseph Fielding Smith (son of Joseph F. Smith), then assistant Church historian and the future president of the Church between 1970 and 1972.[16] This theory, as a justification for racist discrimination against Black members, was repeated in various forms throughout the twentieth century by a variety of Church leaders, including those at the highest levels.

The leadership's attempts to shore up the Church's racist prohibitions against Black members were motivated by the same incentive that had turned the federal government's attention westward and drove its attempts to ban polygamy and the Saints' other nonnormative practices. Even as shifting their attention to the Saints had allowed "the federal government— and northern public opinion more generally" to "tacitly acknowledge[] that its primary interest no longer lay in chastising a defeated South," the Saints themselves evidenced an equal commitment to the ongoing national project of white supremacy, helping to ensure national belonging would continue to be defined in terms of racial hierarchy into the twentieth cen-tury.[17] Sharing predominant ideas about supposed white racial purity and

Black deviance, the Saints engaged in violent practices meant to maintain white supremacy, including lynching.[18] And while interracial marriage, or miscegenation as it was then known, was not formally outlawed in Utah until 1888 when a federally controlled legislature was installed under the 1887 Edmunds–Tucker Act, comments by Church leaders make it clear that the Saints shared an abhorrence for interracial unions.[19] For instance, while decrying the 1882 Edmunds Act, President Taylor argued that the purported fact of "'Washington, where miscegenation has prevailed to so great an extent'" was far and away more disturbing than the religiously motivated polygamous marriages of some Saints.[20] Respected Mormon theologian B. H. Roberts went so far as to claim that "'no other conceivable disaster,' including 'flood and fire, fever and famine and the sword,' could 'compare with . . . miscegenation,'" indicating the extent to which the Saints opposed interracial marriage as a practice that threatened white superiority.[21]

The Saints' acceptance of, and contribution to, anti-Black religious theories was grounded in other long-standing and prosaic forms of racism. One article printed in the *Contributor,* the unofficial magazine of the Church's Young Men's and Young Ladies' Mutual Improvement Associations between 1879 and 1896, offered a typically racist account of Black people, calling them "highly emotional in their natures," "irresponsible," and "childlike" and claiming that, "notwithstanding their seemingly unalloyed happiness, the more ignorant, especially, are harassed with superstition and fears." Indicting the abolition of slavery as "a curse to the country" and "to the colored race" itself, the author argued that freed people were "much better cared for in slavery than they can care for themselves" and that their imprudent behavior, "foolishly spend[ing] all their earnings for whiskey, or at 'gay and festive frolics,' failing to lay in store anything for 'a wet day,'" was evidence of their racial incapacity for self-government.[22] Statements like these show that, like non-Mormon white people, white Saints were invested in maintaining a racial hierarchy with white people on top and Black people at the bottom, justified by a narrative of supposedly benevolent apartheid.

This *Contributor* author was so confident in such a plan that he went so far as to argue that chattel slavery had bestowed upon Black people the unique "gifts" of civilization. "The black men of the South know how to build houses, to raise corn and sweet potatoes," and they should use these gifts in the service of Africa's colonization, he explained:

A population larger than that of the United States, composed of men and women of their own flesh and blood sunk in ignorance, barbarism, and idolatry, are groping for the light. . . . He who teaches his benighted countrymen to raise two stalks of corn where but one now grows will be a benefactor to his race. Africa abounds in natural resources. . . . States and governments [need] to be founded there; cities and railroads to be built, and education, science, and religion to be disseminated among the people.

Ignoring postwar violence and discrimination against Black people, this author insisted that African colonization, rather than "complaining and whining because they do not get a full share of the offices under the government," was a much preferable activity for the formerly enslaved.[23]

Predating U.S. imperial interventions in Cuba, Puerto Rico, Guam, and the Philippines by almost fifteen years, this author's suggested dual programs of Black relocation and African colonization in the service of U.S. empire revealed a thoroughly racist, but utterly typical, agenda that most white people shared after the failure of Reconstruction. These sorts of attitudes about freed people's supposed ungratefulness and immaturity functioned to explain what white people classified as Black people's so-called natural subordination under them, while also justifying U.S. imperial desire. Long before the 1890 Manifesto announced the renunciation of polygamy, both the Church and its followers articulated and acted upon these kinds of racist rationales, placing the Saints in alignment with the white Protestant majority and helping to position them for full assimilation as Anglo-Saxon white people in the post-1890 period. Articles like the one that appeared in the October 1885 edition of the *Contributor* would only increase in frequency and intensity as the nineteenth century gave way to the twentieth.[24]

While the Church's explicit limitations on Black membership were not paralleled by similar official rules regulating other racially marginalized groups' membership, racist Mormon attitudes about other nonwhite groups were common. The most obvious example was the patronizing treatment of Indigenous groups in North America and various Pacific Islander groups.[25] Articles discussing the history and status of Native peoples in the United States appeared frequently in Church publications, contributing to existing Mormon attitudes about their "barbarity." A typical article printed in the February 1881 edition of the *Contributor* asked "whether the red man has the capacity for attaining unto a better life than that of a roaming savage."[26] Similarly, several articles on Hawai'i, Samoa, and Polynesia—

locations where the Church had achieved marked missionary success—appeared in Church publications during the 1890s arguing for U.S. imperial intervention as justified by racial hierarchy and necessary for completing the destiny of white civilization. Joseph M. Tanner, a prominent Saint who had performed missions in Europe and Western Asia and who was a significant figure in the Church's educational initiatives, touted a typical view of U.S. imperialism as inevitable and desirable in one article for the *Improvement Era*, the official magazine of the Church between 1897 and 1970, arguing that "'Westward the course of empire takes its way,' was a perfect expression of the great historical truth when the immense territorial expanse of this western country lay before the vision of the statesmen of a generation ago" and that "that expression may now . . . include an imperial empire whose domains extend beyond . . . the sea."[27]

Other articles explicitly identified certain sites for U.S. imperial intervention. In April 1898, for example, the editors of the *Improvement Era* argued that Hawai'i was ripe for annexation by the United States—a location with a major Mormon missionary presence.[28] Missionaries, who often authored these articles, explained their success in proselytizing in the Pacific by identifying the new converts as distant relatives of the Indigenous peoples of North America whom the Saints believed were descended from the Lamanites of the Book of Mormon and who were themselves descended from Israelites. Hōkūlani Aikau argues that Mormon "notions of whiteness were not disrupted by [the] redrawing of racial lines," which recognized Pacific Islanders as having Israelite lineage, but "instead reiterate[d]" those lines by maintaining that despite "their depraved, barbarous, and treacherous actions, they could be saved" and that it was the job of white Mormon "missionaries to return the gospel to these lost people."[29] For example, W. O. Lee of the Samoan Mission wrote a piece for the *Improvement Era* that detailed evolving Mormon views of Pacific Islanders, explicitly classifying them as racially inferior and in need of white oversight. Lee's differentiation between "the brown Polynesians" and the "Papuans," the latter whom he described as a "negro race" that the missionaries had "nick-named 'Black Boys,'" was clearly based in Mormon notions of race and lineage but also reflected commonly accepted philosophies of supposedly scientific racial distinction and white racial superiority in the United States more generally.[30]

Church publications also printed racist pieces on "Mohammedanism," "Mexicans," "Hindoos," "Turks," "Indians," "Arabs," "Kalmucks," "Filipinos," and "the Chinese," among many others.[31] These articles often juxtaposed gendered relations among other racial-religious-national groups with those of the Saints to verify the latter's whiteness, specifically their Anglo-Saxon heritage, and therefore their Americanness. Gender exceptionalism discourse was often deployed to racially differentiate the Saints from these groups, contrasting them with, for example, a "negro" in "Central Africa . . . [where] children are regarded as merchandise, women as slaves," or from "savages" for whom "marriage . . . consists in carrying off the bride by force, real or simulated."[32] At the same time that anti-Mormons were decrying the gendered "barbarity" of Mormon polygamy, the Saints were distinguishing themselves from those whose skin color would never allow them, because of hegemonic biological understandings of race, to claim or attain the status and privileges of whiteness.

The notion that U.S. white people were more civilized because they treated women with respect was a standard trope of civilization discourse and one that the Saints utilized for their own cause. Not only did the Saints vehemently deny claims that Mormon women were kidnapped, duped, taken advantage of, or abused, but they countered these charges by juxtaposing the freedom of Mormon women with the purported subjugation of women in other cultures, religions, and nations across the globe. Articles in the *Woman's Exponent,* an unofficial Church magazine published between 1872 and 1914, regularly printed claims that women's oppression in "Jew[ish]," "Oriental," "non-Christian," and especially "Mohammedan" cultures was a result of the fact that "all nations over whom the principles of Christianity have either no influence at all or only a partial influence, . . . assign . . . women a place of unwarranted inferiority."[33] This rhetorical move equated Mormonism with Christianity and Christianity with civilization.

Long before 1890, then, the Saints shared and participated in the dominant culture of white supremacy in the United States, even though many non-Mormons did not accept them as white while they maintained certain practices. Equally significant, however, was that the Saints' gradual but complete renunciation of polygamy and other nonnormative practices overlapped with the "closure of the frontier," the attendant extension of U.S. imperial interests overseas, an increasingly vehement antimiscegenation movement, equally fervent lynching campaigns, the escalation of white slavery panic, and an exponentially intense nativist movement mounting in response to the major wave of immigration that occurred between 1880 and 1920. In other words, the combination of the Saints' own racial attitudes and the timing of their capitulation ensured they were able to ride a tidal wave of white supremacist agitation at least thirty years before Jewish,

Irish, Italian, Polish, Russian, and other European immigrant groups would be able to definitively claim whiteness.[34]

While the Church had long articulated a commitment to white nationalism, it embarked on a campaign of economic integration as early as 1877, the year of Brigham Young's death, that would help transform its racial image even more thoroughly. While Young had vigorously advocated for economic independence from the national economy, his successor John Taylor was much less invested in such independence. With his succession to the presidency, Taylor dismantled, or simply let evaporate, the majority of Young's cooperative economic policies and programs. In a startling transformation between the 1880s and the 1890s, Church leaders began to issue warnings against economic radicalism in sermons, the Church's official publications, and counsel to individual members. As the century moved toward its close, these warnings became increasingly vehement. The economic dimensions of civilization discourse that deemed private property a mark of racial development ensured that the Church's capitulation to capitalist values would help to change non-Mormons' views of their racial development.

By 1890, Mormonism was beginning to be discursively defined as a merely religious eccentricity that was safely abstract: belief in the Book of Mormon and other nineteenth-century texts as divine articles, preexistence, God's material form, and man's potential to achieve divinity. Particularly, the Mormon notion that faith by itself is not enough—that deeds must supplement and verify belief—was reinterpreted as a pro-monogamous, pro–two party, and procapitalist doctrine, which contrasted markedly with the Church's former promotion of plural marriage, economic isolation and resistance, and political fiat as divine mandates necessary for building the Kingdom of God on Earth. As the Church adjusted its theological tenets to align with mainstream values and practices, Mormon peculiarity discourse was simultaneously transformed into a positive buoy for the institutions, ideologies, and norms that underlay notions of Americanness that had become dominant by 1900. Thus, by the end of the fourteen-year period that it took the Church to fully forsake plural marriage, bookended by the original 1890 Manifesto and the Second Manifesto of 1904 in which President Joseph F. Smith guaranteed that those entering polygamous unions would be excommunicated, the Saints could accurately identify themselves as in full alignment with the hegemonic ideologies and practices of the nation-state. And, as Thomas G. Alexander points out, because there was "some abatement in the feeling of the immediacy of the millennium" among the Saints during this period, "participation in national politics" began to reflect a more intense "loyalty to the government rather than simply tolerance of its existence."[35]

A reinvigorated patriotism flourished among the Saints after the federal government withdrew its energies from Utah in the early 1890s, reflected in the realignment of Mormon articulations of Mormon and U.S. exceptionalism. While most earlier expressions of Mormon exceptionalism affirmed the Saints' superiority, over and above the nation, their twentieth-century expressions were decidedly more tempered. Answering the question "Are We 'Mormons' Americans?" for the *Improvement Era,* prominent Mormon novelist Nephi Anderson, for instance, characterized the Church as the ultimate example of U.S. exceptionalism:

> "The American nation is the embodiment and vehicle of a divine purpose to emancipate and enlighten the human race." . . . If there be an American religion, "Mormonism" must be that one. No other religious system makes such claims for America as does "Mormonism." No other religion has made America such holy ground by its teachings and history. The "Mormons" have placed America along with Palestine and made the Holy Land to share its honors with the Zion of the West.[36]

While, in the past, the Saints had portrayed the creation of the United States as a precondition for the Church's emergence and eventual supremacy, Anderson's article instead represented Mormonism as having served to enhance the nation's exceptional status, not surpass it:

> Here in the desert valleys of the Rocky Mountains, we have built a great American commonwealth. Converts to "Mormonism" who come to America from abroad soon lose their national characteristics and blend into the one American life. . . . We are inseparably connected with America.[37]

Staking a claim to Americanness in this new way, the Saints linked what they saw as their religion's distinctly American nature to its ability to dissolve the racial and national identifications of (northern and western European) immigrants arriving in the United States (in the melting pot of whiteness). "'Mormonism' makes for good citizenship, don't you see?" Charles W. Nibley, a high-ranking Church official, queried in another *Improvement Era* article. "There is no hyphen with 'Mormonism.' We have in this Church no Scotch-Americans or Danish-Americans, or German-Americans, not one; we are all *Americans*."[38] Nibley's contention not only communicated the Saints' Anglo-Saxon heritage but also hinted at the then-significant distinction between northern and western European immigrants who were considered white—like Nibley himself, who was from Scotland—and southern and eastern immigrants who were not. Increasingly, the leadership of the Church cast Mormonism as a uniquely American influence that could help to combat racial threats to the white nation.

The Saints' significant accommodations to mainstream culture and governance were reflected not just in their own attitudes, policies, and publications but in the national response to the Saints after 1890. Bunker and Bitton note, for example, that between 1890 and "1898 the Mormons seemed to be melting into the national landscape" because they "were less interesting as" subjects of concern, causing "the number of" anti-Mormon representations to "dwindle."[39] Even with a resurgence in anti-Mormon activity between 1898–99 and 1903–7, following the debates over seating both B. H. Roberts and Reed Smoot, respectively, representations of Mormonism took on a distinctly lighter tone in the early twentieth century. The sharp drop off in overt hostility toward the Saints, which had most frequently been couched in charges of racial treason, is less surprising given the foregoing work the Saints had done to pledge their commitment to whiteness and, consequently, prevailing notions of U.S. modernity. No longer geographically or technologically separated from the rest of the country as they had been before the completion of the railroad in 1869, and no longer consumed by the hardships imposed by the federal government's intervention in Utah, the Saints were better able to interact with and represent themselves to non-Mormons as fellow patriotic white people.

ACHIEVING CIVILIZATION THROUGH GENDER DIFFERENTIATION

One of the most significant opportunities for the Saints to challenge prevailing perceptions of themselves and their Church came with the 1893 Chicago World's Fair. The First Presidency of the Church was determined to alter popular opinion through the participation of the Church's choir in the exposition's choir competition.[40] George Q. Cannon was convinced that:

To see and hear this famous choir will be a surprise to many. They will hear music beautifully and harmoniously rendered by a body of interesting, good-looking young people of both sexes, whose skill as singers would do credit to the most cultured community on the continent, a body of singers whom New York or Boston need not be ashamed. . . . Their respect for the Latter-day Saints would be increased, and they would feel that a people who had encouraged and sustained the formation of such a choir, could not be the ignorant, inferior people they had been described. . . . The healthy appearance and good looks of the young ladies and gentlemen of the choir make a very favorable impression. The onlookers see they are bright, intelligent and superior-looking.[41]

Deftly deploying the gendered, racialized, and cultural terms of civilization discourse, Cannon was confident that the combination of the singers' phenotype, talent, and artistic accomplishments would serve as proof of their whiteness. The fact that these "young people" had a "healthy appearance" and were "bright, intelligent, and superior-looking" would counter widespread perceptions that polygamy had produced a degenerate race; evident in their Church's and their own decision to participate in such a cultivated pastime, "these young ladies and gentlemen," Cannon was sure, would represent the Saints as civilized, white Americans.

The overwhelmingly positive response to these young singers, and other Mormon representatives at the fair, indicates that Cannon's confidence was justified. Even those who had previously participated in anti-Mormon agitation found themselves open to embracing the Saints. For example, after hearing Mormon women speak at the fair's National Woman's Relief Society Congress, Rosetta Luce Gilchrist, author of the popular antipolygamy novel *Apples of Sodom* (1883) and previously an avid anti-Mormon, who was working as a journalist for the Ashtabula, Ohio, *News Journal,* reported that the Mormon women's "forbearance and kindness" was "saint-like." In her speech at the congress, Martha Hughes Cannon subtly touted the Saints' racial qualifications by pointing out that "'the delegation from Utah represents two classes, the pioneer women of the Territory and the native born daughters of that region" and that "the pioneer women and leaders of the National Woman's Relief Society of Utah are of distinct New England type of character.'"[42] Stressing the hereditary connections between the Latter-day Saint women and white New Englanders was an indirect but clear assertion of whiteness at the same time these women's very presence was attesting to the "civilized" gendered relations of the Saints.

Prominent women's rights leaders' praise of the Saints at the fair verifies not only that Mormon claims to whiteness were made through the gendered dimensions of civilization discourse but that their claims were increasingly successful. As Gail Bederman and Julian Carter show, the discourse of civilization rested heavily upon the notion of sex/gender binarism—the more differentiated a society's sexes and gender relations, roles, and expectations were, the more racially superior and civilized that society was thought to be. In other words, societies that "had not yet evolved pronounced sexual differences" were considered racially underdeveloped, "and, to some extent, this was precisely what made them savage" and unsuitable for self-government.[43] But, while "polarized gender difference was very widely represented as one of the evolved achievements of civilized modern whiteness," equally important was the notion of respectful gendered relations.[44]

Especially significant was the idea that white cultures' and nations' supposedly more evolved approaches to gender relations were demonstrated in men's treatment of women. It was thought that instead of callously asserting their natural dominance over women, civilized men treated women with respect, by, for example, not hitting them or forcing them to have sex, out of reverence for their important and supposedly natural contributions to society as homemakers, wives, and mothers. But this respect was also thought to be a regard for women's supposedly natural weakness; showing respect in this sense meant men were responsible for caring for women mentally, physically, and financially. Much of anti-Mormonism rested upon the assumption that women's mistreatment under Mormonism was a sign of Mormon men's barbarity; not only were plural marriages thought to be evidence of men's fundamental disrespect for women, but they were often portrayed as abusers, rapists, and slavers. The Church had long countered these representations, using civilization discourse to make its own claims of gender exceptionalism, but it was not until the 1890s that non-Mormons began to accept Mormon claims that "the Latter-day Saints show the refinement of their nature through the treatment of their women."[45]

The attainment of women's suffrage in Utah in 1870 and the meanings attributed to it were therefore couched in the terms of civilization discourse. These terms helped ensure the passage of women's suffrage in

Utah in the first place, and they also helped to guarantee a more open field of debate about women's rights among the Saints between 1870 and 1896.[46] It was harder, but clearly not impossible, for anti-Mormons to preserve the logic that Mormon men's assumed mistreatment of women was a sign of their supposed racial inferiority when Mormon women had been given the right to vote. Thus, the progression of Mormon assimilation in the early twentieth century was shaped by the continuing debate over women's suffrage, both locally and nationally, as well as, by extension, the debate over women's proper place in U.S. society. In the late nineteenth century, given the changes capitalism wrought on the makeup and dynamics of families in the United States, the gendered terms of civilization discourse allowed women to make increasingly extensive claims for participation in the public sphere.

In the Mormon context, although the Saints accepted and perpetuated mainstream nineteenth-century ideas about women as naturally submissive, domestic, pure, and pious, the realities of settler colonialism and the conditions of practicing polygamy in a hostile environment had meant that even earlier than other women in the United States, Mormon women often functioned outside the strict boundaries of mid-nineteenth-century domesticity. Women were frequently encouraged by Church leaders to become educated whenever possible, as well as to pursue careers traditionally only open to men.[47] Moreover, for women in plural marriages, getting an education and establishing a career could be made possible with the help of sister wives who could care for children, run the house, and participate in the Church's strict program of home manufacture, while they attended school and worked outside the home.[48] As a result, by 1890 women were advocating for equality in the pages of Church publications, and after women's suffrage was reintroduced in Utah in 1896 they also began to run for and serve in office.[49]

Throughout the 1870s, 1880s, and 1890s, articles in the *Woman's Exponent* and the *Young Woman's Journal*, the official Church magazine for the Young Ladies' Mutual Improvement Association between 1897 and 1929, reliably featured stories on local and national women's suffrage campaigns, women's achievements worldwide, and pieces advocating women's higher education and career advancement.[50] These articles encouraged a more liberal view of women's place in society, pushing the boundaries of nineteenth-century gender expectations but without ever challenging the fundamentally sexist or racist assumptions of gender exceptionalist civilization discourse. One such article from the March 1890 edition of the *Young Woman's Journal* argued that "woman, without having lost anything of her gentleness and grace, no longer accepts that once famous axiom, 'man should support woman'" and that "to see woman from the homestead alone is to view her from a contracted standpoint." "I believe we thus hinder her progress," the author continued, "for there are social questions that will never be understood until woman shall stand by the side of man to discuss them."[51] The idea that a woman's full capacity could lie outside the home and that she should actively contribute to the solution of major social issues was a drastic departure from mid-nineteenth-century views of women as singularly domestic; yet, the author still emphasized that a woman's focus should be on homemaking, childbearing, and motherhood. As was typical during this period, authors often argued that civic participation and education would enhance women's ability to better meet those supposedly natural responsibilities. As such, the article's arguments for expanding women's rights were tempered by the notion that women must "be honored and respected" because "the fate of humanity depends . . . on woman, since she has [an] all-powerful influence on the fruit she bears."[52] By connecting questions of women's suffrage, education, and work to the apparently natural and distinct responsibilities of womanhood, women's rights advocates effectively argued not just for their acceptability but for their necessity in a truly civilized society, keeping intact underlying assumptions about the relationship between gender, race, and politics.

However, as the women's rights movement gained a broader base of support and started to make substantive political achievements, a cultural reaction to white women's increasing independence—both nationally and in the Church—sought to reassert the essential sexism of gender exceptionalism within civilization discourse. Church publications aimed at women continued to publish articles that pushed social expectations of gender, sometimes clearly contradicting Church authorities' conservative views on the subject, through the first few years of the twentieth century. But after the abandonment of polygamy, two changes narrowed the field of debate over women's rights in Mormon culture. Most evidently, after 1890 the Church had to contend with fewer accusations of Mormon men's mistreatment of women, which meant that there was less need for the hierarchy to prove women were respected in the faith. Put another way, there was no longer a need to expand women's access to the public sphere in an effort to improve the Church's image. Less obviously, but certainly more

significantly, however, there was a shift in the way gender was emphasized in civilization discourse as the nation embraced overseas imperialism. This shift was mirrored by a change in an emphasis on respecting
women's unique qualities as evidence of racial development to a focus on
men's virility and dominance as a sign of white racial supremacy.

Largely a response to the expansion of white women's rights that
had developed over the course of the last century, but also to the increasingly bureaucratic and segmented conditions of middle-class labor, a new
obsession with "the connection between manhood and racial dominance"
expressed through the rhetoric of civilization permeated the nation between
1890 and 1920.[53] Although the 1920s are commonly identified as the decade
in which women gained real independence, James R. McGovern demonstrates that "the great leap forward in women's participation in economic
life came between 1900 and 1910" and that their "individualization resulted
mainly because, whether single or married, gainfully employed or not,
[they] spent more time outside [their] home[s]."[54] The changes resulting
in women's increased participation in the public sphere were met by
a rhetorical backlash that "protested the dangers of 'overcivilization' to
American manhood and thus to American culture, in a not very oblique
reference to the dangers of women's civilizing influence and the effeminization of men."[55]

What was perceived to be women's incursion into the natural domain
of men—their increasingly extensive influence on political issues such
as suffrage, temperance and Prohibition, child labor, and prostitution and
white slavery, coupled with the growth of professional specialties for women
in social work, teaching, and nursing—was represented as the feminization
and therefore weakening of U.S. national culture and politics. Moreover,
concerns about the effeminization of men were paralleled by concerns over
the effects of corporate and consumer capitalism on manhood. By 1910,
the opportunities for substantial wealth accumulation that had once been
available to middle-class men had all but disappeared, while working-class
agitation increasingly threatened middle- and upper-class dominance in
electoral politics.[56] Concerns over the decadent effects of capitalism-as-
civilization were expressed as fears over middle- and upper-class men's loss
of vitality, virility, and strength—attributes more supposedly primitive men
were thought to display in abundance.

Cultural responses to the perceived threats of women's usurpation of
men's natural authority and modern capitalism's disruption to the natural

familial order reasserted assumptions about the connection between gender and race, but with a new twist.[57] A sharp increase in participation and emphasis on sports, especially combative sports such as football and prizefighting, fraternal organizations such as the Freemasons, and youth training organizations like the Boy Scouts were all motivated by the idea that men needed to become reacquainted with their so-called primitive natures. The racial terms of this new take on gendered civilization emphasized certain characteristics thought to be inherent to all men but that were especially obvious in supposedly racially inferior ones whose natures had not been distorted by the displacements and pressures of modern life.[58] "With our Indians," Francis M. Lyman, president of the Quorum of the Twelve Apostles, explained, "the brave who was the most skillful in hunting, and the fiercest in war, [and] who could endure hardship and even torture . . . was looked upon as the best type of manhood." However, "in civilized communities, higher qualities" were also required, "and the Saints have the opportunity to form[] the best standard," he argued.[59] In other words, white manhood was thought to necessitate a balance between primitive virility and modern sensibility. Apprehension about men's effeminization and overcivilization was therefore as much about a reassertion of white supremacy as about a reassertion of patriarchal power under the expansion of twentieth-century capitalism.

While scholars have pointed to the religious dimensions of the early twentieth-century obsession with racial manhood—exemplified by the Men and Religion Forward Movement of 1911–12, for instance—there has been no examination of the role the discursive construction of Mormonism played in advancing these ideas or in the Church's broad influence on the reactive response to the shifting landscape of gender and sexuality between 1890 and 1920.[60] Like their non-Mormon counterparts, the Saints participated in trends that were meant to remasculinize the nation's men and to teach its boys an appropriate balance between responsibility and ruggedness. But unlike their white non-Mormon counterparts, the Saints' investment in these trends was a necessary strategy for their assimilation into the white imaginary of ethnic nationalism in the United States. Even though "millions joined fraternal orders like the Red Men, the Freemasons, and the Oddfellows [and] concentrated on making boys into men through organizations like the Boy Scouts and the YMCA," Mormon participation in these kinds of activities far outstripped the national average.[61] By 1916, "largely because of Mormon sponsorship, Utah had the highest per-capita membership in the Boy Scouts of any state in the Union," only six years after the organization's founding. Mormon commitment to programs like this would only strengthen over the next fifteen years. By 1926, one in three boys in Utah belonged to a Scout organization, compared with a national average of one in five. By February 1930, the Church's investment in scouting and its attendant commitment to the racial-gendered patriotic values promoted by the organization warranted national recognition in the form of a White House invitation extended to then Church president Heber J. Grant.[62]

Fraternal and youth organizations provided an especially efficient vehicle for achieving assimilation because of the correlation that was understood to exist between gender, civilization, and race. Participation in the Boy Scouts allowed the Saints to recuperate their tarnished image by taking advantage of the idea that the rapid, urbanized progression of modern civilization was resulting in an unintended, but nonetheless dangerous, degeneracy that the Saints purportedly already knew how to combat. In an article for the October 1911 edition of the *Improvement Era*, Eugene L. Roberts, head of physical education at BYU between 1910 and 1928, warned that "civilization has of late progressed all too rapidly. Man has created for himself an artificial environment which is making of him an artificial and decidedly superficial creature. . . . As a result . . . a perceptible degeneracy has occurred." Characteristic of Progressive Era literature that warned against the dangers of "overcivilization," the problems with modernization, and the need for responsive social reform, Roberts's article touted "the 'Mormon' pioneer farmer of fifty years ago" as "a type of verile physical manhood and healthy mentality which is too rare at present" but that could be reinvigorated through the Boy Scout program.[63] Repackaging Mormon settler colonial history as exemplary of white men's essential characteristics and emphasizing the Saints' enthusiastic participation in programs like the Boy Scouts not only framed Mormonism as actively adapting itself to the gendered and racial requirements of national inclusion, but it also represented Mormons as more naturally manly than others.

It is a testament to the Church's participation and promotion of the Boy Scouts as a strategy of assimilation that by 1939 then FBI director J. Edgar Hoover was enlisting young Mormon men who participated in "the great army of the Boy Scouts of America" to help in building "a greater nation, a better nation, a cleaner-thinking nation through the constant recruiting of new soldiers in the army of good citizenship." With characteristic alarm, Hoover proclaimed *"it is your job to clean up America"* to fight in the "war of decency—for the safety of our homes, for the sanctity of our ballots, and for the cleansing of the moral fabric of our fellow man." Only fifty years since the Church itself had been branded indecent, a threat to the home, democracy, and morality of the nation, Hoover charged the latest generation of Mormon men with protecting that same nation. Although the explicit language of civilization and race had disappeared, Hoover's speech still evoked notions of white nationalism through gender. "Your achievements will be heartened by a never-ending alliance with the things that are good and noble," he promised, guided by "the traditional virtues that never change," including "character" and "[self-]conquest." He implored Mormon Boy Scouts to "love . . . your home and your church" and to "keep yourselves physically strong, mentally pure, and morally straight."[64] While civilized manliness at the turn of the century was explicitly tied to race by identifying sensibility, control, and responsibility as white characteristics, mid-twentieth-century masculinity was implicitly understood to be white through association with these same qualities.

At the same time that the Church was "out-boy-scouting its Protestant contemporaries" and "caught the wave of 'making men,'" it also began a new campaign to reverse Mormon women's hard-fought gains for independence in the public sphere.[65] Klaus J. Hansen's observation that "it was not until the twentieth century that Mormon women were raised onto the same pedestal from which their nineteenth-century antagonists had barely escaped" reflects the vehemence with which the Church began to push expectations for women that significantly halted social and political progress toward gender equality in Mormon society.[66] Even as Mormon women were articulating more forceful arguments for women's activity outside the home in publications like the *Young Woman's Journal,* Church authorities began to refute those arguments in those very same periodicals. At first, these contradicting viewpoints made for a lively, if unintended, debate, but by the first few years of the 1900s Church authorities began to exercise tighter control over the message the Saints received about acceptable roles for women.

Because Mormon women, like women's activists nationwide, had relied upon notions of gender exceptionalism and civilization discourse to make their case for a woman's right to participate in the public sphere, those trying to steer women back into the home had no trouble modifying arguments for women's suffrage, equality, and education to suit their own ends. Many Mormon feminists had reasoned that increased independence to engage in the public sphere, higher education, and careers outside the home would help women become better daughters, wives, and mothers by preparing them for those roles they were supposedly predisposed to perform. This argument was a slippery slope that allowed Church authorities to restrict women's roles and opportunities after 1900 on the basis that such restriction reflected true equality and mirrored a natural order of gender created by God.

Playing on older versions of gender exceptionalism that asserted women must be respected in order for a society to attain the highest level of civilization, Apostle John A. Widtsoe argued that "woman must be dignified by intelligence and made equal to that of man, else the foundations of society will crumble." But while he accepted that "the intellectual awakening of the world demonstrated . . . the equality in natural endowments of man and woman," he was also sure to emphasize that men and women "temperamentally and physiologically . . . differ in large degree." For Church leaders, the equality of men and women did not mean both genders possessed the same abilities, characteristics, or talents but rather that each gender possessed distinct but equally important and complementary traits as prescribed by God and engrained in biology. Thus, Widtsoe concluded that in "their power of thinking the great thoughts and doing the needed work of the world—that is, in the sum of their powers—they are undoubtedly equal."[67]

Keeping with the theme of giving women "true" equality, Church publications presented women's proper place as standing beside and supporting men: "God said in the beginning, 'It is not good for man to be alone,' so he created the woman as a helpmeet for him. . . . 'She was not made out of his head to surpass him; nor from his feet, to be trampled on; but from his side, that she might be equal to him.'"[68] Widtsoe put it another way: "The place of woman in the Church is to walk beside the man, not in front of him nor behind him." To support his contention that "there is full equality between man and woman" in the Church, even as the leadership pushed women out of the public sphere and back into the home, Widtsoe drew on the history of women's suffrage in both the Church and Utah. He cited Brigham Young's approval of "woman holding public office" but only "if compatible with her other duties" and "the right of woman to develop her native gifts through education" as evidence of that equality but maintained that work and education for women were only appropriate if "the natural differences between men and women" were acknowledged and that those differences were allowed to "determine in a rational society the major duties of man and woman."[69]

In this way, Church authorities deftly manipulated the rhetoric of equality to construct gender parity as God's intention for woman "to be equal with man in her own sphere, not to take the place of the man, but to be a helpmate unto him."[70] According to the priestly authority of the Church, this meant women would reach their "greatest achievement and happiness" by acknowledging "the man as head of the family."[71] The hierarchy went so far as to argue that the Church's urging "that man and woman accept their respective responsibilities as man and woman, husband and wife, father and mother" was evidence of equality between men and women because such a policy "conform[ed] to natural law" and ensured that "greater freedom and power are won by both."[72] This different-but-equal style logic was used to further argue that "the Church has always favored an education to fit man and woman for their respective spheres of activity—that is, a practical education." Despite claims that women were free to get an education in "business, science, mining, medicine, civil government and law," the hierarchy heavily emphasized an education for "homemaking," which was now considered "a well-established applied science and art," as most appropriate for those Saints supposedly destined to become wives and mothers.[73]

The implications of this line of thinking for women's place in Mormon society became quickly apparent. "God never intended woman to be a competitor of man," one lesson printed in the January 1912 edition of the *Young Woman's Journal* declared, "as such woman will fall by the wayside, for she cannot escape the truth of her own nature, by willing or acting in violation of it."[74] Statements such as this actively discouraged women from participating in the public arena for fear that they might violate God's will and nature and thus sabotage his plan for salvation. Yet, Mormon women had been actively engaged in the public sphere for some time and had even comfortably competed with Mormon men without public comment from Church leadership. For example, Angus M. Cannon's plural wife Martha Hughes Cannon ran against and beat her husband for a seat in Utah's senate, serving from 1897 to 1901. But by the mid-1910s such competition was spurned as dangerous to what the Saints considered to be the divinely ordained gendered order.

This danger was, however, couched in the rhetoric of women's equality, even superiority. "Woman is naturally stronger in endurance than man; and yet today untold numbers of them are physical wrecks, because women do not know themselves, because they fail to understand their needs," one author professed. By this logic, even if women were more gifted in certain areas than men, they were unable to take advantage of their superior qualities because they spurned the most basic aspects of their nature: "they reject the greatest gift to woman—children" and instead "they endeavor to compete with man in business."[75] More and more women were encouraged to develop those qualities that were thought to differentiate them from men and thus make them women. "To reach the highest perfection of an ideal womanhood is not (as is sometimes understood with the 'New woman movement,' of today) to imitate man in his character, his habits, and pursuits, whereby she loses all that is essential and best in womanhood," an *Improvement Era* author maintained, "but, on the contrary, to reach the highest ideal of womanhood, she must learn her true nature, duties and privileges, and develop within the place and sphere that God and nature have pointed out for her."[76]

In a throwback to the cult of true womanhood "President [Joseph F.] Smith . . . declared . . . that 'spiritually, morally, religiously, and in faith' woman is as strong as a man." In fact, he argued that "the mother in the family far more than the father is the one who instills in the hearts of the children, a testimony, and love of the gospel," bringing mid-nineteenth-century beliefs about the natural piety of women and their greater influence on children to bear on early twentieth-century struggles over gender roles.[77] And even as Church leaders claimed in one breath that the evolution of society had proven women's equal ability and right to deal with major social issues of the age, in another they maintained that "man, as a rule, is superior to woman in the power of the intellect." This difference was balanced, they claimed, by "woman['s] superior[ity] to man, in the warmth, the purity, and the constancy of the affections."[78]

Beginning in the 1910s, articles began to warn against the dangers of gender fluidity, threatening women with spinsterhood, a particularly cruel fate for a woman in a religion where her salvation is predicated on marriage, for daring to even dabble in behavior that was considered masculine. Reflecting dominant notions of gender, Milton Bennion argued that "man recognizes in women as a class a superior refinement of thought and feeling—a peculiar sensitiveness in the most tender relations of life," which

were best allowed to flourish in the roles of "mother, daughter, and sister."
"Men are no more pleased with masculine women than are women with
feminine men," he insisted.[79] Well into the 1930s, Church publications cautioned against the dangers of masculine women. One writer heavily chas-
tised readers for the trend of women "acting like" men, reasoning that "I
belong to the superior sex. In fact, there seems to be no doubt about it.
The women themselves admit it—by imitating us." Accompanied by a
sketch of a woman dressed in blazer, tie, and slacks, the article rebuked
women for "imitating [men's] vices" rather than their virtues. Again exploit-
ing ideas about women's equality, the author argued that women must be
feminine to exercise their "true" power: "The secret of a woman's power has
always been in her womanliness, not her masculinity." With this reasoning, the author sidestepped challenges to restrictions on women's activity,
arguing there were no "conventions that interfere with a girl's becoming
more womanly," but only those that were for the "purpose of safe-guarding
her modesty, protecting her from insults, and making her fight for chastity
easier."[80]

To counter the threat of gender fluidity, Mormon authors made their
own adaptations to civilization discourse in order to argue that like white
men, white women must also embrace aspects of their nature that had
been forgone in the haste of modern social, political, and economic development. Just as white men were encouraged to rehabilitate the essential
qualities of manliness they had lost, Mormon authors explained that white
women could recuperate their true natures, and therefore true equality,
by observing women from so-called primitive cultures. One author encouraged "white women [who] hold motherhood as a side issue of their
womanhood" to witness "the red man's sacred reverence for . . . motherhood [a]s a gift from the Great Spirit" as evidence that it was an essential
quality of their gender that they should not discard. In a contradictory
twist on standard civilization discourse, this author argued that because
Indigenous people were supposedly more primitive, the essential qualities
of their gendered natures were more, not less, apparent. In other words,
because "womanhood typifies motherhood in [the Native's] breast, a thing
to be revered, a thing to be protected," Native women provided an excellent example of the respect white women should have for their supposedly
natural roles as mothers.[81]

The division between women and men, their talents, proclivities, and
roles, Church leaders were always sure to point out, was evidence of racial,

civilizational, and, therefore, national development. Although "for long ages woman was the drudge or ornament of a man's home," even "his slave," the nineteenth century in the United States had marked "a culmination of an era of human triumphs and brilliant victories over ignorance and prejudice" and "its crown of imperishable glory is the recognition that woman was created to be man's companion and co-laborer."[82] Indeed, the logic used by Church leaders to reinforce gendered differences in the post-Manifesto era was largely a rehearsal of the reasoning behind Manifest Destiny.[83] At a time when U.S. society was concerned with reestablishing male dominance in response to the changes brought by corporate capitalism and imperial intervention, the Saints were successfully employing an earlier version of civilization discourse—particularly one that reinforced naturalized, binarized gender roles—as a tool of assimilation that not only brought them into line with mainstream U.S. society but actually marked them as the epitome of ideal gender relations.

SAVING THE RACE BY LEADING THE RACE FOR HETERONORMATIVE REPRODUCTION

To be certain, the tenets of Mormon religion meant that the Church's campaign for gender differentiation was much more effective in reversing the gains toward gender parity than similar national efforts. In part, this was because authorities could rely on doctrine to support the idea that sexed difference and naturalized gender roles and relations were elemental and necessary. But only after 1890 did Church authorities begin to so regularly and fervently articulate the view that men and women were fundamentally distinct—reflecting the dictates of divine design established even before the moment of conception—and that this distinction was unavoidable. "Man was created, 'male and female,' and only in the union of male and female as one is man found to be in the likeness of his Maker. . . . The union of the two is a necessity, and only by virtue of that union is the divine attainable," one *Woman's Exponent* piece explained.[84] Mormon theologian James E. Talmage underscored what early twentieth-century leaders had started to regard as the divine and eternal nature of sex and gender in another article for the *Young Woman's Journal*:

> The Church of Jesus Christ of Latter-day Saints affirms as reasonable, scriptural, and true, the doctrine of the eternity of sex among the children of God. The distinction between male and female is no condition peculiar to

the relatively brief period of mortal life; it was an essential characteristic of our pre-existent state, even as it shall continue after death, in both the disembodied and resurrected states. . . . There is no accident or chance, due to purely physical conditions, by which the sex of the unborn is determined; the body takes form as male or female according to the sex of the spirit whose appointment it is to tenant that body . . . through which means alone the individual may enter upon the indispensable course of human experience, probation, and training.

Sex and gender were considered natural to the extent that they were divinely determined even before mortal life and remained an essential part of an individual's self after death in postmortal realms. This emphasis on sex and gender as inherent and enduring characteristics transcended even the modern hegemony of science, to which Talmage as a scientist himself was personally committed, ensuring "that the vital distinction of sex characterizes life on earth [and] cannot be questioned."[85]

Equally important, however, was the idea that man and woman were thought to be necessarily complementary entities. This idea was intimately tied to and accompanied by a vehement emphasis on the concept of opposite-sex desire—or heterosexuality—expressed appropriately only within the confines of monogamous marriage. "Every really successful marriage" is necessarily "founded in love—the love of man for woman [and] of woman for man," John A. Widtsoe explained to readers. Equating "physical attraction and spiritual harmony" with heterosexual love, Church authorities in the early twentieth century deemed opposite-sex desire an integral part of the divine plan that would inevitably "lead[] to mating and parenthood" in accordance with God's "command 'to multiply and replenish the earth.'" Thus, early twentieth-century Mormon theology emphasized that "the [physical, sexual] union of the sexes is ordained of the lord, eternal, so that life may ever be multiplied."[86]

Connell O'Donovan argues that Joseph Smith "deified heterosexuality" in the 1840s; however, only after the 1890 Manifesto did Church authorities begin to articulate heteronormativity as a predestined and essential triad of sexed difference, naturalized gender roles, and opposite-sex desire as crucial to Mormon theology.[87] While the Church had always been fundamentally patriarchal, its emphatic insistence on a complementary scheme of sex, gender, and desire expressed exclusively within the bounds of monogamous marriage only emerged in the last ten years of the nineteenth century, coinciding with the emergence of sexuality as a popular and academic concept in U.S. society between 1880 and 1920.[88] More specifically, the advent of the Church's interest in sexuality and its relationship to the sex/gender binary mirrored larger societal patterns that recognized sexuality as a concept of personal identification. Sexuality became an increasingly potent factor for expressing or determining a person's gender during this period, especially for middle- and upper-class men. While "sexual style had long been a crucial aspect of gender style [and] both sexual aggressiveness and sexual self-control—as well as the ability to propagate and support children—had served as markers of manliness among different groups of men," the notion of personal sexuality, specifically heterosexuality, emerged as a new expression of "real" manliness.[89] Consequently, expressions of nonheterosexual desire, in men especially but increasingly for women as well, were understood to be "prominent and volatile signs of the fragility of the gender order," echoing earlier sexological theories of inversion.[90]

Just as women's increasing independence and activity in the public sphere triggered a concern about the stability of the prevailing gender order, so too did the notion of sexuality elicit a need to shore up the hegemony of certain gendered, marital, and familial ideals. As numerous scholars argue, anxieties about gender and sexuality at the turn of the century were closely tied to the project of white supremacist nationalism.[91] The twentieth-century parameters of this project and its ties to the politics of gender and sexuality are reflected in the debates over, and campaigns for, eugenics and birth control, immigration reform, Jim Crow, antimiscegenation statutes, anti–white slavery activism, alien land laws, and imperial intervention abroad. Nayan Shah argues, for instance, that together "miscegenation laws and Alien Land Laws produced state-sponsored family forms and circumscribed participation in the economy" for nonwhite people, further entrenching marriage as "central to the production of citizenship and peculiarly entangl[ing it] in the formation of racialized property-owning citizenship."[92]

Concern about the declining marriage and birth rates of Anglo-Saxon white people, famously coined "race suicide" by Teddy Roosevelt, is perhaps the most recognizable example of the intersection between the project of white nationalism and efforts to regulate gender and sexuality in the United States. Like non-Mormons, the Saints expressed fears about the new woman (the "'flimsy garb of girls spells peril to the race. The sturdy type of American womanhood is becoming extinct and a frail scrawny species is in the process of evolution'");[93] career bachelors ("it is not legitimate for men . . . [to] delay in marriage");[94] racially suspect immigrants (our "country is being overrun with foreigners. The patriots of a hundred years ago are being supplanted by Polish Jews, and Italians, and Irish peasants, who are flocking to America in droves. . . . If this process goes on at the present rate . . . the blood of America will be largely eliminated and foreigners will possess the land which was the birth right of the citizens of America");[95] and sexual "perverts" ("there is an increasing number of men who delay marriage until they become celibates, which often means moral degenerates")[96] as both causes and symptoms of race suicide among Anglo-Saxon white people. In an editorial for the October 1908 issue of the *Improvement Era*, President Joseph F. Smith warned that there was a problematic and "growing tendency to delay marriage" among white people, Mormons included, a tendency that was "growing to be one of the greatest social evils of our country."[97] The Church's new articulation of a heteronormative worldview, which prescribed monogamous marriage and copious procreation as virtual requirements of both Church membership and U.S. citizenship, was largely a response to this sense of racial crisis. "There are multitudes of married people who through selfishness and prevention either have no children, or at most one or two," Smith fretted.[98]

In response to these concerns, Church publications and orations increasingly addressed the necessities and challenges of marriage and parenthood, discussing everything from how to select an appropriate partner; preparation and expectations for marriage and parenthood; sex education; the protocol for courtship, engagement, and weddings; the importance of marriage and procreation for spiritual attainment; to progressive solutions for divorce, adolescent crime, and sexual compatibility.[99] Virtually every post-1890 issue of the *Contributor*, the *Young Woman's Journal*, and the *Improvement Era* included numerous articles on courtship, marriage, and parenthood. Even more vehemently than other early twentieth-century moralizers, the Church successfully encouraged young people to marry early and parent numerous children. This vehemence was such that widely accepted "celebrations of manly self-restraint [that] encouraged young men to postpone marriage until they could support a family in proper middle-class style" were rejected as selfish and dangerous by Church leaders.[100]

As early as 1899, Church authorities pointed to the Saints' commitment to, and high rate of, procreation to argue that in "those points which are acknowledged to be the weakest in American civilization, the 'Mormon' people have achieved their greatest triumphs."[101] By the early years of the twentieth century, Church publications were touting Mormon eugenic efforts to maintain white racial dominance and avoid race suicide through the promotion of heteronormativity. In a May 1903 article, the *Salt Lake Herald,* a pro-Mormon newspaper, "tapped into Roosevelt's 'race suicide' rhetoric [and] . . . trumpet[ed] Mormon fertility."[102] The article was accompanied by an anticipatory image (Figure 31) of President Roosevelt's upcoming visit to Salt Lake City and depicted the U.S. president greeting Mormon men and their plentiful families. A large welcome sign in the background proclaims, "NO RACE SUICIDE HERE." At first, the Saints' high birth rate was fodder for a national press seeking to elicit cheap laughs at the expense of a Church still rumored to be sanctioning polygamous marriages. One caricature (Figure 32) pictured a delighted Roosevelt holding a newspaper reporting on Joseph F. Smith's testimony for the Smoot hearings with various headlines reading, "President Smith Admits Being the Father of 42 Children" and "38 Children in the Merrill Family!!" But

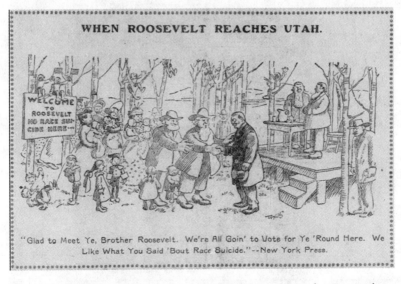

FIGURE 31. *When Roosevelt Reaches Utah.* "'Glad to Meet Ye, Brother Roosevelt. We're All Goin' to Vote for Ye 'Round Here. We Like What You Said 'Bout Race Suicide.'—New York Press." Reprinted from the *Salt Lake Herald,* May 3, 1903, 25. Courtesy of the Library of Congress.

with the abatement of anti-Mormon sentiment after the conclusion of the
Smoot hearings, journalists and social pundits began to admire "Mormon
fertility . . . as a constructive aspect of the religion," with one 1913 pamphlet calling babies "Utah's best crop" and noting that they had "the highest birth rate, the lowest death rate, the lowest percentage of divorce and
the unmarried of either sex."[103]

By 1911, Roosevelt himself praised the Saints for their commitment to
marriage, family, and procreation in *Collier's,* a prominent national magazine. "Among these [monogamous] 'Mormons,'" the former president proclaimed, "the standard of sexual morality was unusually high." Not only
are "their children . . . numerous, healthy, and well brought up," but "their
young men were less apt than their neighbors to indulge in that course of

Roosevelt—That's Bully! No Race Suicide There!

FIGURE 32. *Roosevelt—That's Bully! No Race Suicide There!* Reprinted from the *Salt
Lake Herald,* March 10, 1904, 1. Special Collections, J. Willard Marriott Library,
University of Utah.

vicious sexual dissipation so degrading to manhood and so brutal in the degradation it inflicts on women." Because "they were free from that vice, more destructive to civilization than any other can possibly be, [as well as] the artificial restriction of families, [and] the practice of sterile marriage; . . . which ultimately means destruction of the nation," Roosevelt held the Saints up as setting "a good example of citizenship."[104] The Saints could not have sought a clearer endorsement of their whiteness than Roosevelt's praise of their gender and sexual mores.

Henceforth, Mormon peculiarity discourse shifted to construct the Saints not as sexually deviant and racially inferior but, paradoxically, as exceptionally normal in their gender relations, sexual practices, familial organization, and, therefore, their racial status. "Everyone desires to live happily in married life," future Church president David O. McKay declared, "it is the natural, it is the *normal* life."[105] Julian B. Carter demonstrates that the norm, and the biopolitical discourse of normality that grew out of and drew upon the more established discourses of civilization and eugenics, tacitly communicated whiteness as an ideal aspect of Americanness through what he calls the "race- and power-evasive" language of sexual morality, physical fitness, and gender differentiation.[106] Therefore, by the 1930s invoking the concept of "normal" life allowed McKay to implicitly reference whiteness in his argument that "the stability of government, and the perpetuation of the race" were "depend[ent] upon" a "congenial marriage."[107] Because white supremacy was directly linked to the regulation of sexual reproduction in early twentieth-century discourses of civilization, eugenics, and increasingly normality, Apostle J. Reuben Clark of the Quorum of the Twelve Apostles stressed chastity as "'fundamental to our life and to our civilization'" in an *Improvement Era* piece cautioning that "'if the race becomes unchaste, it will perish' . . . [destroy] chastity, the sanctity of marriage and the holiness of the home" and the "Christian man becomes a brute."[108] While failure to procreate would result in race suicide, so too would sexual impropriety lead to racial, national, and spiritual deterioration.

It is no coincidence that the resignification of Mormon peculiarity discourse coincided with the shift from an explicit discussion of the relationship between sexual practice and racial identity to a "representational collapse of heterosexual love into citizenship" between 1890 and 1940.[109] In fact, Mormon peculiarity discourse, whether articulated by the Saints themselves or by non-Mormons, was integral to realizing this representational collapse, in which heteronormativity came to stand in for the explicitly racial language of white supremacy. The abandonment of polygamy, with all its attendant racial implications, coupled with the Saints' new commitments to sexed difference, heterosexual desire expressed only through monogamous marriage, and abundant procreation transformed the meanings and uses of Mormon peculiarity discourse such that the Saints' assimilation into U.S. society was touted as evidence of the racial power of so-called sexual fitness.

Self-government, which had unequivocally been styled a white racial trait under civilization discourse, was transplanted into modern discussions of gender and sex between 1900 and 1920, solidifying associations between heteronormativity and whiteness without always invoking the explicit language of race. An individual's, especially a man's, capacity for self-government, and therefore his racial status, had long been tied to the possession of qualities such as self-control, self-cultivation, sensitivity, self-sacrifice, and hard work. Like self-government, these virtues had been racialized as definitively white but were now being transformed into ostensibly race-neutral characteristics in cultural discussions of sexual fitness, modern marriage, and normal adjustment. To ensure individual Saints complied with the emergent ideal of normal life, and to avoid any further suggestion of Mormon racial depreciation, Church authorities forcefully emphasized these characteristics as implicitly racial virtues expressed through the gendered obligations of marriage and parenthood.

During the first twenty years of the new century in particular, Mormon theologians placed "a new emphasis on personal character, self-discipline, and morality as the primary pathway to salvation" for both men and women.[110] The Church's increasingly strict attitude about adherence to the Word of Wisdom (a religious health code instituted under Church President Heber J. Grant that required compliance for temple admittance) is frequently cited as the most apposite evidence of this new theological emphasis.[111] However, equal, if not more, weight was given to heteronormative compliance, suggesting that "sexual morality may well have become an even more profound symbol of [Mormon] identity" than the Word of Wisdom during the early twentieth century.[112] Although the Church had always had regulations restricting sexual activity to the confines of the marital union, it was only during the early twentieth century that the Church took unparalleled steps to surveil and manage sexual activity outside of marriage, resulting in an increase in "excommunications due to sexual transgression."[113]

Evidence of the Church's regulation of same-sex sexuality during this period suggests that the leadership was becoming increasingly concerned about deviations from the married, monogamous, heterosexual norm just as they began to emphasize it in Mormon doctrine.[114] As early as 1904, Francis M. Lyman advised young men in the *Improvement Era* that "if a man has evil tendencies in any particular direction, he can conquer them by self-control, prayer, and striving to help others who are similarly tempted,"[115] while Apostle Anthony W. Ivins warned that the "great evil[s] that menace . . . this nation today, the great evil[s] which menace . . . the Church," are "intemperance and sexual sin."[116] Indulgence in intemperance and sexual sin were cast as the absolute opposite of the highly prized characteristics of self-discipline and self-cultivation and were thought to lead to the loss of an individual's sensitivity and work ethic.[117] Apostle Charles A. Callis of the Quorum of the Twelve Apostles, who in 1933 had been assigned to "deal with the flow of interviews with Church members involved in fornication or adultery or homosexuality," penned an article for the November 1939 issue of the *Improvement Era* pushing the spiritual and moral importance of "self-conquest."[118] While the article never explicitly mentions nonnormative sexual desire or practice, Callis's advice directly encourages young men, through the evocation of virtues that had already been heavily associated with sexual self-control in the pages of the *Improvement Era,* to exclusively practice heterosexual sex within the confines of a monogamous marriage. Since "the Gospel teaches self-denial and forbearance from gratifying one's own wrong desires," Callis pronounced, it is "better . . . to go to heaven through much self-denial than to wreck a human life in a course of self-indulgence." Although the language of self-government is delivered under the auspices of religious improvement—"in order for a man successfully to overcome a bad habit he must have in mind an objective. . . . In this manner he will work harder in the spirit of self-restraint and self-mastery to secure the soul-satisfying benefits that will surely come to him as he gets sovereign power over himself"—the article deploys the racially coded language of sexual fitness and modern marriage.[119] Even the image accompanying the article, a knight in shining armor, evokes conventional notions of twentieth-century heterosexual romance and normative masculinity.

The racial import of virtues such as self-conquest was carefully emphasized by Church authorities as fundamentally connected to the foundation of the nation through sexual morality well into the twentieth century, increasingly through racially coded language. For example, on the eve of World War I, John A. Widtsoe counseled that "the effect of moral [sexual] sin does not end with the sinner" but that "it is carried down to the third and fourth generation" and that "the horrible scourge [of] moral looseness now plaguing the country would result in the downfall of the nation" just as other "nations and individuals on the road to greatness have fallen because they failed to observe sexual purity."[120] While the potential for sexual, and therefore racial, transgression haunted authorities' active promotion of heteronormative family life, they also encouraged active participation in the capitalist economy as an avenue for the Saints to enact good racial citizenship.

A CHURCH OF HONORABLE AND INDUSTRIOUS MEN AND WOMEN

Most scholarly accounts of Mormon assimilation regard it as an inevitable process of economic and political integration into the national mainstream.[121] The Church presidency's efforts to encourage members to participate in both the free market and party politics are typically framed as good faith efforts to get the Church out of government, divest its interests in economic planning, and bring it into alignment with democracy and free enterprise. These accounts have left intact the assumption that the Saints were entering a free and open political system, yet the recent history of federal suppression of the Church definitively belies such an assumption. Non-Mormons' objections to Church authorities' control of individual members' political and economic activities in the nineteenth century were not so much a true concern for individual freedom of belief as about controlling the types of ideologies the Church endorsed. The problem was not the Church's extensive influence over its members but its promotion of economic and political alternatives to industrial capitalism.

The significant challenges the Church posed to the rising hegemony of corporate and consumer capitalism during the mid-nineteenth century were abated when federal anti-Mormonism began to quash the Saints' ability to practice economic isolationism. With the creeping financial and cultural effects of Utah's integration into the national economy (precipitated by the completion of the railroad in 1869), the death of Brigham Young in 1877, and the burdens imposed by anti-Mormon legislation in the 1880s, a significant transformation of Mormon attitudes toward the free market had already begun. By the end of the nineteenth century, for example, agriculture in Mormon-dominated areas began to follow "the national trend and became increasingly commercialized," resulting in the discontinuation of Church-run storehouses and the once-common practice of tithing-in-kind by the end of 1908, signaling the collapse of a once thriving barter economy and the communal operation of important common resources.[122] But, as Leonard J. Arrington explains, even though the Church had begun to abandon its commitment to alternative economic policies and practices at least a decade before 1890, "the church was still an active force in the economic life of the community, as a promoter and proprietor," a reality "that was deemed inconsistent with the laissez-faire and free enterprising concepts of national policy" and resulted in attacks on the Church "as a gigantic holding company controlling the strategic industries of the region."[123] Just as flare-ups over whether polygamy was still being practiced continued through the first decade of the new century, so too did concerns about the Church's influence in economic and political matters.[124]

But "that the church was accused of proprietary monopoly rather than of radical progressivism as had been true through much of its earlier history was a sign of" how significantly Mormon economic policy and practice had changed between the 1880s and the first years of the new century.[125] No longer committed to an insulated communal economy, authorities had become thoroughly invested in promoting and supporting capitalist enterprises for the benefit of the Church. These activities, however hyperbolically characterized by anti-Mormons, provoked the ire of the national business community, who engaged in muckraking attacks with "accusations that Church leaders cooperated with monopolistic enterprises and made enormous profits."[126] While President Joseph F. Smith moved to "get the church out of business" and denied these attacks—clarifying in the *Improvement Era* that "not one of the general authorities in the Church . . . draws one dollar from the tithes of the people for his own use"—the accusations in no way dampened the leadership's newfound commitment to capitalism as a fundamental ideology underpinning the greatness of the U.S. nation-state's white civilization.[127]

In their study of economic radicalism in nineteenth- and early twentieth-century Utah, John S. McCormick and John R. Sillito argue that an important strategy used to convince non-Mormons that the Saints were neither dangerous nor subversive, but loyal, law-abiding Americans was to oppose socialism and embrace capitalism.[128] However, this constituted much more than a single strategy of assimilation. The Church hierarchy's openly hostile opposition to not just socialism but all anticapitalist and reformist political economic philosophies and ideologies was part of a much larger rhetorical campaign aimed at demonstrating the Saints' racial and patriotic qualifications for U.S. citizenship. Because capitalism was widely considered to be the most civilized economic system, the Church's open embrace of capitalism had decidedly racial implications that the Church intentionally foregrounded in their own representations of Mormonism in the new century. This campaign was composed of three key tactics: first, the leadership's open opposition to ideologies like socialism; second, an infusion of capitalist rhetoric in Mormon theology; and third, a capitalist reinterpretation of the Church's history. The success of this campaign would culminate in the development of the Church Security Program, later renamed the Church Welfare Program, during the Great Depression.

The first strategy recycled the Church's earlier disapproval of socialism, which rejected the ideology primarily to legitimize its own utopian goals, into a much wider, vehement condemnation of a whole host of anticapitalist ideologies and reformist activities. Church authorities expressed strong disapprobation of organized labor, unionism, strikes, socialism, communism, and Bolshevism in sermons, articles, and private counsel. This increasingly hostile opposition was the earliest indication of what became the Church's commitment to capitalism as a system that the Saints patriotically supported. An admonition given by George Q. Cannon in his March 1894 address at the Salt Lake Tabernacle was typical: "'Let socialism severely alone,'" he warned, instructing the Saints to "reject all radical economic and political philosophies." Identifying "radical political groups as among the 'secret combinations' God had warned his people against in the Book of Mormon," he claimed they sought "'to destroy government, to overturn existing institutions, and to array class against class, community against community,'" echoing non-Mormon objections to socialist and communist organizing that dismissed anticapitalist critiques as mere troublemaking, not legitimate analyses of existing economic conditions.[129] As early as August 1883, official Church publications cautioned adherents from joining unions or participating in walkouts. An editorial in the *Contributor* discouraged Saints from joining in strikes, arguing that they "sometimes seem to be necessary, but they are always wasteful."[130] David O. McKay clarified the Church's stance against unions in another editorial for the *Improvement Era,* calling them "undemocratic" and "un-American," contending that they stifled "individual liberty."[131] The seriousness of the Church's efforts to dissuade Saints' sympathy for economic activists, whether radical or revisionist, is reflected in President Joseph F. Smith's instructions in the spring of 1911 to the *Deseret News*, the Church-owned newspaper, to initiate an editorial campaign against socialism.[132] In the unambiguous words of Cannon, "'our constant effort is to keep our people from joining these organizations.'"[133]

The acceptance of free enterprise as a national ideology was by no means certain during the nineteenth century. Political efforts that sought to expose and combat the deleterious effects of industrial and corporate capitalism became increasingly attractive to many workers across the country. "Between 1881 and 1905" alone "there were nearly thirty-seven thousand strikes, often violent, involving seven million workers—an impressive number in a nation whose total work force in 1900 numbered only twenty-nine million."[134] But, in the late nineteenth century, labor and anticapitalist activity became increasingly associated with southern and eastern European immigrants whose racial status was under intense scrutiny from white Protestant elites. As capitalist ideology became further entangled with the already heavily racialized notion of Americanness, it was progressively viewed not just as an indication of racial development but as an important aspect of good citizenship.[135] Thus, in rejecting and even attacking labor activism, the Church did not simply demonstrate its willing assimilation into the national mainstream after decades of resistance, but it tacitly communicated the Saints' racial allegiance to white nationalism through its promotion of capitalism.

Church leaders had demonized socialism through racial associations as early as 1884. One *Deseret News* piece argued that socialism would precipitate "'chaos and a return to barbarism,'" playing on associations between civilization, race, and economics.[136] Other Mormon authors disparaged socialism for its supposed immorality, specifically citing its association with "free love" as an indication of its threat to the stability of white racial dominance.[137] But as the twentieth century progressed, the explicit links authors drew between economic ideology and racial status were replaced with oblique and indirect references to race. For example, in an article for the April 1913 issue of the *Improvement Era*, Pocatello, Idaho, stake president William A. Hyde argued that "Mormonism 'teaches us *the highest type* of patriotism and love for our country,'" subtly drawing on hierarchal notions of white nationalism.[138]

By the mid-1930s, Church leaders were being commended for their fierce opposition to anticapitalist ideologies. In the *Improvement Era*, one editorial noted with satisfaction that the First Presidency's anticommunist stance had been met "with fervent approval, both within and without the Church, by Americans who love America," even by the anti-Mormon *Salt Lake Tribune*, which announced:

> There is both reason and logic in the recent pronouncement of the Mormon Church against communism. . . . It warns of a menace that drives at the very foundations of American life. Communism has nothing in common with the Mormon Church or any other, this government or any other, this people or any other. It is an enemy to religion, to freedom, and to civilization.[139]

In aligning Mormonism with the U.S. nation-state, the *Tribune* reversed almost seventy years of anti-Mormon writing. Approval of the Church's anticommunist stance, particularly its insistence that "communism is not a political party nor a political plan under the Constitution; it is a system of government that is the opposite . . . and it would be necessary to destroy our Constitution before communism could be set up in the United States" making "support [for] communism . . . treasonable," is perhaps the best confirmation that non-Mormons' concerns about the Church hierarchy's power over members was not actually a concern for freedom of choice or speech but a concern about the economic and political ideologies the Church backed.[140]

Concomitant with the rise of the Church's opposition to unionism, socialism, and communism was an infusion of capitalist rhetoric in Mormon culture and theology. As fervently as Church leaders lambasted radical economic and political philosophies, they were equally avid in their praise and support for the capitalist system, encouraging members to become loyal and hardworking employees, to broker civil solutions between labor and capital, and to engage in the two-party system on which the hegemony of the free market system was based. In the late 1880s, Church publications began to regularly feature articles advising young men on the importance of vocational training and career selection as essential to personal happiness and development: "Work, with an inclination to do it, is the key to success and contentment," one author advised.[141] "No matter what occupation a young man may choose," another claimed, "it will be impossible for him to succeed without unremitting toil."[142] Authors often linked an individual's gender and racial identity to their work ethic under the capitalist system. "If you would have your work count for something, put yourself into it," one writer insisted, "determine that whatever you do in life shall be a part of yourself, and that it shall be stamped with *superiority*."[143]

As a highly prized civilized quality, *superiority* implicitly denoted not just manliness and whiteness but economic productivity and innovation; "superiority of method, progressiveness, and up-to-dateness" were essential characteristics of any modern man, worker, or citizen.[144] Concerns about the effects of industrial and corporate capitalism clearly affected the advice young Mormon men received about the modern workplace. "Be not content to" work hard and "know only a part" of a trade, an *Improvement Era* piece suggested, "for you thus become a machine which must always be governed or controlled by some one else."[145] In order to truly embody the most highly prized qualities of manhood, and therefore American civilization, young Mormon men were encouraged to develop a balance between productivity and individuality. "Something to do! That is the cry and desire of the young and active," an *Improvement Era* editorial declared. "If useful and good employment is not found or given them there is grave danger that they will choose to do that which will perhaps lead them to evil." While "useful employment" was the solution to the temptations of intemperance and sexual sin and resulted in the "development of life and character," young men were also counseled to "leaven[]" their efficiency "with [their] own individuality."[146]

Anticipating the 1911–12 Men and Religion Forward Movement's "insist[ence] that church work should be understood as part of the modern, twentieth-century world of corporate business," the Church not only connected manliness, whiteness, and citizenship to working identity, but authorities adopted the language of business, finance, and entrepreneurship in their theological discussions of morality, man's relationship to God, and salvation.[147] George H. Brimhall, then president of Brigham Young University, explained, "through obedience to the law of tithing, we become the financial elect of God or business partners with the Lord." Describing the relationship between man and God as a "business contract," he expounded on the Saints' spiritual obligation to tithe 10 percent of their income as an investment: "If it is true that giving to the poor is lending to the Lord, then paying one's tithing is investing with the Lord." This was a marked departure from past theological accounts that explained that the Saints did not own but were merely holding the Lord's property in

trust as they worked to build up the Kingdom of God. Failure to tithe
in the nineteenth century had been represented as stealing from God,
whereas twentieth-century theologians were now describing tithing as "a
law of perfect financial liberty" and "a debt of honor."[148] Tithe paying, as
a shrewd and morally correct financial investment, was therefore evidence
of Saints' racial-religious fitness, whereas "the neglect thereof," Brimhall
explained, "cannot fail to affect the greatest of all social units, the family.
Under the law of heredity, what will be the tendency in offspring where
the parents are conscious of not dealing honestly with the Lord?"[149]

If Mormons were good businessmen, then being a Mormon meant
being a good citizen in the Saints' own estimation, and increasingly in
non-Mormons' as well. "This is pre-eminently the age of industry, and
good citizenship requires that each one shall be industrially efficient,"
Ephraim G. Gowans remarked. "The industrial development of the past
two decades is unparalleled in the history of forty centuries, and surely
there is no disposition to minimize the value of America's great industrial
contribution to civilization and the progress of the race."[150] To be labeled
industrially efficient was therefore also to be interpellated as white so that,
as with heteronormativity, the language of capitalism came to stand in for
explicitly racial designators, disguising the extent to which whiteness was
still regarded as an essential for full citizenship in the United States. Just as
the qualities of self-discipline, self-control, self-cultivation, sensitivity, self-
sacrifice, and hard work were used to tacitly affirm the Saints' commitment to heteronormativity as a commitment to white dominance, so too
were these kinds of characteristics deployed to relay the Saints' investment
in capitalism as sign of their whiteness. Waste, idleness, and laziness were
decried by Church authorities as evil, while "independence, industry, thrift,
and self-respect" were "enthroned as a ruling principle of the lives of our
Church membership."[151]

While the Church's economic about-face was widely applauded by
Protestant white elites, it was not easily understood or accepted by its
own members. Decades of teachings that had emphasized equality, fair-
ness, and cooperation could not be erased, nor could they easily be recon-
figured to reflect the Church's new investments. Moreover, as a result of
the Church's history of economic isolation, resistance, and socialistic practice, many Saints were interested in the growing movements for economic
justice, particularly socialism.[152] In addition to the zealous rhetorical campaign against those movements, Church leaders also began to introduce

reinterpretations of Church history, often directly contradicting earlier statements by other Church authorities in order to dissuade such interest. In
1901, the *Improvement Era* went so far as to apply a capitalist lens to the
Bible, arguing that "Jacob's covenant was a business contract with God"
and was therefore an important "element[] of his business success."[153]

It was not until the dawn of the Great Depression that authorities felt
the need to provide an extensive reinterpretation of the Church's economic history. At its depth in October 1932, one *Improvement Era* article
was unafraid to ask the question "Has capitalism failed?" In an apparent
response to lay interest in the nineteenth-century United Order cooperative economic system, as a more equitable alternative to the current economic structure, the article's author, Joseph A. Geddes, compared the two
systems, concluding that "the United Order carries the great principle of
social justice and group righteousness into the dark corners of capitalism
in a surprisingly simple and thoroughgoing manner." Showing no discom-
fort labeling the United Order "communistic," Geddes pointedly argued,
"ownership of private property . . . brings about undue inequality," just as
"granting of full freedom of initiative to the individual brings confusion"
and "conflicts between owners and workers interfere with cooperation
and entail large wastes," whereas "the United Order plan could not help
but stir the spirit and lift the hope, courage, and ambition of that large
number of people to whom the doors of opportunity have been opened
but a very little way and have been closed again all too quickly under the
present system."[154]

Clearly, Geddes's remarks were a dramatic departure from the Church's
recent attacks on socialism and communism, however unsurprising they
were given the catastrophic effects of the Great Depression. But as the
Church struggled to support its congregants, authorities found it necessary to disabuse their followers of any thoughts of abandoning or even
critiquing the present economic system. To do this, they offered up a reinterpretation of the Church's economic history, particularly its experiments with the communal and cooperative efforts of the United Order
that dangerously resembled socialism in many fundamental aspects. "Basic
to the United Order was the private ownership of property," J. Reuben
Clark alleged in a speech during one general conference.[155] Fearing the
growing "sentiment that communism and the United Order are virtually
the same thing," Clark was emphatic in his denial. Repeatedly contending
that "PRIVATE OWNERSHIP [WAS] FUNDAMENTAL" to the United Order and

that "each man owned his portion, or inheritance, or stewardship, with an absolute title," Clark strained to convince listeners that "the United Order is an individualistic system, not a communal" one.[156]

Not content to argue that the history of the United Order demonstrated its basically capitalist essence, Clark went further to offer a theological reevaluation of the revelation that first announced the United Order in 1831. Section 51 "affirms that every man is to be 'equal according to his family, according to his circumstances and his wants and needs,'" but, "obviously, this is not a case of 'dead level' equality," Clark opined. Rather, "it is 'equality' that will vary as much as the man's circumstances, his family, his wants and needs, may vary."[157] Another article, published a few months later, maintained that the United Order was "erroneously refer[ed] to . . . as 'socialistic' or 'communistic'" and that "the principles of the United Order are much more capitalistic." "How these fallacies gained currency is difficult to understand," the author said, but he admitted that he "too, [once] had the idea that socialism and United Order were first cousins, if not identical twins." Nonetheless, he insisted that the "operation" of the order "was carried on in the capitalistic fashion. . . . It was the very opposite of public ownership and control of all the sources of wealth—labor included. Property was privately owned, labor was not regimented, and even the surpluses turned over to the Church were free-will offerings."[158]

Church authorities' unequivocal insistence that the faith's history was capitalist was at the very least willful misrepresentation, but it fit nicely with the faith's twentieth-century commitment to free enterprise. The transformation from one materialist theology to another was punctuated by the elevation of individuality, self-reliance, and hard work. As Mangum and Blumell point out, self-reliance as an economic concept no longer referred to the economic independence of the entire Mormon community but "became primarily individual, while the law of consecration and the United Order gradually became esoteric concepts."[159] Nothing embodied these new values more clearly than the creation of the Church Security Program in 1936.

Developed in response to the Great Depression, the program was instituted, in the words of then Church president Heber J. Grant:

"[to] set up a system under which the curse of idleness would be done away with, the evils of a dole abolished, and independence, industry, thrift, and self-respect be once more established amongst our people. The aim of the

Church is to help the people to help themselves. Work is to be re-enthroned
as the ruling principle of the lives of our Church membership."[160]

The by now familiar references to independence, industry, thrift, and self-
respect would have been instantly recognizable to Mormons who regularly
encountered statements promoting them in connection with the racial,
sexual, and economic fitness thought to be necessary for both spiritual
salvation and good citizenship. The logic of the new program was based
on the idea that "the idle person . . . must be provided with the opportunity of rendering some service of which he is capable so that if and when
he needs assistance it may be given not as a dole to sustain him in idleness
but as a partial compensation for the work he has done or the services
he has rendered."[161] The dole, and not the instability and inequality of capitalism, was seen as the problem. "The fruits of idleness [are] ripening . . .
into indolence, infidelity, and rebellion," head of the program Harold B.
Lee warned, and would become ingrained if the unemployed were not put
to work.[162]

Just as non-Mormons praised the Saints for their promotion and practice
of heteronormativity, the national reaction to the Church Security Program
as a symbol of the Church's commitment to free market capitalism was
overwhelmingly positive. Both the media and the federal government commended the Church's leaders for instituting a program that did not rely
on government funds, promoted the values of hard work and personal
responsibility, and seemed to "show the way out" of the Great Depression,
according to one *New York Times* piece.[163] After the program's initiation
in April 1936, Church officials met with President Franklin Roosevelt to
discuss the plan and promoted it in the national press. J. Reuben Clark's
statements at a press conference in which he claimed, "'the LDS Church
will remove its 88,000 needy members for public relief rolls and launch
cooperative work projects tending to make them self-supporting,'" were
picked up and reported nationally.[164] The mainstream media regularly "published articles as if [Clark's] stated intention[s] were an accomplished fact,
apparently anxious to praise this alternative to the 'liberal' New Deal."[165]

A two-page spread in a May 1937 edition of *Newsweek* featured "the
work of the men and women in their effort to care for themselves and the
worthy poor through the Church Security Program," the *Improvement Era*
happily reported.[166] Even the *Catholic Worker,* a periodical of the Catholic
Church, applauded the Church for its new program, making the surprising

declaration that "Mormons have taken the lead from Catholics in caring for their needy," setting "an example worthy of imitation by their Catholic fellow countrymen." The *Worker* was particularly impressed that the Church "called upon every man, woman, and child to be *personally responsible* for the amelioration" of the economic crisis.[167] The common thread in the overwhelmingly positive national coverage of the Church's new program was its apparent emphasis on self-reliance, self-support, and personal responsibility. These characteristics, which had already been well-established as racialized traits during the first thirty years of the twentieth century, were extolled as definitive evidence of the Saints' absorption into U.S. society and culture.

Church officials immediately recognized the significance of the nation's response to their new program, using it to continue to refurbish Mormonism's reputation and to reaffirm the Church's racial-national commitments. Apostles Reed Smoot, Utah's former senator, and George Albert Smith wrote a letter in response to the *Newsweek* piece, which, although it had praised the Church Security Program, had also included some anti-Mormon prejudice. A testament to the significant shift in non-Mormon attitudes toward the Church, the magazine responded positively to the letter—especially notable given the intense campaign to keep Smoot out of national office only thirty years earlier—and printed a retraction.[168] "The past year has been marked by a warm and generous reception in the world's leading periodicals," the *Improvement Era* was proud to announce, the "slander, historical falsehood, and the willful misconceptions of" decades past had been replaced with the message that "the Church has be[come] wholesome front page news for America—and beyond."[169]

Mangum and Blumell contend that "perhaps the greatest contribution of the [Church] Welfare Plan was that it permanently shifted the church's image from that of a polygamous sect . . . to a solidly middle-class American church that exemplified hard work, family-centered values, and the frontier virtues of neighborliness and self-reliance."[170] In fact, the program assisted Church authorities' efforts to limit and even scale back on women's participation in the public sphere. Arrington and Bitton explain that "church leaders insisted that prevention was more effective than cure and that the best antidote to social problems was a strong home." Continued emphasis on heteronormative family units was therefore advertised by the Church not just as divinely ordained but as a preventive prescription against modern social evils. The previously "widespread involvement of

Latter-day Saint women in social work became a thing of the past" and "monthly lessons which had earlier focused on social work and psychology now dealt with social relations within the Latter-day Saint family."[171] By the 1930s, the Church's economic agenda had become thoroughly intertwined with its social one, just as it had been in the nineteenth century, but now monogamous heterosexual marriage based upon the supposed naturalness of differentiated gender roles was posed as both the solution and perfect complement to the modernization of life in the United States under the free market system.

Thus, Mormon peculiarity no longer signaled a deviant, racially inferior threat to the nation. Instead, it had transformed 180 degrees to communicate a "higher state of morality" than "the general run of people in this country," one non-Mormon commentator opined. Even though non-Mormons now considered Mormons to be a "morally and physically . . . fine people," a clear indication that the Saints were accepted as white by the 1930s, Mormon peculiarity discourse would still be used as a foil against which Americanness was defined in terms of whiteness, only now Mormon's "high state of morality" was what made them peculiar: "they surpass the people in any other part of the country in their high standards of personal conduct" and value "family life . . . to a greater extent than among people generally in this country." In other words, Mormon peculiarity now denoted a peculiar hypernormativity. The Mormons as "a high grade of people," "with high standards of personal conduct," who were above average in their efforts to "bring up their boys and girls to be honorable and industrious men and women," communicated "industry," "sobriety," "self-reliance," "thrift," "hard work," and "clean living" as necessary and implicitly racial attributes of the (white) nation.[172] After World War II, these values would be increasingly associated with Mormonism and come to denote hypernormativity as the prevailing version of Mormon peculiarity discourse just as white supremacy was being challenged by a new civil rights movement.

5 A Thoroughly American Institution, 1936–1962

At times, its members have been labeled a "strange people,"
but they are not strange. They are different, yes, but the right
to be different is the essence of the American dream. . . .
The followers of Joseph Smith and Brigham Young have
assimilated.

> —Hartzell Spence, "The Story of Religions
> in America"

Forms of sociality that do not carve out a "unique" status for
the reproductively directed marital unit can be treated not
simply as inferior within the scope of human history but as
threatening to [hamper], or reverse, the progress of those that
do. The invocation of "civilization" appears less as a residue of
an outmoded nineteenth-century language of Euro-conquest
than a trace of the ongoing enmeshment of discourses of
sexuality in the project of fortifying the United States against
incursions by *uncivilized* formations that jeopardize the
"common sense" of national life.

> —Mark Rifkin, *When Did Indians Become Straight?*

Two years after the end of World War II, The Church of Jesus Christ
of Latter-day Saints claimed one million adherents. In less than twenty
years, by 1963, that number had doubled. Not ten years later, in 1971, the
Church's membership reached three million. The sheer speed with which
the Church grew in the second half of the twentieth century is a testament
to the ways it had and would continue to overcome its infamous nineteenth-
century reputation as a peculiarly racial threat, replaced by a novel sense
that the Saints and their religion were peculiarly normative.[1] As detailed

in the last chapter, this newfound Mormon hypernormativity had racial, gendered, sexual, economic, and political dimensions that communicated— increasingly implicitly, but certainly not exclusively so—the Church's commitment to the white supremacist project of U.S. exceptionalism, a pattern that would continue throughout the Cold War era.

Jan Shipps argues that a mostly negative perception of Mormonism persisted into the late 1920s but was reversed with the onset of the Great Depression and the debut of the Church's Welfare Program in 1936, which the national press unequivocally embraced.[2] As an overview of mainstream perceptions of Mormonism, Shipps's assessment is generally accurate, yet it tends to have an oversimplifying effect, rendering invisible the extensive, racialized work of theologizing and promoting both heteronormativity and free enterprise that the Church had undertaken in the early twentieth century and that served as the foundation for the Saints' assimilation into whiteness by the mid- to late 1930s. Able to attain whiteness, and thus Americanness, as a result of shedding the socially proscribed nonnormative practices of their past, the Saints and their Church's continued commitment to white supremacy throughout the twentieth century served to further cement this newfound status.

This chapter and the next build on chapter 4's examination of how Mormon peculiarity discourse came to construct Mormonism as hypernormative between the Great Depression and World War II, specifically the shift from explicit to implicit forms of racial rhetoric in constructions of U.S. nationalism and empire. It does so by scrutinizing how hypernormativity became the predominant form of Mormon peculiarity discourse, starting in the 1930s, through appeals to mainstream whiteness, made both overtly—expressed through commitments to institutionalized racism and U.S. colonialism—and, increasingly, covertly—expressed through association with the nuclear family, the gender binary, and the prized (racialized, economic, and political) qualities of hard work, self-control, self-sufficiency, and wholesomeness as examples of embodied patriotism in the mainstream press—at a time when the Black freedom movement was beginning to force the nation to confront its anti-Black racism. Thus, this chapter provides a thorough exploration of Mormon peculiarity discourse between the mid-1930s and the early 1960s, while chapter 6 focuses on the century's later cultural conflicts between the 1960s and the early 1980s, in order to argue that Mormon peculiarity was an important driver in the evolution of white supremacy's survival as a fundamental component of U.S. nationalism and empire during the Cold War era. More specifically, this chapter contends that after World War II, Mormon peculiarity discourse functioned as an important mechanism through which the nation-state's investment in white supremacy began to shift from primarily being articulated in terms of biological superiority and segregation to the rhetoric of colorblindness most frequently by ignoring, but sometimes downplaying, the Church's white supremacy while simultaneously constructing Mormonism as a "thoroughly American institution."[3]

Mid-twentieth-century Mormon peculiarity discourse provides a particularly elucidatory vantage point from which to examine this transition because, as a conservative church much like its evangelical fundamentalist counterparts, it was simultaneously represented as both a typical example of and an outsider to mainstream sociopolitical developments, particularly those related to race, gender, and sexuality. At the same time that the Saints were heralded by mainstream media as hypernormative—cast as exemplary in their rugged pioneer past, overcoming adversity, and successfully assimilating into and achieving the American dream to become respectable, patriotic citizens—previous iterations of Mormon peculiarity discourse were occasionally deployed to frame them and their church as particularly backward. However, gone were the days when mainstream media, politicians, and social commentators would effortlessly dismiss Mormonism as deviant, degenerate, or foreign. Indeed, portrayals of Mormonism as backward were no longer primarily negative in tone but were instead equated with being simply outdated, old-fashioned, or traditional. In other words, these negative portrayals were now couched within a significantly altered racial context in which Mormons were definitively racialized as white and therefore seen as fundamentally redeemable, despite (and sometimes because of) the Church's white supremacy. The construction of Mormonism as hypernormative is illustrated by contextualizing that process within the larger frame of racialized Cold War anticommunism and fears of national civilizational decline. As a socially and politically conservative institution, the Church reflected, promoted, and embodied many of the social, economic, and political ideals of Cold War–era conservatism, which mainstream media delightedly extolled.

MIDCENTURY (MORMON) WHITE SUPREMACY

By the start of World War II, the Church, like most white institutions and citizens in the United States, had strongly reaffirmed its commitment to a culture and politics of white supremacy. The articulation and development of white supremacist thought by Church leaders during the last two decades of the nineteenth century, as detailed in the last chapter, was a pattern that persisted into the first three decades of the next century. This is unsurprising, given that the early decades of the century were marked in the United States by a vehement resurgence in white supremacy and xenophobic nativism, perhaps most notably symbolized by the rebirth of the KKK, inspired by the first-ever blockbuster film, D. W. Griffith's *The Birth of a Nation* in 1915, and the successive passage of a number of increasingly restrictive immigration acts, culminating in the 1924 Johnson–Reed Act.[4]

It was also during this period that the Priesthood Correlation Program began, a Progressive-era effort instituted in 1908 by President Joseph F. Smith to centralize and streamline the publications and curriculum of the Church. The effects of correlation—an effort that expanded to consolidate leadership, authority, auxiliary organizations, finances, and other institutional components by midcentury—were numerous, but most significantly for Mormon racial attitudes, resulted in the hardening of institutionalized anti-Black racism and the loss of women's authority and power within the Church. Because, as Joanna Brooks explains, the "systematization of Mormon theology went hand in hand with" this "centralization and bureaucratization of Mormon religious life[,] . . . modern Mormonism instituted one of the most rigidly enforced systems of racial segregation in the history of American Christianity."[5]

It is especially important to note, however, that despite the insistence of Church leaders at midcentury, the Church's theology of Blackness was not based on revelation. Rather, Church leaders, after the death of Joseph Smith, recycled common, but specious, biblical justifications for slavery and segregation used by other Christian groups, primarily the Curse of Cain, in addition to developing their own Mormon-specific justifications, as discussed in the previous chapter. This included the citation of a story from the Book of Abraham in the Pearl of Great Price, a scripture canonized by the Church in 1880, which was connected to the Curse of Canaan (Ham), as well as the preexistence theory. These justifications, developed over time, were also buttressed by nonreligious racist theorizing. For example, behind B. H. Roberts's 1907 *The Seventy's Course on Theology*'s lesson "The Law of the Lord in Ancient and Modern Revelation Applied to the Negro Race Problem" was "Reconstruction-era white supremacist thought, developed in the American South," meaning that the Church's "lay priesthood curriculum relied on Confederate history."[6]

In April 1924, the same year that saw the passage of the Johnson–Reed Act and the height of the KKK's power, Joseph Fielding Smith published an article in the *Improvement Era* called "The Negro and the Priesthood."[7] Although it was much like other writings on the bans, this piece was significant because it was the first time that the Church officially, and falsely, stated the bans were not a product of earthly interpretation but were divinely mandated as a result of a revelation to Joseph Smith. Joseph Fielding Smith would go on to cement this idea in his highly respected theological work *The Way to Perfection,* published in 1931. Thereafter, Church leaders would consistently claim that the Church's bans were God's will and therefore could not be reversed without a revelation. Early twentieth-century Mormon theologians, such as Roberts and Smith, were instrumental, Brooks explains, in also institutionalizing "a new orthodox consensus around the inerrancy or infallibility of Mormon prophets," which she calls a "possessive investment in rightness."[8] This possessive investment in rightness would ensure that the Church would not give up its racist anti-Black bans until 1978 and would not acknowledge until 2013 that human racism, not a divine revelation, was behind their creation and maintenance.

Although the Church's anti-Black racism was perhaps the most formally ensconced of any U.S.-based church, and quite visibly so as a result of Mormon peculiarity discourse, it is important to note that it was not unique. The widespread movement "to create a systematic, Bible-based fundamentalist white American Christianity had white supremacist impulses at its core" and was based on a longer history of proslavery, segregationist Christianity in the United States.[9] Beyond the well-known example of Bob Jones University and its long-standing, overtly racist policies, scholars have cataloged a variety of ways that white supremacy was embedded within and driven by American Christianity.[10] The ubiquity of white supremacist Christianity was reflected in widespread support for and passage of pro-segregation and antimiscegenation laws across the country between the 1860s and the 1930s, including in Utah.[11] While Utah had previously passed laws banning interracial sex and marriage, in 1939 the state updated its law to expand its antimiscegenation restrictions.[12] That same year, Sheldon R. Brewster, a Mormon bishop and real estate developer, presented a petition with one thousand signatures to the Salt Lake City Commission asking for an ordinance that would formally segregate Black people into a single neighborhood.[13]

In 1940, there were only 1,235 Black people residing in Utah, but that number would double by 1950 as a result of migration spurred by post-war economic opportunities. Yet, even that number, 2,729, was less than 1 percent of Utah's population. Despite these numbers, anti-Black racism was motivated by the now entrenched belief of Church leaders—most of whom had no recollection of the early years of the Church, including the ordination and inclusion of Black members—that Black people represented an undesirable and dangerous threat to the priesthood and were fundamentally, in terms of both biology and ancestry (an especially important category within Mormonism), separate from white people. For instance, concern about Black blood potentially "tainting" white blood through intermarriage was expressed by Apostle J. Reuben Clark in 1946 when he warned that the push "to break down all racial prejudice" would lead to "intermarriage."[14] Of course, Clark's stance against interracial marriage was nothing new; Church leaders had been preaching against it since at least 1863, when Young warned that the practice was punishable by death.[15]

Throughout the 1940s and well into the 1960s, high-level Church leaders consistently lent their influence to anti-Black initiatives designed to maintain segregation and to discourage further Black settlement and interracial marriage in Utah. In 1944, Clark, a member of the First Presidency—who effectively ran the Church during the latter part of both Heber J. Grant's and George Albert Smith's presidencies—endorsed local Church leaders joining "civic organization[s] whose purpose is to restrict and control negro settlement," while the next year, Clark and President Smith discussed using Mormon chapels "for meetings to prevent Negroes from becoming neighbors."[16] It was also during this decade that Clark and other Church leaders were involved in advocating for the segregation of hospital blood banks in order to prevent white Mormons from having their blood "mixed" with Black donors and therefore losing eligibility for the priesthood—a practice that lasted well into the 1970s.[17] Challenging the undisguised anti-Black racism of Church and state officials, the Salt Lake chapter of the NAACP, founded in 1919, pushed for civil rights legislation during the Utah legislature's 1945 session, which ultimately failed to pass—a pattern that would persist throughout the 1950s. Of course, white supremacy in Utah was not limited to anti-Black racism. In 1943, both Utah and Wyoming passed alien land laws, like many other western states already had, in order to prevent

those incarcerated in Japanese internment camps from settling permanently in the state after the war.[18] None of these examples is exceptional;
rather, they are testaments to the sheer ordinariness of such racism, not
just within the Church or Utah but within U.S. society generally.

Even as the Saints were strongly committed to anti-Black white supremacy, that commitment was challenged by a Black civil rights movement
that was gaining momentum. Just four months after Clark's admonition
against interracial marriage, President Truman appointed a federal Civil
Rights Commission. The commission's creation was a response both to
intensifying Black activism and to the pressures of the Cold War, which
required the United States to, at least nominally, place itself beyond Soviet
charges of racism in order to retain the nation's claim to moral superiority, functioning to help frame U.S. imperial ambition as benevolence. The
year before the commission reported its findings, a special committee of
the Utah state senate, which had been created to investigate racial discrimination in employment and was formed at the urging of the Salt Lake
NAACP, found that there was "a substantial body of unfair and discriminatory practices in the state's industry, which operates to deny minority
groups among our citizens equal right to gainful employment."[19] In December 1947, the presidential Civil Rights Commission conveyed similar national
findings and proposed several major initiatives, all of which Truman decided
to endorse when he gave an address to Congress in February 1948. In July
he signed Executive Orders 9980 and 9981, which desegregated the federal
workforce and the military, respectively.[20]

At the same time that the Black freedom movement was building up
steam in the late 1940s, directly influencing major legal and social changes
such as Truman's civil rights policy, a rising tide of anticommunism, surg-
ing postwar industrial production and consumption, and evangelical fundamentalist influence were quickly melding together to promote a distinctly
conservative, "ultranationalist Christian identity that celebrated laissez-faire
capitalism, rugged individualism, free markets, and the robust, forward-
deployed militarism that was [considered] needed to defend th[o]se freedoms."[21] This ultranationalist Christian identity, while heavily influenced by
the rising prominence of evangelical fundamentalists like Billy Graham, was
one that aligned with and was exemplified by twentieth-century Mormonism and was openly promoted by many of the Church's leaders, as described
below. Scholars have chronicled the intertwined cultural and political influence of conservative Christianity in terms of both domestic concern and

foreign policy, which increased over the course of the 1940s and 1950s, and culminated in what Sylvester Johnson calls a new "American civil religion" that deftly wed conservative Christian values to imperial ambition.[22]

As a result, the seething ideological conflict between the United States and the Soviet Union that began in the late 1940s, and that would soon boil over into a massive geopolitical realignment of the globe, was rescripted as a transhistorical battle between good and evil. Johnson explains:

> [This rescripting was] an explicit alliance of theology and empire [that] created a major advantage for the foreign policy of the US security state. Why? There now existed an explicit justification for the United States to administer satellite states and to implement murderous policies . . . in Third World countries. Moreover, this rationale had populist potency. . . . The presumptions of American civil religion—purporting that revivalist Christianization and aggressive US militarism were twin episodes of divine will—began to function as common sense. And those who opposed this imperial vision of religion seemed inexplicable, bizarre, or veritable enemies of the United States.[23]

In other words, this new civil religion justified a variety of exploitative and violent imperial strategies and tactics by portraying the populations of certain locales as (racially) unfit for self-governance without the supposedly benevolent oversight of U.S. democratic influence, just as had been done in earlier periods. Not only did this new civil religion infuse U.S. governance at its highest levels, greatly influencing both domestic and foreign policy, but the values that it promoted became embedded in mainstream U.S. culture to such an extent that they were, and often still are, not recognized as ideological but as commonsense principles. Or, as Sara Moslener explains of the early Cold War United States, "the world was thus [seen to be] divided between communists and Christians" and "a spiritual battle" was seen to be playing "out in global politics" in which opposition to certain values or criticism of the U.S. state was easily framed as seditious.[24]

In this context, critiques of U.S. racial politics were frequently regarded as communist and thus anti-American, a trend that was strong within Mormon culture between the 1940s and the 1970s. In fact, it was only two months after Truman's February 1948 civil rights speech to Congress that the *Deseret News*, the Church-owned and -operated newspaper, reported that civil rights organizing was a communist plot, contending that "'many

Negro organizations' were 'signing petitions, introducing resolutions, send-ing protests and joining delegations on matters that have been put up to them by the Communists in their midst.'"[25] This framing, exemplary of anticommunist rhetoric about the civil rights movement, not only dis-missed civil rights as a communist plot meant to divide the country, there-fore delegitimizing anti-Black racism as a serious issue with which the nation needed to deal, but it also painted Black activists as naive, ignorant, and, therefore, dangerous. In doing so, the article subtly implied that Black people, like other nonwhite peoples in locations subject to Soviet influence, were not ready for self-governance without proper guidance. Delegitimiz-ing Black antiracist activism and portraying Black people as unprepared for full citizenship would remain a consistent talking point for Church leaders well into the 1970s.

The Church's anticommunism dovetailed nicely with its commitment to white supremacy, influencing the trajectory of its postwar global mis-sionizing efforts. In 1946, a Nigerian wrote to the president of the Church's South African mission asking that missionaries be sent to Nigeria. While the request was received and actively discussed by the First Presidency, it was not acted upon until 1959 as a result of concerns about finding what was considered to be the necessary white priesthood leadership for such a potential mission.[26] Similarly, in 1947 Heber Meeks, president of the Church's Southern States Mission, was asked by the First Presidency to explore the possibility of missionizing in Cuba. When Meeks consulted his friend, Mormon sociologist Lowry Nelson, about the possibility, Nelson informed Meeks that the island's mixed racial makeup would present a challenge for Church leaders attempting to pin down converts' racial back-grounds. Given Nelson's response, which Meeks reported back to Church leadership, the decision was made not to move forward with missionary efforts in Cuba. That same year, despite the First Presidency's concerns about the racial status of potential converts, missionary work moved for-ward among mixed-race populations in Brazil, a location similar to Cuba in terms of racial heterogeneity. Interestingly, Brazil would become one of the central factors influencing the 1978 revelation lifting the Church's Black priesthood and temple bans.[27]

Upon receiving Meeks's letter, Nelson had been disturbed to hear that the Church's Black priesthood and temple bans were indeed considered doctrine, not merely an unfixed policy. He immediately wrote to the First Presidency expressing his incredulity that the Church could have such a racist doctrine. The First Presidency's response to Nelson reiterated the early twentieth-century justifications for the bans and the falsehood that Joseph Smith had originated them with a revelation.[28] Taylor G. Petrey observes that Nelson's "lack of awareness about the doctrines on race suggested that church leaders had not emphasized [them] . . . in previous decades."[29] At the very least, they had not done so in any systematic way. This seems a well-supported conclusion given that only two years later, in 1949, the Church's leadership felt the need to release a statement clearly articulating its position on the restrictions on Black people's membership.[30]

That statement declared that "the attitude of the Church with reference to Negroes remains as it has always stood," when in reality its position had only been in place for about twenty-five years. "It is not a matter of the declaration of a policy," it went on to explain, "but of direct commandment from the Lord, on which is founded the doctrine of the Church from the days of its organization, to the effect that Negroes may become members of the Church but that they are not entitled to the priesthood at the present time." The statement also formalized two justifications for the priesthood ban, citing the Curse of Cain and the notion of "the conduct of spirits in the premortal existence." Expressing satisfaction with these justifications, the letter ended with the proclamation that "there is no injustice whatsoever involved in this deprivation as to the holding of the priesthood by the Negroes."[31] In historical hindsight, it is clear that the statement was precipitated by a variety of factors including not only members' inquiries about the ban, such as Nelson's, but also the growing population of Black people in Utah and progressively visible civil rights efforts both in the state and nationally. Additionally, in 1948 two higher court decisions would have most likely concerned the Church's leaders. The Supreme Court's decision in *Shelley v. Kraemer* struck down racially restrictive housing covenants as unconstitutional under the Equal Protection Clause of the Fourteenth Amendment, while California's Supreme Court held in *Perez v. Sharp* that that state's law against interracial marriage was also prohibited for the same reason.[32] With the release of the Church's statement, it is unsurprising that the 1949 Utah legislature failed, yet again, to pass proposed civil rights legislation backed by the NAACP.[33]

The logic that allowed the Church to declare there was "no injustice whatsoever" in its Black priesthood and temple bans is evident in Apostle Mark E. Petersen's speech "Race Problems—As They Affect the Church," given at Brigham Young University (BYU) in 1954. Illustrative of the avid segregationist and antimiscegenation views held almost universally by the Church's leadership, the speech opened with an extended quote from an interview with civil rights activist Adam Clayton Powell. Petersen insisted that Powell's comments demonstrated that he was "not just seeking the opportunity of sitting down in a café where white people sit," but rather that he, and Black people generally, sought "absorption with the white race" through "intermarriage."[34] Petersen justified his blatantly racist views by appealing to the uniquely Mormon idea that a person's earthly racial identity was a symbol of their preexistent behavior:

> Is there reason then why the type of birth we receive in this life is not a reflection of our worthiness or lack of it in the pre-existent life? We must accept the justice of God. He is fair to all. . . . With that in mind, we can account in no other way for the birth of some of the children of God in darkest Afrida [sic], or in floodridden China, or among the starving hordes of India, while some of the rest of us are born in the United States? We cannot escape the conclusion that because of performance in our pre-existence some of us are born as Chinese, some as Japanese, some as Indians, some as Negroes, some as Americans, some as Latter-day Saints.[35]

Despite this Mormon-specific logic, the segregationist conclusion was the same as any number of midcentury evangelical fundamentalist preachers.[36] In addition to the preexistence theory, Petersen also justified segregation in biblical terms more common to his evangelical fundamentalist counterparts, asking rhetorically and with circular logic, "Who placed the Negroes originally in darkest Africa? Was it some man, or was it God? And when he placed them there, He segregated them. Who placed the Chinese in China? The Lord did. It was an act of segregation."[37] Petersen maintained that because God instituted and continued to command racial segregation, charges of racial prejudice against the Saints were unfairly leveled. Instead, he claimed, the mercy of God that allows Black people to accept the gospel through free agency (and, presumably, Mormon missionizing, which was a contradiction given the leadership's reluctance to proselytize in places with Black majority populations from 1908 until the late 1970s) supposedly demonstrated the Saints' fundamental humanity and racial empathy. This kind of reasoning, which displaced the realities of racial segregation onto God—as merely *racial* and not *racist* discrimination—was widely employed by conservative Christians.

Throughout the 1960s, many Mormon respondents to public charges of the Church's racism would insist that both the media and critics incorrectly stated the Church's position on Black membership, specifically that the Church's doctrine did not allow Black people to achieve the highest level of Mormon heaven, the celestial kingdom.[38] For these respondents, such claims were indicative of a bigoted anti-Mormon attitude. Yet, in Petersen's speech he explains that "if that Negro is faithful all his days, he can and will enter the Celestial Kingdom. He will go there as a servant, but he will get a Celestial resurrection."[39] Mormon respondents' accusations of anti-Mormon bigotry ignored the inherent racism built into beliefs about Black people's ability to achieve heavenly exaltation only as servants, held and proffered by the Church's leadership.

While Petersen's speech is specifically about the racial position of Black people at the bottom of a racial and ancestral hierarchy specific to Mormonism, his comments also imply a broader idea among Church leaders about an alignment between racial identity and biblical lineage: a notion that had a direct impact on Mormon expressions of racism beyond anti-Blackness. These ideas were reflected in Bruce R. McConkie's highly influential *Mormon Doctrine* published four years later, which repeated and made widely available many of the same justifications for the Church's bans.[40] Ideas about race in McConkie's book were considered "authoritative 'doctrine'" but they were in actuality an "anti-Black speculative theology supporting segregation, opposing interracial marriage, and claiming that African Americans were cursed by God and that white supremacy was God's will."[41] The formalization of this theology as doctrine helps to contextualize the prevention of the enrollment of Black students and the hiring of Black instructors at BYU in the late 1950s and up until the passage of the Civil Rights Act in 1964.[42] For example, in 1960 Ernest Wilkinson, president of BYU between 1951 and 1971, reversed a subordinate's decision to hire a Black professor, noting in his diary that "I wish we could take him on our faculty, but the danger in doing so is that students and others take license from this, and assume that there is nothing improper about mingling with the other races."[43] Church and BYU officials would refute that the exclusion of Black people on campus had ever taken place once they came under fire in the late 1960s as a result of the protests of Black student athletes.[44]

On a larger scale, Church leaders exerted their influence first to prevent and then to slow the process of desegregation in both Utah and around the nation, well into the 1960s. For instance, in 1956 the *Deseret News* published an editorial, "Extremism Is Never the Answer," which conceded that de-segregation was inevitable (and, it implied, unfortunate), but that it must be achieved only very gradually and not through the "extremism" of the civil rights movement.[45] While President McKay had approved the edito-rial, he had also ordered the deletion of a section supporting school de-segregation. This decision may seem curious since Utah schools were not segregated, but his diary entry on the subject explains that his thinking was about supporting the decision of white parents' nationally, not just in Utah, to not send their white children to a majority Black school.[46] This thinking was reflected in his 1958 denial of permission for a local Mormon chapel in Virginia to be used in support of integrated schooling efforts.[47] Similarly, a year earlier, J. Ruben Clark had encouraged Relief Society pres-ident Belle Spafford to "do what she could to keep the National Council [of Women] from going on record in favor of . . . negro equality," while in 1961 Apostle Henry D. Moyle of the First Presidency argued that the Church should persuade the U.S. Department of Defense to deploy troops to an army base in California instead of one in Tooele, Utah, because "there w[ould] be two to three hundred Negro families" residing in the state as a result.[48]

In 1959, the Utah legislature had failed to pass another NAACP-sponsored civil rights bill. Given the rising tide of the civil rights movement, it is unsurprising that the Black press reported on the failure of the bill. Both Chicago's *Daily Defender* and Cleveland's *Call and Post* reported that "all the major religious bodies, except the Mormon Church, supported the mea-sure."[49] This would become a significant pattern in the 1960s and 1970s—only publications aimed at audiences of color, especially the Black press, and a few left-leaning publications like the *Nation* and the *Christian Century* were willing to identify the Church's priesthood and temple bans as racist (even these publications sometimes were reluctant to apply the label), which the mainstream media was almost always reluctant to do, or they simply did not cover the subject at all.[50] Coverage of Mormonism in venues like the *New York Times,* the Associated Press, the *Denver Post, Life, Time,* and *News-week,* among others, were almost never willing to definitively label the Church or its policies as racist, instead using phrases like "an alleged 'rac-ist' doctrine." This pattern illustrates that while the civil rights movement did indeed shift the social acceptability of explicit expressions of racism, a widespread, deeper understanding of racism as an institutional phenome-non was not achieved but was in fact resisted. This reality is indicative of the extent to which Mormonism was firmly and widely considered to be a hypernormative U.S. religion not in spite of but because of its racism. Put another way, despite the Church's racism, the mainstream press continued to portray Mormonism as emblematic of the American dream and the Saints as the embodiment of ideal citizenship, indicating the extent to which white supremacist, anti-Black racism did not contradict but constituted these constructions.

CIVILIZATIONALLY SUPERIOR

As they had during the early decades of the century, Church leaders retained a strong interest in regulating not just racial but gender and sexual norms among its members and in U.S. society generally. As Petrey explains in his analysis of sexuality and gender in modern Mormonism, Church leaders' concern with these issues, like that of their contemporary evangelical fundamentalist counterparts, "was deeply connected to broader American postwar concerns about the status of the new American global power." Petrey and Moslener both note that postwar civilization discourse was deployed in the context of "the religious revival during this period [to] reclaim[] themes of moral purity as a key to national survival," but they fail to fully elucidate the ways that the connections drawn between communism, sexual purity, and U.S. exceptionalism were primarily about race.[51] Both anticommunism and sexual purity had, since at least the late nineteenth century, been connected to broader national concerns about racial, civilizational superiority.[52] Moreover, while sexual purity was a concept tied to evangelical (fundamentalist) Christianity beginning in the late nineteenth century, the regulation of sexual practices—and the corresponding notions of sexual normativity that regulation engendered—had been a central tool for constructing and maintaining notions of white supremacy in the United States since its inception, as the history of Mormon peculiarity discourse itself shows.[53] Thus, the convergence of anticommunism and sexual purity in the early Cold War era must be regarded as a particularly salient catalyst that sped up a transition that was already underway, evident in earlier Mormon theologizing of heteronormativity and capitalism. This transition was a move away from explicit articulations of the nation's commitment to and investment in white supremacy and, instead, increasingly articulated that commitment and investment implicitly, through concerns over sex and gender as barometers of national well-being.

Not only were midcentury Mormons "not immune to th[e] trend in conservatism to situate sexual morality and family life as the bedrock of civilization," but Mormon peculiarity discourse during this period consistently presented the Saints as hypernormative examples of the kind of nuclear, heteronormative families—characterized by gender differentiation, hard work, self-control, self-sufficiency, and wholesomeness—who purportedly embodied a truly anticommunist brand of patriotism.[54] If, as Moslener argues, "sex and national survival are the poles around which evangelicals . . . constructed an American identity, asserting their own value system to be the cornerstone of a thriving nation-state," the Saints were the ones who were presented as most successfully embodying that value system, and indeed they themselves presented it as a uniquely Mormon system.[55]

The widespread perception of Saints as hypernormative, as "higher, . . . on average than the general run of people in this country," which began to manifest in the mid-1930s, was in large part an effect of mainstream media coverage that was echoing the Church's own portrayal of itself as "perhaps the most sturdy and self-reliant religious group in existence today."[56] This trend in coverage grew stronger in the early 1940s and continued throughout the 1950s and 1960s, with mainstream media focusing on four topics as indicative of Mormon peculiarity: first, the Saints' adherence to the Word of Wisdom as evidence of their self-control and wholesomeness; second, the Saints' commitment to heteronormative family units that emphasized gender differentiation; third, the Church's promotion of industriousness, self-sufficiency, and hard work, most commonly exemplified with reference to the Church's welfare system and individual Mormons' business success; and fourth, its settler history as a paradigmatic example of how assimilation into (white) national culture and politics could lead to the achievement of the American dream.

For instance, in a 1950 *Saturday Evening Post* profile of successful Mormon businessman J. W. Marriott, with the telling title "Good Mormons Don't Go Broke," journalist Greer Williams waxed poetic on Marriott's business acumen with a focus on his "self-reliance," "inability to stop working," and efficiency and tidiness, noting that Saints like Marriott "are advised to be practical, thrifty and industrious" and that he had "learned the Mormon Word of Wisdom on cleanliness from his mother," while "his father, he figures, gave him a running start on success by assigning him man-sized chores and leaving him to work them out for himself." The article communicates not only that Marriott embodied the virtues preached by his Church and regarded by the country as fundamental to 1950s national culture but that he was taught those values in the context of a gendered division of labor. Marriott's only "peculiarity," according to Williams, seemed to be that "he drinks neither tea nor coffee, nor anything harder. Nor does he smoke." In other words, what made Marriott's Mormonism peculiar was not any negative quality but an unusual religious commitment that fostered a wholesomeness that came to be widely associated with white American-ness during the 1950s. Even Williams's brief presentation of nineteenth-century Mormon history in the article rescripted it through the rhetoric of midcentury evangelical Christian (fundamentalist) capitalism, calling the Saints' migration from Illinois to Utah "the most successful religious migration since the exodus of Moses."[57]

Perhaps the most cited article from this period is Andrew Hamilton's "Those Amazing Mormons," printed in the April 1952 edition of *Coronet* magazine, a *Reader's Digest*–style periodical. While the article is represen-tative of the positive trend that "undercut the negative image that had been central to the coverage of the Saints" in the nineteenth century, what is most telling about it is its continued reliance on peculiarity discourse to construct an image of Mormons as intriguingly American.[58] Indeed, even the subhead proclaims the Saints "'a peculiar people'— . . . vigor-ous, independent, paradoxical." Hamilton exploited this well-trod sense of Mormonism as peculiar, noting that "even devout members say . . . 'We're a peculiar people.'" Not ready to relinquish the sensationalism that came with earlier versions of Mormon peculiarity discourse, Hamilton contends throughout the piece that "what is puzzling about this made-in-America religion is its amazing contradictions." Yet, the overall tone of the piece is admiring, even laudatory.[59]

In particular, Hamilton, like Williams, recasts both Mormon and U.S. history, actually taking up a version of Mormon peculiarity discourse that the Saints themselves pushed throughout the nineteenth century by declar-ing their experiences of settler hardship exactly the kinds of racial and gen-dered experiences that were necessary for molding hardworking Americans. "Many scholars have tried to analyze the secret of Mormonism's astonish-ing growth and present-day vigor," Hamilton explained, but it could "be summed up in two words: *persecution* and *participation*." Ignoring the real-ities of settler colonialism and the ongoing exploitation and violent perse-cution of Indigenous peoples, he contended that "no other religious group in the U.S. has been hounded, vilified, slandered, and ostracized like the Mormons," even portraying Native peoples as the primary and unprovoked perpetrators of violence. These settler colonial experiences of hardship and toil, Hamilton claimed, were essential for generating the conditions that made "the Church . . . a purring dynamo" holding "title to vast quantities of real estate, while prominent churchmen serve as directors of well-known American companies." Yet "in spite of its wealth and power," he pointed out, "the Church is keenly aware of the value of independence and self-sufficiency. Hard lessons were learned when its people were threatened by Indians and rattlesnakes rather than inflation and taxes."[60]

Hamilton's mediation on the Saints' experience as agents of U.S. settler colonialism is, of course, no accident, but it repeats a contemporary narrative that framed 1950s U.S. national culture, economy, and governance as civilizationally (i.e., racially) superior, especially in relation to Native peoples. This was a narrative the Church itself would repeat as it established a variety of programs at midcentury, discussed below, designed to assimilate Indigenous peoples and instill in them the supposedly civilized values and practices they themselves had mastered. One of these so-called civilized values, or what Hamilton called "pioneer virtue[s]," was exhibited by the Saints' belief in "taking care of their own when trouble strikes." "During the depression of the 1930s," he clarified, "Church leaders were distressed by the number of members on relief. They quickly realized that government handouts were blunting initiative. In 1936 . . . they launched their unique Welfare Program, and since then it has served 225,000 persons."[61] Thus, Hamilton concluded that Mormonism was an example of U.S. exceptionalism because it had "demonstrated again the great lesson of America—that there can be diversity within unity, one faith among many, individuality within the bounds of cooperation."[62]

Hamilton's article had actually received what Shipps describes as "a devastating prepublication critique" from a Mormon reviewer whose "reservations about the article ranged from what he regarded as inaccuracies in the historical portions of the manuscript to a romanticized picture of contemporary Mormonism," yet the editors of *Coronet* moved forward with publication.[63] This decision is interesting not because it was an unusual move on the part of the editors (it was not) but rather because it illustrates how Mormon peculiarity discourse, even in its newer, more positive iteration, was still viewed as a potentially lucrative, sensationalist narrative. Press coverage of raids on a fundamentalist Mormon enclave in Short Creek,

Arizona, in 1953 could not even dampen the positive regard the media had developed for the mainstream Church. Rather, these pieces made efforts to distinguish between the fundamentalist and mainstream churches, framing polygamy in terms of the early twentieth-century preoccupation with white slavery and a focus on the fundamentalists' supposed exploitation of the dole.

Even rural Mormon life in Utah was romanticized, and not denigrated as it could have been, in a photo essay shot by Dorothea Lange and Ansel Adams, published in *Life* in September 1954. Instead, the photos and their captions linked the experience of rural Mormonism to a sense of pastoral beauty and timelessness that was being quickly overtaken by the rapid pace of industrial production and modern consumer life. Reiterating the historical narratives proffered by Williams and Hamilton, the essay portrayed the Saints as "old-fashioned," but endearingly so. No mention was made of the conflicts between the Saints and non-Mormons in the nineteenth century, nor was there any acknowledgment of the racism that continued to permeate these all-white communities.[64] Letters to the editor confirmed that both Mormon and non-Mormon readers were pleasantly impressed with the image portrayed in the essay. One reader who had made her own visit to Saint George, Utah, one of the "Mormon towns" featured in the essay, explained that she was favorably impressed with the Saints' hard work and mastery of the desert landscape—"when I thought of the toil it must take to keep that church looking as if it had just come fresh from the builders' hands, and to keep its park green in that arid land, I felt there was in that humble little Western town a spirit akin to that which in past centuries raised the great cathedrals"—rehearsing the same theme of Mormon peculiarity as emblematic of U.S. exceptionalism.[65]

Articles that framed Mormon history as indicative of "the American experience" were not the only ways that earlier versions of Mormon peculiarity discourse were recycled to construct the Saints as hypernormative. One June 1955 *New York Times* article, about a study reporting on the increased birth rate among college graduates, proclaimed that "Mormons, Averaging 3.19 Offspring in 25 Years, Lead in the Survey." The article tellingly opened with the line, "college graduates appear to be checking a trend toward race suicide" and devoted an entire section to Mormon fertility. Harkening back to Teddy Roosevelt's praise for Mormon fertility as a cure to white Anglo-Saxon race suicide at the turn of the century, the article presented midcentury Mormons as leading the charge against challenges to U.S. dominance by ensuring numerical, and therefore, implicitly, white racial supremacy. Quoting the report, the article noted that "'perhaps a real change in attitude toward children and family is also involved'" and that "the graduates of two Mormon colleges still tend to average more children than do those of Roman Catholic, Protestant, private or Government colleges."[66] Even as evangelical fundamentalists were actively promoting sexual purity and a commitment to the nuclear heteronormative family in revivals and on radio sermons across the country, the Saints were presented as outpacing them in their enactment of those values.

More significantly, those values certainly did not clash with explicit commitments to white supremacy, nor was the mainstream press willing to condemn such commitments among those who were seen to embody those values. Despite Lowry Nelson's indictment of his Church's racist policies and teachings in an article published in the *Nation* only a month after Hamilton's *Coronet* piece appeared, the mainstream press did not pick up the story.[67] Moreover, the *Nation,* as a left-of-center publication, only reached a selected audience and was coming under attack as procommunist under McCarthyism. While the publication gave space for Nelson to call out his Church's racism, it also printed a letter to the editor, written by BYU religion professor Roy W. Doxey, countering Nelson's piece and defending the Church's bans on prosegregationist grounds.[68] Given the context of early 1950s U.S. racial politics, this is unsurprising, but it is telling since it was already in the 1950s that the national mainstream media was beginning to report on anti-Black racism, presenting it as a quickly waning phenomenon, the last vestiges of which were only to be seen in the South. This portrayal of the nation's racism as regionally exceptional, confined to the South, was of course a key factor that resulted in the ultimate rejection of overt, segregationist racism, but not in a more comprehensive acceptance of racism's institutionalization in the United States.

Repeating this pattern, only a few days later, a front-page *New York Times* piece reported on a "marked decline in racial bias in the far west" based on a survey conducted by the newspaper and enthusiastically declared that "while controversy seethes about desegregation in public schools below the Mason-Dixon line, unspectacular but marked progress is being made toward elimination of racial discrimination in the West." The article portrayed this supposedly steadily improving racial climate as a result of inevitable progression toward civil rights. Reviewing the repeal of segregationist laws and the passage of various civil rights bills in the thirteen states covered in the survey, the article made no mention of civil rights activism or the opposition that such activism faced. In its review of Utah specifically, the article suggested, but did not go so far as to directly claim, that the Church's Black priesthood and temple bans were connected to the segregationist conditions in the state. After chronicling numerous examples of racial discrimination in Utah—including on the part of Church-owned entities like Hotel Utah—the article was still obliged to maintain, given its headline and generally hopeful tone, that "there has been a general informal decrease in prejudice in Utah in recent years."[69]

Like white people in Utah, the New York Times willfully ignored, or simply did not care to review, the abundance of evidence chronicling the terrible civil rights situation in the state. In 1953, for instance, Wallace R. Bennett published a report in the Utah Law Review relating the entrenched anti-Black segregation that dominated recreation and public accommodation, employment, housing, marriage, and other areas of life in the state.[70] Similarly, in 1954, W. Miller Barbour, a field director for the National Urban League, had published a report in Frontier magazine asserting that racism in rural sections of some western states, including Utah, was as bad as the South.[71] These reports would not have been hard to obtain, nor would the relationship between the racist teachings of Church leaders and the general attitudes of lay Saints have been hard to ascertain.

When examined in the context of the era's racial politics, not only in terms of the Supreme Court's decision in Brown v. Board of Education (1954) but in terms of early anticommunism's convergence with conservative Christianity's—including the Church's—concern about gender's and sexuality's connections to national well-being, Mormon peculiarity emerges as a primary discourse of midcentury white supremacy.[72] The four-point focus in media coverage of the Saints' adherence to the Word of Wisdom, the importance of the heteronormative family unit in Mormonism, the Church's promotion of attributes associated with capitalist individualism, and the Church's settler past as indicative of the Saints' achievement of the American dream was reflected in explicitly and tightly regulated public relations campaigns that the Church began to launch in the late 1950s. Once leaders realized the intertwined value of public relations as a way to control the Church's image and promote conversion to the faith system, an entire public relations department was created in 1957.[73]

While the complimentary coverage of the Church and its members continued in 1956 and 1957 with stories that portrayed the Saints as "a stouthearted Christian people" and Utah as a "model state, leading the other forty-seven in a number of ways," such coverage reached new levels in the last two years of the decade with the involvement of the Church's public relations department.[74] In 1958, two major stories, one published in *Look* magazine and the other in the *Saturday Evening Post,* were encouraged and helped along by employees of the newly minted Church Information Service.[75] Hartzell Spence's fourteen-page article for *Look* provided a thorough and largely affirmative overview of the Church and its members, complete with color illustrations and photographs. The article only retained a few notes of nineteenth-century Mormon peculiarity discourse—for example, referring to the Saints as living "rather clannishly in close-knit communities" such that many "Mormons have difficulty in breaking away or nonconforming."[76] Yet, these notes were hardly recognizable to an audience that prized conformity and other valued attributes that were apparently exemplified by the Saints.

As with Williams's and Hamilton's pieces earlier in the decade, Spence empahsized the Church as "a thoroughly American institution" by describing its gendered pedagogy ("for the boys, there are sports, Boy Scouting and hobby instructions; for the girls, dramatics, music, homemaking and preparation for the role of mother of a maximum family"), hyperbolizing about its welfare plan ("No Mormon ever has to go hungry. . . . The Church Welfare Program, for example, raises, stores and distributes staggering quanities of food for needy Mormons everywhere"), and reframing nineteenth-century Mormon settler colonalism as exemplarly of U.S. exceptionalism ("The 30 years from 1847 to 1877 qualify Brigham Young for the distinction of being one of the great colonizers of all time").[77] Significantly, Spence downplayed the Church's history of polygamy as "highly exaggerated" and its racial doctrines as almost unimportant.[78] The piece must have pleased the Church by promoting a notion of Mormon peculiarity that was in line with the Saints' own understanding of their distinctiveness and place in the nation: "At times, its members have been labeled a 'strange people,' but they are not strange. They are different, yes, but the right to be different is the essence of the American dream. . . . The followers of Joseph Smith and Brigham Young have assimilated," Spence declared.[79]

Wedding Mormon peculiarity to the achievement of the American dream as a manifestation of U.S. exceptionalism, Spence's piece was complemented by Frank J. Taylor's coverage of the Church's Welfare Program later that year in the *Saturday Evening Post*. As with almost all articles about the program from the 1930s onward, Taylor's coverage emphasized the hard work, industriousness, and self-sufficiency of the Saints, repeating the false but oft-cited claim that "without calling on relief agencies" the Saints "rolled up their sleeves and worked their way out of hard times."[80] Echoing the notion that "one of the present peculiarities of the Mormons is that they do not go on public relief rolls when hardship descends," an article in the *New York Times* observed that, while in the nineteenth century when the Saints were called "peculiar" "it was a term of derision and led to persecution"; by midcentury, calling a Mormon "odd" or "peculiar" was done with a tone "of respect."[81] Although the Church's program was certainly successful, claims that no Saints utilized federal relief were untrue, yet they nonetheless helped to undermine federal welfare programs in an anticommunist climate that emphasized, and framed success or failure as a product of, individual responsibility, not wealth inequality or structural racism.

Amid this glowing coverage, in 1958 the Utah State Advisory Committee to the U.S. Commission on Civil Rights published a report connecting racist segregation in Utah to the Church's priesthood and temple bans. Describing the committee's scathing report on the generally deplorable state of racist discrimination in Utah, *Time* informed readers that "widely accepted statements by [Mormon] leaders in years past, has led to the view among many Mormon adherents that birth into any race other than white is a result of inferior performance in pre-earth life, and that by righteous living dark-skinned races may again become 'white and delightsome.'"[82] Published in the same period as the *Look, Saturday Evening Post,* and the *New York Times* laudatory articles, *Time's* piece also coincided with the release of the Mormon Tabernacle Choir's hit rendition of "Battle Hymn of the Republic." The choir's version of the song, Brooks argues, would by the early 1960s seal "the association between Mormonism, religious 'wholesomeness,' and Cold War patriotism."[83] *Time's* report on the Church's racial politics was certainly overshadowed by the vast majority of media coverage that overwhelmingly regarded Mormonism as a religion to be admired and emulated.

TEACHING AND POLICING ASSIMILATION

The creation of the Church's public relations department—which furiously championed an image of the Saints as exemplars of the heteronormative nuclear family unit whose members personified the values of the nation's new civil religion—was paralleled by Church leaders' increasing concerns with both lay members' sexually sinful behavior and assimilating Indigenous peoples into white American culture, concerns that were reflected in the broader society. Thus, it was in the late 1940s and early 1950s that the Church began to take not only a more active interest in policing non-normative sexual practices and identities, homosexuality specifically, but in actively addressing what the Saints viewed as their "prophetic responsibility to elevate American Indians to their former status as members of the House of Israel."[84] While at first glance these dual concerns appear unrelated both to one another and the ongoing transition from explicit to implicit expressions of white supremacy, they were in fact deeply intertwined as expressions of both Mormon and U.S. investment in a racially implicit sense of civilizational superiority.

As Mark Rifkin explains, invocations of "civilization" at midcentury were indicative of "the ongoing enmeshment of discourses of sexuality in the project of fortifying the United States against incursions by uncivilized formations that jeopardize the 'common sense' of national life." But "while homosexuality may serve as the most prominent foil" for the metaphor of the heteronormative, nuclear family unit as a stand-in for a dominant, capitalist nation-state, there is "a more multivalent history of heteronormativity in which alternative configurations of home, family, and political collectivity are represented as endangering the state." More specifically, "the effort to *civilize* American Indians and the attendant repudiation of indigenous traditions," he argues, should certainly be understood as a significant component of the "institutionalization of the 'heterosexual imaginary' . . . helping to build a network of interlocking state-sanctioned policies and ideologies that positioned monogamous heterocouplehood and the privatized single-family household as the official national ideal."[85]

Viewing the discourses of sexuality that communicated midcentury concern about civilizational dominance not just from the perspective of the hetero/homo binary but from the perspective of ongoing settler colonial capitalism helps to illuminate the significance of, and the relationship between, the projects taken on by Church leaders during this period. In 1947, Apostle Spencer W. Kimball, future Church president whose revelation would end the Church's Black priesthood and temple bans in 1978, received a special assignment to deal with cases of sexual sin among Church members, including those related to fornication, adultery, and homosexuality. It was also that year that Kimball began to develop the framework for a

program that would eventually become the Church's Indian Student Placement Program (ISPP) in 1954, the same year that Apostle Mark Petersen—
who would later become Kimball's assigned partner in addressing sexual
sin—gave his "Race Problems" speech.[86]

The First Presidency's 1947 decision to assign Kimball the responsibility
of dealing with cases of sexual sin marked a significant transition from
earlier eras. Before Kimball, Apostle Charles A. Callis had dealt with such
cases quietly, but over the course of the first half of the century the Church's
theological focus on gender differentiation and heteronormativity had been
steadily incubating.[87] By the mid-1950s, that incubation period had produced a full-blown phobia of homosexuality on the part of Church leaders
as one of the most profound problems facing both the Church and U.S.
society.[88] This was, of course, not a unique development but was in fact
connected to the broader social panic around sexual purity's relationship
to civilizational health that helped to both produce and fuel McCarthyism
and specifically the Lavender Scare's attention to "homosexual" government workers' purported vulnerability to potential communist blackmail
schemes.[89]

Within the Mormon corridor, the 1955–57 Boys of Boise scandal rocked
local and Mormon communities with the knowledge that "a widespread
homosexual underworld that involved some of Boise's most prominent
men," some of whom were Mormon, "had preyed on hundreds of teen-
age boys for the past decade."[90] Such reporting, both locally and nationally,
was not only sensationalistic but unsubstantiated, as John Gerassi shows
in his book-length investigation of the scandal published in 1965; yet, it was
typical rhetoric for the Lavender Scare and the fear that permeated U.S.
and Mormon society at the time. As a result, during the 1950s and early
1960s, both the Church and Utah began implementing initiatives to identify,
police, discipline, and increasingly "treat" homosexuality. These initiatives
were also grounded in contemporary Mormon theology like McConkie's
Mormon Doctrine, which, in addition to interracial marriage, condemned
sodomy, onanism, and homosexuality. Public anxiety about the Boys of
Boise scandal specifically, and the Lavender Scare generally, coalesced with
the hiring of ardent anticommunist Mormon W. Cleon Skousen as the head
of the Salt Lake City police department in 1956 to produce a generally homophobic and sex-negative climate in the city.[91] Skousen, who was a former
BYU professor and assistant to FBI director J. Edgar Hoover, embodied the
Cold War conservative Christian ethos of the nation's new civil religion,

evident in speeches where he discussed "the breakdown in many of the fundamental American concepts which are based on spiritual values."[92] Soon after being hired, Skousen instigated a push to catch and imprison "sexual deviates" and "moral perverts," using surveillance and entrapment to identify gay men at local bars.[93]

Using similar tactics, Ernest Wilkinson, BYU's president during this period, simultaneously began to make concerted efforts to identify, through surveillance and interviews, "homosexuals" on campus, as part of a series of actions taken that year by Church leaders meant to deal with their increasing concerns about homosexuality.[94] More specifically, Church leaders, led by Kimball, developed an extensive "religio-psychological framework," between the late 1950s and the 1970s, for interpreting homosexuality as a sin and, in turn, providing pastoral counseling as a "cure."[95] By the early 1960s, the study and practice of aversion therapy, including electrical shock therapy, began at BYU and would last into the early 1980s.[96] By 1962, BYU instituted a formal policy of not admitting to the school any student who they had "convincing evidence [wa]s a homosexual."[97] By 1975, the school would actively pursue, with the help of the SLPD, the expulsion of all "homosexual" students.[98]

This increased concern with homosexuality among Church leaders was the result of a variety of factors, including the Lavender Scare and the explosion in scientific and political attention to homosexuality, and it was also probably in reaction to the publication of Allen Drury's best-selling political thriller *Advise and Consent,* which was made into a film starring Henry Fonda in 1962.[99] The plot featured a storyline in which a Utah senator, Brig Anderson, is exposed as having had a clandestine wartime same-sex sexual relationship. Petrey implies that Church leaders may have been concerned with Mormonism's public image, given thinly veiled implications in both the book and the film that Anderson was Mormon.[100] Yet, Petrey's interpretation does not necessarily square with the general image that the public had of the Church and its members at this time. While Church leaders may have been concerned with how the book would reflect on the Church's sexual morals, given U.S. society's past criticism of polygamy, it seems more likely that they were genuinely concerned that Brig Anderson's character reflected a reality in both Mormon and U.S. society that they felt had to be confronted head-on: the susceptibility of white men to homosexuality as a threat to national and civilizational superiority—a threat heightened by its depiction on screen.

In response, Kimball, as a primary developer of the Church's religio-psychological framework for dealing with homosexuality, took a "preventive approach to [sexual] sin with strict moral guidelines" and an emphasis "on the proper roles of men and women."[101] This reflected a broader societal interest in monitoring, regulating, and policing changing gendered and sexual behavior as indicative of civilizational (i.e., racial and national) breakdown. With Apostle Harold B. Lee's appointment as head of the Priesthood Correlation Committee in 1960—the same man who had become director of the Church Welfare Program in 1932 and who was "one of the most outspoken opponents of civil rights among McKay's advisors," evidenced in his warning to Wilkinson, the same year of his appointment to head the Correlation Committee, that "if a granddaughter of mine should ever go to the BYU and become engaged to a colored boy there, I would hold you responsible"—came concerted efforts to "ensure that the proper household patriarchal order would be carried out . . . and that gender roles would be maintained."[102] But for Lee and most of the Church's leadership, the proper household patriarchal order was not only heteronormative, it was white.

As Petrey cogently illustrates, over the course of the 1960s Lee's efforts to centralize administrative power, decision-making, and finances resulted in the weakening of women's authority in the Church, largely through the curtailment of the Relief Society's independence, the implementation of initiatives designed to "strengthen the home" and patriarchal power (such as programs like Family Home Evening), and increasing urgency to emphasize and teach gender differentiation as the best protection against sexual deviance.[103] Of course, these efforts were made possible by the fact that Church leaders had been theologizing gender differentiation and heteronormativity for at least sixty years. Lee's efforts as head of the Correlation Committee were also paralleled by ongoing Mormon teachings that intermarriage was to be avoided because God had created a system of racial segregation that humans were commanded to maintain.[104]

Reflecting the general importance of patriarchal gender roles in Mormon theology, Kimball applied a similar approach of emphasizing those roles as indicative of "advanced" civilization in his work concerning the conversion of Indigenous people. The ISPP and other similar Church programs, such as those at BYU, focused on providing "civilizing" education meant to assimilate Indigenous youth into white American culture, with an emphasis on gendered norms and roles.[105] This approach was evident in the ISPP's drive to house and educate Native children in Mormon homes in order to "save" them from their "primitive" culture, "living in 'poverty, . . . filth and . . . indolence and ignorance,'" by "'teach[ing] them the gospel and hopefully to win them from their "Indian" ways to where they would become completely like'" white Saints.[106] One of these so-called Indian ways was the false notion that Native women were more promiscuous than white women. A Mormon woman, Myrtle Hatch, remembered hearing her fellow Relief Society members comment at one meeting, "'Don't let your daughters hang around with Claude Hatch's girls. Their mother is an Indian, and you know how those Indian kids are. They get pregnant. They'll lead them astray. They're not whole people; they're half.'"[107] These comments reveal not only that some Saints' attitudes toward Native peoples were based on racial stereotypes of laziness and hypersexuality, among others, but that they did not even regard Indigenous people as fully human.[108] Of course, both Mormons' and non-Mormons' racist views of Native people were also a product of a century and a half of federal policy that produced extreme poverty and cultural corrosion, conditions that had long been attributed to their supposed savagery.

These long-standing, racist notions of savagery influenced much of twentieth-century Mormon and federal Indian policy. In fact, Church leaders and Mormon politicians (including the architect of federal termination policy, Senator Arthur V. Watkins; Ute tribal attorney John S. Boyden, who wrote the Ute Partition Act that terminated about a third of that tribe's members; H. Rex Lee, a high-level bureaucrat in the Bureau of Indian Affairs; and, Wilkinson, BYU president and Ute tribal claims attorney) universally supported termination and relocation based on the idea that "federal guardianship over Indian assets fostered dependency."[109] These policies aligned perfectly with Mormon views of Native groups as a "people in a fallen state," therefore resulting in the consistent devaluation and dismissal of "the intrinsic legitimacy of Indigenous cultures" between the 1940s and well into the 1980s.[110]

While Mormon historians frequently portray Kimball as a great supporter of and advocate for Indigenous people in the Church, it is critical to note that his support was based on a fundamentally racist premise that Native peoples were racially "redeemable," a religious concept frequently paired with the idea that Native persons who did convert would not just symbolically but also physically become "white and delightsome" as the Book of Mormon promised.[111] Moreover, the view that Indigenous people's

skin and circumstance reflected the poor decisions of their ancestors and
their preexistent spirits, as Petersen had indicated in his 1954 speech, was
reflected in Kimball's view that "the Lord's hand" was evident in "the limited opportunities that the Navajo faced" after World War II. In Kimball's
mind "through the Navajo's deprivation, the Lord was 'bringing the Lamanites back to us,'" as many Navajo people were forced to engage in itinerant
farm work on Mormon-owned farms as well as in other kinds of migrant
or seasonal labor. In short, Kimball viewed these circumstances as providence, "a 'great opportunity' for missionary work" provided by God.[112]

Kimball firmly believed that Native people would be able to achieve
assimilation into white cultural standards with the appropriate educational
opportunities. Thus, he developed, fostered, and encouraged the adoption of the ISPP. The basic structure of the program opened volunteer
Mormon homes to foster Native children between the ages of six and eigh-
teen during the nine months of the school year, while during the summer
months the children lived with their families. In the first few years of the
program's official existence, starting in 1954, Native parents complained
that their children were subject to mass unapproved baptisms, which were
indeed being performed, and that the program had severe effects on the
participants' sense of Native cultural and familial belonging.[113] In 1958, the
Church shifted the program to target only Native peoples who were already
baptized in the Church and thus raised the minimum age for participation
from six to eight.[114]

Despite the concerns of Native parents and governments, the program
continued and was regularly praised by the press as a creditable effort to
"civilize" Indigenous peoples. While such coverage was perhaps incredulous
about the scripture upon which the Saints' views of Indigenous people
was based, it was not critical of the Book of Mormon's racial politics.
For example, in an article reporting on the recent opening of a temple in
New Zealand and the organization of the Church's first stake outside the
United States in 1958, *Time* explained that Mormon "missionaries find an
ancient kinship with the Pacific's brown-skinned peoples in a passage from
the Book of Mormon." Rather than taking issue with the notion that "the
white-skinned, 'delightsome' members of the Israelite tribe of Lehi gr[e]w
quarrelsome and sinful after arriving in America from Israel," causing
them to "turn dark-skinned and 'loathsome,' thereby producing the American Indians," who many Mormons assumed were the ancestors of Pacific
Islanders, the article presents these ideas as curious but not particularly

problematic. Indeed, the article notes that "Mormon missionaries from Hawaii to New Zealand . . . give thousands of natives hope that they may once again become 'white and delightsome'" and quotes New Zealand Mormon President Ariel S. Ballif's telling assertion that "'as they take up the righteous way of living, they become more attractive and acceptable to white people and lose their dark skin.'"[115]

Ballif's comment indicates that Kimball's belief, that conversion would not just symbolically turn Indigenous people's skin white but would literally do so, was not his alone and was quite widespread among Church leaders. Even more significantly, his comment demonstrates that conversion was contingent upon assimilation into and practice of white cultural values, including those related to "heterocouplehood and the privatized single-family household as the official national ideal."[116] Another article in *Time* published in 1959 played on the Book of Mormon phrase "white and delightsome." The article, entitled "Red & Delightsome," praised the ISPP as an efficacious "experiment in interracial living and education" that "successfully bridged the two civilizations." Describing the program through the eyes of the Mormon foster parents and Church officials who ran it, the article presented the ISPP as a commendable charitable program that "rescued" Native children from "primitive" conditions. Reiterating popular ideas about individual responsibility under conditions of equal opportunity, Margaret Keller, head of the program, explained, "'The Indian youngsters are just like all our children; some succeed, some don't. But the important thing is that they be given an opportunity to succeed.'"[117] While the article did note that the ISPP was "hailed by Mormons as living rebuttal of the charge that they discriminate against races whose skins are not what the Book of Mormon calls 'white and delightsome,'" the author in no way refuted that interpretation of the program. In fact, both the Church and the press pointed to the Church's programs for Native people to counter charges, which became more prevalent in the 1960s, that the Church was racist.[118]

In September 1960, the most complimentary article on the ISPP appeared in the *Saturday Evening Post*. The author concluded that "the Mormon Church's unique educational and sociological experiment has demonstrated again—if proof is needed—that peoples of different racial and cultural backgrounds can live together harmoniously." Indicative of the generally patronizing and racist cultural attitudes toward Native peoples at the time, Hamilton unselfconsciously quoted President McKay's declaration that

"'Brigham Young gave us the key more than a century ago. . . . He said, 'It is better to feed the Indians than fight them'" as evidence of the Church's charitable humanity.[119] Peppered with suggestions that Indigenous peoples were culturally deficient and needed to be guided through the process of assimilation, Hamilton reported that the program was "well accepted by the Indians" and that he could find no evidence of discrimination, backing up white Mormons' own claims that they were not racist.[120] This conclusion ignored the fact that many who participated did so "because they considered placement 'the least immediately painful solution' to financial difficulties and limited educational choices" on reservations and that "while many Indian parents voluntarily signed consent forms . . . that d[id] not negate the power dynamic between Indian parents and LDS officials."[121]

Hamilton even went so far as to state there was no truth to the rumors circulating early in the program's history that "Indian children were being torn from their families, that they were treated as slaves, [and] that the program was nothing but a Mormon scheme to gain new converts," despite the fact that Church officials were indeed performing mass baptisms and that the primary impetus for the program was to "redeem the Lamanites."[122] Moreover, Hamilton's claim that "the Mormons have wisely encouraged their foster Indian children to retain a pride in native language and customs" is contradicted by historical evidence that both program officials and foster families generally discouraged foster students from speaking their native languages, practicing their native customs, and visiting their families in order to ensure assimilation into white culture.[123] For example, one program official, in a letter to parents, discouraged visiting over the winter break, stating, "'I hope you will not do this. Most of the time it is not good for you or your child. . . . As you know *no* student is allowed to go home for any reason during the school year and children should not be kept away from their foster families for more than a few hours and definitely not overnight.'"[124] The connection between the Church's programs targeting Native conversion and assimilation and its interest in teaching and promoting gender differentiation and heterosexuality among its members is illuminated by the fact that both were praised for the same reasons by the mainstream media. In other words, both were seen as evidence of the Church's and the Saints' civilizational and, therefore, national credentials as hypernormative exemplars of the nation's new civil religion.

As the civil rights movement gained momentum and grabbed national attention in the 1960s, and other social and political justice movements gained traction, the mainstream press would continue to rely on the trope of Mormon hypernormativity in order to interpret these increasingly fraught national conflicts. Continuing to render Mormonism as an exemplar of U.S. citizenship and exceptionalism—despite its continued commitment to overt, institutionalized racism, demonstrated most potently in its Black priesthood and temple bans and colonialist programs targeting Native peoples—proved to be a powerful tool that precipitated a rhetorical rejection of overt expressions of white supremacy while maintaining institutionalized forms of racism that were rebranded through the narratives of equal opportunity and the American dream over the course of the 1960s and 1970s.

6 Making Mormon Peculiarity Colorblind, 1960–1982

"Elsewhere they burn the flag or the ROTC building," one university official remarked. "Here we are expanding our ROTC, and everybody stands and faces the flag when the national anthem is played mornings and evenings." The reason Brigham Young is different is that it is run by the Church of Jesus Christ of Latter-day Saints (Mormons) and conforms to Church policies. . . . The discipline of their religion affects almost every university activity. . . . The young people at BYU were all clean-cut, good-looking. There was no beatnik atmosphere. . . . Instead of finding fault, they were accepting leadership.

—"No Flag-Burning at Brigham Young,"
   U.S. News and World Report

Blacks can more easily appreciate the honesty of the Church of the Latter Day Saints when compared with the subtle, unconscious, rhetorical forms of discrimination usually directed at them, for what Mormons claim is basically honest and true. At least in America, because of the color of his skin, the direct descendants of Ham are indeed, a cursed people.

—Diane Perry, "Race Bias Bans Blacks
   from Heaven"

By the late 1950s, Mormon peculiarity discourse had firmly constructed Mormonism as a "thoroughly American" religion, citing what was characterized as the Saints' hypernormative commitment to values and practices that were regarded as elemental to patriotic citizenship in the early Cold War era. As the civil rights movement gained momentum in the early 1960s, the Church's Black priesthood and temple bans also acquired increased media attention as prominent Mormons, George Romney in particular, walked onto the national political stage. It is frequently assumed that this increased attention to the Church's bans had a detrimental impact on non-Mormon perceptions of Mormonism, accomplishing a retreat to nineteenth- and early twentieth-century portrayals of the Saints as problematically, and irrevocably, out of step with the nation's social and political sensibilities, especially given Church leaders' refusal to overturn the bans before 1978. This chapter challenges this assumption, revealing it to be an example of the fundamentally flawed but common understanding of racism in the twentieth-century United States as characterized by an ongoing, progressive evolution toward equality and colorblindness.

As numerous scholars illustrate, there has been no neat history of racial progress in the United States, no clear or total transformation from overt to embedded racism; rather, an examination of the nation's racial past and present reveals a much more complex and rhizomic reality in which racism is manifested simultaneously in both explicit and colorblind ways, progress and retrenchment ebbing and flowing throughout the nation's history.[1] While explicit manifestations of racism were previously accepted and expected, the social and geopolitical changes brought on by World War II, both internally and externally, fueled the burgeoning civil rights movement and, over the course of the 1950s and 1960s, resulted in shifting social mores that made it less and less acceptable to express explicitly racist views. Yet this decline in the social acceptability of explicit racism was mirrored by an increase in implicit racist expressions, practices, and policies in U.S. society and politics, most famously exemplified by the southern and suburban strategies.[2]

As one of only a handful of conservative Christian institutions, and certainly the largest, to retain explicitly racist policies, in the form of bans on Black men's priesthood ordination and Black participation in certain temple rites—well past the height of the Black freedom movement—the Church's racial politics simultaneously served as what Joanna Brooks calls "a spectacle of innocence that normalized anti-Black racism as unremarkable of a 'wholesome' morality" and as a foil against which the nation could establish its supposedly nonracist or postracist (i.e., colorblind) credentials.[3] Thus, this chapter, in conjunction with the preceding one, argues that Mormon peculiarity discourse was deployed in the service of constructing white racial innocence, as well as delegitimizing antiracist activism between the 1940s and the early 1980s. This argument not only challenges common colloquial and historical assumptions that Mormons were more racist than their non-Mormon counterparts, assumptions that some scholars of Mormonism have taken pains to disprove, but also confronts the equally problematic assumption that evidence showing the similar racial views shared by white Mormons and white non-Mormons is, in turn, verification of the Saints' relative racial tolerance.[4]

By following the trajectory of Mormon peculiarity discourse in relation to the social and political movements of the 1950s, 1960s, and 1970s, this chapter elucidates the links between the reassertion of white racial innocence and the growing dominance of colorblind racism to anxiety about the demonization of, and resistance to, changing gender norms, nonnormative sexual subcultures, and feminism. The overwhelmingly complimentary and admiring response from mainstream media and non-Mormon white people to the Church as a socially and politically conservative institution—which reflected, promoted, and embodied the ideals of Cold War–era conservatism, including a shift in focus from explicit racial segregation to emphasizing so-called family values (i.e., patriarchal gender binarism, antifeminism, and heteronormativity)—not despite but regardless of its explicitly racist priesthood and temple bans (and sometimes even because of its resistance to public pressure to reverse those bans) provides a particularly valuable vantage point from which to examine how colorblindness became the paradigm through which white supremacy was reasserted through articulations of U.S. exceptionalism.

In other words, this chapter embarks on an analysis of Mormon peculiarity discourse between the 1960s and the early 1980s, revealing it to be an important driver in the evolution of white supremacy's survival as a fundamental component of U.S. nationalism and imperial policy during the Black freedom movement's transition from a focus on civil rights to a focus on Black power and the rise of various other social justice movements during the later Cold War era. Examining how Mormon peculiarity discourse functioned as an important means through which the nation-state retained its investment in white supremacy—transitioning from emphasizing claims of biological racial hierarchy and segregation, to those of cultural superiority, assimilation, and equal opportunity (in short, to the language and rhetoric of colorblindness)—provides a necessary historical background for

understanding how twenty-first-century biopolitical governance in and by
the United States proceeds through the supposedly "race neutral" categories of heteronormative neoliberal capitalism.[5]

A WHOLESOME, PATRIOTIC, AND HARDWORKING RACISM

The trend of laudatory media coverage of Mormonism, which had developed between the mid-1930s and the 1950s, continued over the course of
the 1960s, almost always emphasizing Mormonism as hypernormative.[6]
For instance, in 1962 the *New York Times* insisted that "no other religious
group in America 'lives' its religion with such emphasis" and that visitors
come "away from Utah with the conclusion that the primary virtues which
made the nation what it is are [t]here more honored than in most regions
of America."[7] Similarly, *Time*'s assessment was that "more than most religious believers, Mormons seem to keep busy seeking perfection from the
cradle to the grave," while in 1966 *U.S. News and World Report* informed
readers that "since 1940, Mormons have tripled membership at home and
abroad," because Mormonism is not just a religion but "also 'a way of
life.'"[8] Media emphasis on Mormonism's fundamental Americanness continued throughout the decade and into the next, even today remaining one
of the most dominant forms of Mormon peculiarity discourse.

At the same time that Mormonism continued to be presented as hypernormative, several developments ensured that increased attention would
be paid to the Church's racial policies as well. Just as the civil rights movement gained widespread attention and achieved various successes—making
it increasingly socially unacceptable to openly hold and promote racist
views—George Romney's success in the car industry morphed into political aspirations for the Michigan governorship, bringing further press attention to Mormonism. Even as the press began to report on the civil rights
situation in Utah and its connection to the Church, mainstream outlets
generally lauded Romney and added to his wholesome reputation, calling
him, as head of the American Motors Corporation, "a sort of Johnny Apple-
seed of the auto industry," asserting that "his religion explains that too-
good-to-be-true quality which irritates scoffers."[9]

Mainstream press profiles of Romney in the 1960s tended either to not
mention his Church's racial policies or to do so in such a way that downplayed them and played up both Mormonism and Romney as hypernormative. For instance, *Life*'s profile declared:

[Mormons] are sturdy and proud folk, the Romney's with roots in the pioneering and evangelizing Mormon past. George Romney embodies family traditions that would bolster any statesman—enterprise, daring, service to church and community, loyalty to convictions.[10]

Avoiding any suggestion that the Church's racism might be a negative influence on Romney, the article instead claimed that "the deep influence of the emphasis that Mormon church places on fundamental value and individual self-reliance shows in George Romney's beliefs."[11] Indeed, Romney's successful rise to head a major corporation was typically presented as entirely a result of his own initiative, supposedly even more impressive given his start as the grandson of a polygamist in Mexico. Romney served as an individual example of how Mormonism had risen above its polygamous past to achieve greatness through individual Saints' commitments to faith, family, and hard work.

Nonetheless, coverage of his campaigns did elicit curiosity about, but not disdain for, his Church's racial policies. In a complimentary profile of Romney from 1962, for example, *Time* noted that "around Michigan . . . the word was being spread that the Mormon Church looks on Negroes as an inferior race, cursed by God," but it quickly transitioned to Romney's own civil rights record, explaining that "he has been outspoken in his opposition to segregation and prejudice."[12] Similarly, the *Saturday Evening Post* noted the Church's racial policies as a potential stumbling block for Romney's campaign but, as in the *Life* profile, repeated Romney's statement that he had "'always opposed discrimination and favored civil rights' and that he can prove it."[13] Indeed, Romney, was able to consistently fend off charges of racism by pointing to his own civil rights record, a tactic the mainstream press (and sometimes even the Black and left-leaning press) accepted and endorsed.

This tactic rested upon two key premises, which foreshadowed the late 1960s and early 1970s transition to colorblind racism during the Nixon administration, under which Romney served as Secretary of Housing and Urban Development. First, Romney differentiated between his Church's policies and his own views and actions related to civil rights. In the *Time* profile, for instance, he explained that "'I believe that the real issue—if there is to be an issue—is what George Romney feels about bias and discrimination against the Negro. No one can point to any word, act or attitude on my

part that involved discrimination or discriminatory feelings.'"[14] His contention that he was not himself racist was premised upon no one being
able to "point to any word, act or attitude" that was explicitly racist. In
other words, he did not actively promote segregationist ideas or policies.
Yet, the policies he promoted and implemented as both Michigan's governor and U.S. Secretary of Housing and Urban Development were certainly
racist in that they rested on premises of what Ibram X. Kendi calls assimilationist racism, which identifies racial inequity as a consequence of personal failings directly resulting from the inferior cultural standards of the
racial group to which one belongs.[15]

Second, Romney differentiated between the Church's Black priesthood
and temple bans and its general teachings about civil rights. He maintained
on more than one occasion that he would not belong to any religion that
would require him to support civil (as opposed to religious) segregationist
policies. For instance, one *Christian Century* piece, titled "Book of Mormon
Enters Politics," noted that Romney declared "his record on race matters
is clear (as indeed it is) and that he would allow no dogma of his church to
interfere with his political responsibilities."[16] As a liberal Protestant publication, the *Christian Century* was generally critical of Mormonism and the
Church's racism, yet in this instance the magazine accepted such a distinction, rhetorically asking, "Must candidates for high office in the U.S.
either be secularists or deny some of their church's ultimate teachings?"[17]
Similarly, *Life* declared Romney "at his best" while campaigning for the
U.S. presidency in 1967 as he explained, "'If my church prevented me as
a public official from doing those things for social justice that I thought
right . . . I would quit the church. But it does not.'"[18] In a preview of early
twenty-first-century racial discourse, Romney also repeated his Church's
increasingly prevalent line that the institution's policies were not actually
discriminatory, a line that the Black media, but certainly not mainstream
media, consistently challenged.[19]

In the early 1960s, Black press coverage on both sides of the political
spectrum did not mince words in calling out Mormon racism. For example, conservative commentator George S. Schuyler referred to Mormonism as a "cult" and concisely explained that "the Mormons are mum about
[civil rights] because they don't believe in any of it. All they have ever wanted
is to be left alone, being sure of taking care of themselves. . . . They are
bigoted but basic."[20] A 1962 article in the *Call and Post* explained how "by
reason of their numerical strength, the Mormons elect most of the public

officials throughout the state," and therefore "in most instances those elected public officials adhere to their religious doctrines and beliefs . . . and refuse to employ or appoint any Negroes in any position of authority or trust."[21] Another piece, in Chicago's *Daily Defender,* similarly noted that "despite the claims of Romney and other prominent Mormons including Interior Secretary Stewart Udall that Mormons do not practice racial hatred, actual studies of racial patterns in Utah contradict their claims."[22]

The Church's leadership resented the media's attention to its Black priesthood and temple bans and met criticism, blunted as it generally was in the mainstream, with incredulity and charges of hypocrisy. On July 14, 1962, just over a week before the Mormon Tabernacle Choir appeared on a "US government-backed propaganda . . . special filmed at Mount Rushmore and broadcast in Europe via satellite," Joseph Fielding Smith responded to such criticism in the *Deseret News,* asking, "Why should the so-called Christian denominations complain? How many Negroes have been placed as ministers over white congregations in the so-called Christian denominations?"[23] The segregation of U.S. Christianity was certainly not on the minds of most white readers when, a mere three days before the choir's televised appearance, *Time* featured a story about "a group of prosperous-looking" Mormons who gathered early one morning to volunteer their time in constructing a local chapel building. Among them were Utah's governor George Dewey Clyde and Apostle Henry D. Moyle, "an oil company millionaire."[24] *Time*'s clearly admiring attitude toward their ethic of hard work, community commitment, and faith, despite their "high-salaried" careers "as lawyers, bankers, doctors, and businessmen," was supplemented by the choir's July 23 television appearance dedicated to demonstrating the hegemony of U.S. culture and nationalism.[25]

Jan Shipps argues that, while print media's attention to the Church's racial policies during the period between 1962 and 1974 was significant and increasingly critical, it was "usually overlooked in radio and television broadcasts." Instead, throughout this period radio and television "featured all sorts of images of Mormons as neat, modest, virtuous, family-loving, conservative, and patriotic people."[26] Brooks takes Shipps's important observation about broadcast media a step further, arguing that the Church's racial policies were not just being overlooked but that "White American audiences openly *embraced* the most visible public emissaries of an officially racially segregated faith . . . the Mormon Tabernacle Choir," and beginning in the early 1970s the Osmonds, the popular Mormon family pop group.

Both the choir and the Osmonds "enacted a spectacle of innocence that normalized anti-Black racism as an unremarkable element of a 'wholesome' morality."[27] Of course, the choir had been performing this kind of racialized and gendered work since at least the 1893 World's Fair. But in the 1960s and 1970s, the choir's image as emblematic of wholesome, patriotic, hardworking Mormonism merged with a variety of other discursive signs to construct the Saints as hypernormative, at first because of, but increasingly despite, the Church's open racism.[28]

The choir, like other portrayals of Mormon hypernormativity, "offered a patriotism defined by willed obliviousness to contemporary political struggles, especially to the thorny moral responsibility entailed in institutional racism."[29] However, it was not just a "willed obliviousness" that allowed white Americans to embrace Mormonism and hold it up as paradigmatic of the nation. A closer discursive analysis of print media's increasingly critical stance on the Church's racial policies is required. Such an analysis illustrates that during the period between 1962 and 1974, while attention to the Church's racial bans did indeed increase, it was not necessarily backed by a widespread social rejection of anti-Black racism on the part of the Church, or any other entity for that matter. Rather, what U.S. society was rejecting in its attention to the Church's racial policies was the explicitly racist form those policies took.

In 1963, the Church experienced a significant shift in its public stance on civil rights, largely as a result of more direct tactics on the part of Black activists in Utah and the resulting intervention of liberal Mormons Sterling McMurrin, a philosophy professor at the University of Utah who served as U.S. Commissioner of Education under President Kennedy between 1961 and 1962, and Apostle Hugh B. Brown, a liberal and outspoken supporter of civil rights who was called to serve in the First Presidency in 1961. Brown would remain the sole tempering voice in the Church's highest leadership body, contrasting sharply and often publicly with figures like the far-right Apostle Ezra Taft Benson of the Quorum of the Twelve and future Church president. McMurrin and Brown were among a small group of high-profile Saints who dissented from the racist views of the majority of the Church's leadership and who publicly threw their support behind civil rights activists. Yet, the voices of people like McMurrin and Brown were certainly overshadowed by the weight and power of the Church's predominantly segregationist hierarchy. In fact, members of the Quorum of the Twelve and the First Presidency not only attempted, but ultimately failed, to excommunicate McMurrin in the late 1960s but also successfully pushed Brown out of the First Presidency after McKay's death in 1970.[30]

In June 1963, Brown gave an unauthorized interview to Wallace Turner, a correspondent with the *New York Times* who regularly covered the Church in the 1960s and who would publish an exposé, *The Mormon Establishment,* in 1966.[31] The article, "Mormons Consider Ending Bar on Full Membership for Negro," blindsided McKay and the rest of the Church hierarchy. As Gregory A. Prince and Wm. Robert Wright document, McKay had only two days earlier determined that "'we shall make no concession to the NAACP. They are trying to take advantage of this situation to make the Church yield equality.'"[32] In his diary, McKay reiterated his segregationist stance by declaring his opposition to laws that would "make the Hotel men violators of the law if they refuse to provide accommodations for a negro when their hotels are filled with white people, or restaurant men made violators when they decline to serve colored people."[33] In contrast, the *New York Times* declared that the Church was "seriously considering the abandonment of its historic policy of discrimination against Negroes" based on Brown's statement that the hierarchy was "'in the midst of a survey looking toward the possibility of admitting Negroes.'"[34]

The rumors spurred by the article were further fueled by two other events. First was Governor Romney's appearance at the head of an anti-segregation march in the suburb of Grosse Point, Michigan, during which he commented that "'there is an excessive amount of discrimination in housing.'"[35] The other event was the appearance of an incendiary article in *Look,* written by a young Mormon Jeff Nye. Nye's piece insisted that the Church taught racial inequality, and in it he systematically reviewed the Church's instruction on the subject and the scriptures upon which that instruction rested. Confirming what activists and some journalists had long maintained, Nye asserted that the Church's policy gave "Mormons a God-sanctioned reason for feeling superior to the Negro. This is where the Mormon question about the Negro merges into the larger question of racial prejudice. . . . The Mormon's Negro doctrine reinforces the ignorance of most Mormons about Negroes."[36] But what was perhaps most notable about Nye's piece was not actually its content but the comment the magazine elicited from Apostle Joseph Fielding Smith in response. After insisting that "the Mormon Church does not believe, nor does it teach, that the Negro is an inferior being," he concluded by saying, "'Darkies' are wonderful people, and they have their place in our Church."[37] Unsurprisingly, this racist and tone-deaf comment was reprinted repeatedly by the press as evidence that the Church's leadership did not understand, or simply willfully ignored, the links between segregationist policies, racial inequity, and racial animosity.

While Brown's rogue interview had angered his colleagues, it also helped to spur action by activists who were already frustrated by the Church's lack of support for civil rights. The NAACP informed the First Presidency, after being denied a meeting to discuss the fact that Utah was the only western state not yet to have passed any significant civil rights legislation, that they planned to picket both the Church's October general conference and its missionary headquarters around the country.[38] Given his association with the NAACP and his membership in the Church, McMurrin mediated between the two groups. The two parties agreed that the NAACP would not picket if Brown would read a statement in support of civil rights at conference. Brown asked McMurrin to write the statement and, after it was approved by McKay, delivered it on October 6.[39]

The statement indicated that the Church had "no doctrine, belief, or practice that is intended to deny the enjoyment of full civil rights by any person regardless of race, color, or creed" and implored "all men everywhere, both within and outside the Church, to commit themselves to the establishment of full civil equality for all of God's children."[40] While the statement was intended by both McMurrin and Brown to be strongly supportive of civil rights, the increasingly vehement insistence of other Church leaders that the bans did not actually constitute racist discrimination— exemplified by Joseph Fielding Smith's comments for *Look*—helped to undercut that intention.[41] The fact that such a claim was considered valid by a significant portion of the country's population indicates the extent to which common understandings of what racist discrimination actually constituted was, and would remain, incredibly murky, setting the stage for a colorblind interpretation of racism to emerge full force in the early 1970s.

In a review of the tumult over the Church's stance, *Time* fell back on Mormon peculiarity discourse to interpret the events of 1963. "'The Peculiar People,' as Mormons call themselves," *Time* declared, "have often found that their peculiar doctrines put them at odds with their fellow citizens. . . . Today, the problem is the Mormon attitude toward the Negro." Yet, nothing in the article definitively identified the Church's bans as racist. Instead, the article explained that while "non-Mormons are prone to infer from this that Mormons are segregationists," the "church replies that it has a right to set the qualifications of its own priesthood, and that excluding Negroes is no more discriminatory than the refusal of many churches (including the Mormons) to ordain women."[42] While the bans themselves, the documented teachings of Church leaders, and de facto segregation in Mormon communities all testified to the fact that the Church was a white supremacist, segregationist institution, *Time* was still reluctant to present it as such, instead falling back on a "both sides" mentality in the presentation of the cultural contest over the Church's racial policies. The article even reiterated the common perception that "Mormons make almost ideal citizens," who were "wholesome, industrious and thrifty, devoted to social welfare and higher education," and then went on to present the bans as mere curiosities of the religion's belief system. The Saints "are unsympathetic toward the Negro, largely as a consequence of the strange church doctrines," the piece concluded.[43] These "strange" doctrines, racist or not, did not stop the Mormon Tabernacle Choir from receiving invitations to perform at the funeral of President Kennedy or President Johnson's 1965 inauguration.

In a December 1963 speech, before his departure to a mission in Europe, Apostle Ezra Taft Benson warned listeners that the civil rights movement was "'fomented almost entirely by the communists'" and that "the pending 'civil rights' legislation" was "about 10 per cent civil rights and 90 per cent a further extension of socialistic federal controls."[44] He even went so far as to say that Americans could "no longer resist the Communist conspiracy as free citizens but can resist the Communist tyranny only by themselves becoming conspirators against established government."[45] A clear reflection of the politics he shared with Robert Welch, founder of the John Birch society, Benson's comments were also a thinly veiled counterpoint to Brown's pro–civil rights statement. While Mormons like McMurrin and Brown advocated for the Church's support of civil rights, Benson just as vehemently warned against the Black freedom movement as not only illegitimate but a dangerous threat to the nation, echoing earlier Church statements from the late 1940s.

George Romney's January remarks at a Republican campaign event in Salt Lake City contrasted sharply with Benson's. While Romney spoke in favor of civil rights, he also warned against the far-right wing of the party, which Benson certainly represented, contending that if the party "'mounts a white horse and carries a white standard into the . . . campaign, it may win an election but it will lose forever its claim to Lincoln.'"[46] These kinds of skirmishes between prominent Church officials, the passage of the Civil Rights Act in July 1964, and the continued activism of the Utah chapters of the NAACP kept the Church's racial policies in the national news throughout the mid-1960s.[47] President McKay's remarks at the dedication of a temple in November further fueled confusion about the Church's stance when he insisted that the Black bans would not be lifted during his lifetime, nor anyone else's at the press conference.[48]

In early 1965, the NAACP once again threatened to picket the Church, but this time it followed through after the Church would not agree to publicly support civil rights legislation that was pending in the Utah legislature. The NAACP's recruitment of Roy Jefferson, a Black football star who had played for the University of Utah and who had just been chosen for the Pittsburgh Steelers, to participate in the protest foreshadowed the importance of Black student athletes in bringing increased pressure to the Church between 1968 and 1970. Jefferson attested to the difficulty he had finding housing in Salt Lake City due to racial prejudice just as the legislature was contemplating the passage of fair housing and employment laws.[49] In response, unlike what McMurrin and Brown had originally intended, the Church used Brown's 1963 conference statement to respond to the protests by printing it in the *Deseret News* and designating it an "official" Church statement that they claimed made the hierarchy's position clear. Doing so allowed the Church to claim support for civil rights without actively engaging in any supportive actions at the same time that leaders continued to "quietly" support segregation.[50]

This "quiet" support was reported on in September 1965 by *Christian Century* journalist Glen W. Davidson, who described how local Mormon leaders preached in support of segregated housing in California, while local Utah "bishops and stake presidents openly preached against [civil rights legislation]—on 'theological grounds,' but always in the vocabulary of the militant anticommunist sects."[51] Benson had further stoked tensions when he reiterated his condemnation of the civil rights movement during the April 1965 conference.[52] Encouraging the Saints to oppose the civil rights movement, he asked, "'When are we going to wake up? What do you know about the dangerous civil rights agitation in Mississippi? Do you fear the destruction of all vestiges of state government?'"[53] In fact, Davidson's reporting suggested Benson's reasoning and language, specifically the implicit racist language of anticommunism to oppose civil rights, was being replicated by lower-level Church leaders in Utah and California and likely elsewhere. Davidson also reported that the segregationist positions of the Church were producing an "influx of die-hard segregationists" into the faith.[54] One such convert Davidson interviewed complained that she was "'fed up with being told by some preacher that these n*gras are equal to me,'" while missionaries were reporting that "there has never been more interest in Mormonism and that 'our race doctrine is of the greatest interest.'"[55]

Increasingly in the mid- to late 1960s, as the achievements of the civil rights movement became cemented in the national consciousness and explicit racism was no longer deemed acceptable, the national press began to frame the Church's bans through Mormon peculiarity discourse in one of two ways: by continuing to downplay them in favor of admiring the Church's "wholesome" and "patriotic" qualities or as an unfortunate, backward doctrine that was a remnant of the religion's deleterious past but not a reason to denounce the faith. The first method is evident in a September 1966 *U.S. News and World Report* piece that acknowledged, "once again [this] unique faith . . . is moving into the spotlight," but barely discussed the reasons for that movement. Rather, the article focused on the "peculiar" characteristics typically associated with the Saints, especially their hard work and wholesomeness.[56] Indicative of the second method, the *Denver Post* contended that the "Mormons are . . . prisoners of their history, in the sense that they have inherited . . . a number of doctrines that set them apart from normative Christianity and stamp them in the minds of many as a peculiar sect" and identified the Church's views on Blackness as the most "embarrassing" of these doctrines.[57] However, for the mainstream media, what was regarded as the Church's "backwardness" was not irredeemable; on the contrary, it was entirely fixable since what was considered backward was not the underlying white supremacy of the institution, which just as fundamentally continued to characterize the nation itself, but was rather the explicitly racist form that the Church's bans took.

Despite the relatively benign criticism of the Church's racial politics in the mid-1960s, Church leaders continued to be disturbed and angered by charges of racism. In his study of the Mormon image during this period, J. B. Haws asserts that "Mormons had good reason to be worried about the 'racist' label."[58] Citing the work of Mormon sociologist Armand Mauss, who contemporaneously examined "several late-1960s opinion studies that 'Mormons could not be considered outside the national consensus in their external civic attitudes toward African Americans'" and that "'Mormon ethnic attitudes' were *not* 'at variance with ethnic attitudes in the "general" culture,'" Haws overlooks the overwhelming evidence that sharing racial attitudes with the general (white) culture did not equate with the Saints holding antiracist attitudes. His contention that the "study implied that religious belief, not racism, drove most Mormons' opinions about the prospects of blacks being admitted to the priesthood" evidences a willful obliviousness, to use Brooks's phrase, about both the nation's and the Church's history of white supremacy.[59] What is significant about the fact that Mormons were no more and no less racist than their non-Mormon counterparts is that this fact helps to explain the relatively toothless criticism of the Church, which predominated in mainstream media, by illuminating how the expression of explicitly segregationist ideas, and not necessarily all racist policies, especially assimilationist, colorblind ones, were at issue.

Indeed, Benson's extreme anticommunist speeches, another of which he made at the October 1967 general conference, illustrate how the transition to colorblindness, which allowed the distinction between explicitly segregationist ideas and assimilationist racist policies to function practically, was achieved. His warnings against the civil rights movement as a communist plot portrayed Black people as naive and susceptible to dangerous anti-American influence without directly stating, and instead implying, their racial inferiority as incompetent citizens incapable of rationale thought.[60] The not-so-subtle racial implications of Benson's remarks are evident in the fact that he provided the foreword to the 1967 tract *The Black Hammer: A Study of Black Power, Red Influence, and White Alternatives,* written by Wes Andrews and Clyde Dalton. This occurred at the same time that various political factions were reportedly trying to encourage Benson to run for the U.S. presidency with Strom Thurmond as his running mate, and that George Wallace was considering Benson as his vice presidential choice.[61]

Thus, even as the Church and, by extension, Romney, as a result of his membership in the institution, came under renewed scrutiny during the 1967–68 presidential campaign, both continued to enjoy a generally wholesome reputation.[62] Of course, Romney's appeal directly connected to his embodiment of the qualities associated with Mormonism—mainly industriousness, family-oriented faith, and patriotism, all of which were implicitly racialized as white and male. Romney's appeal was often frustrating for his opponents since "the appearance of the man, the impression he gives, the earnestness, sincerity and just plain goodness which Romney fairly exudes, are vital assets," the *Saturday Evening Post* explained.[63] Romney's strong morality was demonstrated in his passionate earnestness about "the decline in family life" or the "'decline in moral and religious commitment,'" which one opponent characterized as "'like running against God.'"[64] If Romney was considered "an intensely moral man" and "his religion [wa]s the key to the man," then Mormonism, despite what most of the mainstream press viewed as its supposedly idiosyncratic stance on race, was certainly not being dismissed as immoral by a society continuing to grapple with the realities of white supremacist anti-Black racism. "Mormonism," remained "the most 'American' of all religions" despite its continued explicit commitment to that racism—a commitment that both the Saints themselves and (white) U.S. society generally would not concede.[65]

BOYCOTTING BYU

Romney's withdrawal from the presidential race in February 1968 had nothing to do with his Mormonism; rather, it was the result of an unscripted comment about the Vietnam War that tanked support for his candidacy.[66] The fervor over the Church's racial politics may have then died down if it were not for a precipitous rise in Black student athlete activism around the country. Generally, Mormon historians have identified this activism as primarily aimed at BYU and, as time wore on, the Church itself, citing the infamous Wyoming 14 or Black 14 incident that occurred in October 1969 as exemplary of the boycotts that characterized the 1968–69 and 1969–70 seasons. This activism was part of a broader trend in the late 1960s of Black athletes, many of them college students, engaging in coordinated actions to bring attention to the ongoing anti-Black racism of U.S. society, and higher education in particular, even after the passage of federal civil rights legislation.[67]

The links between these protests and BYU are evident when one examines their roots in the activism of Olympic track stars Tommie Smith and John Carlos, who both attended San Jose State University, one of the first schools to boycott competition with BYU. Famous for their Black power salute protest during their medal ceremony at the October 1968 Mexico City Olympics, Smith and Carlos were part of a year-long effort to organize a Black boycott of the 1968 games, with the help of their sociology professor Harry Edwards. As they attempted to organize the boycott, called the Olympic Project for Human Rights, throughout 1967, the athletes and their mentor received national press coverage that was predominately disparaging. Indeed, Douglas Hartmann explains that "White sportswriters and reporters across the country condemned the boycott initiative and all athletically-based protest from the beginning and almost universally, as did leaders and elites within the athletic establishment."[68] These protests were designed to combat the view of Black athletes, who were becoming more numerous and prominent in the late 1960s, as "symbols of the openness of American race relations" and in turn being "used to legitimate the racial status quo."[69] Recognizing the context of a broader social drive in the late 1960s to call for an end to the Black freedom movement, and especially Black power activism, because of a sense that "the race problem" had been "solved" by federal civil rights legislation helps to explain the tepid condemnation of Mormon racism during this same period.

An exclusive focus on the boycotts aimed at BYU between 1968 and 1970 paints a misleading portrait of the perception of Mormonism during these years. In contrast, Haws asks us to consider if "anti-BYU activity simply blend[ed] into the larger national scene of widespread campus protests" and therefore that "the impact of the negative publicity against BYU [was] thus blunted?"[70] Analysis of contemporary press coverage suggests that this is indeed the case when both the larger context of Black athlete activism in the late 1960s and the generally complimentary press coverage of Mormonism between the 1930s and the 1970s—despite the moderated criticisms of the Church's racial bans—is taken into account. A close examination of the content of the protest coverage during this period also illustrates that while the protests helped maintain a focus on the Church and its racial policies, this focus was not paired with a deeper criticism of those policies or of the societal racism that was reflected in university conditions that athletes were protesting. In fact, non-Mormons were relatively sympathetic to both the universities' punitive response to players' protests and the Church's defenses against the protesters' criticism of its policies.

This pattern is evident from the very first protest against BYU in the spring of 1968, when, just a week after Dr. Martin Luther King Jr. was assassinated and only a few days after the Civil Rights Act of 1968 was signed into law, eight Black members of the University of Texas at El Paso track team announced they would boycott an upcoming meet with "the Mormon-operated BYU" because it "believes 'that the blacks are inferior and that we are disciples of the devil.'"[71] As a result of their action, the players were kicked off the team and lost their scholarships.[72] The Church responded by claiming that the protest was staged by "some extremists who have gotten the wrong idea of what the church position is."[73] Reflecting the same rhetoric Benson used in his anticommunist speeches, the Church's response sought to delegitimize the athletes' actions through reference to their extremity and by claiming they misunderstood the Church's policies altogether. While the Church did not formally teach the idea that Black people were "disciples of the devil," a lay myth to that effect did circulate within Mormon society. Formal responses that focused on that discrepancy missed the point of the athletes' protests.

By 1968, the Church's claim that it did not believe in or promote the inferiority of Black people was widely accepted in mainstream media and would appear in most of its responses to athlete protests of BYU. While BYU had started to allow the attendance of Black students—Church leaders' concerns about the prospect of interracial dating and marriage not withstanding—and occasionally recruited a few Black athletes, the number of Black students on the campus was minute.[74] This became a sticking point for Black activists and, by extension, the Western Athletic Conference of which BYU was a part. In November, another boycott of BYU by Black players on the San Jose State University football team made headlines when some of the team's white players threatened to quit if the Black players were not punished. In response, Black players on the track and basketball teams vowed to give up their scholarships if the Black football players lost theirs as a result of their boycott.[75]

Although the most intense spate of Black student athlete protests against BYU had yet to occur, by January 1969 the press began to present laudatory profiles of BYU, countering and distracting from activists' claims that the campus reflected the Church's racism. *U.S. News and World Report* informed its readers that "no 'hippies,' miniskirts or riots make the scene at Brigham Young University. The Mormon school is an oasis of calm amidst campus turmoil. Its secret: high standards, strict discipline," where students "are unusually hard-working and devout," implying that student activism like that of Black college athletes was merely a whim of whiny, undisciplined, lazy extremists.[76] In doing so, the article presented Mormonism's peculiarity, in this case symbolized by BYU, as hypernormative:

It's a different kind of university. . . . At a time when students everywhere seem to be on the warpath, Brigham Young University is undisturbed. It has never had a serious demonstration. There are no "hippies" here. Everybody dresses up to go to class. Beards are a rarity and you don't see any miniskirts.

There is no smoking on campus. Rules against drinking include not only alcohol but even tea and coffee. "Elsewhere they burn the flag or the ROTC building," one university official remarked. "Here we are expanding our ROTC, and everybody stands and faces the flag when the national anthem is played mornings and evenings." The reason Brigham Young is different is that it is run by the Church of Jesus Christ of Latter-day Saints (Mormons) and conforms to Church policies. . . . The discipline of their religion affects almost every university activity. . . . "The young people at BYU were all clean-cut, good-looking. There was no beatnik atmosphere. . . . Instead of finding fault, they were accepting leadership."[77]

Such reporting repeated the typical tropes of midcentury Mormon peculiarity discourse to construct Mormonism as the model of wholesome, white, capitalist nationalism specifically in the context of and in contrast to anti–Vietnam War and civil rights college campus protests.

By the spring of 1969, the number of anti-BYU protests increased exponentially. In February, students boycotted a BYU–University of New Mexico basketball game, while in March University of Texas at El Paso students pushed for an investigation into charges of racism at BYU, which was denied by the University of Texas at El Paso administration.[78] Later in the season, both California State College at Hayward and Stanford canceled athletic events with BYU, while the Riverside Baseball Tournament informed BYU it would not be invited back in 1970 because of potential "racial unrest."[79] Yet it is clear from exchanges between administrators at these various institutions that the unwillingness to engage BYU in competition was motivated not by any sense of conscience but by a desire to avoid negative press.[80] In other words, without the efforts of Black student athletes, racism on campus—any campus—would not have been addressed by administration or the press.

The most well-known incident related to Black student athlete activism occurred in October 1969, when fourteen Black players on the University of Wyoming football team walked into their coach's office in order to ask permission to wear armbands in protest during their upcoming game with BYU. Before the players had a chance to deliver their request, Coach Lloyd W. Eaton, upon seeing their armbands, rescinded the players' scholarships and kicked them off the team.[81] Scholars have generally identified the Wyoming incident as different from previous actions because up to that point most of the protests had targeted BYU specifically, while the student

activists at Wyoming directly targeted the Church itself, calling its policies "inhuman and racist."[82] But the Wyoming situation was also different because, as part of a broader action organized by the Black Student
Alliance at the school, the students were up against a much more conservative and openly racist environment in Laramie.[83] The protests elicited
responses from everyone, including the student activists, the athletes, the
NAACP, both schools' administrations, Wyoming's faculty senate, Wyoming
alumni, and even Wyoming's governor. The incident also elicited much
public debate, evident in editorials and letters to the editors of various newspapers, which focused on whether Eaton's dismissal of the players was warranted, as opposed to the legitimacy of the athlete activists' grievances.[84]

These responses from the public illustrate that white tolerance for the
athletes' protest was extremely low, generally not affording them any belief
in their sincerity, legitimacy, or agency. For example, one editorial in the
Denver Post, with the tagline "BYU Has Right to Policies," contended that
"the most disturbing thing about it all" was "that the 14 Negro players
involved are not making up their own minds, but being used as a cats-paw
by the same kind of movement that would use the athletic field as a sociology laboratory," and accused the students of being subject to "extrem-
ist" activist scholar Harry Edward.[85] In his letter to the editor three days
later, W. Daley contended that the *Post*'s editorial had not been harsh enough
on the athletes, who, in his view, were "proposing a restriction on a civil
right of a minority group, i.e., the freedom of religion of the followers
of the Mormon Church." A fact he accused the author of "completely
ignor[ing]."[86]

The freedom of religion argument was frequently deployed by Church
leaders as a result of the athlete protests against BYU and the Church, and
also quickly became widely accepted—another indication of how weak
the public's condemnation of the Church's racial policies up to that point
had really been. Even editorials that somewhat sympathized with the athletes ultimately came down on the side of Eaton, citing his authority to
make decisions about students' ability to participate in protests on campus or the field.[87] One University of Denver professor's satire of Eaton's
position was the exception that proved the rule.[88] Continued references
to the "calm" on BYU's campus served to further create the illusion that
the protests were merely meant to stir up trouble as opposed to address
pressing social issues. For instance, one article described the situation by
contrasting "the winds of dissent swirl[ing] through the West" with "the

BYU campus" as "an eye of quiet. No protests—just thousands of young Mormons pursuing learning in a homey central Utah town. 'There's no prejudice here,' says Floyd Millett, BYU athletic director. 'It seems so un-justified.'"[89] Millett's statement belied the very real climate of racist prej-udice and institutionalized racist discrimination at BYU and in Mormon society generally. Another article presented a similar narrative describing how "racial demonstrations aimed at BYU have occurred with increasing frequency at other schools over the past year, while the BYU campus itself remained as serene as the mountains which surround it."[90]

Mormon responses to the protesters' charges of racism were increas-ingly likely to cite the presence of "Jews, Indians, Spanish-Americans and two Negroes among BYU's 24,000 students" as evidence that the school did not practice racist discrimination.[91] These numbers were meant to prove the institution's tolerance without having to address and transform the anti-Black segregationist views of most of its administration, faculty, and students or the racist, assimilationist logic that drove the university to have nonwhite students on its campus in the first place.[92] While some articles documented evidence of such racist discrimination on campus, that evi-dence was never labeled as such by journalists. But the racist attitudes of many Mormons were evident in letters to the editor about the Wyoming controversy, such as one man's statement addressed directly to Black people: "God is the one who created you with a black skin and not the Mormons. So don't try to blame us for the 'curse' that was placed upon you."[93]

Spurred by the coverage of the Wyoming controversy, student activists at several schools pushed the Western Athletic Conference to expel BYU from the conference. One BYU faculty member retaliated by asserting, "'If we're racist because we only have half a dozen Negroes, then other schools are racist because they don't have enough Indians.'"[94] Attempting to deflect attention away from the charges against the university, this BYU instructor falsely equated admitting students of color as proof of a lack of racism on campus. Indeed, "at the time, BYU" frequently "claimed to have the largest university enrollment of American Indians in the United States, with approximately 600 on campus."[95] This claim belied the racist ideas that underlay programs for Indigenous students at BYU, which had grown out of the Church's assimilationist Indian Student Placement Program, discussed in chapter 5. Although BYU had created the Institute of Ameri-can Indian Studies and Research in 1960, administrators had "little con-cern for tribal needs or the cultural moorings of Native students."[96] Their

pedagogical approach, lacking any "inclusion or awareness of the culturally specific needs of Native students," instead "defined Indian 'success
in terms of becoming successful, like other students on campus. Indian
students would be integrated into the mainstream'" and given the chance
to be "'free to fail.'"[97] Some defenses of the Church even went so far as
to deny the Saints had ever practiced any kind of racist discrimination
at all.[98]

In November, the controversy reached new levels when both Stanford
and the University of Washington announced they would no longer compete with BYU. Stanford's statement declared that it was its policy "not to
schedule events with institutions which practice discrimination on a basis
of race or national origin, or which are affiliated with or sponsored by
institutions which do so."[99] BYU's president, Ernest Wilkinson, who had
been instrumental in maintaining anti-Black racial segregation on campus
up until the passage of the Civil Rights Act of 1964 and who, like his superiors, continued to preach against interracial marriage while upholding the
Church's Black bans, crafted a hard-hitting response that centralized the
Saints' right to freedom of belief and denied that BYU practiced racist discrimination. The response took Stanford's president "to task for dropping
BYU for alleged discriminatory practices when in fact BYU's 'compliance
with the Civil Rights Act [had] been certified by the Department of Health,
Education, and Welfare.'" Moreover, the statement said that BYU "fully
agreed with the Stanford standard" and that if "Stanford could not reason-
ably have severed ties with BYU over discriminatory *practices,* the break
must have been because of the religious *beliefs* of the LDS Church."[100]

Simultaneously, both BYU and the Church were instituting several public relations measures meant to quell the widespread criticism of its racial
policies that the activists' protests had instigated. For example, only two
days after Stanford announced it would no longer compete with BYU, the
Mormon school reportedly "rolled out the red carpet . . . for a black leader
from Los Angeles[,] Phil Watson," who was invited to speak on campus.[101]
And in December, the Mormon Tabernacle Choir appointed its first Black
member. By the end of January, the group would have a total of three Black
singers. BYU also began to actively recruit Black players for its teams.[102]
These measures, BYU's retaliatory statement, the context of (at best) luke-
warm disapproval of the Church's racist policies, and a generally negative
response to Black athlete protests nationwide meant that most mainstream
press coverage, and even some of BYU's competitors, actually sided with

the Saints or, at the very least, did not fully dismiss or discount the Church as racist but rather as "anachronistic" in its explicitly racist policies.

In his review of the "rising militancy among black athletes" at colleges around the country, Anthony Ripley described, on the front page of the *New York Times,* Black student athlete activists as "gambling their principles against their education." Not in the least approving, Ripley asserted that their activism included "an element of self-destruction" that had and would continue to lead "to dismissals and a cutback in recruiting," stymieing the one chance "many blacks from poor families [had at] a college education[,] a football scholarship."[103] Rather than question what structural factors restricted poor Black students to football scholarships, Ripley's analysis paradoxically blamed the athletes for potentially restricting their already limited access to college, thereby dismissing their activism as illegitimate and unwise. Later in the article, Ripley quoted a college administrator who repeated the idea that Black activists were mere pawns subject to the political machinations of others, in this case "white liberals."

This latter accusation was repeated in at least two *Denver Post* editorials, which also continued to deny that the Church's racial bans were discriminatory, and an editorial for the *National Collegiate Athletic Association News.* One of the *Post* editorials even went so far as to claim that "Mormon Church teaching is that a white priesthood must serve the Negro temporarily: perhaps this is because the Negro was forced to serve others for so long," while the *NCAA News* editorial, according to the *Post,* insisted that college athletes' protests were part of a "revolutionary" conspiracy. The NCAA editorial also claimed, as reported by the *Post,* that "evidence is clear that there is operating in this country a hard-core revolutionary force designed to destroy the present governmental and educational system," yet the *Post,* reporting on the NCAA editorial's claims, did not assess what that evidence was.[104] Similarly, a piece in Stanford's student paper, reporting on the controversy caused by the university's decision to end athletic competition with BYU, quoted Dudley Swim, president of the school's alumni association, who insisted that Stanford "should be 'learning' from BYU" because "'at BYU, unlike so many schools, happily campus life does not embrace chainwalking to far left bigotry, homage to alien ideologies, disrespect for the American flag, arrogant, traitorous flaunting of enemy flags, championing of drug use, dedication to debauchery, and physical violence.'"[105]

As with Ripley's article, which disapprovingly reviewed the general state of Black athlete student activism, most articles, editorials, and letters to the editor about the Wyoming 14 incident barely referenced the Church and its racial policies, shifting the focus to the legitimacy of the protests themselves.[106] Those that did focus on the Church's racial policies repeated tropes of Mormon hypernormativity and attributed the institution's racial policies to its peculiarity. For example, another *New York Times* piece declared that "it's hard to imagine a more typically American religion" because "the faith was born on the frontier [and] tells the story of the American Indian in its Scriptures."[107] The author explained:

> For many onlookers, the dispute is extraordinary, not so much as a racial confrontation, but because the church's position seems so wildly anachronistic. How in this age can any American institution with nearly three million members (some 200 of them Negroes) raise second class citizenship to the level of principle?[108]

The author's question illustrates that what was at issue was not racial conflict, or even the practice of racist discrimination—that was as American as apple pie—but the Church's explicitly racist policy.[109] No mainstream venues challenged these perspectives, and the Black press alone was left to challenge them, and the Church's bans, as racist.[110]

Given the protests, press coverage, and controversy, in December 1969 the Church's First Presidency decided to send a letter reiterating its racial doctrine to local leaders. The letter, which compared historical Mormon experiences of oppression with experiences of anti-Black racism, emphasized its support for civil rights, religious freedom, and the role of divine revelation in its racial bans. Originally intended only for internal circulation among Church leaders, the letter was soon leaked to the press.[111] But neither this reiteration of its racist policies nor ongoing protests in the spring of 1970 dampened public support for the Church. Despite a few pointed pieces in *Newsweek, Time,* the *New York Times,* and *Sports Illustrated* that did come close to identifying the Church's bans as racist but did not actually do so, mainstream coverage of the Church was quite generous.[112]

Indeed, Haws observes that "the initial explosiveness of the protests" quickly died down after the 1969–70 season. "Part of that change was due to growing public distaste for the protest movement" but most importantly was because of "growing public ambivalence about the need for continued emphasis on racial issues after the seeming success of the civil rights legislation of the 1960s."[113] This "growing distaste" and the public sense of having definitively "dealt" with racism were not simply reasons the public moved its attention away from the Church's racial bans, but they were effects of tactics the Church and other conservative figures and institutions were using to challenge mainstream coverage of and conversation about institutionalized racism. In leveraging perceptions of Mormon hypernormativity, Church leaders and lay members alike had successfully countered Black student athlete protests by discrediting them as indicative of society's growing immorality, laziness, and anti-Americanism (exemplary of the era's newfound colorblind rhetoric) and by altogether denying charges of institutionalized racism within the Church despite its continued commitment to the anti-Black priesthood and temple bans. An article in the *Tucson Daily Citizen* reflected white society's unwillingness to hold BYU to account given that it concluded BYU, and by extension Mormonism, was "no more racist than any other university" or religion.[114]

By 1971, the same year the Osmonds began to enjoy unprecedented success and were extending the "willed obliviousness" of white innocence into the 1970s, the press was back to printing laudatory pieces about high-profile Saints.[115] For instance, *Forbes* featured an implicitly racialized article about J. W. Marriott, insisting that "if you're one of those cynics who doubt that a combination of native shrewdness, hard work, a good product and dedicated employees is still a viable American success formula, you won't believe this story. But it's true, nevertheless."[116] "The unity and success of the Marriott family," the article insisted, was "a testimonial to the unity and thriving success of Mormonism" as well as the virtues of "bee-like thrift and industry," which "the largest strongest, and certainly the richest made-in-America faith" promotes.[117] Articles such as those covering one of the Mormon Tabernacle Choir's first Black members, who insisted that the Church was not racist, and the lack of mainstream press coverage of other accusations of Mormon racism—such as the complaints filed against the Intermountain Indian School in Brigham City, Utah, by Navajo students alleging that not only did the "predominantly Mormon staff . . . discourage[] the practice of native Navajo religions in favor of the Mormon religion," but students were subject to "neglect," "brutality," "physical abuse," and "drugging"—supplemented the willed obliviousness of white readers and the wholesome reputation of the Church.[118]

MORMON OPPOSITION TO THE ERA AND THE
RISE OF COLORBLIND FAMILY VALUES

In January 1970, in the midst of Black student athlete protests, an article in the conservative evangelical *Christianity Today* evinced the ongoing transition from a focus on explicit forms of societal racism to widespread concern about changing gender roles and sexual norms. The editors commended the Church "for refusing to let popular protest shape its [racial] doctrine" and affirmed the social acceptability of any religion's right to promulgate racist beliefs as long as they were separate from civil liberties.[119] Such a view was paramount, they insisted, because with the rise of the "women's rights movement, one could expect future demands that not only blacks but women also be admitted to the Mormon priesthood!"[120] This kind of statement has been regarded as evidence that "as racial separation receded in importance in the renewed conservative movement," a focus on sexuality and gender took its place in the 1970s.[121] But this interpretation misconstrues the importance and embeddedness of white supremacy in both religious and secular U.S. culture.

It would be more accurate to say that what receded was not the importance of racial separation, although that reading is itself certainly a testament to the power of the colorblind narrative, but actually the acceptability of calls for racial separation and, as a result, the importance of explicit anti-Black racist discrimination. As such *Christianity Today*'s comments hint at how concern about both the feminist movement and sexual liberation among conservative Christian groups did not just replace a waning national interest in the civil rights movement; rather, rising concern with family values was indicative of the new methods being used to reinforce the racial status quo. In other words, white supremacy was shifting away from a reliance on explicitly segregationist ideas and policies and instead was more regularly maintained through colorblind and assimilationist ones, most often expressed through an emphasis on the need to maintain and protect family values, specifically patriarchal binary gender norms and heteronormative family units. Family values, as a fundamental component in the rise of the Religious Right and the political power it wielded during the 1970s, 1980s, and 1990s, was fundamentally connected to the rise of colorblind racism, which condemned those who were unable or unwilling to enact such values, primarily marginalized racial and sexual groups.[122] The fact that the Church maintained its explicitly racist priesthood and temple bans, while simultaneously helping to construct an implicitly racialized notion of family values, provides a useful angle from which to recognize and explain how the mid- to late twentieth-century transition from explicit to colorblind racism occurred.

As early as the mid-1960s, white people's tolerance for the civil rights movement had already begun to wane, and a new mainstream focus on gender and sexuality was overtaking racial issues, even as Black activists and press continued to push for social and legal changes. During the mid-1960s, the feminist movement had just started to capture national attention, but by the early 1970s it would produce a significant cultural backlash, fueled by the earlier theorizing and activism of conservative religious figures such as Billy Graham and Jerry Falwell. The early inklings of this trend were evident in March 1966 when the *Daily Defender* featured a short piece on Mrs. America, Alice Buehner, a Mormon who warned against women losing their femininity "in the 'drive for emancipation and equality.'" Repeating contradictory notions of women's submission to patriarchal authority and gender equality that were being articulated by the Church's leaders at the time, Buehner asserted that "'American men are strong and dependable . . . mak[ing] you feel secure . . . but they accept women as equals'" and that "women should realize that" in marriage "the man is the dominant person, the head of the house, that he makes the final decisions, and that if 'she's smart she'll keep herself as attractive to him as possible.'"[123] Buehner's comments reflected, almost verbatim, Church leaders' statements on women's and men's roles, statements that were identical to those being made by evangelical fundamentalist leaders, just as both the Religious Right and the Church were preparing to stake out a new, politically active role in social debates about gender, sexuality, and family.

While it was not until the mid-1970s that the Church joined other conservative Christian groups in explicit political challenges to the supposed threat of feminism, by the mid-1960s Church leaders were already engaged in pedagogical projects meant to insulate against what they saw as the dangers of changing gender norms, homosexuality, and interracial marriage. For example, in 1964 Apostle Spencer W. Kimball had begun to preach that homosexuality was an excommunicable offense, and by 1968 he was insisting "that homosexuality could be cured by the strength of the patient's desire to change." In other words, "masculine self-mastery [had become] an important concept for" Mormon understandings of "both the causes and the cures of homosexuality."[124] Self-mastery was, of course, a highly prized virtue that had a long history in both Mormon and U.S. culture of signaling racialized and gendered notions of personhood, individual agency, and self-governance.[125] Thus, the earlier transition from explicitly racialized language in the late nineteenth and early twentieth centuries, through discourses of gender and sexual hypernormativity to implicit racialized meaning, was being recycled as an important tool in efforts to refigure white supremacy's institutionalization in U.S. culture and governance. Buehner's ideas about binarized and hierarchical gender roles and Kimball's ideas about homosexuality as a failure of self-mastery each helped to communicate an implicitly white ideal of faith and citizenship, which as a result of Cold War politics had been firmly coupled with commonsense notions of U.S. nationalism.

At the same time that the Church became more outspoken about the idea that homosexuality could be prevented and cured, primarily by teaching and practicing differentiated gender roles grounded in women's submission to men's authority (even as the mainstream psychiatric community was moving toward declassifying homosexuality as an illness), a Mormon housewife named Jacquie Davison founded a group called Happiness of Womanhood (HOW). Predating Phyllis Schlafly's organization, STOP ERA, by two years, HOW was an antifeminist group inspired by Davison's attendance at a workshop given by Mormon author Helen B. Andelin and based on Andelin's bestselling book *Fascinating Womanhood* (1965), which taught that women would find fulfillment in "accepting their divinely ordained roles and responsibilities," specifically through "wifely submission" to their husband's sexual, intellectual, and economic authority.[126] Andelin's book and workshops reflected many of the lessons she had learned about gender, sexuality, and marriage from both her Church and popular culture, lessons that were themselves steeped in racialized notions of sex/gender differentiation and heterosexuality as emblematic of the highest order of civilization.[127]

By 1973, a year after the Equal Rights Amendment (ERA) had been passed by Congress and sent to the states for ratification, HOW had ten thousand members across all fifty states and opposed not only the ERA but "abortion, homosexuality, pornography, sex education, busing, and the removal of school prayer," arguing that "the women's movement's false promises of liberation and equality and the sexual revolution's assaults on traditional monogamous heterosexuality threatened women's happiness and endangered the family."[128] These events overlapped with the publication

of a variety of texts explaining and justifying the Church's Black priesthood and temple bans and the continued insistence by leaders that the
institution was not racist.[129] Upon his installation as Church president
in 1972, for instance, Harold B. Lee, who had been the architect of the
Church's midcentury Correlation program that worked to promote patriarchal households and gender differentiation, was quoted widely when he
asserted, "'It is ironic we are called 'racist' in light of all the work we have
done with minorities throughout the world.'"[130] Similarly, when Spencer
W. Kimball, who would eventually lift the Church's bans, became president in 1973, he insisted, "'We do love these [Black] people. . . . We think we
treat them better than most people do.'"[131] The mainstream press generally let these kinds of statements stand without investigation, comment,
or criticism. Despite a variety of smaller events and controversies related
to the Church's bans, for the most part the mainstream press moved on
to other foci, leaving Black and left-leaning publications to point out the
Church's racism.[132]

Articles like Judy Klemesrud's 1973 New York Times piece highlighted
the Church's new family home evening program as a genius solution to
the problems of "divorce, drugs, venereal disease, alcohol, adultery and
group sex."[133] Articles like this one played off earlier Cold War versions
of Mormon peculiarity, as well as the rising tide of family values rhetoric,
to "implicitly mobilize[] a racialized notion of wholesomeness that position[ed] white patriarchal, heterosexual families against 'delinquency' and
'deteriora[tion]' evidenced in behaviors associated in the white national
imagination with counterculture, urban, and minority communities."[134]
Featuring a photograph of the Osmonds but failing to mention the Church's
Black bans served to further cement a notion of Mormon hypernormativity through an implicit notion of white cultural superiority in the realms of
faith and family.

These images were etched into the minds of millions of people through
both the popularity of the Osmonds and a series of Church-produced public service announcements that began to air on national radio and television
in 1972.[135] These short spots, referred to as the Homefront series, promoted
heteronormative family values through brief skits such as those encouraging parents to spend more time with their children, advocating family
bonding, and providing tips on how to avoid divorce. Featuring white,
middle-class families who embodied patriarchal gender roles, the ads won
national awards and reached millions of people, firmly shifting previous

perceptions of Mormonism from a religion associated in the popular imagination with terms like *polygamy* and *racist* to a Church "that believes in families," as evidenced by the Church's own surveys.[136]

Thus, by 1974 Mormon peculiarity discourse shifted to focus on the Church's leaders' outspoken and overtly political dive into debates over feminism and homosexuality. Press coverage of the Church's leaders' statements about both women's liberation and family values illustrate this shift. In October, the *Daily Defender* ran two articles highlighting Mormon opposition to the feminist movement evident in Apostle N. Eldon Tanner's declaration "that women's liberation is the work of the devil." "'Satan and his cohorts are using scientific arguments and nefarious propaganda,'" Tanner claimed, "'to lure women away from their primary responsibilities as wives, mothers and homemakers.'"[137] Similarly, *Time* reported on the likelihood that newly installed President Kimball would "change Mormon views on the family or race," noting that as "a devoted husband and father" he "insists that under normal circumstances 'the place of women is in the home'" while "the controversial Mormon doctrine that keeps blacks from full membership in the church . . . 'is the policy of the Lord.'"[138]

These reports also reflected the ideas outlined in Benson's new book *God, Family, Country: Our Three Great Loyalties* (1974), which "forward[ed] a conservative political vision based on traditional gender roles, opposition to welfare, and promotion of free markets" that never explicitly mentioned race but still promoted an intensely racialized view of heteronormative family units engaged in free market capitalist production and consumption as essential to U.S. superiority.[139] In 1976, when the battle over ratification of the ERA had heated up considerably, the *Denver Post* reported that Benson acknowledged "that he felt ERA would 'weaken men'" and that in the family, as "'the cornerstone of society' . . . 'men are dominant' . . . because 'someone must be in charge and take leadership.'"[140] Although Benson's logic was reflective of not just his own but the rest of the Church's leaders' views on the subject, "in a separate interview, another church official said the question 'hasn't anything to do with male supremacy,'" suggesting that as with the Church's racial doctrines, the institution had learned that denials of its positions were just as effective, if not more so, as justifying those positions when social mores were in the process of changing.[141]

Mormon peculiarity discourse continued to be used to explain away the Church's Black bans as anachronistic in the mid- to late 1970s ("What makes the LDS church 'peculiar' among American religions is that portion of its doctrine which is considered by many to be racist") while still allowing the public to widely embrace its family values as hypernormative.[142] "Many" may have considered the Church's policies racist and the "Change in Rules on Blacks" may have "Fail[ed] to Satisfy [the] N.A.A.C.P.," but this mattered little to a public widely, though certainly not universally, enamored of the religion's family values.[143] In a widely reported UPI piece, the Church's decision to not join the World Council of Churches was attributed to its "puritanical sexual standards," and the author noted that when "asked why the Mormons haven't joined," President Kimball had "said, 'We're different than all the others.'"[144] While Kimball chose "his words carefully" in December 1974, "eschew[ing] the criticism other Mormon leaders . . . made of the women's liberation movement," still emphasizing that "the church believes the 'primary role' of women is wife and mother" and noting that "the church stays out of politics and thus has not taken a stand on the" ERA, by early 1975 the Church would come out full force against the amendment, shifting almost all press coverage of Mormonism to the topic.

When Congress had first sent the ERA to be ratified in 1972, states heavily populated by Mormons, such as Idaho, easily voted in favor of it. Indeed, by 1974 the ERA had been approved by thirty-three of the thirty-eight states needed for ratification. In November, a *Deseret News* poll found that 64 percent of Utah Mormons actually favored ratification. Both the widespread success of the amendment and Mormon support for it would reverse in four short months, after a November meeting between Phyllis Schlafly and Relief Society president Barbara Smith that marked the beginning of a formal relationship between the Church and the Religious Right. Convinced by Schlafly that the Church should come out in opposition to the ERA, Smith convinced President Kimball of the same. Although Kimball had previously refused to comment on the ERA because he considered it a "political issue," on January 11 an anonymous editorial appeared in the *Deseret News* arguing that the ERA was too vaguely worded, that it might harm long-standing benefits to women like maternity leave and government aid to single mothers, and that its consequent breadth would harm "traditional" gender roles—arguments similar to those Schlafly was making and had presented to Smith.[145] After the editorial's publication, by February only 31 percent of Mormons supported the ERA. Unsurprisingly, the Utah legislature voted down the amendment that same month.[146]

The battle to defeat the ERA by conservative Christian groups, including the Church, was widely reported by the press. Coverage noted the role the Church played in, as well its relationship to, evangelical fundamental-ist groups working for the ERA's demise. For example, *U.S. News and World Report* asked in one headline, "Equal Rights for Women—Doomed?," noting that "a Utah legislator dropped his support of ERA and said: 'It is my Church, and . . . I'm not going to vote against its wishes.'"[147] Reversing its position that it would stay out of politics by designating the ERA a "moral" rather than a "political" issue, the Church's "male leaders brought greater organization and disciplinary approaches to the early national [anti-ERA] political strategy, creating their own anti-ERA organizations and directing members into them." Aware the Church's foray into the political arena created the potential for bad press, leaders also instructed these groups "to appear as 'grassroots' collections of 'concerned citizens' and not to reveal backing from the LDS church."[148] But the press was quick to report on the Church's active opposition to the ERA and interpret it through the lens of Mormon peculiarity. For instance, Grace Lichtenstein of the *New York Times* observed that even some Mormon women thought their Church's sexism was exceptional: "'Even though I'm an LDS . . . I think Mormons are the most male chauvinist society anywhere.'"[149] In fact, a significant portion of Mormon women identified as feminists and supported the ERA.[150] The press quickly picked up on what it character-ized as the contradiction of being both a Mormon and a feminist, using Mormon peculiarity discourse to frame it as a paradox.[151]

By the mid-1970s, Church leaders had shifted to a new interpretation of homosexuality that posited "failure of the family and the blurring of sexual difference," and not lack of self-mastery, as the cause of homosexuality.[152] This new interpretation, which came into vogue among Church leaders at the same time that Kimball (formally the one in charge of the Church's approach to homosexuality) became president, in part drove the Church's desire to defeat the ERA. For the Church's leaders, what they viewed as the "breakdown of family values explained the apparent rise in the prac-tice of homosexuality" and demonstrated a need to protect and nurture "a fragile heterosexuality and fragile masculinity."[153] This helps to explain why leaders were actively dismantling women's authority in the Church in the 1960s and 1970s, through Correlation, in an attempt to ensure sup-posedly proper patriarchal roles and authority within the home. To these leaders, the ERA threatened such an order and would result in an increase in same-sex sexuality if that order was not protected. Thus, in October 1976 the First Presidency issued a statement against the ratification of the

ERA, pointing to an increase in homosexuality and lesbianism as possible by-products of the legislation, a line that would be repeated again and again for the press.[154]

These developments illustrate that while the Church still maintained a stance against interracial marriage, and would continue to do so even after the Black bans were lifted in 1978, it had shifted from primarily focusing on preventing interracial sex as a way to maintain white supremacy to focusing on protecting heteronormative families, and especially white men, from the vulnerabilities and fragilities of normative sex and gender. These priorities also served to maintain and promote white supremacy since they were fundamentally tied, both historically and politically, to notions of civilizational and national health, especially concerns about sex/gender differentiation and sexual practices. Thus, "by focusing on the possibility that gender norms could change and positing that as a source of danger and a cause for fear rather than liberation, LDS political activism in the 1970s framed gender and sexuality as the province of government regulation."[155] However, it is also important to recognize that these changes also reflected broader cultural patterns embraced and perpetuated by religious conservatives, especially evangelical fundamentalists. Indeed, *Newsweek* deemed 1976 not the year of the Mormon but "the year of the evangelical."[156]

By 1977, as a result of the Church's opposition, Idaho rescinded its passage of the ERA.[157] As a result of intense lobbying, Nebraska and Tennessee also rescinded ratification with "some senators" noting that the "issue generated the most intensive lobbying they'd been subjected to" and that the Church "was among the strongest opponents of the ERA."[158] Saints, at the direction of Church leaders, successfully organized in Florida, Virginia, Hawai'i, Montana, Nevada, and Washington to help defeat state ratification and undermine the organizing efforts of feminist groups.[159] The racial and class dimensions of this kind of political organizing were rarely referenced in the media, if at all then only in passing, and were never investigated in mainstream coverage. This was the case in Klemesrud's fleeting observation of an antifeminist rally held in Houston and attended by fifteen thousand people, including many Saints, that "the rally's participants, most of them white and well-dressed, unanimously passed resolutions against abortion, the proposed equal rights amendment and lesbian rights."[160]

However, reporting on the demise of the ERA generally framed the Church's opposition to, and its role in stopping, the ERA's ratification in relation to other conservative groups and institutions. In other words, in the mainstream press the Church was generally not singled out as peculiarly conservative in its views on gender and sexuality but was rather linked with the Religious Right.[161] In the late 1970s, Mormon peculiarity continued to be occasionally articulated in the vein of early coverage from the 1950s and 1960s, which identified the Church as a particularly good example of national values and success but with the added twist that the Church was now being represented as a good model for tackling problems of "moral and social disarray." These problems were of course implicitly racialized as Black or nonwhite as a result of the southern strategy, especially references to "poverty," "welfare," and "violent crime" being coded as nonwhite.[162]

MORMONS "SOLVE" THEIR "BLACK PROBLEM"

On June 1, 1978, while praying in the Salt Lake City Temple, President Kimball received a revelation reversing the Church's Black priesthood and temple bans. Publicly announced on June 9, the reversal of the Church's bans made front page news across the country. Black men were given the priesthood and Black people almost immediately entered temples for various rites previously denied them.[163] Very soon after the announcement, the Church also declared plans to start missionizing in predominantly Black locations such as Nigeria, where interest in the Church had long been high. Many scholars have pointed to this interest outside of the United States, especially the success of the Church in Brazil, as a major factor that contributed to the revelation. Analysis of Mormon peculiarity discourse during this period also reveals that although public pressure did indeed significantly affect how the Church responded to and framed its racism, it did not directly affect the timing of the revelation. While occasional reports were still covering the Church's racial policies, and popular news shows such as 60 Minutes had begun to challenge the wholesome image of the Church in the late 1970s, both white people and the mainstream press had largely forgotten about, begrudgingly accepted, or were only sporadically grumbling about the Church's explicitly racist bans.

In February, four months before the revelation, Barbara Walters interviewed Donny and Marie Osmond on television and asked about the bans. The interview utilized typical hypernormative images of Mormonism, featuring the large Osmond family together on family home evening night, and the interview included questions that highlighted the normative values and apparent success of the faith. When Walters finally asked about the bans, Donny Osmond repeated the now rote response that the Saints "are not prejudiced people" and that the faith "'offer[s] more I think than any other religion to the Black person.'"[164] In this context, the press responded glowingly to the Church's reversal, consistently featuring the responses of faithful Black Mormons.[165] Expressing a collective sigh of relief, journalists reported on the reversal with almost no attention to ongoing racism within the Church, only to quickly move on to the Church's role in the fight over the ERA.

The reporting on the bans' reversal tended to reinforce the now widely accepted idea that once explicitly racist policies were lifted, that was the end to the race question, as exemplified in the *Denver Post*'s headline: "Mormon Revelation Solves Black Problem."[166] As usual, the only challenge to this type of thinking was evident in the Black press. One exasperated reporter sarcastically explained:

> While we join with others around the country in welcoming the Mormon religion into the enlightened attitudes of the 20th century, we cannot but offer this jibe: Who cares? Racism exists and will continue to exist. Some aspects of racism are worth fighting and some are not. That the Mormon Church has, in the year 1978, begun to end its racist practices of more than a hundred years is of little consequence to us.[167]

Anticipating a quick shift back to the issue of the ERA, mainstream journalists noted in their coverage of the revelation that the Church still banned women from the priesthood.[168] Only *Time* pointed out in the immediate coverage of the event that the Church had printed a statement discouraging interracial marriage alongside the revelation in *Church News*.[169]

By the fall of 1978, Sonia Johnson, Mormon feminist and founder of Mormons for ERA (MERA), was taking hold of the press's attention as a figure symbolizing the supposed contradictions of being both a feminist and a Mormon. As a result of the publicity that her group received when it participated in a Washington, D.C., march in support of the ERA, Johnson was invited to testify as a part of the Senate hearings on the floundering amendment. Johnson's heated exchange with Mormon Senator Orrin Hatch of Utah drew even more press attention to Mormonism's role in the ERA debate.[170] Her public support of the ERA and her open criticism of the Church's position would result in her excommunication in December 1979—a story that received widespread coverage.[171] MERA's increasingly flamboyant tactics, used to counter the Church's well-organized anti-ERA efforts, ensured that the press remained focused on the gendered, rather than the racial, politics of Mormonism at the beginning of the new decade.[172] Given Congress's extension of the ERA ratification deadline from March 1979 to June 1982, coverage of the conflict between pro- and anti-ERA Mormons continued into the early 1980s and was primarily focused on Johnson and MERA.

The early 1980s were also marked by another shift in Mormon peculiarity discourse, constituted by evangelical fundamentalist attacks on the validity of the Church's Christianity, most notably exemplified in the release of the sensationalist anti-Mormon documentary *The God Makers*.[173] According to Haws, many Protestants worried "that Mormons' social morality would grant Mormonism legitimacy in the eyes of religious Americans" and that "such legitimacy would only increase the threat of Mormon proselytizing, since it would simultaneously decrease perceptions of Mormon peculiarity and thus open more doors for Mormon missionaries."[174] But this is not quite right, because perceptions of Mormon peculiarity did not actually decrease but had instead shifted to firmly construct the Saints as hypernormative citizens by the early 1980s. Or as one 1980 *New York Times* article put it, "the Mormon church is now a burgeoning and influential religion whose members eagerly espouse the traditional values of patriotism and capitalism" and are "the highly respected embodiment of a clean-living, old-fashioned set of principles."[175]

Mormonism as the ultimate example of both the American dream and U.S. exceptionalism had been reiterated since the 1930s and was now firmly embedded, reflected in the views of the evangelical fundamentalists' political darling Ronald Reagan. In 1982, he proclaimed the Church's welfare system as "'one of the great examples in America today of what people can do for themselves if they hadn't been dragooned into the government's doing it for them.'" "'If more people had had this idea back when the Great Depression hit,'" he insisted, "'there wouldn't be any government welfare today or any need for it,'" making Mormonism a sharp contrast to the implicitly racialized figure of the Black "welfare queen" who he had so famously conjured up during his 1976 presidential campaign and continued to exploit.[176] With the decline of the civil rights movement and the rise and acceptance of colorblindness, Mormon peculiarity discourse had completed its transition away from explicit discussions of racial, civilizational health, and superiority. Instead, normative ideas about gender, sex, family, and economy became the main conduits through which racial meaning could be culled from Mormon peculiarity discourse in the 1990s and early 2000s as the Church waded deeper into political battles related to LGBTQ rights, particularly same-sex marriage.

PART III

Regulatory Queer Varieties of Mormon Peculiarity

7 Polygamy, or The Racial Politics of Marriage as Freedom

> If "[t]here is dignity in the bond between two men or two women who seek to marry and in their autonomy to make such profound choices," . . . why would there be any less dignity in the bond between three people who, in exercising their autonomy, seek to make the profound choice to marry?
>
> —Supreme Court Chief Justice Roberts's dissent in
> *Obergefell v. Hodges*

On December 20, 2013, a federal court judge ruled that Utah's ban on gay marriage was unconstitutional.[1] Making Utah the eighteenth state to allow same-sex marriage, *Kitchen v. Herbert* was one of dozens of cases that followed in the wake of the Supreme Court's rulings earlier that June, *Hollingsworth v. Perry* and *United States v. Windsor*—dealing with the constitutionality of Proposition 8 in California and the federal Defense of Marriage Act respectively.[2] Taken as only part of the larger push to legalize gay marriage in the United States, *Kitchen* is unremarkable; however, the reactions to the reversal of Utah's law reveal that for many the meaning of the decision was somehow different, and drastically so, from those in other states.[3] Take, for example, popular MSNBC news anchor Rachel Maddow's reporting on the decision:

> I don't know why this one feels different, but this one feels different. Today a *federal* judge in *Utah, yes that Utah*, struck down the state's ban on same-sex marriage. . . . And so the ruling came down, surprising everyone, at two o'clock local time in Utah and by three o'clock local time in Utah *people were getting married in that state*. People who probably thought they would never,

ever, ever in their entire lives, ever, be able to get married in Utah, let alone today. . . . Does this Utah decision today just feel like it's a bigger deal than all the others because, forgive me, *it's freaking Utah?* . . . Am I just having an emotional reaction to the word Utah?[4]

Maddow's comments invoke—through the inability to express what exactly is different but the certain knowledge that something is different—a long history of exceptionalist rhetoric that identifies Utah, via Mormonism, as peculiar. Her reaction is typical of late twentieth- and early twenty-first-century articulations of Mormon peculiarity discourse that equate Utah with the influence of The Church of Jesus Christ of Latter-day Saints. In this account, an apparently unprecedented religious influence character-izes the religious and political atmosphere of the state, rendering any and all forms of queer life and activism therein totally inconceivable. Consequently, even though the *Kitchen* decision was legally probable, if not predictable, it remained notable exactly because Mormon peculiarity discourse deemed it (im)possible.

Just seven days later, on December 27, another federal court judge struck down the central component of Utah's antipolygamy law in *Brown v. Buhman.*[5] Brought to court by the polygamous Brown family featured on TLC's popular reality TV series *Sister Wives,* the decision altered 150 years of marriage law in Utah by declaring the state's criminalization of "cohabitation" unconstitutional.[6] Although media coverage of *Brown* was extensive in Utah, its reverberations were not as widespread as those of *Kitchen.* Given the historical context of Utah's antipolygamy law, the cen-trality of antipolygamy activism to federal marriage law, and widespread concern that the legalization of gay marriage would lead to the legalization of polygamy, it is ironic that its decriminalization, at first, garnered such limited attention from the national press.[7]

The concurrent timing of these decisions and the respective reactions to them are revealing, but not as examples of a newfound acceptance of sex-ual nonnormativities in the United States; rather, these decisions mark a subtle yet powerful recentering of heteronormative whiteness in U.S. cul-ture and politics vis-à-vis Mormon peculiarity discourse. As courts across the country affirmed the rights of same-sex couples to marry, culminating in the Supreme Court's *Obergefell v. Hodges* (2015) decision, narratives of U.S. (sexual) exceptionalism have applauded the nation for the formal accep-tance and supposed cultural integration of yet another marginalized group.[8]

However, a close analysis of the *Kitchen* and *Brown* decisions reveals that despite the legalization of gay marriage and the potential future legalization of polygamy in the United States, these decisions were not watershed victories for "sexual freedom" but rather signal a reassertion of heterosexuality, monogamy, marriage, and, ultimately, whiteness as vested interests of the nation-state.[9]

Analyzing these decisions in relation to one another and within the historical context of their development helps to demonstrate how the ostensible inclusion granted to sexual and religious minorities through legal recourse is at most selective and at least (and most usually) cursory. Moreover, when read together, these decisions symbolically bookend the development of Mormon peculiarity discourse from its nineteenth-century beginnings to its twenty-first-century iterations. Both decisions, and their proximity to one another, underscore the continued elaboration of Mormon peculiarity in relationship to sexual nonnormativities: in each instance Mormonism is framed as abnormal either because of its promotion of polygamy or in its abhorrence of same-sex sexuality and kinship. As a result, Mormon peculiarity discourse ensured that *Kitchen,* more than any other state-based gay marriage decision, functioned as proof of the apparently substantial progress that the United States has achieved in protecting, including, and even embracing sexual minorities. "If Utah," so the thinking goes, "whose politics is dominated by the ultraconservative Mormon Church, legalized gay marriage, then the United States has certainly achieved a completely progressive and inclusive state." And while it may be tempting to read *Kitchen* as progressive and *Brown* as evidence that the decriminalization of sodomy and the legalization of gay marriage have paved the way for greater sexual and religious freedom in the United States, a closer look reveals a limited view of sexual freedom, as well as a willful disavowal of the nation's persecution and exclusion of sexual, religious, and racial minorities, past and present.

Accordingly, this final chapter analyzes contemporary articulations of Mormon peculiarity discourse, in relation to both *Kitchen* and *Brown,* as potent examples of U.S. (sexual) exceptionalism's ingrained ideological power. Both cases exemplify how the discourse is still used to reinforce claims of U.S. moral superiority and ultimately serves as justification for U.S. imperial policy and practice—specifically in terms of both the nation-state's ongoing biopolitical governance and its foreign policy—through the negation of racism in the contemporary moment.[10] My analysis of these decisions focuses on two points: first, that legal claims to sexual and religious freedom in the United States inevitably require a willful erasure of the nation's racial-colonial legacy and any acknowledgment of its racial-colonial present, and second, that Mormonism remains a vital assemblage justifying U.S. colonialism and imperialism.

To make this argument, I draw on a body of queer, legal scholarship about *Loving v. Virginia* (1967) and *Lawrence v. Texas* (2003), two Supreme Court cases that decriminalized interracial marriage and same-sex sodomy, respectively.[11] I engage this work because *Loving* and *Lawrence* were precedent-setting cases that were crucial to the findings in *Kitchen* and *Brown* and, even more important, because this scholarship helps to illuminate the complex ways that discourses of U.S. sexual exceptionalism and racial equality have become intertwined and perpetuated within the law. In addition to providing a more complete contextualization for the development of marriage case law in the United States, particularly the haunting but often underemphasized importance of the Supreme Court's *Reynolds v. United States* (1879) decision, it becomes apparent how the rearticulation of Mormon peculiarity discourse in recent marriage case law reinforces an implicit investment in whiteness, couched in the extension of a conservative set of rights to private sexual conduct.[12]

BACKGROUND: RACIALIZING MORMONISM IN THE POST-9/11 ERA

Secular Sexual Rights versus Backward Religious Discrimination

Early twenty-first-century articulations of U.S. sexual exceptionalism have typically contrasted the successful secular legalization of same-sex sex and marriage with the failure of conservative religious bigotry to prevent such changes, ostensibly proving that the United States has achieved, or will very soon achieve, a complete inclusion of sexual minorities.[13] *Kitchen* is merely one example from a pattern of rulings legalizing gay marriage nationwide that trades in such discourse. However, one significant fact separated this judgment from others like it: both in the decision itself as well as in media coverage of the decision, a furtively racialized conception of religion generally, and of theocratic governance rooted in sexual underdevelopment specifically, was deployed as the boogeyman to blame for the proscription of same-sex marriage. *Kitchen* particularly embodied this concept, contrasting "one of the hearts of conservative religion in America," a state that "just *hates* homosexuals in every form and certainly doesn't want them getting married," with the assumed inevitably of the U.S. legal system's triumph over discrimination.[14]

Kitchen began when a local gay man in Utah, Mark Lawrence, decided through a grassroots effort to put together a test case to challenge the state's anti–gay marriage laws. Lawrence's efforts and those of Peggy Tomsic, the local attorney who took the case on, are notable because they were not supported by any formal nonprofit organization or fundraising. In fact, they had been told by multiple national legal and LGBTQ organizations that any attempt to bring such a case in Utah would be futile, given the political power of The Church of Jesus Christ of Latter-day Saints. After Lawrence recruited three same-sex couples—Karen Archer and Kate Call, Derek Kitchen and Moudi Sbeity, and Kody Partridge and Laurie Wood— they, with the help of Tomsic, petitioned to find the state's ban on gay marriage unconstitutional.[15] The six plaintiffs argued that Utah's prohibition against same-sex marriage denied them access to rights that were protected under the Due Process and Equal Protection clauses of the Fourteenth Amendment of the U.S. Constitution. Judge Shelby of the U.S. District Court of Utah, agreeing with the plaintiff's reasoning, found resoundingly in their favor. In and of itself, Shelby's reasoning is not necessarily noteworthy; however, unlike the multitude of other same-sex marriage cases, the religious backgrounds of the plaintiffs—Sbeity's and Call's, most obviously—play a critical role in how the judgment is framed and how it should be interpreted.

Located in the requisite background section at the beginning of the decision, Shelby's selected personal history of the plaintiffs is easily overlooked, but upon contextualized reflection it is quite revealing. Shelby's selected discussion of the plaintiffs' relevant personal histories, which pulled from their individual affidavits to the court, highlights their coming out experiences and the discrimination they faced as a result of their sexuality. Shelby reiterates the particularly religious nature of the discrimination that most of the plaintiffs experienced, but this carefully worded section avoids any specific indictment of a single religion as the cause of the plaintiffs' suffering. For example, Sbeity's religious background is omitted, yet Shelby mentions that he was "born in Houston, Texas," but "grew up in Lebanon" and came to the United States "during the war between Lebanon and Israel."[16] It is also explained that in reaction to his coming out, Sbeity's "mother took him to a psychiatrist." Even after his mother accepted his sexuality, "he was careful about whom he told because he was concerned that he might expose his mother to ridicule."[17] It is unclear from this brief account why and by whom Sbeity's mother, as opposed to Sbeity himself, would be ridiculed; however, mentioning his childhood and adolescence in Lebanon, especially in the post-9/11 context, inevitably invokes the specter of a stereotypically homophobic and sexist Islam, even without ever explicitly identifying Sbeity's religious background.[18]

Sbeity stands out as the sole plaintiff of color whose personal history drastically differs from the other petitioners. The allusions to his upbringing in Lebanon and coming out experience subtly reference stereotypes of Islam (regardless of whether or not he or his family identifies as Muslim) as not just homophobic but as supposedly backward in its approach to gender, marriage, and kinship more generally. These stereotypes, lurking in the foreground of the background section, were confirmed by various media reports, such as the *Huffington Post*'s narration of Sbeity's history. The *Post* confirmed that Sbeity's Lebanon-based family is in fact Muslim and reiterated a formulaic depiction of Islamic cultures and nations as inherently more homophobic, and therefore less secular, than any Christian culture or nation, especially the United States:

> Sbeity was raised in Lebanon, where until this year, being caught having sex with someone of the same gender was punishable by up to one year in jail. So as a gay teen, Sbeity was careful to hide his orientation to avoid being thrown in jail and because he feared his mother's Muslim family would turn against her.[19]

While the facts of his history may or may not be presented accurately in the *Post* article, they perpetuate a narrative of regressive Islamic morality contrasted with an implicit acceptance and inclusion of same-sex sexuality in the secular United States, embodied in the *Kitchen* decision itself. But what the *Post*'s version of events elides, in addition to ignoring Lebanon's own religious diversity, is that sodomy was criminalized in the United States until 2003 and that, as in Lebanon, LGBTQ people are still subject to discrimination, harassment, and violence, often at the hands of evangelical fundamentalist Christians, among others. Clarifying Judge Shelby's vague reference to Sbeity's fear that his mother would be "ridiculed," the article echoes criticisms that Islam is inherently and irretrievably patriarchal and despotic—situating Sbeity's mother as a target of cultural and religious intolerance, perhaps even more so than her gay son.[20]

Shelby's judgment is subtly framed by the establishment of the discursive formulation of the United States as a tolerant and progressive nation-state in contrast to the supposedly fanatical and backward space of Lebanon, specifically, and Islamic cultures and nations more generally. Yet, in the decision, U.S. sexual exceptionalism is not solely articulated through references to Sbeity's cultural background; it is also paradoxically reinforced by parallel narratives of Mormonism's intolerance of same-sex sexuality. In fact, it is clear that the majority of the plaintiffs came from conservative religious backgrounds, most of them from families who were a part of The Church of Jesus Christ of Latter-day Saints. This is best reflected in Call's personal history: she grew up in the Church, her parents serving as mission presidents in Wisconsin and Mexico, and her father working as a professor at BYU. Call herself attended BYU, graduating in 1974, and served a mission in Argentina. Shelby notes that Call was outed, without her permission, to Church authorities and her parents by her mission president in South America.[21] Although these facts might be dismissed as mere details of Call's personal history, they reference a long history of specifically Mormon homophobia. The Church's notorious history of regulating and violently suppressing its LGBTQ members reached a fever pitch in the 1970s, the time when Call came to embrace her lesbian identity.[22]

At first glance, references to the Church's repression of same-sex sexuality might seem to allay the claim that *Kitchen* trades in commonly held ideas of U.S. secular tolerance and Islamic backwardness; however, this assertion must be read in light of the historical racialization of Mormons and Mormonism, specifically often as analogous to Muslims and Islam, and by extension the space of Utah, as nonwhite, un-Christian, undemocratic, and therefore un-American, a history recounted in earlier chapters.[23] Shelby's recurrent allusions to Mormon intolerance in the decision, as well as the media's continual references to Mormon bigotry in coverage of the gay marriage debate, reinforce a lasting stereotype of Mormonism as perpetually regressive when it comes to social issues related to gender and sex—a state of affairs that is traceable back to nineteenth-century representations of Mormon polygamy as backward. This history has continuously been regurgitated since the 1970s and since at least 2001 specifically through a "neo-Orientalist framework" evident in news coverage of Mormon fundamentalist polygamy that "relies on racialized and sexualized codes to . . . Muslimize" various Mormon fundamentalist traditions.[24] The racial implications of this framework are made clear when news coverage in the 2010s, following federal investigations into child abuse and subsequent raids on the Fundamentalist Church of Jesus Christ of Latter-Day Saints (FLDS), continually referred to the church, a group that split from the mainstream Church in the early twentieth century, as "North America's Taliban" or to its leader Warren Jeffs's "harem."[25]

Communication scholars Courtney Bailey and Adam Zahren point out that contemporary media coverage of the FLDS recalls nineteenth-century conceptualizations of Mormons as a separate race by highlighting how the media cast FLDS members—whose dress and demeanor were tightly regulated by Jeffs—as having a "peculiar, quasi-foreign look," a look that was in turn used to help justify state surveillance and intervention in that community.[26] Media coverage and cultural representations of The Church of Jesus Christ of Latter-day Saints and its members follow a similar pattern by consistently repeating stereotypes about their family size, clothing, tastes, and, paradoxically, their whiteness, despite the international and racial diversity of the Church. This trend is evident in much of the coverage of Mitt Romney during his presidential campaigns in 2008 and 2012, coverage that often featured photographs of himself with his wife and five sons next to images of his great-grandfather's much larger polygamous household.[27] Efforts to frame Mormonism as racially akin to Islam not only conflate religion, ethnicity, and race, but they also reinforce stereotypes of both religious traditions as fundamentally opposed to the progressive achievements of twenty-first-century U.S. jurisprudence.

The simultaneous likeness and distinction between the plaintiff with an Islamic background and those with Mormon backgrounds echoes a familiar refrain about domestic tolerance, contrasted with foreign persecution of LGBTQ people. All in all, the personal details Shelby highlights about each plaintiff are central to Kitchen's significance, both locally and nationally. For the plaintiffs, homophobia—and, by extension, their restricted access to gay marriage—is understood to be a direct result of these two repressive (and implicitly racially suspect) religious traditions, traditions that are represented as antithetical to the supposed U.S. pattern of acceptance and inclusion that is said to characterize the nation-state as exceptional. Explicitly in the media, and more subtly in Kitchen, Muslims and Mormons are presented as outside of proper belonging and citizenship despite narratives of religious liberty, racial equality, and sexual freedom. What is significant about Kitchen in particular, then, especially in its proximity to the Brown decision, is that Mormonism is once again being constructed as an Orientalist religious tradition that promotes outdated approaches to gender and sex, whether that be in its commitment to polygamy as a religiously necessary practice or in attitudes that regard same-sex sexuality as an abomination.

This is especially ironic given Shelby's assertion that expanding the fundamental right of marriage to include same-sex couples would actually expand, not limit, religious freedom. According to Shelby, *Kitchen* "does not mandate any change for religious institutions, which may continue to express their own moral viewpoints and define their own traditions about marriage."[28] A clear attempt to placate religious institutions, especially the mainstream Church of Jesus Christ of Latter-day Saints, that (incorrectly) claimed that legalizing same-sex marriage would infringe on their right to religious freedom, Shelby's statement is haunted by the fact that *Reynolds v. United States* (1879)—the case, first discussed in chapter 3, that inaugurated the belief–action distinction based on racist-colonial tropes that likened Mormonism to Islam and the United States to the supposedly civilizing influence of colonial Britain in India in order to justify the federal government's restriction of certain religious practices—still ensures that both state and federal governments can legally criminalize polygamous marriages, even if those unions are a matter of religious belief.

"An Orientalist Mindset among Ruling Elites"

As the first Supreme Court case to interpret the First Amendment guarantee of religious freedom, *Reynolds*'s differentiation between religious belief and practice set the standard in the realm of religious freedom for the next two centuries, upholding the federal government's right to criminalize polygamy. As Sarah Barringer Gordon observes, "subsequent decisions sustained and amplified the essential premise of *Reynolds,* which remains a frequently cited precedent." Moreover, the "staying power of anti-polygamy jurisprudence is remarkable, for many nineteenth-century cases were buried under the weight of twentieth-century rights doctrines that consciously eschew the nineteenth-century Court's restrictive interpretation of civil rights."[29] Since it was decided in December 2013, *Brown* has incorrectly been interpreted as a decision that legalized polygamy, implying that *Reynolds* is no longer valid. On the contrary, *Brown* did not legalize polygamy in Utah; instead, it invalidated a major component of the state's antipolygamy law—excising any criminalization of cohabitation—which had been a part of Utah's legal code since the late nineteenth-century federal campaign against Mormonism resulted in the criminalization of the practice.

Previously, the term *marry* in Utah's antipolygamy statute had been interpreted to mean both legally recognized marriages and those that are not state sanctioned. In other words, an individual need not have two (or more) marriage certificates to run afoul of the law, but merely cohabitating with a second partner, when legally married to a first, constituted a violation of Utah's antipolygamy statute. The Browns claimed that this interpretation of the statute violated their constitutional rights—first and foremost, their right to due process under the Fourteenth Amendment. They did not assert a constitutional right to practice polygamy (i.e., a constitutional right to engage in bigamy) but instead asserted a right to a "'carefully described' liberty interest in religious cohabitation," which Judge Waddoups agreed was constitutionally protected.[30] *Reynolds* remains binding precedent, allowing the government to regulate bigamous marriages but not necessarily religious cohabitation.

Premiering in 2011, the reality TV series *Sister Wives* follows the marriage of polygamist Kody Brown and his four wives, Meri, Janelle, Christine, and Robyn Brown.[31] Garnering significant media coverage after its premiere, the show followed the family's everyday lives in Lehi, Utah, and documented Kody's proposal to Robyn, his fourth wife, and their subsequent marriage in its first season. As a result of the show's massive popularity and the extensive media coverage that it received, the Brown family came under investigation by Utah County for engaging in polygamy. While the state was aware that the Brown family was polygamous before the show aired, "state officials acknowledged that 'The Sister Wives' program triggered their investigation."[32] Season Two recounted the shock and terror of the family as the state investigated the family, leading Kody to make the decision to move himself and all four of his wives and seventeen children to Las Vegas. The overdramatization of reality television notwithstanding, audiences witnessed the family's fear and misery as they frantically packed their belongings and desperately drove toward the Nevada border. In one telling scene, Robyn, Kody's fourth wife, tearily realizes, "This is not the America I learned about when I was in school."[33] This realization drove the Mormon patriarch and his wives to file their lawsuit in July 2011, contending that Utah's antipolygamy statute was unconstitutional.

While every U.S. state bans bigamy, as a result of the protracted social, cultural, and political battle of the nineteenth century, Utah's statute banning bigamy contains an extra prohibition forbidding "cohabitation."[34] As discussed in chapter 3, this supplementary ban was specially designed by the federal government to assist in successfully prosecuting polygamist patriarchs without having to prove that a legal marriage had taken place.[35] The *Brown* decision was based on three premises: first, that Utah's antipolygamy statute was facially unconstitutional (meaning it was obviously discriminatory because it only applied to a certain group of people— religious polygamists and, more specifically, fundamentalist Mormons) and as a result the court struck the phrase "or cohabits with another person" from the statute as a violation of the Free Exercise Clause of the First Amendment;[36] second, that the statute was without a rational basis under the Due Process Clause of the Fourteenth Amendment; and third, Judge Waddoups determined that the terms *marry* and *purports to marry* in the statute must be interpreted to mean only those marriages that are legally recognized and do not include relationships that are defined by cohabitation, religion, or other nonlegal criteria.[37] Key to the decision was Waddoups's determination that there is a crucial difference between polygamy and what he labeled "religious cohabitation." According to the court, the former is simply another name for bigamy—the knowing acquisition of multiple marriage licenses—while the latter refers to a relationship defined by "private 'spiritual' marriages not licensed or otherwise sanctioned by the state."[38] With this distinction at its heart, Waddoups's decision dealt an apparent deathblow to the historic regulation of polygamy in Utah, functionally determining that a statute banning bigamy already prohibits polygamy and that Utah cannot legally ban religious cohabitation.

I do not highlight the significance of this sea change in Utah's polygamy policy in order to praise the state's recognition of individuals' liberty interest in "religious cohabitation." Because the decision did not expand the right of legal marriage to religious polygamists but self-consciously demands the recognition of an individual's right to make private, personal decisions about their life, it might be easily mistaken for, or read as, a queer template for individuals' relationship to the state. Instead, this decision's significance must be understood as an extension of, rather than a break from, the state's investment in both heteronormativity and white supremacy. Discourses of U.S. (sexual) exceptionalism, particularly Mormon peculiarity, are deployed in *Brown* to camouflage and ultimately downplay the racial implications of both the remaining ban against bigamy and the state's interest in regulating marriage.

This is evident in the fifteen-page historical preamble to the actual analysis of the decision. Because *Reynolds* is still binding precedent and, as Waddoups noted, "it would [have been] an easy enough matter for the court to do as the Defendant urge[d] and find against the Plaintiffs on the question of religious cohabitation under the Statute,"[39] he took the time to contextualize both the constitutional developments since *Reynolds* and some of the racial dynamics of the nineteenth-century polygamy debate leading up to it. In this section, Waddoups, like Gordon, noted that *Reynolds* has had a remarkable staying power in the context of constitutional law, leading him to contend that it "would not be the legally or morally responsible approach [to ignore] the current contours of the constitutional protections at issue" in which "the Supreme Court has over the [intervening] decades assumed a general posture that is less inclined to allow majoritarian coercion of unpopular or disliked minority groups, especially when blatant racism (as expressed through Orientalism/imperialism), religious prejudice, or some other constitutionally suspect motivation, can be discovered behind such legislation."[40] Thus, Waddoups understood the jurisprudence of the post-*Reynolds* era to have necessitated a reexamination of the polygamy question in light of modern constitutional standards that protect individuals' rights, especially when proposed restrictions on those rights are based in suspect motivations, such as racism.

Relying heavily on academic treatments of the history of the Latter-day Saint tradition, the battle over polygamy, and the concept of Orientalism, Waddoups launched into a detailed outline of the ideological framework that yielded *Reynolds*. Narrating the context that produced the 1879 verdict as "an orientalist mindset among ruling elites" that would be "unthinkable as part of the legal analysis in a modern Supreme Court decision," Waddoups correctly characterized the *Reynolds* court as both subject to and advancing the prevailing racial and imperial logic of its day.[41] Nineteenth-century citizens saw, and the *Reynolds* court articulated, "a social treason against the nation of White citizens when Mormons adopted a supposedly barbaric marital form, one that was natural for 'Asiatic and African' people, but so unnatural for Whites as to produce a new, degenerate species."[42] This transgression was doubly threatening, since nineteenth-century logic held that engaging in the patriarchal practice of polygamy would ipso facto lead to despotism—a logic that is still repeated in modern deployments of U.S. gender and sexual exceptionalism, especially in relation to certain Islamic countries, especially those in southwestern Asia, in which

the United States has political and economic interests.[43] Implicitly rejecting nineteenth-century articulations of Mormon peculiarity as based in
Orientalism, Waddoups's history provided crucial context for any consideration of the ways sexual exceptionalism is deployed in modern legal
decisions. Despite his attention to Orientalism as a major historical factor
in the treatment of Mormonism, polygamy especially, his analysis frames
racism as an unfortunate mistake that must be expunged from the legal
record given more recent developments in civil rights and constitutional
law. His account of the ideological basis for *Reynolds* retains a problematic,
but unsurprising, approach to race that uses gender and sexual exceptionalism to justify contemporary U.S. imperial power.

First and foremost, such an approach frames "Orientalism/imperialism"
as firmly located in the past, legacies that have been expunged by more
recent civil rights jurisprudence—a narrative that is, of course, common if
not historically factual. This framing, whether intentional or not, works to
reaffirm a linear, progressive narrative of U.S. history and tacitly disavows
any modern imperial motivations, policies, or actions on the part of the
nation-state. But as Siobhan Somerville reminds us, Orientalist thinking
directed at the practice of polygamy was not left behind in the nineteenth
century. In *Boutilier v. INS* (1967), the Supreme Court confirmed the federal
government's right to restrict immigration on the basis of homosexuality.[44]
The 1952 Immigration and Nationality Act, at issue in the decision, was the
first time overt references to and restrictions against immigration and naturalization based on race were removed, replacing them with limitations
based on national origin. The removal of explicitly racial language was not
evidence of the irrelevance of race to immigration policy; rather, as Somerville argues, exclusions based on nationality and "sexual deviance" came to
stand in for race, allowing the state to continue to exclude certain populations without having to endorse an explicit policy of white supremacy. It is
no coincidence, then, that sexual deviance came to stand in for race, excluding people, for example, based on their (purported) practices of not only
same-sex sex but also adultery and, most significantly here, polygamy.[45]

Second, identifying Orientalism as the defining ideology for the *Reynolds*
court restricts a broader understanding of the racial context that fueled
the decision. Put another way, Waddoups's failure to position Orientalism
as a piece and not the whole project of white supremacy problematically
ignores key components of both nineteenth- and twentieth-century racism. In fact, the United States, as an empire, had been engaged in colonial

projects long before 1879, and the uses and applications of Orientalist thinking deployed against the Saints were also regularly used against Chinese
and Irish immigrants and Black and Indigenous peoples, among other
groups. Gordon's argument that the battle over Mormon polygamy was
an extension of Reconstruction policies demonstrates how labeling the
Saints as racial others was intimately tied to the anti-Black logic of the
postbellum United States and the need to reassert white supremacy after
the passage of the Thirteenth, Fourteenth, and Fifteenth Amendments.
The same court that decided *Reynolds* also decided *Pace v. Alabama* (1883),
which upheld antimiscegenation statutes as constitutional, and the more
famous *Plessy v. Ferguson* (1896), which sustained the legality of "separate
but equal."[46] Nathan Oman argues that the Reconstruction-era racial thinking that was employed against the Saints, and to reaffirm white racial dominance in the United States more generally, was both a justification and an
outline for implementing new forms of U.S. imperialism.[47]

As articulated in *Late Corp. of The Church of Jesus Christ of Latter-day
Saints v. United States* (1890)—a Supreme Court decision that solidified the
criminalization of polygamy by upholding the disincorporation of The
Church of Jesus Christ of Latter-day Saints—polygamy was dubbed "a
return to barbarism" and was understood to be "contrary to the spirit of
Christianity and of . . . civilization," reflecting the racist-colonial logic of
the period.[48] According to Waddoups's idealistic view:

> [This Supreme Court's] assessment arising from derisive societal views about
> race and ethnic origin prevalent in the United States at that time has no place
> in discourse about religious freedom, due process, equal protection or any
> other constitutional guarantee or right in the genuinely and intentionally
> racially and religiously pluralistic society that has been strengthened by the
> Supreme Court's twentieth-century rights jurisprudence.[49]

But the move to declare this logic outdated and long retired is, unfortunately,
overly simplistic and fails to grasp the role of race in ongoing U.S. colonial
governance[50] Waddoups's bold, if well-worn, sentiment negates the central role of race in regulating land, citizenship, labor, and political power
throughout the nation's history and the ways it continues to do so today.

As a lower court decision, Waddoups's ruling could not and does not
overrule *Reynolds* (1879) or *Late Corp.* (1890).[51] Despite his good-faith declaration that it "is not, [and] should not be considered, good law," *Reynolds*

retains a privileged position in constitutional jurisprudence, especially given its status as the first case to address a provision of the First Amendment's guarantee of religious freedom.[52] As Waddoups himself admitted, the case is still regularly cited by the Supreme Court. He claimed that references to *Reynolds* "can mistakenly give the impression of endorsing the morally repugnant reasoning [there]in"—but can 111 years of precedent really be dismissed as a mistake?[53] Given the legacy of racial oppression in the United States, enabled by multiple Supreme Court decisions, this claim is less than convincing, yet the necessity of such an assertion is clearly tied to the logic of U.S. exceptionalism. Any nation that claims to be postracial, religiously pluralistic, and sexually tolerant must excise and renounce any explicit institutional racism or bigoted ideologies. This need is particularly acute in the *Brown* decision with a claim brought by white plaintiffs seeking the redress of the state in the post–civil rights era.

Bailey and Zahren argue that white Christians, exemplified by the Browns, are problematically portrayed as the logical beneficiaries of the civil rights successes of the LGBTQ movement.[54] Even as the Browns pushed to receive the type of legal acceptance extended to other sexual minorities, their religious and marital nonnormativity is reconciled through their dedication to a supposedly neutral (i.e., white and Western) brand of conservative Christianity. The family adheres to strict dietary and modesty standards, attending church weekly and touting a strong patriotic commitment to the United States (at least two of the oldest Brown children are affiliated with the military), despite their own experiences of discrimination at the hands of the state. Kody maintains sexually monogamous relationships with each of his wives, Meri, Janelle, Christine, and Robyn—all five of whom emphatically insist that they do not "go weird," presumably denying engaging in group sexual activity.[55] Robyn Brown's explanation that "plural marriage is like monogamy on steroids" conveys the sense that white, Christian-based polygamy might even be superior to monogamy in its reaffirmation of a patriarchal authority that allows women "the right to choose polygamy but also the right to assert their 'authentic' heterosexual desires in an increasingly queer world."[56] Placed center stage, both on television and in the justice system, the Browns' attempts to gain the rights afforded to same-sex couples recenters "white heterosexuality as the normal and natural default" of U.S. citizenship.[57]

Yet Waddoups's disavowal of the "morally repugnant reasoning" in *Reynolds* ignores contemporary Orientalist and racist approaches to Islamic cultures in modern U.S. foreign policy and law. Instead, Waddoups framed Orientalism only as a contemporary extension of nineteenth-century European colonialism. Illogically, despite his own statement that *Reynolds*'s reasoning and the history of anti-Mormonism demonstrates that Utah's ban against polygamy is no longer acceptable, Waddoups still attempted to justify the ban in purely historical terms. Citing regulations as far back as AD 673, Waddoups claimed that the "prohibition against polygamy has . . . ancient roots in Anglo-American law."[58] However, he was unable to avoid pointing out that injunctions against polygamy were grounded in attempts to punish those who would defraud both the state and an innocent spouse and not in the nature or morality of polygamy. He even acknowledged in a footnote that "as early as the 1760s . . . an orientalist understanding of polygamy" motivated laws against the practice.[59] It is telling that his desire to conclusively determine that polygamy is not a fundamental right overrides his weak logic and his own in-depth consideration of the racist history of laws against plural marriage. Despite his consideration of the historical racialization of polygamy, Waddoups was unable to acknowledge that the practice might still be racialized as a specifically nonwhite, non-Christian custom. In this way, the continued criminalization and regulation of polygamy becomes an important way for the state to discriminate against and police nonwhite and non-Christian populations.[60]

REINVESTING IN HETERONORMATIVITY:
THE PARADOX OF INCLUSION AS REGULATION

Waddoups's assertion that the emergence of civil rights jurisprudence post-*Reynolds* relegates Orientalist discourse (and, I would add, other forms of racist discourse) to the nineteenth century is at best wishful thinking and at worst willful erasure. The very act of consigning the racist history of *Reynolds* and its bearing on *Brown* to a preliminary section of the decision titled "Historical Background" reflects the prevalence of postracial thinking and demonstrates the damaging effects that such thinking has on constitutional interpretation. But once again, as Somerville points out, the condemnation and resulting removal of explicit racial language in the law does not necessarily, or even likely, translate to a state that is oblivious to race. In fact, the opposite is often true: the erasure of racial language from the law has led to a more implicit application of racism, one that is conducted in and through the regulation of sexuality (among other sites), as discussed in chapters 4, 5, and 6.[61] Thus, it is significant that even though

Waddoups's decision decriminalized cohabitation, it did so by reasserting that the institutions and logics of heteronormativity, culminating in a marital relationship, can and should be favored by the state:

> At a time of much discussion in society about problems arising from the decline in rates of people marrying or the increased age at which people decided to marry, the Statute penalizes people for making a firm marriage-like commitment to each other, even though they know that their religious cohabitation does not result in state-sanctioned or recognized marriages. . . . Encouraging adulterous cohabitation over religious cohabitation that resembles marriage in all but State recognition seems counterproductive to the goal of strengthening or protecting the institution of marriage.[62]

In other words, by decriminalizing cohabitation Waddoups sought to more effectively promote the state's avowed interest in regulating sexual and familial relationships by strengthening the institution of marriage as the purportedly proper location in which sex should take place.

Waddoups's reasoning directly parallels Judge Shelby's declaration in *Kitchen* that Utah's prohibition of same-sex marriage was not rationally related to its objectives. According to Shelby, denying marriage licenses to same-sex couples encouraged sex outside of marriage, inhibited the formation of "traditional" families, and stifled religious freedom.[63] The reasoning of both *Brown* and *Kitchen* reinforces the legitimacy of the fundamental objectives of both Utah and the federal government—promoting supposedly traditional families in which raising children is the ultimate objective—by accepting them without question. Thus, these decisions do not encourage the liberty to make sexual and familial choices but rather perpetuate heteronormativity, and provisionally homonormativity, as an agenda of the state.[64]

Jasbir Puar argues that cases like *Kitchen* and *Brown* are so deceptive because they purport to include sexual others, particularly gay, lesbian, and queer people—and in this case polygamists too—when in actuality that inclusion is fleeting and conditional, reliant upon the exclusion of sexual and racial others who do not fit the narrow requirements of heteronormative ideals. Puar points out that those seeking to assimilate into "U.S. heteronormative citizenship" are consistently required to disavow bodies or figures that represent a "perverse queerness" and, more often than not, this disavowal involves a process of racial othering.[65] Accordingly, Waddoups's and Shelby's reasoning demonstrates how extending rights to privacy and marriage to some is not so much about individuals' access to rights and freedoms guaranteed to all U.S. citizens but is instead about preserving social norms that encourage prescribed sexual expression and normative conceptions of family and belonging that are most usually associated with whiteness and Christianity. The historical context of these cases reveals that while they purport to expand privileges and rights to all people, they merely extend conditional acceptance of a small number of privileged sexual minorities.[66] This provisional inclusion has troubling implications for racial justice in the United States, especially considering that marriage is one of the central ways that the state has consistently maintained an investment in whiteness, even after eschewing explicit commitments to white supremacy in the twentieth century.[67]

Because the Constitution guarantees that the law will be applied equally to all citizens but that individual statutes must also inevitably distinguish between classes of persons, the court is charged with determining whether the law in question permissibly discriminates against those inhibited by the law. Judge Shelby's verdict in *Kitchen* that Utah's ban unfairly and illegally discriminated against a class of persons based on their sexual orientation (gays and lesbians) was made based on the application of rational basis review, the lowest level of review courts use.[68] Rational basis is used "when a law creates a classification but does not target a suspect class or burden a fundamental right"—a class such as race, for example, or the constitutional right to the freedom of religion—leading courts to presume the law is reasonable and "uphold it so long as it rationally relates to some legitimate governmental purpose."[69] Despite the fact that rational basis is the lowest level of review and the least burdensome for the state to justify, the state must still articulate a legitimate reason for discriminating between citizens. The state of Utah claimed that it had an interest in prohibiting same-sex marriage in order to promote "responsible procreation" and "optimal child-rearing."[70] Shelby summarily rejected those reasons, pointing out that there is no clear relationship between denying same-sex marriage and promoting those interests.

In fact, Shelby concluded that the ban results in the opposite, actually inhibiting the promotion of "responsible procreation" and "optimal child-rearing." As in *Brown*, the court's reasoning reveals how the legalization of same-sex marriage actually promotes rather than challenges the state's underlying commitment to heteronormativity through its implicit endorse-ment of the state's interest in how children are raised. Taking this logic even further, Shelby asserted:

> Both opposite-sex and same-sex couples model the formation of committed, exclusive relationships, and both establish families based on mutual love and support. If there is any connection between same-sex marriage and respon-sible procreation, the relationship is likely to be the opposite of what the State suggests. Because Amendment 3 does not currently permit same-sex couples to engage in sexual activity within a marriage, the State reinforces a norm that sexual activity may take place outside the marriage relationship.[71]

The extraordinary linkage Shelby weaves between couples, marriage, pro-creation, and sexual activity—regardless of sexuality—is astonishing, espe-cially given the history of LGBTQ activism that has sought to disentangle such cultural logic that assumes commitment as a necessary and desirable prerequisite for sex. Rather than question the state's right or investment in discouraging or encouraging certain sexual activities, relationships, families, or kinship formations, Shelby's reasoning explicitly ties same-sex marriage to the state as a vehicle to achieve normative family formations. Consider-ing that federal and state agendas list "responsible procreation" and "opti-mal child-rearing" as justifications for sanctioning and withdrawing support from nontraditional families, particularly to households with women (espe-cially Black women) at their head, the court's easy incorporation of same-sex marriage into the folds of legal marriage requires a reexamination of the LGBTQ community's investment in the institution.[72]

Although Shelby does not explicitly engage in a discussion of Utah's "gold standard," what the state defines as children who are raised in a state-sanctioned marriage with a mother and a father in a stable family unit, he argues that prohibiting same-sex marriage does not forward the goal of having children raised in such an environment.[73] Not only did Shelby's rea-soning implicitly endorse the state's gold standard—including the idea that children should be raised by a heterosexual couple—but he goes so far as to say that the state could have legitimately prohibited gays and lesbians from adopting or raising children in more effective ways: if "the State wishes to see more children in opposite-sex families, its goals are tied to laws con-cerning adoptions and surrogacy, not marriage."[74] The apparent problem of whether or not to accept homosexuality as a benign variation or as a less than desirable disadvantage is not solved but is in fact reasserted and even heightened in decisions such as *Kitchen* and *Lawrence*. As Nan Hunter argues, the legalization of sodomy and gay marriage increases the scrutiny paid to "the question of whether homosexuality actually causes harm in any given situation" and "will require more, not less, judicial scrutiny."[75] Allowing same-sex couples to marry, in other words, will ensure that the state maintains an investment in assessing, defining, and regulating same-sex sexuality when it comes to the issue of child care and custody.

While the state of Utah did not question the plaintiffs' fundamental right to marry, the state did assert that the plaintiffs' rights had not been abridged because they were at liberty to marry a person of the opposite sex. Lambasting the state's argument, Shelby denounced this choice as an "illusion" because it infringed upon their right to dignity, intimate association, and privacy. What is noteworthy about his critique of the state is that Shelby takes the time to point out the plaintiffs' choice is a choice grounded in essentialist notions of sexual identity:

> The State fails to dispute any of the facts that demonstrate why the Plaintiffs' asserted right to marry someone of the opposite sex is meaningless. The State accepts without contest the Plaintiffs' testimony that they cannot develop the type of intimate bond necessary to sustain a marriage with a person of the opposite sex. . . . The Plaintiffs' testimony supports their assertions that their sexual orientation is an inherent characteristic of their identities . . . and the State presents no argument or evidence to suggest that the Plaintiffs could change their identity if they desired to do so.[76]

Under this logic, if the plaintiffs were willing and able to develop a heterosexual bond, it would be preferable and would apparently negate their right to dignity, choice, and privacy. One hesitates to ask what rights are afforded to those who identify as bisexual or any other sexual or gender minority identity. Ironically, given the focus on choice, the court's inability to see beyond "born this way" discourses evidences its continued inability to take the intersectional and fluid nature of identity into account. Following the law's approach to other questions of identity, most notably race, this court was only able to find the plaintiffs' rights grounded in their inherent (i.e., unchangeable) characteristics. By enshrining sexuality's essentialism in the law, Shelby was able to confer rights and responsibilities by avoiding moral questions about choice and failed to engage other frameworks for understanding sexual activity beyond essentialized identity. Following and fortifying the chain of associational rights established by the Supreme Court in *Lawrence*—dignity, choice, and privacy—Shelby's refutation of the state's arguments reinforces a limited or "privatized conception of liberty" tied to the ideal of heteronormative marriage.

Shelby's conclusion that the state of Utah did not have a rational basis on which to discriminate against gays and lesbians in denying them the right to marry should therefore not be read as an unequivocal victory. Not only did the decision provide a contingent acceptance only of those willing and able to engage in homonormativity, but it provided for the extended surveillance and regulation of those who fall outside those norms. In this way, *Kitchen* reinforced a conservative state agenda that paradoxically limited rights. *Kitchen*, like *Loving* and *Lawrence* before it, serves to further cement privacy, liberty, and association as attendant rights of marriage rather than, say, individual choice, reinforcing a privatized conception of liberty, one that is implicitly racialized. It is not a mistake that Shelby closes his historic judgment by invoking *Loving*: "The contentions [in *Loving*] are almost identical to the assertions made by the State of Utah in support of Utah's law prohibiting same-sex marriage."[77] Glossing over important contextual and historical facts, explored in the next section, this parallel reinforces the false notion that state-sanctioned racism is a thing of the past and that gays and lesbians now deserve those same rights and privileges that people of color have already gained. Such a narrative ignores the ongoing ways that contemporary marriage law "reinstate[s] white privileges and rights."[78]

REINVESTING IN WHITENESS: ANALOGIZING RACE AND SEXUALITY IN *KITCHEN* AND *BROWN*

In the aftermath of the Supreme Court's *Lawrence v. Texas* decision that decriminalized sodomy, many scholars critiqued the decision's use of analogizing logic that compared race to sexuality. Scholars such as David Eng, Katherine Franke, Somerville, and Puar argue that portraying race and sexuality as parallel forms of difference in which "gays and lesbians are the last recipients of civil rights that have already been bestowed on racial minorities" is problematic for many reasons, not least of which because it forwards a selective and overly optimistic reading of the history of racial justice in the United States.[79] Moreover, analogizing race and sexuality ignores the inextricable ways in which those identities are experienced and produced in society.

Analogy is as an essential tool in legal argumentation, especially for those
cases that invoke the Fourteenth Amendment. Somerville explains:

> It is important to recognize that "like race" comparisons are more appeal-
> ing because of the distinctive argumentative power of race in federal con-
> stitutional reasoning. . . . Because the Fourteenth Amendment was created
> in 1868 on behalf of a specific racialized group, previously enslaved African
> Americans, "like race" arguments implicitly refer to this constitutional appa-
> ratus for challenging identity-based discrimination.[80]

This suggests that the law requires a simultaneous and paradoxical uplift-
ing and forgetting of race. In other words, legal analogy makes race an
essential (the highest level of scrutiny is reserved for assessing race-based
laws) yet paradoxically virtually empty point of reference (the state's determination to be colorblind allows it to ignore race when it is in fact opera-
tive).[81] In his critique of the analogizing logic used in *Lawrence,* Eng asks,
"As race disappears, how will the law ever come to see [it]?"[82] In other words,
Eng highlights how the law can only attain colorblindness through an explicitly sanitized narration of the history of race and racism in the United States.
In order to understand the importance of analogy in law "even though
specific cases about homosexuality may seem to have nothing to do with
race," as in *Lawrence, Kitchen,* or *Brown,* it is imperative to uncover the tacit
ways that race is invoked through juridical discourses concerning homosexuality and other nonnormative sexual practices, particularly, in this case,
polygamy.[83]

Somerville examines the appeal and effects of what she calls the miscegenation analogy, a popular rhetorical and legal tactic used in cases dealing
with the rights of sexual minorities, that equates the repeal of antimiscegenation laws with antisodomy and anti–gay marriage laws. By situating
the *Loving* decision in relation to other legal and political developments
of the period, she draws attention to the ways that the legal discourses
have produced sexuality and race in relation to one another. For example,
she notes that *Loving* was not just a case about race in its legalization of
interracial marriage but "it also effectively consolidated heterosexuality as
a privileged prerequisite for recognition by the state as a national subject
and citizen."[84] The analogizing logic that invokes *Loving* as a decision in
need of replication for the rights of gays and lesbians demonstrates that
the racialization of intimacy—a process Eng describes as the ways that

"race becomes occluded within the private domain of family and kinship today"—is a significant and problematic effect of such analogizing.[85]

In *Lawrence*, this occlusion is evident in the very circumstances that brought the case to the attention of the authorities. Several scholars have pointed to the probable racist motives of the call that brought police to the house of John Lawrence, a white man. Lawrence and Tyron Garner, a Black man, were together in the former's house when the police were informed of a weapons disturbance and a "black man 'going crazy.'"[86] The precipitation of a police investigation and the ultimate indictment of the two for engaging in sodomy is an example of the continued criminalization of Blackness that repeatedly brings Black people under state management.[87] Relatedly, Puar argues that the parallel drawn between *Loving* and *Lawrence* must be examined in light of a post-9/11 Orientalist mindset that links sodomy, perversion, and Islam. Contending that "the politics of racism, empire, and warmongering" cannot be disconnected from the legalization of same-sex sodomy, Puar argues that analogizing in the law glosses over continued racial injustices and justifies the nation-state's imperial ambitions by exceptionalizing the United States as inherently progressive, a progressiveness that must be spread to "less developed" nations.[88] Of course, analogizing race and sexuality in contemporary case law also relies upon the forgetting of historical precedents of U.S. (sexual) exceptionalism—in particular, the criminalization of Mormon polygamy as a racial threat that was used to help justify nineteenth-century imperialism in the *Reynolds* and *Insular* decisions.[89]

While I certainly agree with scholarship that examines how analogies between interracial and same-sex marriage disguise the complicated ways race and sexuality are produced through one another, and that we must work to contextualize what is lost in the historical forgetting of these decisions, we must also pay attention to the specific ways that the law relies on analogy. This is critical for undoing the logic of comparison that permeates popular understandings of race and sexuality in the contemporary world. It is also necessary for understanding the law primarily as a vehicle of exceptionalist narratives, not for the resolution of social justice concerns. In the *Kitchen* decision, for example, the plaintiffs' equal protection claim required Judge Shelby to determine whether the state of Utah had unreasonably restricted their rights by denying them access to marry a person of the same sex. As with all equal protection arguments, the court had to determine which of three levels of scrutiny was appropriate when assessing the reasonableness of the state's restriction of the rights in question:

rational basis review, intermediate scrutiny, or strict scrutiny. Jurisprudence in the United States requires that different classifications used to restrict citizens' rights (for example, classifications based upon nationality or class) be subject to different levels of examination by courts. As a result of the Fourteenth Amendment, race is a classification that is subject to the highest level of scrutiny, strict scrutiny, while over time it has been determined that other classifications such as sex are subject to a lower level of review, intermediate scrutiny. In the case of sexual orientation, the law only requires the application of the lowest level, rational basis review, to determine whether a law restricting sexual minorities' constitutionally protected rights is permissible. This system of analysis, which has developed as a process for determining whether a law or state has unduly infringed upon a particular group's rights, reveals the hierarchal nature of the law's understanding of and approach to issues of identity and oppression. This tiered method of legal reasoning is one that has been critiqued by critical race scholars for its inability to comprehend the intersection of multiple identity categories and forms of oppression.[90] Although the law's purported objective is equality in its application, its inability to register identity and oppression as nuanced and intersectional betrays its inevitably unequal and inequitable application. The unequal, and in fact disproportional, attention that the law produces is evident in both *Kitchen's* and *Brown's* limited protection of only certain sexual minorities.

Like *Lawrence*, *Brown* and *Kitchen* both reference *Loving* as an analogy that validates the legalization of same-sex marriage and the decriminalization of cohabitation in Utah. In *Kitchen*, because the Supreme Court has definitively determined marriage to be a fundamental but unenumerated right, Shelby's reasoning sought to link marriage to a series of other recognized rights.[91] The Supreme Court has repeatedly articulated liberty, privacy, and association as rights intertwined with marriage.[92] Both Puar and Franke describe these rights as deceptively conservative because they display "a narrow version of liberty that is both geographized and domesticated—not a robust conception of sexual freedom or liberty, as is commonly assumed."[93] Such a conservative version of liberty helped Shelby to hold out monogamous marriage as the ideal form for both heterosexual and same-sex couples, in which the very dignity of gays and lesbians became fundamentally linked to their ability to access the institution.

By formulating a chain that links dignity with choice and choice with privacy, *Kitchen* reinforces the occlusion of race within the domain of the

privatized family.[94] The decision conveniently ignores the history of institutional racism in the United States—from immigration restrictions to
criminalization practices—that have made it extremely difficult for nonwhite populations to maintain supposedly traditional (i.e., heteronormative)
family units at the same time that the choice to marry and have children
is upheld as the best possible choice.[95] Puar argues, however, that "a taken
for granted access to privacy raises many questions about the unacknowledged forms of privilege necessary" to make particular choices.[96] And as
Franke points out, "put most bluntly," the choice to marry means that
"the state acquires a legal interest in your relationship," an interest that is
especially consequential for those who are already heavily managed by the
state.[97] Given the well-documented history of the state's intervention into
the lives and (the purportedly protected right to) privacy of nonwhite populations, the court's reliance on such a chain of related rights must be
taken with more than a grain of salt. Even more telling is the fact that
the state's intervention is often motivated by a desire to force compliance
with (hetero)normative ideals of sex, sexuality, marriage, family planning,
and kinship. Thus, the formulation of "liberty" in these decisions is not
a positive or substantive right but a negative one; one that encompasses
the "right to be left alone from state interference, surveillance, and criminalization" only as long as one is able and willing to engage in heteronormative ideals of sexuality, family, kinship, and support.[98] And as numerous
scholars demonstrate, populations that are unable or unwilling to comply
with state-sanctioned (white, heterosexual) norms of family and kinship
consistently come under the purview of state management.[99]

Hunter's point that "decriminalization is not deregulation[,] it is one
stage in a regulatory process" gestures toward the ways that the regulation of sex and family formation is an important way that the state can still
racialize and legally manage certain populations, particularly nonwhite,
immigrant, poor, and queer ones, without resorting to explicitly racial justifications.[100] In other words, the regulatory process is not necessarily only,
or even primarily, about those individuals who gain inclusion or rights in
cases like *Kitchen* and *Brown*. In *Kitchen*, for example, same-sex couples will
come under the purview of the state and its regulatory apparatuses—for
example, family law (including divorce, custody, and adoption), tax law,
inheritance law, etc.—but those most likely to suffer under the duress of
the state's supervision are those who have traditionally been subject to its
regulatory and disciplinary gaze: nonwhite, poor, immigrant, and queer

populations. Opening access to marriage for same-sex couples, and possibly to polygamous people in the future, reaffirms the importance and centrality of marriage, providing the state with continued justification for the
evacuation of privacy and rights of those who cannot or do not choose to
engage in normative, state-sponsored relationships.

As Franke notes, same-sex couples who choose not to marry in states
that attain gay marriage often lost privileges, economic and intimate, that
they had previously gained.[101] For example, many employers that previously provided health insurance coverage to same-sex partners no longer
provide coverage unless the couple legally marries. As Shelby confidently
claims in his conclusion to *Kitchen,* "the Plaintiffs' desire to publicly declare
their vows of commitment and support to each other is a testament to the
strength of marriage in society, not a sign that, by opening its doors to all
individuals, it is in danger of collapse."[102] By opening the doors of marriage
to gays and lesbians, the loss of viable alternative kinship models is justified and reinforced.

Similarly, the Browns argued that they had a "fundamental liberty interest in choosing to cohabit and maintain romantic and spiritual relationships, even if those relationships are termed 'plural marriage,'" based on
the establishment of "'a fundamental liberty interest in intimate sexual
conduct'" in *Lawrence.* Despite finding this argument compelling (he spent
six pages positively reviewing the *Lawrence* court's decision), Waddoups was
bound by the Tenth Circuit Court's interpretation of *Lawrence* in *Seegmiller v.
LaVerkin City* (2008), which determined that no fundamental right to sexual privacy exists.[103] In *Seegmiller,* the court determined that "'the [Supreme]
Court has never endorsed an all-encompassing right to sexual privacy
under the rubric of substantive due process,'" reflecting Franke's assertion
that the *Lawrence* decision was not the vigorous protection of sexual privacy rooted in choice as many have claimed.[104]

But in a similar line of argumentation, the Browns also asserted that
Utah's statute violated the guarantee to the free exercise of religion. Despite
this constitutional guarantee, the Supreme Court has held that individuals
are required to adhere to laws that are "generally applicable" or "neutral,"
prohibiting conduct that a person's religion prescribes. More simply put, if
a law prohibits conduct equally for all individuals and does not target one
religious group, then it may outlaw a practice even if it is prescribed by
a particular religion. Although "it would be ludicrous to suggest that the
federal legislation at issue in [*Reynolds*] and [*Late Corp.*] did not specifically

target the LDS Church and its practice of polygamy," Utah repealed all of its criminal statutes and entirely replaced its penal code in 1973.[105] This meant that the pre-1973 statute directly targeted Mormon polygamy but that the rewritten post-1973 statute did not. In other words, while the pre-1973 anti-polygamy statute would have been unconstitutional because it explicitly targeted Mormon polygamists, the post-1973 statute was not because it was, at least facially, neutral, targeting anyone who practiced polygamy or cohabited.

The distinction between Utah's two antipolygamy statutes (pre- and post-1973) is especially important because common law marriage was recognized in Utah until 1898. This meant that "'after 1852, when the Church publicly recognized the doctrine of plural marriage, ceremonies of plural union performed according to Church practice were *legally valid marriages* under territorial law until the Morrill [Anti-Bigamy] Act [of 1862] declared otherwise.'"[106] These historical circumstances explain why attempts to criminalize polygamy required the simultaneous criminalization of cohabitation. But because Utah no longer recognizes common law marriages, Waddoups found that the cohabitation portion of the 1973 statute violated individuals' right to the free exercise of religion under the First Amendment. While Utah's antipolygamy statute did not explicitly refer to any one religion, its application unduly targeted a specific religious group: practitioners of the Latter-day Saint tradition. This is clear in the state's practice of only utilizing the statute against religious, specifically Mormon, cohabitation. In fact, the last prosecution for nonreligious cohabitation in Utah (also known as adultery) was in 1928. Yet, the state deviated from its own openly stated policy of only prosecuting cohabitation cases that involve underage girls in order to pursue those individuals that "openly discuss[] their religious cohabitation in the media."[107] This deviation reflects both the state's and the mainstream Church's investment in perpetuating discourses of Mormon peculiarity that continue to emphasize polygamy as a supposedly backward practice that reflects the (racially) suspect nature of fundamentalist Mormons.

Like Shelby in *Kitchen*, Waddoups identifies the apparent "absurdity" in the state's position of prosecuting religious cohabitation when it is trying to "protect" the institution of marriage: "[If] the Statute penalizes people for making a firm marriage-like commitment," then the state is "encouraging adulterous cohabitation over religious cohabitation that resembles marriage."[108] Just as Judge Shelby's reasoning in *Kitchen* outlines a clear investment in a conservative agenda that promotes "marriage-like commitments"—long-term relationships and family forms that include procreation and care of children as the primary objective—so too does Judge Waddoups's castigation of the state articulate a preference not only for marital commitment but for a specifically religious one at that. The selective inclusion of certain sexual minorities that both judges advocate is contingent upon the obfuscation of the racial politics of the state's regulation of marriage and kinship.

For example, why do so many opponents of gay marriage cite the legalization of polygamy as the next inevitable, and apparently terrifying, step after the legalization of same-sex marriage? What exactly is so frightening about polygamy that it is referenced as one of the primary reasons that gay marriage should have remained prohibited? To answer these questions, it is crucial to recall the ways in which the practice has and continues to be racialized in the United States. For example, in an interview about the threat of gay marriage in April 2013, Fox television host Bill O'Reilly asserted that polygamy would induce "chaos in the family," a chaos akin to the "disintegration of the African American family when 71 percent of babies are born out of wedlock" without a father in the home.[109] O'Reilly's claims that the legalization of (Mormon) polygamy would mirror the supposed breakdown of the Black family eerily echoes nineteenth-century claims by anti-Mormon activists that polygamy produced racial deterioration and collapsed proper gender roles to the detriment of society.

Keeping this history in mind, the Browns' litigation can be read as a call to reinstate the privileges of whiteness that were lost to Mormon (i.e., Christian) polygamists. In this light, Robyn Brown's comment that "this is not the America I learned about when I was in school" takes on new meaning, as a recognition that the inclusion promised under the law has not been realized. The Browns' access to both informal and formal privileges of whiteness—evident in their legal success after almost 150 years of formal discrimination against Mormon polygamy—reflects the ascendency of whiteness in the age of neoliberalism. As Eng asserts, "in the era of late capitalism . . . whiteness as property has now evolved to create new queer subjects for representation, demanding a more thorough investigation of the degree to which (homo)sexuality and race constitute and consolidate conventional distinctions between the time and space of civilization and barbarism."[110] While Eng makes his observation in relation to the inclusion of certain gay and lesbian individuals, he could just as easily be describing white polygamists, particularly Mormon fundamentalists.

As the Browns are increasingly interpellated as queer subjects in the supposedly posthomophobic era, represented in the mainstream media as simply another example of the diversity of the United States, their inclusion is contingent upon the othering and exclusion of nonwhite and non-Christian populations that practice polygamy or fail to adequately adhere to the requirements of heteronormativity. For example, would the Browns' claim have been as successful if they were a Muslim family? While the rule of law dictates its equal application, numerous scholars have effectively demonstrated that the law, and by extension the state, is not oblivious to race (or religion) or the racialization of certain (sexual and religious) practices. Thus, Waddoups's conclusion that the cohabitation prong "actually inhibits the advancement of th[e] compelling" interests of the state indicates a desire to formally allow a practice in order to better regulate certain populations but also to forward the narrative of diversity and inclusion at the root of twenty-first-century U.S. exceptionalism.[111]

In addition to finding that the cohabitation prong of Utah's antipolygamy statute violated the Free Exercise Clause of the First Amendment, Waddoups also considered and accepted the plaintiffs' claim that the statute violated their right to due process under the Fourteenth Amendment. In applying the rational basis level of review, the lowest level of scrutiny, for claims that deal with consensual private sexual activity as dictated in *Lawrence* and *Seegmiller,* the court concluded that the state cannot equate private sexual conduct with marriage as was being done in the antipolygamy statute. Waddoups concluded that in *Lawrence,* "the individual liberty guarantee essentially draws a line around an individual's home and family and prevents governmental interference with what happens inside, as long as it does not involve injury or coercion or some other form of harm to individuals or society."[112] In the case of the Browns, both sexual activity and personal choices about family and kinship are protected exactly because they have chosen a "marriage-like commitment" that is promoted by the interests of the state. But any activity or relationship that falls outside of those heteronormative boundaries is likely to come under scrutiny by, and intervention from, the government.

In a similar line, perhaps the most suggestive argument that Utah forwarded and Shelby rejected in *Kitchen* was that the plaintiffs were seeking access to a new rather than an existing right. Because it is very uncommon for a court, especially any court other than the Supreme Court, to establish a new right, the state's argument that same-sex marriage was a new one was meant to negate any constitutional claim the plaintiffs could make. Unfortunately for Utah, Shelby determined that "the Plaintiffs here do not seek a new right to same-sex marriage, but instead ask the court to hold that the State cannot prohibit them from exercising their existing right to marry on account of the sex of their chosen partner" just as the *Loving* court held that the plaintiffs in that case could not be stopped from exercising their existing right to marry due to the race of their chosen partner.[113] Once again, the logic of analogy is deployed in order to establish the state's investment in ensuring a domesticated, geographized liberty that the court describes as "the right to make a public commitment to form an exclusive relationship and create a family with a partner with whom the person shares an intimate and sustaining emotional bond."[114] The overly romantic description of marriage aside, the court points out that to qualify as a new right, same-sex marriage would have to make new (i.e., additional) protections and benefits available to all citizens. Shelby's rationality, while it did not have a direct bearing on the outcome of the *Brown* case, has interesting implications for the state's future ability to regulate polygamous marriages. If the right in question is a fundamental one that is guaranteed by the Constitution, and not a new right to same-sex marriage, then that same reasoning could be applied to those seeking the state's validation of their polygamous unions. A reasonable claim for the legalization of polygamy could be made on the grounds that the prohibition of plural marriage unduly infringes upon an individual's right to access the existing fundamental right to marry based upon religious persecution (a violation of the First Amendment).

It is tempting to conclude that *Kitchen* and *Brown* signal a broader and more vigorous move toward the defense of private sexual conduct couched in the condemnation of the explicitly racist history of antipolygamy legislation, but upon closer inspection it is evident that these decisions are essentially conservative in scope. While *Brown* did temporarily invalidate a central and historically significant portion of Utah's antipolygamy law— an action whose impact cannot be discounted—it did not decriminalize polygamy, it did not overturn *Reynolds,* and it did not confirm or expand the right of individuals to make choices about personal sexual conduct, family, or kinship free from government interference. What it did do was to recast the historical narrative of the nineteenth-century antipolygamy movement as long since passed, inaccurately characterizing its racist foundations as distinctly outmoded and unconnected to modern law and policy. A careful reading of both Shelby's and Waddoups's reasoning reveals a subtle yet powerful support for regarding the intimacy protected in marriage as a racialized property right, one that is "unequally and unevenly distributed" to gays, lesbians, queers, polygamists, and others that engage in nonnormative kinship practices and relationships.[115]

MORMON PECULIARITY IN THE TWENTY-FIRST CENTURY

Ultimately, what *Kitchen* and *Brown* reveal is the extent to which, in the twenty-first century, Mormon peculiarity, as a resilient strain of U.S. (sexual) exceptionalist discourse, functions to promote the nation-state's ongoing investment in white supremacy, most obviously through the continued elaboration of heteronormativity as natural and normal. While this chapter examined the construction of Mormonism as inherently peculiar in its negative views of sexual nonnormativity—views that are framed as in opposition to the purportedly inevitable wave of progressive judicial rulings that expand the civil rights of sexual minorities—in order to illustrate the ways that liberal commitments to tolerance, inclusion, and equality are fundamentally bound to the biopolitical (i.e., racial) governance of U.S. colonialism, it could have just as easily examined the mainstream Church's own contemporary deployment of Mormon peculiarity that represents the Church as uniquely positioned and destined to protect the integrity of the heteronormative family unit. Thus, the point here is not to identify the mainstream Church, or any Latter-day Saint church for that matter, as inherently or especially conservative, homophobic, or theocratic but rather to expose the discourse of Mormon peculiarity as part and parcel of the ideological apparatuses that buttress the continuation of U.S. empire.

Although Mormon peculiarity has changed course and form since the nineteenth century, it has consistently been a tool through which the nation-state has been articulated as Protestant, secular, capitalist, and heteronormative, all characteristics that are meant to establish a fundamental distinction between Euro-Americanness (whiteness) and non-Euro-Americanness (nonwhiteness). In other words, Mormon peculiarity, as an important variety of U.S. exceptionalist discourse, functions to racialize and therefore justify the political rule of white people over nonwhite people, even, perhaps most especially, within the colorblind strictures of late twentieth- and early

twenty-first-century U.S. jurisprudence. Regarding Mormonism as a racializing civilizational assemblage, and not as a fundamentally peculiar religion, is especially important for understanding the nuances of how race
functions as "a system of governing through the colonial relation of power"
exactly because it helps to deconstruct the vast and long-standing ideological apparatus that has constructed Euro-Americanness (i.e., whiteness)
as humanness.[116]

Coda

What Mormonism Can Tell Us
about Critical Theory

> Playing on this difference, between the subject being queered
> and queerness already existing within the subject (and thus
> dissipating the subject as such), allows for both the temporality
> of being (ontological essence of the subject) and the tempo-
> rality of always-becoming (continual ontological emergence,
> a Deleuzian *becoming without being*).
>
> —Jasbir Puar, *Terrorist Assemblages*

In her seminal 1997 essay "Punks, Bulldaggers, and Welfare Queens," Cathy
Cohen argues that "a truly radical or transformative politics ha[d] not resulted from queer activism" and instead called for a new kind of politics
"where one's relation to power, and not some homogenized identity, is privileged in determining one's political comrades . . . where the *nonnormative*
and *marginal* position of punks, bulldaggers, and welfare queens, for example, is the basis for progressive transformative coalition work."[1] Reflecting
twenty years later on her earlier article's proposition about the radical potential of queerness, Cohen recenters the context of 1970s, 1980s, and 1990s
radical Black writing and activism that was responding to not only (or even
primarily) the HIV/AIDS crisis but also the implementation of neoliberal
policies that devastated poor communities of color under the Reagan and
Clinton administrations. She does this in order to remind readers that Black
feminist knowledge production during those decades was about confronting the "urgency of Black death" and articulating a future in which "punks,
bulldaggers, and welfare queens" would be accepted as "full members of
Black communities, connected in struggle and helping to produce a new
era in the Black radical tradition."[2]

As I write this in October 2020, confronting what Cohen so precisely terms the "urgency of Black death" remains an ongoing struggle—especially in the wake of the deaths of George Floyd, Ahmaud Arbery, Breonna Taylor, Dion Johnson, and Tony McDade earlier this year. In Cohen's formulation of queer politics, Floyd, Arbery, Taylor, Johnson, and McDade all constitute queer subjects "not because of their sexual practice, identity, or performance but because they, as well as other young and poor folks of color, operate in the world as queer subjects: the targets of racial normalizing projects intent on pathologizing them across the dimensions of race, class, gender, and sexuality, simultaneously making them into deviants while normalizing their degradation and marginalization until it becomes what we expect—the norm—until it becomes something that we no longer pay attention to."[3] Cohen's formulation reflects Jasbir Puar's reconceptualization of queerness in *Terrorist Assemblages* where she explores how "the connectivities that generate queer, homosexual, and gay disciplinary subjects . . . concurrently constitut[e] queerness as the optic through which perverse populations are called into normalization for control."[4] For both Cohen and Puar, perverse (i.e., racialized) populations are the subjects of U.S. colonial and imperial production, surveillance, control, and, ultimately, necropolitical management.

Both the utility and risk of identifying Mormonism and Mormons as queer—queer as in a kind of politicized identity, a practice or set of practices, and as antinormative (all of which articulate queerness as a kind of exceptionalism)—is made evident when race and not sex, gender, sexual practice, or sexuality is the primary category through which such a formation and the people it adheres to is prioritized. For instance, Peter Coviello argues that "modern Mormonism's ever more seamless identification with American religiosity" is inevitably disrupted by an underlying "perversity"—a perversity identifiable, he insists, in both early Mormonism's commitment to polygamous marriages as indicative of an extravagantly embodied theology of the human as divine and in modern Mormons' insistence on their own hypernormativity.[5] Significantly, Coviello arrives at this conclusion by reading into the 2017 General Conference remarks of Apostle Dallin H. Oaks, who reiterated the teachings of the Church's 1995 document "The Family: A Proclamation to the World."

The proclamation further institutionalized a heteronormative worldview within the Church, declaring that "marriage between a man and a woman is ordained of God and that the family is central to the Creator's plan"; that "gender is an essential characteristic of individual premortal, mortal, and eternal identity and purpose"; and that "by divine design, fathers are to preside over their families in love and righteousness and are responsible to provide the necessities of life and protection for their families" while "mothers are primarily responsible for the nurture of their children."[6] Oaks's reiteration of these dictates was supplemented with a statement that simultaneously identified those engaged in same-sex sexual activity or relationships as "apostates" but still deserving of tolerance and love and went on to use Mormon peculiarity discourse to charge individual Saints with the special task of staying true to God's requirements for earthly life in preparation for the celestial kingdom. "'Even as we must live with the marriage laws and other traditions of a declining world,'" Oaks proclaimed, "'those who strive for exaltation must make personal choices in family life according to the Lord's way whenever that differs from the world's way.'"[7]

Reading in these comments the specter of early polygamy and "a whole unruly tradition of dissident Mormonism," Coviello tends to overdetermine both the practice of polygamy specifically and early Mormon theology generally as exceptional—in other words, as fundamentally deviant, errant, and perverse, making it impossible for the Saints to ever, however much they insist upon their own hypernormativity, truly expurgate their queerness.[8] Thus, Coviello identifies the history of a certain practice, alongside a kind of theological essence ("the early Mormons were the purveyors of what was all but universally recognized as a deviant carnality"), as what made early Mormons queer and continues to overshadow their claims to normativity.[9] While Coviello's approach does indeed "trace out a different story of secularism" as part and parcel of nineteenth-century biopolitics in which Mormon queerness becomes concomitant with that project, he slips into his own construction of both queerness and Mormonism as exceptionally perverse.[10] In contrast, *Exceptionally Queer*'s approach moves beyond an examination of the theological and material practices of a particular religious tradition to attend to the discursive construction of that tradition as itself a racializing civilizational assemblage in order to recenter the production and management of unexceptional—or what Puar calls nonexceptional—queer subjects. Approaching Mormonism this way—and potentially other racial-religious formations as well—provides a different perspective through a more holistic treatment.

For example, like many scholars of Mormonism, Coviello focuses his attention on its early history and inevitably, without more comprehensive attention to its later instantiations, overdetermines the meaning of Mormon polygamy as indicative of a grandiose theology of the body, while paying less attention to its deeper racial-national-colonial dimensions. A comparative analysis of nineteenth- and twentieth-century Mormonism reveals the extent to which twentieth- and twenty-first-century claims of Mormon hypernormativity were and are not solely those of the Saints themselves but were and are actively and sincerely forwarded by non-Mormons, thereby functioning to maintain the nation-state's commitment to white supremacy through the enactment of new kinds of biopolitical governance during the transition to colorblind rhetoric and policy. Thus, approaching Mormonism from a perspective that does not prioritize sex, gender, or sexuality and instead relies upon an understanding of queerness primarily in relation to racialization, alongside multiple processes of normalization that intersect with but also move well beyond those categories, is better able to comprehend the simultaneity of both queerness and Mormonism's resistance to and complicity with dominant formations. These dominant formations, of course, operate continuously through the surveillance, control, and management of queer subjects (i.e., those subject to processes of racialization that draw on "a series of onto-colonial taxonomies of land, climate, history, bodies, customs, language, all of which became sedimented metonymically, metaphorically, and normatively as the assembled attributions of 'race'") in the service of U.S. empire.[11]

The racial-national-colonial implications of Mormon hypernormativity are made evident in current Church president Russell M. Nelson's statement about racism, posted to his Facebook page on June 1, 2020, after the protests that arose following the deaths of Floyd, Arbery, Taylor, Johnson, and McDade. "We join with many throughout this nation and around the world who are deeply saddened at recent evidences of racism and a blatant disregard for human life," Nelson announced.[12] Commentators, both Mormon and non-Mormon, have generally regarded his statement as strongly condemning racism and a significant change given the Church's legacy of anti-Blackness.[13] Despite the largely local praise of his comments (in general, the national press did not cover Nelson's statement and focused instead on the ongoing protests, as well as the Covid-19 pandemic), Nelson's statement relied on a fundamentally individualized view of racism as expressed through personal prejudice and action. Thus, after first denouncing "recent evidences of racism," Nelson continued by noting that the Church "abhor[s] the reality that some would deny others respect and the most basic of freedoms because of the color of his or her skin" and declared that "the Creator of us all calls on each of us to abandon attitudes of prejudice against any group of God's children. Any of us who has prejudice toward another race needs to repent!" Nelson's focus on individual racist attitudes and actions—and individualized solutions to those sins—reflects the prevailing Enlightenment conceptualization of sin as "an individual act to be expiated through transaction with the church," leaving behind earlier notions of sin "as a collective condition to be redeemed."[14] As Brooks reminds us, this individualized notion of sin was a significant component of European colonialism in North America; it underwrote early articulations of U.S. exceptionalism and "provided the framework for the US Supreme Court's deliberation of cases involving school desegregation and affirmative action."[15]

In other words, such a conceptualization of sin within U.S. Christianity, Mormonism included, is predicated upon the same governing racial logics that drove European colonialism in the Americas, the development of racial capitalism, and the biopolitical governance of the U.S. settler colonial nation-state. As indicative of modern U.S. Christianity, Nelson's comments about racism as an individual sin reflect any number of statements made not only by religious leaders but also by corporations and politicians around the country after the Black Lives Matter protests erupted in late May. Unsurprisingly, then, Nelson's statement did not just condemn individual racism as a sin but also "assaults on human dignity [which] lead to escalating violence and unrest." "Any nation can only be as great as its people," Nelson declared, insisting, "that requires citizens to cultivate a moral compass that helps them distinguish between right and wrong." In Nelson's statement, racism is only solvable through the development of individuals' personal moral compasses, not through the communal redress of institutionalized racist segregation and discrimination, and what is right and wrong does not account for ongoing U.S. settler colonialism. Significantly, his appeal to individuals to develop such a compass was followed by the strong chastisement of "illegal acts such as looting, defacing, or destroying public or private property," which he asserted "cannot be tolerated" since "evil has never been resolved by more evil."[16] The equation of racist killings with looting and destroying of property as evil illustrates the differing extent to which white property and Black life are prioritized by both the modern state and the Church, reflecting the earliest instantiations of modern democracy in the form of company-states that developed through European colonialism in the Americas and the Atlantic slave trade.[17]

As an expression of the governing logic not only of U.S. Christian notions of sin but of how race and racism function in the United States, Nelson's statement is a decidedly normative assessment of the nation's racial politics. Given the history of Mormon peculiarity discourse in the development of colorblind racism in the United States and the normative racial views of both nineteenth- and twentieth-century Mormons, it is not surprising that the Church continues to articulate such ideas about race. Moreover, read with this context in mind, the Church's statement "The Family: A Proclamation" and continued references to it (often tethered to condemnations of same-sex sex or marriage) should be read as a document that helps to reinstantiate white supremacy by dictating heteronormativity's universality, especially given the Church's global reach.[18] Thus, Mormon hypernormativity, as the predominant version of twentieth- and twenty-first-century Mormon peculiarity discourse articulated by both Mormons and non-Mormons, works to reaffirm the prevailing frameworks of biopolitical governance both within and on behalf of U.S. empire.

To this same end, we can see how nineteenth-century versions of Mormon peculiarity discourse are sometimes resurrected to portray Mormonism as other (frequently through reference to polygamy but also often through reference to the mainstream Church's financial and political power and a variety of nonnormative religious practices not deemed appropriately Protestant/secular) and how these portrayals are in turn used as proof of U.S. sexual/secular/religious exceptionalism. Most frequently, these portrayals work to present Mormonism as a foil against which the U.S. nation-state can proclaim its tolerance and inclusivity: compared to the Church's treatment of gender and sexual minorities, the nation-state appears progressive. The revivification of these nineteenth-century versions of Mormon peculiarity help to exemplify how "many of the roots of heteronormativity are in white supremacist ideologies which sought, and continue, to use the state and its regulation of sexuality, in particular through the institution of heterosexual marriage, to designate which individuals were truly 'fit' for full rights and citizenship."[19] In both opposition to and alliance with the state, assemblages of Mormonism evidence the extent to which challenging the ongoing projects of U.S. colonialism and imperialism—including racial capitalism—must rely upon coalitions built around one's relation to dominant systems of power, and not identity or practice.

Puar echoes Cohen's interest in distinguishing between a "queer politics of identity" in which *queer* is regarded as "an embodiment of sexual positionality" or sexual practice and "the queer politics of positionality" in which *queer* is regarded as a form of political organization against systems of hegemonic power and oppression, specifically the biopolitical governance of the state and racial capitalism.[20] Puar further extends Cohen's already expansive notion of queer coalitional politics by asserting that we must "consider nation and citizenship to be implicit in the privilege of heteronormativity" and attend "to affective processes, ones that foreground normativizing and resistant bodily practices beyond sex, gender, and sexual object choices," so that "queerness is expanded as a field, a vector, a terrain, one that must consistently, not sporadically, account for nationalism and race within its purview."[21]

Exceptionally Queer has sought to facilitate that expansion. In approaching Mormonism as an assemblage, I have followed Puar's model, which, regarding "queerness as assemblage," facilitates a move "away from excavation work, deprivileges a binary opposition between queer and not-queer subjects, and instead of retaining queerness exclusively as dissenting, resistant, and alternative . . . underscores contingency and complicity with dominant formations."[22] Mormonism as assemblage, as opposed to Mormonism as an inherent aspect of the Latter-day Saint tradition, moves away from the stabilizing, ontological project of determining what exactly constitutes Mormon peculiarity and pinpointing exactly where such peculiarity resides in time and space. It also deprivileges a variety of binary oppositions—including queer versus nonqueer subjects (and especially the question of whether Mormons are queer or not)—as fundamental to the elaboration of Americanness under the auspices of U.S. exceptionalism. Lastly, in taking this approach, Mormonism emerges as simultaneously, and paradoxically, challenging and conforming, resisting and submitting to the dominant formations of modern biopolitical governance in and by the United States. Examining Mormonism as a racializing civilizational assemblage helps to account for how notions of Mormon peculiarity have functioned as particularly potent versions of U.S. exceptionalism, in turn allowing us to better attend to how race functions as *the* system of governance—frequently constituted in and through the social formations of sex, sexuality, and queerness—within U.S. empire.

Acknowledgments

Although I expected to write a book with queerness at its center, I did not expect to write a book about Mormonism. Looking back, however, this result was entirely predictable. My personal history has enabled me to stay committed to this project, and it is why I still feel so strongly that scholars of critical theory should pay attention to Mormonism. Despite the frequent responses of momentary curiosity that quickly faded, confusion, or just plain disinterest upon the mention of Mormonism as my subject of analysis in the critical and interdisciplinary fields in which I was trained and now work, intuition told me to keep going. That intuition was fostered by a core group of mentors whose support has allowed me to complete the text now in your hands. Thus, it is only right that I start by thanking my dissertation committee: Kevin Murphy, Regina Kunzel, Tracey Deutsch, and John Gustav-Wrathall. Without their sincere interest and investment, as well as their insistence that I should and could push myself further, this book would not exist. I owe special thanks to Kevin for his unwavering support of this project. At every turn, he has introduced and included my work in venues where it would not otherwise have been known, insisting that others need to pay attention to it.

In addition to this strong group of mentors who fostered my intellectual development, I was also fortunate to encounter a critical core at the University of Minnesota who modeled practices of ethical scholarship, liberatory pedagogy, and professional care that still serve as both guides and ideals for me, including Jigna Desai, Tracey Deutsch, Miranda Joseph, Malinda Lindquist, Kevin Murphy, Richa Nagar, Elliott Powell, and Sandy Soto. The support and camaraderie of fellow graduate students—and their partners—was also an important ingredient in this project. Thanks to Jackie Arcy, Cohen Gamboa, Scott Makstenieks, Kate Ranachan, and David Tucker for their friendship. My participation in the Graduate Interdisciplinary Group in Sexuality Studies and the Critical Gender and Sexuality Studies Dissertation Writing Group at the University of Minnesota helped to refine several aspects of this text. Thanks to colleagues and friends Myrl Beam, Angela Carter, Mia Fischer, Lars Mackenzie, Andrew McNally, the late Jesús Estrada-Pérez, Tom Sarmiento, Libby Sharrow, Jayne Swift, Karisa Butler-Wall, and Elizabeth Williams for not only reading but also providing detailed feedback on early drafts of several chapters. I think a great deal about you, Jesús. Your activism and spirit provide a compass for many, including myself.

After completing my dissertation, I was lucky enough to be selected as the inaugural Postdoctoral Fellow in Mormon Studies in the Religious Studies Department at the University of Virginia. It is not an understatement to say that without that opportunity, this book would not have become what it is, for several reasons. Thanks to Kathleen Flake for taking a chance on me and teaching me so much about Mormonism and its history. Matt Hedstrom provided me with an excellent example of how to bridge work in American and religious studies, as well as valuable advice whenever it was needed. He was responsible for organizing opportunities for me to present and receive feedback on earlier drafts of this book. Teaching in a religious studies department was an invaluable experience that allowed me to more fully develop my thinking about Mormonism as a racialized assemblage—articulated primarily through reference to normative visions of heteropatriarchy and capitalism—not as peculiar but typical in U.S. history and culture. Thank you to the University of Virginia students, both undergraduate and graduate; you had essential and difficult conversations in the aftermath of the white supremacist violence of the Unite the Right rally in August 2017.

I sincerely needed to be thrown into the deep end of religious studies in order to fully appreciate the disservice that is done when scholars in other fields ignore or diminish the significance of religion. This was an unconfirmed hypothesis I developed when writing my dissertation, but it was proved definitive by my time at UVA. The problems with such dismissive attitudes are ones that I have tried to make plain in this book. I am so appreciative for the community I had while in Charlottesville not only because William Boyce, Brandy Daniels, Kasey Keeler, Bradley Kime, and

Mel Pace provided me with indispensable intellectual community but also because that community came with their friendship. I could not be more grateful to have met you all and to count you as friends.

I will not sugarcoat it: it is hard to try to finish a book while working as a nontenure-track faculty member with a focus on teaching and service. I certainly would not have been able to complete this journey under the circumstances if I had not been welcomed into the Ethnic Studies Program at the University of Colorado Denver. Thank you to Faye Caronan, Sothary Chea, Paula Espinoza, Dennis Green, Rachel Harding, and Donna Martinez for bringing me into your tight-knit circle and allowing me to learn from you all. I can say absolutely that my book is better because its final chapters were written as I got to know you all, witnessed your unwavering support for the ethnic studies project, and, best of all, began to work closely with students in the program. It also would not have been possible without the colleagues I have come to know and appreciate through the Women's and Gender Studies Program and beyond. Chris Carson, Amy Ferrell, Sarah Fields, Lisa Forbes, Rachel Gross, Sarah Hagelin, Amy Hasinoff, Megan Hurson, Marjorie Levine-Clark, Jacob McWilliams, Katherine Miller, Brandon Mills, Chad Shomura, Shea Swauger, and Sarah Tyson have variously provided me with personal, intellectual, and organizing inspiration and community, as well as much-appreciated advice and support at various stages of this project. A special thanks to Sarah Tyson for the last-minute discussions that helped me to refine my argument in chapter 3.

I owe a great debt to the two reviewers of this manuscript whose close reading and pinpoint feedback ensured I said what I meant and meant what I said. Special thanks to Hokulani Aikau for such caring reading of my work and the detailed feedback that made it so much more precise and readable for a wider, interdisciplinary audience. Thanks to my editor, Leah Pennywark, for believing in my project and following it through even though it was dropped in her lap by others. Deep and sincere thanks to Anne Carter, Eric Lundgren, Rachel Moeller, Jeff Moen, Mike Stoffel, Ziggy Snow, and Anne Wrenn for their diligent work throughout the review and publication process. Without the financial support of the Schochet Interdisciplinary Fellowship in Queer, Trans, and Sexuality Studies, I would not have been able to complete this project. Thank you to both the Steven J. Schochet Endowment and the Gender and Sexuality Center for Queer and Trans Life at the University of Minnesota. This project also received important financial support from the University of Colorado Denver's College of

Liberal Arts and Sciences' Dissemination Grant program. Without the archival and investigative brilliance of librarians and archivists at the American Antiquarian Society; the Bancroft Library at the University of California, Berkeley; the California State Library; The Church of Jesus Christ of Latter-day Saints' Church History Library; the Harold B. Lee Library at Brigham Young University; the J. Willard Marriott Library at the University of Utah; and the Library of Congress, especially those working in the Prints and Photographs Division, this book would have been much poorer. Special thanks to those at these institutions who helped me identify, locate, and reproduce the images in this book, including Brianne Barrett and Nathan Fiske; Elena Smith; Abby and Eva; Lyuba Basin; and Hanna, Sheree Budge, Andrew Gaudio, and Tomeka Meon Myers. Also, thanks to Tom Tryniski, as well as Paul Reeve, who kindly shared images I would not otherwise have been able to access.

A small but indispensable group has sustained me in a variety of ways throughout the completion of this project. Some have always been there, others came later, while still others drifted in and out but remained critical all the same. My thanks and love to Deborah and Michael Mohrman, Gita Varner, Maren Delap, Chris Adamson, Megan Jones, and Evelyn Volz. A special thanks also to Bernice Digre, who served as a kind of surrogate grandmother during my time in Minneapolis. My own grandmother Peggy Tregoning recently passed away. Every time my mother or I would call, she would, without fail, ask how my work was going and whether I was happy. Grandma, I am so incredibly happy to have been able to complete this project, and I hope you would have been proud. There is one last person I need to thank: Mia Fischer. You have been a champion for the completion of this book from the beginning—always reminding me to stay focused, encouraging me to remain confident, and pushing me to do better in ways big and small. Thank you for your willingness to live with and listen to a scholar of Mormonism—your pessimism and skepticism about religion in general has been, unexpectedly, exactly the kind of barometer I needed to gauge the strength and focus of my argument. I am still so grateful that you enabled me to understand what the late José Esteban Muñoz meant when he wrote, "queerness is a structuring and educated mode of desiring that allows us to see and feel beyond the quagmire of the present." Thank you for helping me to see not only my own value but the "then and there."

Notes

INTRODUCTION

1. "I Believe," featuring vocalist Andrew Rannells and ensemble, track 12 on Parker, Lopez, and Stone, *Book of Mormon*.

2. A note on terminology: The Latter-day Saint movement includes several different churches that identify the Christian restorationist tradition founded by Joseph Smith, along with the Book of Mormon, as the basis for their faith. The Church of Jesus Christ of Latter-day Saints (formerly abbreviated as the LDS Church) is only one, albeit by far the largest and most well-known, of these groups. Others include the Community of Christ (formerly known as the Reorganized Church of Jesus Christ of Latter-day Saints, or RLDS), the Church of Christ, the Apostolic United Brethren, and the Fundamentalist Church of Jesus Christ of Latter-Day Saints (FLDS) Church. The terms *Mormon* and *Mormonism* are commonly used to refer to all of these groups, although they are most closely associated with The Church of Jesus Christ of Latter-day Saints given that institution's dominance.

While *Mormon* and *Mormonism* were originally coined as derogatory terms in the early nineteenth century, over the course of that century they became quotidian monikers with which to refer to followers of and churches within the Latter-day Saint tradition, not just The Church of Jesus Christ of Latter-day Saints; even adherents themselves adopted these terms. However, it is important to remember that *Mormon* and *Mormonism* retained derogatory undertones well into the early twentieth century and that various Latter-day Saint churches have embraced and/or rejected these terms over time.

Throughout the book, I refer to The Church of Jesus Christ of Latter-day Saints either by its full name or simply as the Church, in keeping with its most recent style guidelines (see "Style Guide—The Name of the Church," The Church of Jesus Christ of Latter-day Saints, https://newsroom.churchofjesuschrist.org/style-guide, for more information). The phrases *LDS Church* and *Mormon Church* only appear in direct quotations from outside sources. However, I do use the terms *Mormon* and *Mormons* to refer to members of The Church of Jesus Christ of Latter-day Saints, as well as members of other churches that are part of the Latter-day Saint tradition. Although this goes against the wishes of The Church of Jesus Christ of Latter-day Saints, I have made this choice for a couple of reasons: first, their recent style guidelines that ask that their members be referred to in particular ways are either impractical, overly general, or confusing, making them untenable for use in a manuscript of this length, depth, and breadth. Thus, I use *Mormon, Mormons,* and *Saints* to refer to those who were or are a part of the Latter-day Saint tradition, regardless of church affiliation. When necessary, I explicitly differentiate between members of various churches.

I use two terms to refer to those who are not part of the Latter-day Saint movement. I use the term *non-Mormon* as a broader label and the more specific term *anti-Mormon,* rather than *antipolygamist,* to describe the Church's nineteenth-century opponents. This is because *antipolygamist* implies that polygamy was the only issue at play in the conflict over nineteenth-century Mormonism, which it was not. Moreover, I use *anti-Mormon* for those who actively regarded, denounced, or attacked Mormonism as uncivilized, fraudulent, or dangerous and therefore as expendable or deserving of destruction.

Polygamy is commonly understood to describe the marriage of multiple women to one man. However, the term technically refers to two forms of multiple marriage: polygyny, in which one man is married to two or more women, and polyandry, in which one woman is married to two or more men. In keeping with the accepted form of usage, I employ *polygamy* to describe the polygyny practiced by various Latter-day Saint groups.

I am fully aware of the constructed nature, as well as the political implications, of the terms *America, American(s),* and *Americanness* when they are used to refer to the U.S. nation-state and its citizens. Therefore, I only use these terms when quoting directly from a source or to highlight them as discursive constructions.

3. Parker, Lopez, and Stone, *Book of Mormon*; Parker, *South Park,* "All About Mormons"; Kushner, *Angels in America*; Olsen and Scheffer, *Big Love*; Gibbons et al., *Sister Wives*; and Cohen et al., *Real Housewives of Salt Lake City*.

4. See Brodie, *No Man Knows My History,* 148; Reeve, *Religion of a Different Color,* 4, 20; and Quinn, *Mormon Hierarchy,* 616, 674.

5. Descriptions from various northeastern papers published between 1831 and 1835, cited in Reeve, *Religion of a Different Color,* 20. By the end of the 1830s, *Mormons* and *Mormonism* had largely replaced *Mormonites* as the standard terminology by which non-Mormons referred to the faith tradition and its adherents.

6. Between 2011 and 2018 the "I'm a Mormon" campaign sought to attract potential converts by featuring diverse profiles of individual Mormons from all over the globe in television commercials, online advertisements, and on billboards. Typically, these profiles attempted to dispel common stereotypes about Mormonism and Mormons, although they sometimes paradoxically reinforced them. See "'I'm a Mormon' Campaign," The Church of Jesus Christ of Latter-day Saints, https://newsroom.churchofjesuschrist.org/article/-i-m-a-mormon-campaign. This campaign was abandoned and replaced with the more generic Come unto Christ campaign when the Church officially changed its style guidelines and stopped using the word *Mormon* to

refer to its members. See "Come unto Christ," The Church of Jesus Christ of Latter-day Saints, https://www.churchofjesuschrist.org/comeuntochrist.

7. This practice was maintained well into the twentieth century.

8. Brigham Young, "Peculiarity of 'Mormons,'" in *Journal of Discourses* (June 27, 1858), 7:54.

9. See The Church of Jesus Christ of Latter-day Saints Bible Dictionary, s.v. "peculiar," accessed May 11, 2017, https://www.lds.org/scriptures/bd/peculiar?lang=eng.

10. 1 Peter 2:9 (KJV) and Deuteronomy 14:2. Also see Exodus 19:5, Deuteronomy 7:6, Deuteronomy 10:15, Deuteronomy 26:18, Psalms 135:4, Isaiah 41:8, Amos 3:2, and Titus 2:14 in the Old and New Testament; 2 Nephi 1:19 in the Book of Mormon; and 101:39 and 115:5 in Doctrine and Covenants (D&C) for references to a chosen, peculiar, special, or favored people.

11. Shipps, "Difference and Otherness," 82.

12. Lunceford, "'One Nation under God,'" 49; Wood, "Evangelical America and Early Mormonism," 386.

13. For discussions of the exceptionalist paradigm in American studies and U.S. history, see Adas, "From Settler Colony to Global Hegemon"; Appleby, "Recovering America's Historic Diversity"; Haskell, "Taking Exception to Exceptionalism"; Jay, "White Out"; Kammen, "Problem of American Exceptionalism"; Rauchway, "More Means Different"; Shafer, *Is America Different?*; and Tyrrell, "American Exceptionalism in an Age of International History."

14. For example, see Bellah, "Civil Religion in America"; Caplow, "Contrasting Trends in European and American Religion"; Demerath, "Excepting Exceptionalism"; Greeley, "American Exceptionalism"; Lipset, *American Exceptionalism*; Tiryakian, "American Religious Exceptionalism"; and Wald and Calhoun-Brown, *Religion and Politics in the United States*.

15. McLoughlin, *Revivals, Awakenings, and Reform*, 19.

16. D. Madsen, *American Exceptionalism*, 8.

17. The original reference to "a city upon a hill" comes from Jesus's Sermon on the Mount, found in Matthew 5:14 (KJV): "Ye are the light of the world. A city that is set on an hill cannot be hid." Reagan's adaptation of the phrase was a reference to visitors' perceptions of Washington, D.C., as the symbolic seat of the nation. See Reagan, "Election Eve Address."

18. See D. Madsen, *American Exceptionalism*, esp. 35–38.

19. D. Madsen, 37.

20. D. Madsen, 17.

21. See the tenth article in the Articles of Faith printed in the Pearl of Great Price, one of four sacred texts used by the Church, among other Mormon denominations. The tenth article reads: "We believe in the literal gathering of Israel and in the restoration of the Ten Tribes; that Zion (the New Jerusalem) will be built upon the American continent; that Christ will reign personally upon the earth; and, that the earth will be renewed and receive its paradisiacal glory." See also Lunceford, "'One Nation under God.'"

22. See Coviello, *Make Yourselves Gods*; Flake, *Politics of American Religious Identity*; Fluhman, *"Peculiar People"*; Givens, *Viper on the Hearth*; Gordon, *Mormon Question*;

Haws, *Mormon Image in the American Mind*; Mason, *Mormon Menace*; Mueller, *Race and the Making of the Mormon People*; Neilson, *Exhibiting Mormonism*; Reeve, *Religion of a Different Color*; Talbot, *Foreign Kingdom*; Walker, *Railroading Religion*; and Weber, *Latter-day Screens*.

23. Flake, *Politics of American Religious Identity*, 1; Coviello, *Make Yourselves Gods*, 4, 13. Also see Walker, *Railroading Religion*.

24. Gordon, *Mormon Question*; Talbot, *Foreign Kingdom*.

25. Reeve, *Religion of a Different Color*, 6.

26. Haws, *Mormon Image in the American Mind*, 4.

27. Haws, 4–5.

28. Givens, *Viper on the Hearth*, 20, 19.

29. Coviello, *Make Yourselves Gods*, 217, 236.

30. Gibbons et al., *Sister Wives*; Haslam and Lundgren, *Escaping Polygamy*.

31. Francis Lieber, *A Manual of Political Ethics: Designed Chiefly for the Use of Colleges and Students at Law*, 2 vols. (Boston: C. C. Little and J. Brown, 1839–47), 234, quoted in Talbot, *Foreign Kingdom*, 133.

32. "The Mormons," *Putnam's Monthly*, March 1855, 234, quoted in Coviello, *Make Yourselves Gods*, 2.

33. Ferguson, *Aberrations in Black*, 149.

34. Here, I am relying on both Sylvester A. Johnson's and Jodi A. Byrd's analogous conceptualizations of the United States as a nation-state whose imperial nature is fundamentally tied to its commitment to democratic freedom and multicultural/postracial liberalism. In his study of Black religion's deep ties to empire, *African American Religions*, Johnson asserts that "to examine the colonial status of African Americans requires one to call into question the fundamental paradigm of the United States as a noble, democratic, freedom-loving society," a requirement that "conflicts with the liberal integrationist paradigm through which African Americans are viewed as always having been members of the United States" and necessitates an "intellectual study of the West that makes visible the ties that bind freedom and democracy to colonialism" (3). While Johnson's focus is on dispelling the assumptions that ground deep-seated attachments to the notion of inclusion for Black people in the United States, Byrd argues in *The Transit of Empire* that, in addition to its colonialist practices and policies, the very essence of the U.S. nation-state has functioned "to make 'Indian' those peoples and nations who stand in the way of U.S. military and economic desires," thereby transforming "indigenous sovereign nations into 'domestic dependent' nations where, according to Joanne Barker, 'the erasure of the sovereign is the racialization of the 'Indian'" (xxi). Thus, both scholars theorize what they acknowledge is the deeply mutually implicated relationship between colonialism and race, although Byrd is more attentive to the ways that colonization and racialization are frequently conflated, resulting in the often paradoxical and unintentional, but nonetheless damaging, erasure of "the territoriality of conquest by assigning colonization to the racialized body, which is then policed in its degrees from whiteness. Under this paradigm, American Indian national assertions of sovereignty, self-determination, and land rights disappear into U.S. territoriality as indigenous identity becomes a racial

identity and citizens of colonized indigenous nations become internal ethnic minorities within the colonizing nation-state" (xxiv).

35. It is important to note that increasingly since the 1960s these claims to superior racial status have been predominantly articulated through colorblind discourse but are, nonetheless, racial in nature. I examine the transition from predominantly segregationist to assimilationist, or colorblind, forms of racism in the United States vis-à-vis Mormon peculiarity discourse in chapter 5.

36. See, for example, Abu-Lughod, *Do Muslim Women Need Saving?*; Al-Ali and Pratt, *What Kind of Liberation?*; Mepschen, Duyvendak, and Tonkens, "Sexual Politics, Orientalism, and Multicultural Citizenship in the Netherlands"; and Werner, "Reaping the Bloody Harvest."

37. Puar, *Terrorist Assemblages*. Although scholarship on gender exceptionalism has predominantly focused on the contemporary context, researchers often cite historical examples in varying colonial contexts. In particular, there is a striking resemblance between modern forms of U.S. and European gender exceptionalism and nineteenth-century British colonialist arguments that cited the so-called oppressive treatment of women and children in southern and western Asian and North African cultures as proof of the need for colonial rule (an argument that was, not incidentally, recycled and adapted to justify federal control of Utah in the 1879 Supreme Court ruling on the constitutionality of Mormon polygamy discussed in chapter 3). See Grewal, *Home and Harem*; Mohanty, "Under Western Eyes"; and Spivak, "Can the Subaltern Speak?"

38. Puar, *Terrorist Assemblages*, 3–4.

39. Pérez, "Rough Trade of U.S. Imperialism," 1081. Also see Pérez's *Taste for Brown Bodies*.

40. Coviello, *Make Yourselves Gods*, 229.

41. While not in any way the central concern of this book, it is relevant to mention that regarding early Mormonism's anti-Pauline emphasis on the body as queer also risks placing Joseph Smith and certain other early Mormon figures on pedestals, while ignoring or smoothing over other aspects of early Mormon belief and practice, particularly those related to race.

42. Wilcox, "Outlaws or In-Laws?," 94; Puar, *Terrorist Assemblages*, 13.

43. Coviello, *Make Yourselves Gods*, 7.

44. Cobb, "Pioneer, Polygamy, Probate, and You," 278–79.

45. Cobb, 278–79, 282.

46. Somerville, "Queer," in *Keywords for American Cultural Studies*, 203–4.

47. Puar, *Terrorist Assemblages*, 22.

48. Weheliye, *Habeas Viscus*, 46.

49. In the context of post-, de-, and anticolonial theory, Sylvester A. Johnson defines the colonial relation of power as "the form of political order through which a polity (viz., a state, be it monarchical or democratic) rules a population by treating its members as political aliens." S. Johnson, *African American Religions*, 394.

50. S. Johnson, 394.

51. S. Johnson, 394.

52. For examples of this work, see Blythe, *Terrible Revolution,* esp. chaps. 1 and 2; Brodie, *No Man Knows My History*; Bushman, *Joseph Smith and the Beginnings of Mormonism*; W. Davis, *Visions in a Seer Stone*; Fluhman, *"Peculiar People"*; and Quinn, *Early Mormonism and the Magic World View.*

53. Kitchen v. Herbert, 961 F.Supp.2d 1181 (D. Utah 2013); Brown v. Buhman, 947 F.Supp.2d 1170 (D. Utah 2013).

54. Reynolds v. United States, 98 U.S. 145 (1879).

1. BECOMING PECULIAR, 1830–1852

1. See Arrington and Bitton, *Mormon Experience*; J. B. Bennett, "'Until This Curse of Polygamy Is Wiped Out'"; Bentley, "Marriage as Treason"; Bigler, *Forgotten Kingdom*; Bowman, *Mormon People*; Burgett, "On the Mormon Question"; Ertman, "Race Treason"; Flake, *Politics of American Religious Identity*; Fluhman, *"Peculiar People"*; Givens, *Viper on the Hearth*; Gordon, "Liberty of Self-Degradation"; Gordon, *Mormon Question*; Gordon, "'Our National Hearthstone'"; Iversen, *Anti-polygamy Controversy in U.S. Women's Movements*; C. Madsen, *Battle for the Ballot*; Mason, *Mormon Menace*; Mason, "Opposition to Polygamy in the Postbellum South"; Oman, "Natural Law and the Rhetoric of Empire"; Reeve, *Religion of a Different Color*; Talbot, *Foreign Kingdom*; and Talbot, "'Turkey Is in Our Midst.'"

2. Coviello, *Make Yourselves Gods,* 11.

3. See Arrington, *Great Basin Kingdom*; Arrington and Bitton, *Mormon Experience*; Bitton and Bunker, "Phrenology among the Mormons"; Foster, *Religion and Sexuality*; Foster, *Women, Family, and Utopia*; Hardy and Erickson, "'Regeneration'"; Kern, *An Ordered Love*; Mason, "Prohibition of Interracial Marriage in Utah"; Neilson, *Exhibiting Mormonism*; Quinn, *Same-Sex Dynamics among Nineteenth-Century Americans*; Reeve, *Religion of a Different Color*; and Umbach, "Learning to Shop in Zion."

4. See Matthew Frye Jacobson's *Whiteness of a Different Color* for a discussion of the shift from internal hierarchies of whiteness established and negotiated between the 1840s and 1920s in response to European immigration, to the solidification of a monolithic whiteness labeled "Caucasian" between the 1920s and the 1960s.

5. Significantly, I mostly avoid discussion of the religious, and specifically theological, differences and similarities that the Latter-day Saint tradition shares with other forms of Christianity. This is because examples of scholarship that do so are legion. However, it is important to note that the differences are substantial enough that it is much debated if Mormonism constitutes another break in Christianity, much like the emergence of Protestantism in the sixteenth century.

6. Sellers, *Market Revolution,* 204.

7. Smith's church was soon renamed The Church of Jesus Christ of Latter-day Saints.

8. The Articles of Faith are, in the Church's own words, "thirteen basic points of belief to which Mormons subscribe" and are as follows: "1) We believe in God, the Eternal Father, and in His Son, Jesus Christ, and in the Holy Ghost; 2) We believe that men will be punished for their own sins, and not for Adam's transgression; 3) We believe that through the Atonement of Christ, all mankind may be saved, by obedience

to the laws and ordinances of the Gospel; 4) We believe that the first principles and ordinances of the Gospel are: first, Faith in the Lord Jesus Christ; second, Repentance; third, Baptism by immersion for the remission of sins; fourth, Laying on of hands for the gift of the Holy Ghost; 5) We believe that a man must be called of God, by prophecy, and by the laying on of hands by those who are in authority, to preach the Gospel and administer in the ordinances thereof; 6) We believe in the same organization that existed in the Primitive Church, namely, apostles, prophets, pastors, teachers, evangelists, and so forth; 7) We believe in the gift of tongues, prophecy, revelation, visions, healing, interpretation of tongues, and so forth; 8) We believe the Bible to be the word of God as far as it is translated correctly; we also believe the Book of Mormon to be the word of God; 9) We believe all that God has revealed, all that He does now reveal, and we believe that He will yet reveal many great and important things pertaining to the Kingdom of God; 10) We believe in the literal gathering of Israel and in the restoration of the Ten Tribes; that Zion (the New Jerusalem) will be built upon the American continent; that Christ will reign personally upon the earth; and, that the earth will be renewed and receive its paradisiacal glory; 11) We claim the privilege of worshiping Almighty God according to the dictates of our own conscience, and allow all men the same privilege, let them worship how, where, or what they may; 12) We believe in being subject to kings, presidents, rulers, and magistrates, in obeying, honoring, and sustaining the law; 13) We believe in being honest, true, chaste, benevolent, virtuous, and in doing good to all men; indeed, we may say that we follow the admonition of Paul—We believe all things, we hope all things, we have endured many things, and hope to be able to endure all things. If there is anything virtuous, lovely, or of good report or praiseworthy, we seek after these things."

9. In addition to the King James version of the Bible, The Church of Jesus Christ of Latter-day Saints considers the Book of Mormon, the Doctrine and Covenants, and the Pearl of Great Price to be sacred texts.

10. Lunceford, "One Nation under God," 54.

11. Quinn, *Mormon Hierarchy*, 4.

12. When I refer to The Church of Jesus Christ of Latter-day Saints as a U.S. religion, I apply that description in historic context and in the most literal sense possible. The Church was created within the newly erected borders of the U.S. nation-state, and its system of belief, as explained above, was (and continues to be) inextricably linked to the ideological underpinnings of the country. Mormonism was a discursive construction with roots, like the Church itself, in the Second Great Awakening.

13. See chapter 1 of Fluhman, *"Peculiar People,"* for an in-depth analysis of early representations of Smith and Mormonism as fake.

14. By 1834, over sixty anti-Mormon articles had appeared in newspapers across the Northeast and Midwest United States. See chapter 1 of both Reeve, *Religion of a Different Color,* and Fluhman, *"Peculiar People."*

15. Ruether, *America, Amerikkka,* 72.

16. For an in-depth examination of the relationship between racial sciences and Manifest Destiny, see Horsman, *Race and Manifest Destiny,* esp. chaps. 3 and 7.

17. Horsman, 120–21.

18. Horsman, 58–59.

19. Although subject to a long-standing debate, numerous scholars have convincingly argued that race is not a modern formation, nor should it be defined solely in relationship to bodies and biology, as so many scholars have done. To do so ironically and problematically reasserts both the hegemonic influence of scientific racism's account of race and a linear narrative of temporality that casts modernity as telos. See Heng, *Invention of Race in the European Middle Ages*; Hesse, "Racialized Modernity"; and S. Johnson, *African American Religions*.

20. The early Saints claimed to be direct descendants of Ephraim.

21. Mauss, *All Abraham's Children*, 18–21.

22. Bitton and Bunker, "Phrenology among the Mormons."

23. Bitton and Bunker, "Phrenology among the Mormons."

24. I discuss the development of this belief in-depth in chapters 4 and 5.

25. This would not always be the case, especially after Brigham Young moved the Church and its followers to Utah. Like other early European settlers, missionizing and conversion, along with enslavement and genocidal war, were the common tactics of U.S. and Mormon settler colonialism. Matthew Frye Jacobson's observation that in the country's early years "what a citizen really was, at bottom, was someone who could help put down a slave rebellion or participate in Indian wars" demonstrates the necessity of viewing not only Native peoples but Black people as colonial subjects and U.S. colonialism as the driving force behind racial formation. See Jacobson, *Whiteness of a Different Color*, 25.

26. Mauss, *All Abraham's Children*, 18.

27. In the Book of Mormon, God cursed the Lamanites with "a skin of blackness," distinguishing them from the Nephites, as a sign of their wickedness and corruption. See 2 Nephi 5:21: "And he had caused the cursing to come upon them, yea, even a sore cursing, because of their iniquity. For behold, they had hardened their hearts against him, that they had become like unto a flint; wherefore, as they were white, and exceedingly fair and delightsome, that they might not be enticing unto my people the Lord God did cause a skin of blackness to come upon them." References to both *whiteness* and *Blackness* were excised from the Book of Mormon in the early 1980s, reflecting a widespread move toward colorblind ideology in the United States. This move is discussed at length in chapters 5 and 6.

28. See Max Perry Mueller's reading of the Book of Mormon and his discussion of how it was differently marketed to Indigenous, Black, and white peoples in *Race and the Making of the Mormon People*, chaps. 1 and 2.

29. For a history of early settler colonialism in North America, see Dunbar-Ortiz, *Indigenous Peoples' History of the United States*, esp. chaps. 1–4.

30. This was especially the case in Ohio and Missouri. For example, in Hiram, Ohio, on the night of March 14, 1832, Joseph Smith was kidnapped by an angry mob, stripped, beaten, and tarred and feathered. In July 1833, another mob in Independence, Missouri, tarred and feathered two Saints, Bishop Edward Partridge and Charles Allen; drove scores of Mormon women and children from their homes; and destroyed the

property and printing equipment of Mormon businessmen. In perhaps the most infamous example, on October 30, 1838, at Haun's Mill in Missouri, a state militia massacred a mobile settlement of Mormon families, indiscriminately killing men, women, and children. Anti-Mormon mobs often formed to prevent the Saints from voting and pushed them out of the territories at the behest of state leaders. Governor Lilburn Boggs of Missouri even took out an "extermination order" against the Saints in 1838. Mormon appeals for protection to other state or federal authorities were always denied. For an account of this persecution, see Arrington and Bitton, *Mormon Experience,* esp. chap. 3. As these examples attest, there are undeniable parallels between the treatment of some groups of Saints and sovereign and marginalized racial groups during this era, yet it is critical to recognize that the Saints' cultural and political similarities with white non-Mormons (most obviously, both groups were settler colonialists) helped to insulate them from the widespread genocidal violence enacted against Native peoples.

31. Reeve, *Religion of a Different Color,* 20, 21.

32. Fluhman, *"Peculiar People,"* 31.

33. For the relationship between race and religion in justifying colonization of the Americas and the Atlantic slave trade, see H. Bennett, *Africans in Colonial Mexico;* GhaneaBassiri, *History of Islam in America;* Goetz, *Baptism of Early Virginia;* S. Johnson, *African American Religions;* Kidd, *Forging of Races;* Martínez, *Genealogical Fictions;* and Kopelson, *Faithful Bodies.*

34. Reeve, *Religion of a Different Color,* 23–24.

35. Reeve, 20.

36. See Allen, *Invention of the White Race;* Jacobson, *Whiteness of a Different Color;* Ignatiev, *How the Irish Became White;* and Roediger, *Wages of Whiteness.*

37. Jacobson, *Whiteness of a Different Color,* 4.

38. George A. Smith, "Liberty and Persecution—Conduct of the U.S. Government, Etc.," in *Journal of Discourses* (July 24, 1852), 1:45.

39. For a representative sample of these types of sermons, see Brigham Young, "The Constitution and Government of the United States—Rights and Policy of the Latter-Day Saints," in *Journal of Discourses,* vol. 2 (February 18, 1855); Brigham Young, "Peculiarity of 'Mormons'—Obedience to the Dictates of the Spirit—Knowledge of the Truth, Etc.," in *Journal of Discourses,* vol. 7 (June 27, 1858); and Joseph F. Smith, "Embarrassments in Arising to Speak—The Different Religions—None Perfect Except Revealed by God," in *Journal of Discourses,* vol. 11 (February 17, 1867).

40. The priesthood is the lay ministry organization of the Church. The Church does not have a formally trained or paid clergy.

41. In order to recognize the full significance of this policy, it is necessary to understand both the structure and doctrine of the Church's ministry system. Under the Church's established system of lay ministry, men (but not women) may be part of two different priesthoods: the lesser Aaronic priesthood or the higher Melchizedek priesthood. Women gain a version of priesthood authority and privilege through marriage to a man with the priesthood. Under the ban, Black men, and by extension Black women (given long-standing cultural, and later religious, restrictions against

interracial marriage), were unable to access the religious privileges—including full attainment of salvation and exaltation—as well as the social acceptance and prestige that comes with membership in the priesthood.

42. Reeve, *Religion of a Different Color,* 114.

43. Reeve, 119.

44. For the concept of race treason as it was applied to the Saints, see Ertman, "Race Treason."

45. Examples of such scholarship include Donovan, *White Slave Crusades*; Ferguson, *Aberrations in Black*; Kandaswamy, "Gendering Racial Formation"; Kitch, *Specter of Sex*; Newman, "Gender, Sexuality, and the Formation of Racial Identities"; Snorton, *Black on Both Sides*; and Somerville, *Queering the Color Line.*

46. For the argument that the Saints' simultaneous insider-outsider status is what made them so threatening to anti-Mormon white people, see Ertman, "Race Treason"; Givens, *Viper on the Hearth*; Reeve, *Religion of a Different Color*; and Talbot, *Foreign Kingdom.*

47. See Baym, *Woman's Fiction*; Brown, *Domestic Individualism*; Cott, *Bonds of Womanhood*; Douglas, *Feminization of American Culture*; Kelley, *Private Woman, Public Stage*; Ryan, *Cradle of the Middle Class*; Ryan, *Empire of the Mother*; Samuels, *Culture of Sentiment*; Sklar, *Catherine Beecher*; Tompkins, *Sensational Designs*; and Welter, "Cult of True Womanhood."

48. This is not to suggest, as some Mormon studies scholars have done, that the practice was insignificant and ultimately not essential to the faith; on the contrary, it was essential to it. Rather, I am acknowledging the realities of how plural marriage was introduced and under what constraints it was developed in early Mormonism.

49. Foster, *Religion and Sexuality,* 230.

50. Hardy and Erickson, "'Regeneration.'" Also see Kyla Schuller's discussion of how the affective and medical elaboration of sexual difference in the nineteenth-century United States was fundamentally part and parcel of the projects of white supremacy, biopolitical governance, and feminism. She calls this process of knowledge production about sexual differentiation "the sentimental politics of life." Schuller, *Biopolitics of Feeling,* 103.

51. The vast majority of revelations were received and recorded by Joseph Smith.

52. D&C, sec. 132.

53. D&C, sec. 132.

54. Foster, *Religion and Sexuality,* 233.

55. Women in Utah gained the right to vote in January 1870, less than a month after women in Wyoming, the first state or territory to grant women's suffrage. I discuss Utah's women's suffrage movement, its relationship to anti-Mormonism, and its implications for understanding gender and sexuality in Mormon history in chapters 2 and 3.

56. There continues to be both a historical and a faction-based debate about the relationship between eternal and plural marriage. Much of this debate takes place informally, online, and in other nonacademic spaces. The position that eternal and plural marriage are not fundamentally linked is overrepresented in scholarship

because it reflects the official view of The Church of Jesus Christ of Latter-day Saints. See Coviello, *Make Yourselves Gods*, esp. chap. 3; Daynes, "Celestial Marriage"; Flake, *Politics of American Religious Identity*; and Hansen, *Mormonism and the American Experience*.

57. D&C, sec. 132.

58. D&C sec. 132 explains that those who abide by the eternal marriage covenant will "be gods, because they have no end; therefore shall they be from everlasting to everlasting, because they continue; then shall they be above all, because all things are subject unto them. Then shall they be gods, because they have all power, and the angels are subject to them."

59. Hartog, *Man and Wife in America*, 93.

60. The Church teaches that all beings have a material existence that transcends birth and death—including mortals, angels, and even God—and that all are at different stages on a scale of eternal progression. The stages of eternal progression include preexistence as a spirit, mortality on earth (constituted by the veil of forgetfulness), the spirit world (constituted by positive and negative levels reached after death where spirits reside before the resurrection and final judgment), and, finally, heaven. There are three levels of heaven in the Church's cosmology: the lowest, the telestial; the second highest, the terrestrial; and the highest, the celestial. Lower levels of exaltation (telestial and terrestrial) are characterized by less perfect forms of embodiment. God created mortals first by "organizing" his spirit children out of "intelligences," or the material that God himself is made from. Then, through procreation, God and his wife (or wives) gave the spirit beings bodies on Earth. Like man, God was once mortal and achieved the highest level of exaltation, godhood (or the celestial level of heaven), by partaking in essential rites and rituals while he was mortal, including baptism, confirmation, washing and anointing, receiving endowment, and eternal marriage. After the resurrection and final judgment, it will be determined which spirits achieve what levels of exaltation and who will be cast into "outer darkness" (the Mormon version of hell). Women do not become Gods in the same sense that men do, but through the security of marriage they are assured a place in the celestial kingdom as a Mother in Heaven or as angels in the lower forms of heaven. For a more thorough description see Mitchell, "Good, Evil, and Godhood."

61. Samuels, *Culture of Sentiment*.

62. Lystra, *Searching the Heart*, 231.

63. Epstein, *Politics of Domesticity*, 84.

64. Arrington, Fox, and May, *Building the City of God*, 15.

65. Arrington and Bitton, *Mormon Experience*, 69.

66. It is notable that Bennett was the first known person to be publicly accused of sodomy in Mormonism (see Quinn, *Same-Sex Dynamics among Nineteenth-Century Americans*, chap. 9) and that Smith dealt incredibly leniently with the accusations against Bennett (before Bennett's defection from the Church). It would be fair to argue that Bennett's accusations of sexual impropriety among the Church's leadership were an attempt to deflect attention away from his own sexual escapades, of which he was accused before, during, and after his time as a Saint, with both women and men.

67. J. C. Bennett, *History of the Saints,* 306.

68. See Fluhman, *"Peculiar People,"* and Givens, *Viper on the Hearth.* It is worth noting here that even though Nauvoo did function as a theocracy, its city charter ensured religious liberty to all creeds, including Islam—an unprecedented, if nominal, extension of religious liberty in the United States at that time.

69. Fluhman, *"Peculiar People,"* and Givens, *Viper on the Hearth.*

70. For an analysis of Mormon ethnicity, see Shipps, "Difference and Otherness."

71. Horsman, *Race and Manifest Destiny,* 204.

72. Horsman, 210.

73. This point is especially well established by those working in queer nineteenth-century Native studies who chart how various Native gendered and sexual practices, often in conjunction with economic ones, were categorized by colonizers as barbaric and uncivilized and therefore racially inferior. For two representative examples (among many), see Rifkin, *When Did Indians Become Straight?,* and Kauanui, *Paradoxes of Hawaiian Sovereignty.* For an explanation of the late nineteenth- and early twentieth-century conflation of racial science and sexology in solidifying both racial and sexual categories, see Somerville, *Queering the Color Line.*

74. S. Johnson, *African American Religions,* 394.

2. A PECULIAR RACE WITH PECULIAR INSTITUTIONS, 1847–1874

1. Wenger, *Religious Freedom,* 2.

2. Wenger, 3.

3. S. Johnson, *African American Religions,* 2. Also see Patrick Wolfe's discussion of settler colonialism as "a structure, not an event" in "Settler Colonialism and the Elimination of the Native," 388; as well as J. Kēhaulani Kauanui's elucidation of how Native studies scholars—such as Jean O'Brien, Mark Rifkin, and Joanne Barker—have provided detailed elaborations of the concept in her essay "'A Structure, Not an Event.'"

4. S. Johnson, *African American Religions,* 394.

5. Byrd, *Transit of Empire,* xxiii.

6. For excellent examples of this scholarship, see Cady and Fessenden, *Religion, the Secular, and the Politics of Sexual Difference*; Justice, Rifkin, and Schneider, "Introduction"; Kauanui, *Paradoxes of Hawaiian Sovereignty*; Miranda, "Extermination of the Joyas"; and Rifkin, *When Did Indians Become Straight?*

7. See D'Emilio and Freedman, *Intimate Matters,* 35–36, 86–87, 93; Godbeer, *Sexual Revolution in Early America*; Justice, Rifkin, and Schneider, "Introduction"; Miranda, "Extermination of the Joyas"; Kauanui, *Paradoxes of Hawaiian Sovereignty,* chap. 4; Leavelle, *Catholic Calumet*; Mohrman, "Polygamy"; Pearsall, "Native American Men"; Rifkin, *When Did Indians Become Straight?*; Smithers, "'Pursuits of the Civilized Man'"; Spear, *Race, Sex, and Social Order in Early New Orleans*; Tuttle, *Conceiving the Old Regime*; and White, *Middle Ground.*

8. See Reeve, *Religion of a Different Color.* The most prominent and widely cited of these somatic theories of race is Michael Omi and Howard Winant's theory of racial formation in which they define race as "a concept that signifies and symbolizes

social conflicts and interests by referring to different types of human bodies." Omi and Winant, *Racial Formation in the United States*, 110.

9. S. Johnson, *African American Religions*, 391.

10. Hesse, "Racialized Modernity," 653.

11. Wilford Woodruff journals and papers, MS 1352, Church History Library, Salt Lake City, Utah.

12. *Deseret*, meaning "honeybee," is a name derived from the Book of Mormon. The Compromise of 1850 actually comprises five different federal laws: An Act Proposing to the State of Texas the Establishment of Her Northern and Western Boundaries, the Relinquishment by the Said State of All Territory Claimed by Her Exterior to Said Boundaries, and of All Her Claims upon the United States, and to Establish a Territorial Government for New Mexico of 1850, 9 Stat. 446; An Act for the Admission of the State of California into the Union of 1850, 9 Stat. 452; An Act to Establish a Territorial Government for Utah of 1850, 9 Stat. 455; An Act to Amend, and Supplementary to, the Act Entitled "An Act Respecting Fugitives from Justice, and Persons Escaping from the Service of Their Masters," approved February 12, 1793, of 1850, 9 Stat. 462; and An Act to Suppress the Slave Trade in the District of Columbia of 1850, 9 Stat. 467.

13. Arrington, *Great Basin Kingdom*, 50.

14. The Poland Act, 18 Stat. 253 (1874).

15. Firmage and Mangrum, *Zion in the Courts*, 126.

16. Arrington and Bitton, *Mormon Experience*, 136.

17. The Saints entered an already complex network of exchange, enslavement, and empire when they arrived in present-day Salt Lake City and began to colonize surrounding lands. Alliances, conflicts, and trade and trafficking routes were well established between the powerful equestrian Utes, New Mexican traders, the Shoshones, and nonequestrian Southern Paiutes, who were subject to enslavement by both the Utes and New Mexicans. Ned Blackhawk explains that as a result of the Mexican–American War and the sour relationship between the Saints and the federal government, "Utah's Indian wars were unique in that the settlers themselves became the initial agents of violence, followed by the U.S. Army. Whereas federal officials usually handled the messy process of Indian dispossession in the West, in Utah Mormon settlers challenged Native equestrians for control of the fertile portions of central Utah." The Saints viewed the Utes as "savage," while they considered the Southern Paiutes "unredeemed children" subject to conversion and assimilation (what amounted to servitude or, at the very least, restricted social and economic opportunities) through adoption schemes, marriage, and charitable programs. See Blackhawk, *Violence over the Land*, 230–31. For more on nineteenth-century Mormon–Native relations, see Mueller, *Race and the Making of the Mormon People*, esp. chaps. 5 and 6.

18. Brigham Young quoted in Reeve, *Religion of a Different Color*, 77.

19. Reeve, 77.

20. Bayoumi, "Racing Religion." Also see the following scholarship on the racialization of minority religions in the United States: Brodkin, *How Jews Became White Folks*; Franchot, *Roads to Rome*; Ignatiev, *How the Irish Became White*; Jacobson, *Whiteness of*

a Different Color; Joshi, "Racialization of Hinduism, Islam, and Sikhism in the United States"; Moore, *Religious Outsiders and the Making of Americans*; Orsi, "Religious Boundaries of an In-Between People"; Reeve, *Religion of a Different Color*; and Takaki, *Strangers from a Different Shore*. For scholarship on racing religion between the late fifteenth and eighteenth centuries, see Goetz, *Baptism of Early Virginia*; S. Johnson, *African American Religions*; Kidd, *Forging of Races*; Martínez, *Genealogical Fictions*; and Kopelson, *Faithful Bodies*.

21. Welke, *Law and the Borders of Belonging*.

22. Reports of this kind were circulating several years before the Utah War (1857–58) when Church leaders sought to forge explicitly military alliances with tribes "in the face of . . . impending federal invasion." Reeve, *Religion of a Different Color*, 90.

23. "The Mormons in Utah," *National Era* (Washington, D.C.), June 28, 1855, quoted in Reeve, *Religion of a Different Color*, 93.

24. Heber C. Kimball, "Obedience—The Priesthood—Spiritual Communication—The Saints and the World," in *Journal of Discourses* (September 17, 1854), 2:211–20.

25. Kimball, "Obedience."

26. Coviello, "Plural," 237.

27. Schuller, *Biopolitics of Feeling*, 2. For work on sentimental literature about Mormonism and polygamy, see Arrington and Haupt, "Intolerable Zion"; Bentley, "Marriage as Treason"; Burgett, "On the Mormon Question"; C. Cannon, "Awesome Power of Sex"; Gordon, "'Our National Hearthstone'"; Gordon, *Mormon Question*; Iversen, *Anti-polygamy Controversy in U.S. Women's Movements*; Lynn, "Sensational Virtue"; Nussbaum, "Other Woman"; and Talbot, *Foreign Kingdom*.

28. I agree with Coviello that much is to be learned by examining what he calls "the movement before [the] coordination" of sexuality during the Wilde trials, when ephemeralities, transient assemblages, and differential emphases around sex during the nineteenth century were not completely restricted by the notions of being or belonging—in a word, by a notion of identity. While Coviello examines the "bewildering extravagance of the literature" of that era in order to chart "styles of erotic being that may not rise to the level of 'discourse' as it is traditionally understood," I am interested here in examining the preliminary conceptual categories that allowed sexuality to emerge so forcefully in relationship to race during and after the 1880s. Coviello, *Tomorrow's Parties*, 10–11.

29. It is evident that polygamy and monogamy functioned as critical categories for racialization and colonization in early colonial North America, well before scientific racism was formally developed. See, for example, D'Emilio and Freedman, *Intimate Matters*; Godbeer, *Sexual Revolution in Early America*; Leavelle, *Catholic Calumet*; Pearsall, "'Having Many Wives' in Two American Rebellions"; Smithers, "'Pursuits of the Civilized Man'"; Spear, *Race, Sex, and Social Order in Early New Orleans*; Tuttle, *Conceiving the Old Regime*; and White, *Middle Ground*.

30. Sexual inversion was a theory prevalent in the late nineteenth and early twentieth centuries that posited that transposition of binary gender traits and impulses occurred in some individuals (with the assumption that the binary was biological and preferable) and therefore caused same-sex attraction.

31. See, for instance, Briggs, *Reproducing Empire.*

32. Burgett, "On the Mormon Question," 77.

33. Beginning in 1851, federal officials abandoned their posts due to various disagreements with the Saints and reported to Washington that the Saints were disloyal. Charges ran the gamut from polygamy to theocracy to murder. While several of the officials simply reported that the nonnormative practices of the Saints (including polygamy, theocracy, an ecclesiastical court system, proselytizing to Indigenous peoples, and communitarian economics) were in conflict with the norms and laws of the United States, many of the officials gave hyperbolic accounts of so-called Mormon treason in response to the Saints' unwillingness to stomach the officials' political corruption and sexual improprieties. One appointed official, for example, caused a scandal among the Saints by bringing his mistress to Utah, a particularly aggravating breach of propriety to the Saints' moral sensibilities, especially at a time when anti-Mormons were increasingly apt to characterize polygamy as a form of adultery or prostitution.

34. For a discussion of the ways that the cult of domesticity, and by extension white women's labor, was critical to advancing U.S. settler colonialism, see Amy Kaplan's "Manifest Domesticity."

35. For an analysis of how Mormon polygamy was viewed as a threat to the erection of a public/private binary in the industrializing nation, see Talbot, *Foreign Kingdom.*

36. The connections made between Mormon polygamy and prostitution are discussed at length in chapter 3 in relation to representations of Chinese immigrants.

37. *Vanity Fair*, February 11, 1860, quoted in Bunker and Bitton, *Mormon Graphic Image*, 30.

38. Thomas Lawson and Richard H. Coolidge, "Sanitary Report—Utah Territory," in *Statistical Report on the Sickness and Morality in the Army of the United States, Compiled from the Records of the Surgeon General's Office, Embracing a Period of Five Years from January 1, 1855, to January 1860*, S. Exec. Doc. No. 52, 36th Cong., 1st Sess., 281–316.

39. Quoted in Bunker and Bitton, *Mormon Graphic Image*, 24; and see Bush, "Peculiar People." For the full Surgeon General's Report, see Lawson and Coolidge, *Statistical Report on the Sickness and Morality in the Army of the United States*, S. Exec. Doc. No. 52, 36th Cong., 1st Sess.

40. Givens, *Viper on the Hearth*, 127. Also see Givens, chap. 6; and Talbot, *Foreign Kingdom*, 87.

41. Givens, *Viper on the Hearth*, 127.

42. Lawson and Coolidge, "Sanitary Report," 301.

43. Lawson and Coolidge, 301–2.

44. Lawson and Coolidge, 302.

45. Lawson and Coolidge, 309.

46. C. G. Forshey, Comment on Roberts Bartholow's "Hereditary Descent; or Depravity of the Offspring of Polygamy among the Mormons," *DeBow's Review*, February 1861, 211–12.

47. Forshey, "Hereditary Descent," 211–12.

48. George Q. Cannon, "Stirring Times—The Latter-Day Work," in *Journal of Discourses* (January 8, 1871), 14:27.

49. It is important to keep in mind that race was equated with nationality during this period and would certainly have been used to describe what are now called ethnic groups.

50. Brigham Young, "The Saints Are a Strange People Because They Practice What They Profess," in *Journal of Discourses* (February 20, 1870), 13:233, 236.

51. Laurel Thatcher Ulrich notes that Young formally requested the reinstatement of the Female Relief Society in 1854, "simultaneously validat[ing] the [women's] work and absorb[ing] it into an ecclesiastical and hierarchal system at least formally under his control." Minutes of Meeting, Salt Lake City, June 4, 1854, quoted in Ulrich, *House Full of Females*, 289.

52. Wards in the Mormon Church are akin to parishes in the Catholic Church.

53. Talbot, *Foreign Kingdom*, 51–52.

54. Jacobson, *Barbarian Virtues*, 50–51.

55. Morrill Anti-Bigamy Act, 12 Stat. 501 (1862). This mutually agreed-upon policy was the result of Lincoln's need to ensure Mormon loyalty during the Civil War. Such loyalty was essential for facilitating both the new, northern transcontinental stage line, which passed through Salt Lake City, and the protection of the new transcontinental telegraph that allowed Washington to communicate easily with California. While the Morrill Anti-Bigamy Act of 1862 and the Morrill Land Grant Act of 1862 are two distinct pieces of legislation, they are often confused or conflated because they were named after the same senator—Justin Smith Morrill, representative of Vermont from 1855 to 1867 and senator of Vermont from 1867 to 1898—and signed into law within days of one another. Although they are two distinct laws, they are related in that they utilize similar logics and tactics of settler colonial governance, most especially forced assimilation. Comparisons between various nineteenth-century laws targeting both Indigenous peoples and Mormons consistently bear this relationship out (an issue further discussed in chapter 3). However, there is no question that as a result of their commitment to and enactment of U.S. settler colonialism, as well as their phenotypical and cultural similarities with non-Mormon white people, Mormons were not subject to the same level of enforcement of these laws as Native peoples, nor to the violent force used against them.

56. Porter, *Rise of Big Business*, 2–3.

57. See Ginzberg, *Women and the Work of Benevolence*; Hartigan-O'Connor, "Gender's Value in the History of Capitalism"; and Zakim and Kornblith, *Capitalism Takes Command*.

58. Talbot, *Foreign Kingdom*, 105.

59. Justin Morrill, "Utah Territory and Its Laws—Polygamy and Its License," App. Cong. Globe, 34th Cong., 3rd Sess., at 285 (1857).

60. Morrill, "Utah Territory and Its Laws," at 288.

61. For example, the Church appeared to comply with the economic directives of the new law by transferring significant properties and various enterprises into the hands of individual members. However, this transfer did little more than result in a

change of paperwork, since individual leaders simply held the Church's financial assets in trust.

62. The Saints have always referred to all non-Mormons, including Jews, as Gentiles. Brigham Young quoted in Arrington, *Great Basin Kingdom*, 47.

63. Arrington, 247.

64. Arrington, 293.

65. See sermons in *Journal of Discourses*, especially between the years of 1856 and 1875. Frequent titles include: "Cooperation," "Home Manufacture," "Word of Wisdom," "Women and Fashions," and "Retrenchment."

66. The Cullom Bill was a federal anti-Mormon bill debated in 1870 that would have rescinded the right to vote and serve on a jury for anyone who believed in polygamy. H.R. 696, 41st Cong., 2nd sess. (1870).

67. See Van Wagenen, "In Their Own Behalf."

68. Rep. Daniel W. Gooch, "Polygamy in Utah. Speech of Hon. Daniel W. Gooch, of Mass," Cong. Globe, 36th Cong., at 3 (1860).

69. The Wade Bill, S. 404, 39th Cong., 2nd sess. (1866); the Cragin Bill (1867), S. 24, 40th Cong., 1st sess. (1867); the Cragin Bill (1869), S. 286, 41st Cong., 2nd sess. (1869); the Julian Bill, H.R. 64, 41st Cong., 1st sess. (1869); the Ashley Bill, H.R. 1625, 40th Cong., 3rd sess. (1869); the Cullom Bill, H.R. 696, 41st Cong., 2nd sess. (1870); the Voorhees Bill, H.R. 2158, 42nd Cong., 2nd sess. (1872); the Logan Bill, S. 1400, 42nd Cong., 1st sess. (1873); and the Poland Act, 18 Stat. 253.

70. Allen and Leonard, *Story of the Latter-day Saints*; Arrington and Bitton, *Mormon Experience*; Bentley, "Marriage as Treason"; Bigler, *Forgotten Kingdom*; Firmage and Mangrum, *Zion in the Courts*; Flake, *Politics of American Religious Identity*; Gordon, *Mormon Question*; Hansen, *Mormonism and the American Experience*; Lyman, *Political Deliverance*; Reeve, *Religion of a Different Color*; Talbot, *Foreign Kingdom*; and Walker, *Railroading Religion*.

71. Rep. Jasper D. Ward, "Courts in Utah," 43 Cong. Rec. 4474 (1874).

72. Rep. Clarkson N. Potter, "Courts in Utah," 43 Cong. Rec. 4470 (1874).

73. Hepworth Dixon, *Harper's Weekly*, October 12, 1889, 807, quoted in Bunker and Bitton, *Mormon Graphic Image*, 131.

74. Talbot, *Foreign Kingdom*, 50.

75. Umbach, "Learning to Shop in Zion," 33.

76. Brigham Young quoted in Arrington, *Great Basin Kingdom*, 323.

77. Whitney, *History of Utah*, 601.

3. THE PROBLEMS OF (MORMON) EMPIRE, 1874–1896

1. Jacobson, *Barbarian Virtues*, 13.

2. For the role Mormonism played in white reconciliation after the Civil War, see Blum, *Reforging the White Republic*, and Mason, *Mormon Menace*.

3. In addition to Nancy Bentley's ("Marriage as Treason") and Sarah Barringer Gordon's ("'Our National Hearthstone'") work on antipolygamy sentimental literature, see Bruce Burgett's cogent analysis in "On the Mormon Question."

4. Talbot, *Foreign Kingdom*, 135.

5. S. Johnson, *African American Religions*, 394.

6. Reynolds v. United States, 98 U.S. 145 (1879).

7. Bentley, "Marriage as Treason," 341.

8. Stoler, *Carnal Knowledge and Imperial Power*, 23.

9. Talbot, *Foreign Kingdom*, 135.

10. See, for example, Martha Ertman's contention that "casting overwhelmingly White Mormons as non-White required rhetorical slights of hand" in her article "Race Treason." For other examples of Mormon studies scholarship that make similar claims, see Givens, *Viper on the Hearth*, Reeve, *Religion of a Different Color*, and Talbot, *Foreign Kingdom*.

11. The "'Boss' Squash Head" refers to William M. "Boss" Tweed, a Democrat from New York, whose political corruption caused a scandal in the 1870s. The "'Champion' Cabbage Head" represents Montgomery Blair, a southern politician who sided with Lincoln during the Civil War and was involved in the trader post scandal of 1876.

12. Jacobson, *Barbarian Virtues*, 4.

13. Reeve, *Religion of a Different Color*, 220.

14. Reeve, 222.

15. The Page Act, 18 Stat. 477 (1875).

16. Report of the Joint Special Committee to Investigate Chinese Immigration, S. Rep. No. 689, at 405 (1877).

17. Even though the Saints were constructed variously as degraded white people or nonwhite people in media, they still retained a privileged racial status in Utah Territory by virtue of both their numbers and, for many, their phenotype. As such, racial prejudice against them outside Utah had limited immediate effect locally. However, missionaries were harassed and even lynched elsewhere in the United States. For a discussion of the violence experienced by Mormons in the south during this period, see Mason, *Mormon Menace*.

18. Talmage, "Mormonism," in *Brooklyn Tabernacle*, 56.

19. Talmage, "Must the Chinese Go?," in *Brooklyn Tabernacle*, 374–77.

20. Talmage, "Mormonism," 55.

21. Talmage, 56.

22. Talmage, 56.

23. On the development of the social purity movement, see Pivar, *Purity Crusade*. On the role of anti–white slavery campaigns in the construction of racial formation and hierarchy in the United States, see Donovan, *White Slave Crusades*.

24. Also see Blum, *Reforging the White Republic*.

25. Concerning the definition of the term *white slavery*, see Langum, *Crossing Over the Line*, 156–60.

26. See Givens's analysis of nineteenth-century genre and discursive authority in *Viper on the Hearth*, esp. chap. 6.

27. This extremely brief list is representative of a much larger sample.

28. See W. Johnson, *Soul by Soul*, esp. chaps. 4 and 6.

29. Hardy and Erickson, "'Regeneration.'"

30. Burgett, "On the Mormon Question"; and Reeve, *Religion of a Different Color*.

31. Blum, *Reforging the White Republic*, 17.

32. Gordon, *Mormon Question*, 14.

33. Johnson and Porter, *National Party Platforms*, 27.

34. Mamdani points out in "Settler Colonialism" that the development of a strong central government in the United States resulted directly from the conflict over slavery, focused on two seemingly paradoxical, yet tightly related, objectives: "to destroy slavery and to wage colonial wars—first against Indian tribes, then against neighbors, and then in the world at large" (605).

35. See Turner, "Significance of the Frontier in American History"; and H. Smith, *Virgin Land*.

36. For scholarship that has debunked this myth, see Byrd, *Transit of Empire*; Chang, *Color of the Land*; Dunbar-Ortiz, *Indigenous Peoples' History of the United States*; Dunbar-Ortiz, *Not a Nation of Immigrants*; Goldstein, *Formations of United States Colonialism*; Hixson, *American Settler Colonialism*; Limerick, *Legacy of Conquest*; Mamdani, "Settler Colonialism"; Mamdani, *Neither Settler nor Native*; O'Brien, *Firsting and Lasting*; Pease, "New Perspectives on U.S. Culture and Imperialism"; Robertson, *Conquest by Law*; Slotkin, *Fatal Environment*; Slotkin, *Gunfighter Nation*; Slotkin; *Regeneration through Violence*; Thornton, *American Indian Holocaust and Survival*; Watson, *Buying America from the Indians*; R. White, *"It's Your Misfortune and None of My Own"*; and Witgen, "Nation of Settlers." For an example of the stubborn persistence of this myth in mainstream U.S. popular and political culture, see Gingrich, *Nation Like No Other*.

37. An Act to Punish and Prevent the Practice of Polygamy in the Territories of the United States, and Other Places, and Disapproving and Annulling Certain Acts of the Legislative Assembly of the Territory of Utah of 1860, H.R. 7, 36th Cong., 1st sess. (1860).

38. For a discussion of modern liberalism and U.S. democracy as historically and fundamentally colonialist enterprises, see S. Johnson, *African American Religions*, and Byrd, *Transit of Empire*. See also Lowe's succinct explanation of how "'freedom' was central to the development of what we could call a modern racial governmentality in which a political, economic, and social hierarchy ranging from 'free' to 'unfree' was deployed in the management of the diverse labors of metropolitan and colonized peoples; this racial governmentality managed and divided through the liberal myth of inclusive freedom that simultaneously disavowed settler appropriation and symbolized freedom as the introduction of free labor and the abolition of slavery." *Intimacies of Four Continents*, 24.

39. Rep. Daniel W. Gooch, "Polygamy in Utah. Speech of Hon. Daniel W. Gooch, of Mass," Cong. Globe, 36th Cong., at 1540 (1860).

40. This question was asked by Rep. William Barksdale of Mississippi. Gooch, "Polygamy in Utah," at 1541.

41. It would be a mistake to assume that because both polygamy and slavery were labeled "barbaric" in the Republican platform that those practices were understood to be morally or racially equivalent. As the Mormon question makes plain, polygamy's alleged barbarity stemmed from its association with the assumed inferiority of nonwhite groups, specifically Islamic, Asian, African, and Indigenous cultures. It

should not be practiced by white Americans, so the logic went, because it inherently belonged to less racially and civilizationally developed groups whose immaturity was evident in their supposedly brutal treatment of women. Such a practice could not be tolerated in a racially progressed society where women were appreciated and revered for their status as wives and mothers. In contrast, slavery's barbarity derived from its outdated quality; such a practice could not be allowed in a nation whose divinely exceptional nature meant that it should continue to spread democracy, while also taking care of those considered to be supposedly inferior peoples. In other words, polygamy was simply a practice inherent to so-called lesser races, while slavery was to be practiced and later abandoned by white people as more advanced civilization was perfected. Under this logic, slavery was to be discarded for newer and better tactics of management, but ones that still maintained white supremacy and paternalistic oversight.

42. Gooch, "Polygamy in Utah," at 1541.

43. For a discussion of liberalism's unspoken but deep reliance on racial logics that continue to perpetuate colonial governance and promote the imperial interests of racial democracies, see Byrd, *Transit of Empire*; and Johnson, *African American Religions*. See also Lowe, *Intimacies of Four Continents,* especially her observation that "modern hierarchies of race appear to have emerged in the contradiction between liberal aspirations to universality and the needs of modern colonial regimes to manage work, reproduction, and the social organization of the colonized. Racial governance was underwritten by liberal philosophies that at once disavowed the violence of settler colonialism and narrated modernity as the progress from slavery to freedom" (36).

44. Hesse, "Racialized Modernity," 656.

45. For a parallel reading of the reasoning for the abolishment of the transatlantic slave trade and the promotion of Chinese labor in Britain's empire, reasoning that in many ways mirrored Talmage's, see Lowe, *Intimacies of Four Continents,* esp. chaps. 1 and 2.

46. Gooch, "Polygamy in Utah," at 1541.

47. See D'Emilio and Freedman, *Intimate Matters,* 6–7, 35–36, 86–87, 92–93; Godbeer, *Sexual Revolution in Early America*; Justice, Rifkin, and Schneider, "Introduction"; Kauanui, *Hawaiian Blood*; Kauanui, *Paradoxes of Hawaiian Sovereignty,* chap. 4; Leavelle, *Catholic Calumet*; Miranda, "Extermination of the Joyas"; Mohrman, "Polygamy"; Morgensen, *Spaces between Us*; Morgensen, "Biopolitics of Settler Colonialism"; Pearsall, "Native American Men"; Rifkin, *When Did Indians Become Straight?*; Smithers, "'Pursuits of the Civilized Man'"; Spear, *Race, Sex, and Social Order in Early New Orleans*; Tallie, *Queering Colonial Natal*; Tuttle, *Conceiving the Old Regime*; and White, *Middle Ground*.

48. D'Emilio and Freedman, *Intimate Matters,* 87. In fact, during debate over the bill Representative Samuel S. Cox of Ohio inquired not only if the bill "includes the crime of adultery committed in the Territory of Kansas, where, I understand, one hundred and twenty divorces were granted in one year, on account of the practice of free-love principles" but also if it "will cover the Indians in the Territories of the

United States, who now, in Minnesota and other Territories, are living in bigamy and polygamy?" Gooch, "Polygamy in Utah," at 1540.

49. Gooch, "Polygamy in Utah," at 1541.

50. Gooch, at 1542.

51. Gooch, at 1542.

52. Gooch, at 1542.

53. Gooch's proposal of this parent–child dynamic was adopted by the federal government in its treatment of Utah. It proved an incredibly accurate predictor of the conditions required for Utah to achieve statehood.

54. Morrill Land Grant Act, 12 Stat. 503 (1862). Byrd, *Transit of Empire*, xxvii.

55. See Dunbar-Ortiz, *Indigenous Peoples' History of the United States*.

56. Morrill Anti-Bigamy Act, 12 Stat. 501 (1862). As was first clarified in chapter 2, the Morrill Anti-Bigamy Act of 1862 and the Morrill Land Grant Act of 1862 are two distinct pieces of legislation but are frequently confused or conflated because they were named after the same senator, Justin Smith Morrill of Vermont, and were signed into law within days of one another. I also want to reiterate that although they are two different laws with significantly differing effects, they are related in their similar logics and use of assimilationist tactics characteristic of U.S. colonial governance. As this chapter argues, comparisons between various nineteenth-century laws targeting Indigenous peoples, Mormons, and other racially marginalized groups consistently bear this similarity out; however, there is no question that as a result of the combination of most Mormons' (perceived) Euro-American heritage, somatic presentation, and their commitment to and enactment of (U.S.) settler colonialism, they were not subject to the same level of enforcement of these laws or to the physically violent force used against Native peoples. The Saints in no way experienced the brutally violent treatment and dispossession Indigenous groups bore at the hands of both settlers and U.S. government officials—indeed, as settlers themselves the Mormons consistently enacted such violence against Native peoples.

57. Morrill Anti-Bigamy Act, 12 Stat. 501 (1862).

58. For the eight anti-Mormon bills debated between 1865 and 1874, see the Wade Bill, S. 404, 39th Cong., 2nd sess. (1866); the Cragin Bill (1867), S. 24, 40th Cong., 1st sess. (1867); the Cragin Bill (1869), S. 286, 41st Cong., 2nd sess. (1869); the Julian Bill, H.R. 64, 41st Cong., 1st sess. (1869); the Ashley Bill, H.R. 1625, 40th Cong., 3rd sess. (1869); the Cullom Bill, H.R. 696, 41st Cong., 2nd sess. (1870); the Voorhees Bill, H.R. 2158, 42nd Cong., 2nd sess. (1872); and the Logan Bill, S. 1400, 42nd Cong., 1st sess. (1873). For the 1860 bill, see An Act to Punish and Prevent the Practice of Polygamy in the Territories of the United States, and Other Places, and Disapproving and Annulling Certain Acts of the Legislative Assembly of the Territory of Utah of 1860, H.R. 7, 36th Cong., 1st sess. (1860); and Gooch, "Polygamy in Utah." Morrill Anti-Bigamy Act, 12 Stat. 501 (1862).

59. The Poland Act, 18 Stat. 253 (1874). Morrill Anti-Bigamy Act, 12 Stat. 501 (1862).

60. Rep. Lorenzo Crounse, "Courts in Utah," 43 Cong. Rec., 4469 (1874).

61. Rep. Jasper D. Ward, "Courts in Utah," 43 Cong. Rec., 4474 (1874).

62. Gordon, *Mormon Question*, 14.

63. Arrington, *Great Basin Kingdom,* 255.

64. See Stoler, *Carnal Knowledge and Imperial Power.*

65. Stoler, 42.

66. The logics that linked race, gender, and sexuality in the imperialist-style management of Utah were not unique. They were also deployed in the everyday governance of various marginalized populations whose sexual and gendered practices (both purported and actual) were used to construct racialized assemblages that justified their subjugation. For example, prostitution, rape, same-sex sexual practices, fornication, and polygamy were all practices associated with various racial groups during this period. Such stereotypes were used to cement conceptualizations of biological racial difference both within and beyond the nation.

67. Gordon, *Mormon Question,* 115.

68. Fluhman, *"Peculiar People,"* 38.

69. Talbot, *Foreign Kingdom,* 131, 133.

70. Naphey quoted in Reeve, *Religion of a Different Color,* 224.

71. Reynolds v. United States, 98 U.S. 145 (1879).

72. See, for example, Fanny Stenhouse's *Tell It All: The Story of a Life's Experience in Mormonism* and Ann Eliza Young's *Wife No. 19, or The Story of a Life in Bondage, Being a Complete Exposé of Mormonism, and Revealing the Sorrows, Sacrifices, and Sufferings of Women in Polygamy,* both published in 1875.

73. A typical title for magazine and newspaper stories about Salt Lake City. This one appeared in *Harper's Weekly* in 1857.

74. Gordon, *Mormon Question,* 121.

75. Oman, "Natural Law and the Rhetoric of Empire."

76. Gordon, *Mormon Question.*

77. Oman, "Natural Law and the Rhetoric of Empire."

78. There is debate as to which cases constitute the *Insular* decisions. At a minimum, six cases are included: De Lima v. Bidwell, 182 U.S. 1 (1901); Goetze v. United States, 182 U.S. 221 (1901); Dooley v. United States, 182 U.S. 222 (1901); Armstrong v. United States, 182 U.S. 243 (1901); Downes v. Bidwell, 182 U.S. 244 (1901); and Huus v. New York and Porto Rico Steamship Co., 182 U.S. 392 (1901). Other scholars argue that the following cases should also be considered part of the *Insular* decision block: Fourteen Diamond Rings v. United States, 183 U.S. 176 (1901); Hawaii v. Mankichi, 190 U.S. 197 (1903); Gonzales v. Williams, 192 U.S. 1 (1904); Kepner v. United States, 195 U.S. 100 (1904); Dorr v. United States, 195 U.S. 138 (1904); Mendozana v. United States, 195 U.S. 158 (1904); Rasmussen v. United States, 197 U.S. 516 (1905); Trono v. United States, 199 U.S. 521 (1905); Grafton v. United States, 206 U.S. 333 (1907); Kent v. Porto Rico, 207 U.S. 113 (1907); Kopel v. Bingham, 211 U.S. 468 (1909); Dowdell v. United States, 221 U.S. 325 (1911); Ochoa v. Hernández, 230 U.S. 139 (1913); and Ocampo v. United States, 234 U.S. 91 (1914).

79. *Reynolds,* at 164.

80. U.S. Const. art. IV, § 3, cl. 2.

81. Gordon, *Mormon Question,* 125.

82. *Reynolds,* at 164.

83. Devens quoted in Gordon, *Mormon Question*, 126.

84. *Reynolds*, at 166.

85. Oman, "Natural Law and the Rhetoric of Empire," 689.

86. Oman, 681.

87. Lieber quoted in Talbot, *Foreign Kingdom*, 133.

88. *Reynolds*, at 166.

89. *Reynolds*, at 168.

90. Talbot, *Foreign Kingdom*, 134.

91. Reeve, *Religion of a Different Color*, 231.

92. Willard quoted in Talbot, *Foreign Kingdom*, 134.

93. Pace v. Alabama, 106 U.S. 583 (1883).

94. *Reynolds*, at 168.

95. The Edmunds Act (also known as the Edmunds Anti-Polygamy Act), 22 Stat. 30 (1882); Chinese Exclusion Act, 22 Stat. 58 (1882).

96. "Punishment of Bigamy," Sen. George H. Pendleton, 47 Cong. Rec. 1211 (February 16, 1882). Also see Firmage and Mangrum, *Zion in the Courts*, chap. 7. Bills of attainder, or laws that single out an individual or group for punishment without a trial, are prohibited under Article I and Sections 9 and 10 of the U.S. Constitution.

97. See "Punishment of Bigamy," Sen. Wilkinson Call, 47 Cong. Rec. 1207 (February 16, 1882). Also see Firmage and Mangrum, *Zion in the Courts*, 165.

98. Oman, "Natural Law and the Rhetoric of Empire," 695.

99. "Punishment of Bigamy," Sen. Joseph E. Brown, 47 Cong. Rec. 1202 (February 16, 1882).

100. Oman, "Natural Law and the Rhetoric of Empire," 696.

101. Gordon, *Mormon Question*.

102. See Arrington, *Great Basin Kingdom*, chap. 12.

103. Bender, *American Abyss*, 2.

104. Jacobson, *Barbarian Virtues*, 50–51.

105. See Hixson, *American Settler Colonialism*, 140–42.

106. The Dawes Act (also known as the General Allotment Act or the Dawes Severalty Act), 24 Stat. 388 (1887).

107. See the Dawes Act, 24 Stat. 388 (1887).

108. Brigham Young quoted in Arrington and Bitton, *Mormon Experience*, 148.

109. Rep. John Tucker, "Suppression of Polygamy in Utah," 49th Cong., 1st sess., H.R. Rep. No. 2735, pt. 1, at 3 (1886).

110. Tucker, "Suppression of Polygamy in Utah."

111. See Foner, *History of the Labor Movement in the United States*, 15.

112. Strong, *Our Country*, 86.

113. Blum, *Reforging the White Republic*, 16.

114. Strong, *Our Country*, 106.

115. Strong, 106. Strong was probably referencing the Godbeite schism in which several prominent Mormon men broke with the Church leadership over disagreements about economic policy. But the Godbeites did not renounce religion, nor even

the Latter-day Saint faith tradition. And they certainly did not embrace socialism; in fact, they formed their own Mormon church that embraced free market capitalism.

116. Lum, *Social Problems of To-day*, 7.

117. Lum, 6.

118. Lum, 89.

119. See Gordon, *Mormon Question*, esp. chap. 6.

120. Tucker, "Suppression of Polygamy in Utah," 7.

121. Tucker, 7; and Marchmont, *Appeal to the American Congress*, 7.

122. The Edmunds–Tucker Act, 24 Stat. 635 (1887).

123. Gordon, *Mormon Question*, 188.

124. Gordon, 202.

125. C. Madsen, *Battle for the Ballot*, esp. chap. 7.

126. Firmage and Mangrum, *Zion in the Courts*, 202.

127. Late Corporation of The Church of Jesus Christ of Latter-day Saints v. United States, 136 U.S. 1 (1890). The Sherman Antitrust Act, 26 Stat. 209 (1890).

128. As Gordon points out, "by any reading of the charter itself, this was an exaggeration." *Mormon Question*, 210.

129. *Late Corporation of The Church of Jesus Christ of Latter-day Saints v. United States*, 18.

130. *Late Corp.*, 12.

131. *Late Corp.*, 13.

132. Bradley understood "Christian" to be equivalent to Protestantism. *Late Corp.*, 51.

133. See Blum, *Reforging the White Republic*, esp. chap. 7.

134. *Late Corp.*, 13.

135. The Manifesto is included as a revelation in the Doctrine and Covenants.

136. In fact, at the time, the Manifesto was regarded as a necessary measure to appease federal authorities but was in no way considered an absolute surrender. See Hardy, *Solemn Covenant*, esp. chap. 4.

137. See Flake, *Politics of American Religious Identity*, and Quinn, "LDS Church Authority and New Plural Marriages."

138. Arrington and Bitton, *Mormon Experience*, 158.

139. The 1894 Enabling Act, 28 Stat. 107 (1894).

140. Harrison and Tullidge were Godbeites. See note 115 in this chapter for more on the Godbeites. Quoted in T. Alexander, "An Experiment in Progressive Legislation," 108.

141. Women's suffrage was only included in Utah's constitution after women's activists, many of them Mormon, strongly lobbied constitutional delegates. See C. Madsen, *Battle for the Ballot*, and J. White, "Women's Place Is in the Constitution."

142. Arrington, *Great Basin Kingdom*, 403.

4. RESIGNIFYING MORMON PECULIARITY, 1890–1945

1. Patten typically published under the pen name Burt L. Standish.

2. Bunker and Bitton, *Mormon Graphic Image*, 58–59.

3. Gilbert Patten, "Frank Merriwell among the Mormons or the Lost Tribe of Israel," *Tip Top Weekly*, June 19, 1897, quoted in Bunker and Bitton, *Mormon Graphic Image*, 59.

4. Patten, "Frank Merriwell among the Mormons."

5. Petrey, *Tabernacles of Clay*, 7.

6. Duggan, *Sapphic Slashers*, 2.

7. Roberts, who was a practicing polygamist, was elected to the U.S. House of Representatives for Utah in 1898, but his seating was contested and eventually prevented because of his plural marriages. While Roberts clashed politically with the Church's highest leaders in the 1890s, he became a prominent leader and important Mormon theologian, writing several influential books. Smoot, a monogamist, served as a member of the Quorum of the Twelve Apostles from 1900 until his death in 1941. Unlike Roberts, he was eventually seated and served as one of Utah's senators from 1903 until 1933.

8. To be clear, I am referring here to the white majority within the Church, as well as the Church's official views, which directed policy and practice among the Saints. While the Church was by no means racially or nationally homogenous at the turn of the century, the vast majority of Saints resided within the western United States and identified as white Americans. More work needs to be done on the ways that converts who were considered or identified as nonwhite were situated in the Church and how they negotiated both their relationship to the faith's white majority and the Church's openly white supremacist views.

9. For examples of how Church leaders used such literature to argue for polygamy as a practice of "superior" peoples, see Hardy and Erickson, "'Regeneration.'"

10. Blum, *Reforging the White Republic*, 6.

11. As Utah's governor, Young presided over a territorial legislature that was populated entirely by Mormon members. Practically, although not legally, the Utah legislature was a Mormon body and was also an extension of the Church's hierarchy. See Brigham Young, Speeches before the Utah Territorial Legislature, January 23rd and February 5th, 1852, George D. Watt Papers, Church History Library, Salt Lake City, transcribed from Pitman shorthand by LaJean Purcell Carruth; "To the Saints," *Deseret News*, April 3, 1852, 42; and Rich, "True Policy for Utah."

12. Elijah Abel was one of a handful of Black men to be ordained before the 1852 ban. Although they could not access the priesthood in the same way because of gendered restrictions, Black Mormon women also requested access to temple rites during the nineteenth century, including, most famously, Jane Manning James. The limitations on Black membership would last until 1978. See Reeve, *Religion of a Different Color*, esp. chaps. 4, 5, 6, 7; and Mueller, *Race and the Making of the Mormon People*, esp. chap. 4.

13. It is interesting, and, I would argue, as Joanna Brooks does, telling that Joseph F. Smith did not reverse his testimony until after the death of Jane Manning James on April 18, 1908. She would have been one of the last people to be able to recall Joseph Smith's views on race and his ordination of Abel. Two days after her death, an article titled "'The Negro and the Priesthood'" appeared in *Liahona*, the Church's missionary

publication, providing several rationales for the bans, including the Curse of Cain, citing the Pearl of Great Price, and the preexistence rationale. See "The Negro and the Priesthood," *Liahona*, 1908, 1164–67; as well as Brooks, *Mormonism and White Supremacy*, 61–65, 75; and Reeve, *Religion of a Different Color*, 209–10. Five months later, on August 26, 1908, during a Council meeting of the First Presidency and the Quorum of the Twelve Apostles over which Smith presided as Church president, in response to a letter from the Church's South African mission, the decision was made to give instruction that missionaries should not proselytize to Black people. From that point forward, the Church was consistent in its instruction that Black populations should not be proselytized to, until a sudden, and ultimately unsustained, reversal in the early 1960s. See Bush, "Mormonism's Negro Doctrine," 38; and Bringhurst, *Saints, Slaves, and Blacks*, 144.

14. Black people continued to be baptized into the Church, but in extremely small numbers. This change in missionary policy at the turn of the century also helps to explain the extraordinary success of early twentieth-century Mormon missionaries in the South, who had previously been demonized and even lynched by Southern white people in the nineteenth century. See Reeve, *Religion of a Different Color*; and Mason, *Mormon Menace*.

15. The Curse (or mark, as it is sometimes referred to) of Cain refers to the biblical story in which Cain was cursed by God with black skin for killing his brother, Abel. The Curse of Canaan/Ham is the biblical story of Canaan, the son of Ham and grandson of Noah, who was cursed to be a servant to his fellows by his grandfather (Noah) for punishment for his father's (Ham's) transgression against Noah.

16. Joseph Fielding Smith to Alfred M. Nelson, January 31, 1907, Church History Library, Salt Lake City, Utah.

17. Mason, "Prohibition of Interracial Marriage in Utah," 111.

18. In December 1866, a Black man, Thomas Colbourn, was lynched in Utah with a message pinned to his body reading: "'Notice To All N***ers! Warning!! Leave White Women Alone!!!'" See Mason, "Prohibition of Interracial Marriage in Utah," 115.

19. The 1888 law banned marriages not just between a "negro" and a "white person" but also between "a white person" and a "Mongolian," reflecting anti-Asian racism so prevalent on the West Coast at the time. For this law see Chapter XLV, "Marriage. An Act Regulating Marriage," Sec. 2, *Laws of the Territory of Utah, Passed at the Twenty-Eighth Session of the Legislative Assembly* (Salt Lake City: Tribune Printing and Publishing Co., 1888), 88. Also in Chapter V, "An Act Regulating Marriage," Sec. 2584, *The Compiled Laws of Utah* (Salt Lake City: Herbert Pembroke, 1888), 2:92. The Edmunds–Tucker Act, 24 Stat. 635 (1887).

20. Taylor quoted in Mason, "Prohibition of Interracial Marriage in Utah," 115. Edmunds–Tucker Act, 22 Stat. 30 (1882).

21. B. H. Roberts, *Seventy's Course in Theology* (Salt Lake City: Deseret News, 1907–12), 1:165–66, quoted in Mason, "Prohibition of Interracial Marriage in Utah," 125.

22. "Our Colored Brethren," *Contributor*, October 1, 1885, 32.

23. "Our Colored Brethren," 33.

24. See, for example, Joseph M. Tanner's contentions that "negroes . . . were grossly incompetent, they were unsuited for self-government, and above all, they had proven no capacity for rule in a government such as ours. That was no fault of theirs, unless it may be said that it was a race incapacity" and that "all practices of intermarriage have brought the offspring of the two races completely on the side of the colored man, and even when this intermarriage is carried on for a number of generations, eliminating almost entirely the color of the skin, the so-called 'taint of the blood' is there. The gulf between them is impassable." Joseph M. Tanner, "Problems of the Age: Dealing with Religious, Social, and Economic Questions and Their Solution. A Study for the Quorums and Classes of the Melchizedek Priesthood: *XXXV-The Negro Question,*" *Improvement Era,* November 1, 1918, 36.

25. As discussed in the first two chapters, the Mormon attitude toward Native peoples was different from non-Mormons in that they viewed them as their biblical relatives who must be converted back to the true Church. This did not erase Mormon racism toward Indigenous peoples but rather influenced the way that racism was expressed.

26. "Washakie and Friday," *Contributor,* February 1, 1881, 157.

27. J. M. Tanner, "Territorial Expansion," *Improvement Era,* April 1, 1899, 425.

28. The Church had established several successful missions throughout the Pacific Islands, including on the Hawaiian Islands, during the nineteenth century. Also see Benjamin Cluff Jr., "The Hawaiian Islands and Annexation," *Improvement Era,* April 1, 1898, 435–47.

29. Aikau, *Chosen People, A Promised Land,* 10, 38.

30. W. O. Lee, "Samoa and Her Neighbors," *Improvement Era,* March 1, 1899, 335. For an overview of how colonialization in Polynesia was predicated upon a version of white supremacy that dovetailed with Mormon-specific views of Pacific Islanders' religious-racial identity as Lamanites, see Arvin, *Possessing Polynesians.*

31. R. W. Young, "External Strength of Mormonism," *Contributor,* April 1, 1880, 153–55; R. W. Young, "Mahomet and His Religion," *Contributor,* February 1, 1880, 102–5; Moses Thatcher, "Mexico and the Mexicans Part I," *Contributor,* October 1, 1880, 1–4; Moses Thatcher, "Mexico and the Mexicans Part II," *Contributor,* November 1, 1880, 33–35; Moses Thatcher, "Mexico and the Mexicans Part III," *Contributor,* December 1, 1880, 65–67; Moses Thatcher, "Mexico and the Mexicans Part IV," *Contributor,* February 1, 1881, 129–32; Moses Thatcher, "Mexico and the Mexicans Part V," *Contributor,* March 1, 1881, 161–65; Feramorz L. Young, "Peculiarities of the Mexicans," *Contributor,* October 1, 1882, 6–7; William Fotheringham, "Chronology of the Hindoos Part I," *Contributor,* October 1, 1881, 14–16; William Fotheringham, "Chronology of the Hindoos Part II," *Contributor,* November 1, 1881, 42–44; William Fotheringham, "Chronology of the Hindoos Part III," *Contributor,* December 1, 1881, 74–76; "The Hindoos," *Contributor,* March 1, 1889, 184–87; and "Some Savage Fancies," *Contributor,* December 1, 1881, 95–96.

32. "Some Savage Fancies," *Contributor,* December 1, 1881, 95.

33. J. M. S., "The Women in the Orient," *Woman's Exponent,* November 1, 1890, 77–78.

34. See Jacobson, *Whiteness of a Different Color*; and Roediger, *Working toward Whiteness*.

35. T. Alexander, *Mormonism in Transition*, 14.

36. Nephi Anderson, "Are We Americans?," *Improvement Era*, October 1, 1900, 935–36.

37. Anderson, "Are We Americans?," 935–36.

38. Charles W. Nibley, "'Mormonism' Makes for Good Citizenship," *Improvement Era*, June 1, 1916, 742–43. Nibley was the Church's fifth presiding bishop, from 1907 to 1925, and served in the First Presidency from 1925 until his death in 1931.

39. Bunker and Bitton, *Mormon Graphic Image*, 59.

40. The First Presidency is the highest-ranking governing body of the Church.

41. George Q. Cannon, "Topics of the Times : The Tabernacle Choir at the World's Fair," *Juvenile Instructor*, September 15, 1893, 567.

42. Martha Hughes Cannon's speech quoted in Nielson, *Exhibiting Mormonism*, 96.

43. Bederman, *Manliness and Civilization*, 28.

44. Carter, *Heart of Whiteness*, 83.

45. 7th Ward, S.L.C., "The Latter-day Saint Opinion of Woman," *Young Woman's Journal*, September 1891, 573.

46. See C. Madsen, *Battle for the Ballot*.

47. Young was especially open to women pursuing careers in medicine to support the Saints' need for doctors, nurses, and midwives. See Derr, "Eliza R. Snow and the Woman Question"; and Beecher, Madsen, and Derr, "Latter-day Saints and Women's Rights."

48. For a description of how such arrangements could work in polygamous families, see O'Donovan, "'Abominable and Detestable Crime against Nature.'"

49. Women's suffrage in Utah had been rescinded by the Edmunds–Tucker Act, 22 Stat. 30 (1882).

50. See the following issues for examples from the 1890s: *Woman's Exponent*, September 15, October 1, October 15, November 1, 1890; and *Young Woman's Journal*, March 1890, July 1890, September 1890, October–December 1890, January–February 1891, April 1891, October–December 1891, March 1892, April–September 1892, March 1893, February 1895, March 1895, June 1895, October 1895, February 1896, September 1896, March 1897, August–October 1898, January 1899, March 1899, October 1899, and November 1899.

51. Lizzie Smith, "Our Girls: The Equality of the Sexes," *Young Woman's Journal*, March 1890, 176.

52. Smith, "Our Girls," 176.

53. Bederman, *Manliness and Civilization*, 4.

54. McGovern, "American Woman's Pre-World War I Freedom in Manners and Morals," 320.

55. Chauncey, *Gay New York*, 113.

56. Bederman, *Manliness and Civilization*, 12–14.

57. For examples of how capitalism was understood to be negatively affecting gendered and sexual relations between 1890 and 1940, see Carter, *Heart of Whiteness*, esp. chap. 2.

58. For a discussion of the racial basis of this discourse, see Bederman, *Manliness and Civilization*, esp. chaps. 1, 3, 5; Deloria, *Playing Indian*, chap. 4; and Kaplan, "Black and Blue on San Juan Hill."

59. Francis M. Lyman, "Manhood," *Improvement Era*, 1904, 175–76. Lyman served on the Quorum of the Twelve Apostles from 1880 until his death in 1916.

60. See Bederman, "'Women Have Had Charge of the Church Long Enough.'"

61. Bederman, *Manliness and Civilization*, 16.

62. In May 2017, the Church announced that it was cutting ties with the Boy Scouts of America. The Church's announcement came after the Boy Scouts' decisions to allow gay and transgender membership and openly gay troop leaders, although the Church denied these changes had any influence on the Church's decision. T. Alexander, *Mormonism in Transition*, 144–45.

63. Eugene L. Roberts, "The Boy Pioneers of Utah," *Improvement Era*, October 1, 1911, 1,084, 1,089.

64. J. Edgar Hoover, "Men of Tomorrow: The Chief of the 'G' Men Talks to Boys," *Improvement Era*, November 1, 1939, 690–93.

65. Hoyt and Patterson, "Mormon Masculinity," 84.

66. Hansen, "Changing Perspectives on Sexuality and Marriage," 37.

67. John A. Widtsoe, "Education for Women in Utah," *Young Woman's Journal*, August 1909, 385–86. A scientist and academic by trade, Widtsoe would serve on the Quorum of the Twelve Apostles from 1921 until his death in 1952, writing several influential theological works on Mormonism.

68. Lauretta Nielson, "The Measure and Destiny of Woman," *Improvement Era*, August 1, 1916, 880.

69. John A. Widtsoe, "Evidences and Reconciliations xlvii. What Is the Place of Woman in the Church?," *Improvement Era*, March 1, 1942, 161–62.

70. Nielson, "Measure and Destiny of Woman," 880.

71. Nielson, 880.

72. Widtsoe, "Evidences and Reconciliations xlvii," 161.

73. Widtsoe, 161.

74. "Optional Studies. IV. The Woman," *Young Woman's Journal*, January 1912, 61.

75. "Optional Studies," 61.

76. Nielson, "Measure and Destiny of Woman," 880.

77. Widtsoe, "Evidences and Reconciliations xlvii," 161.

78. Nielson, "Measure and Destiny of Woman," 881.

79. Milton Bennion, "Observations Concerning Women," *Young Woman's Journal*, June 1913, 330–31. Bennion would become the general superintendent of the Church's Sunday school union between 1943 and 1949.

80. Rey L. Smith, "Girls Will Be Boys—But Why?," *Improvement Era*, June 1, 1937, 366.

81. Lizzie S. Welker, "Some Legends, Characteristics, and Customs of the Indians," *Young Woman's Journal*, June 1922, 339.

82. Nielson, "Measure and Destiny of Woman," 882.

83. See Kaplan, "Manifest Domesticity."

84. "Woman's Rights," *Woman's Exponent*, October 15, 1890, 71.

85. James E. Talmage, "The Eternity of Sex," *Young Woman's Journal*, October 1914, 600. Talmage would serve as a member of the Quorum of the Twelve Apostles from 1911 until his death in 1933 and wrote several theological works at the request of other Church leaders.

86. John A. Widtsoe, "Woman's Greatest Career: A Consideration of Home, Marriage, Love, and Some Perversions of Love," *Improvement Era*, October 1, 1940, 635.

87. O'Donovan, "'Abominable and Detestable Crime against Nature,'" 124.

88. See D'Emilio and Freedman, *Intimate Matters*; D'Emilio, "Capitalism and Gay Identity"; and Chauncey, *Gay New York*.

89. Chauncey, *Gay New York*, 117.

90. Chauncey, 115. Also see Quinn's observation that "Mildred Berryman blamed the publication of Radclyffe Hall's 1928 lesbian novel *The Well of Loneliness* for creating 'a storm of talk' and a climate of homophobia in Salt Lake City. . . . According to Berryman, this resulted in an 'effort being made to classify' as homosexuals 'every woman who wore a suit and was seen in the company of a girl companion more than once, and every man who had curly hair and might have a little more than feminine walk or a flair for bright colored ties.'" Quinn, in *Same-Sex Dynamics among Nineteenth-Century Americans*, 57.

91. For an incomplete but representative list of examples, see Bederman, *Manliness and Civilization*; Bender, *American Abyss*; Blum, *Reforging the White Republic*; Carter, *Heart of Whiteness*; Duggan, *Sapphic Slashers*; Jacobson, *Whiteness of a Different Color*; Pascoe, *What Comes Naturally*; Pérez, *Taste for Brown Bodies*; Roediger, *Working toward Whiteness*; Shah, *Stranger Intimacy*; Somerville, *Queering the Color Line*; and Welke, *Law and the Borders of Belonging*.

92. Shah, *Stranger Intimacy*, 10, 186.

93. "In the Realm of Women: Peril of Present Day Dress," *Young Woman's Journal*, July 1922, 414.

94. Joseph F. Smith, "Editor's Table: A Vital Question," *Improvement Era*, October 1, 1908, 959–61.

95. George W. Middleton, "The Real Eugenics Problem of America," *Young Woman's Journal*, July 1913, 408–9.

96. Smith, "Editor's Table."

97. Smith.

98. Smith.

99. An illustrative sample of titles includes: Amethyst, "Husband, Home, Motherhood," *Contributor*, May 1, 1890, 269–70; S. W. Richards, "The Duty of Marriage Part I," *Contributor*, December 1, 1891, 91–92; S. W. Richards, "The Duty of Marriage Part II," *Contributor*, February 1, 1891, 165–67; "Courtship and Marriage," *Young Woman's Journal*, October 1894; "An Ideal Home," *Young Woman's Journal*, November 1894; "Editorial: Courtship Conduct," *Contributor*, August 1, 1895, 642–43; Elijah Farr, "Marriage and Divorce," *Contributor*, September 1, 1896, 678–82; "Editorial: Marriage and Divorce," *Contributor*, October 1, 1896, 740; J. M. Tanner, "Some Leading Events in the Current Story of the World: Marriage Statistics," *Improvement Era*, September 1, 1902, 891–95;

"Don't for Wives" and "Don't For Husbands," *Young Woman's Journal*, May 1904; "Editor's Table: Waywardness and Its Remedy," *Improvement Era*, September 1, 1906, 900–02; E. G. Gowans, "The Boy Problem I: Juvenile Faults," *Improvement Era*, 1908, 194–97; E. G. Gowans, "The Boy Problem II: Some Suggestions for Its Solution," *Improvement Era*, 1908, 296–98; E. G. Gowans, "The Boy Problem III: What the Schools Can Do," *Improvement Era*, 1908, 369–73; E. G. Gowans, "The Boy Problem IV: An Ideal," *Improvement Era*, 1908, 456–60; Susa Young Gates, "Timely Topics: Concerning the Girl Who Marries," *Young Woman's Journal*, February 1908; Lella Marler Hoggan, "Preparation for Marriage," *Young Woman's Journal*, November 1908; Amey B. Eaton, "Eugenics and Parenthood," *Young Woman's Journal*, January 1913; John Henry Evans, "How to Get Married," *Young Woman's Journal*, June 1915; A. Lee Brown "Education for Parenthood: The Right of Child to Be Well Born," *Young Woman's Journal*, March 1916; Levi Edgar Young, "Parenthood and the Family," *Young Woman's Journal*, May 1916; Newel K. Young, "Moral Education of the Adolescent," *Improvement Era*, March 1917, 406–14; Newel K. Young, "Moral Education of the Adolescent," *Improvement Era*, April 1917, 523–26; Newel K. Young, "Moral Education of the Adolescent," *Improvement Era*, May 1917, 626–33; Rudger Clawson, "Marriage an Investment," *Young Woman's Journal*, June 1920; "Our June Conference: D. The Wife in the Home-Building Partnership," *Young Woman's Journal*, August 1920; "Lesson XII. Conjugal Love," *Young Woman's Journal*, December 1921; "An Everlasting Covenant: Lessons on Marriage and Family Life: Senior Course of Study: Lesson XIV: The Destiny of the Unmarried," *Young Woman's Journal*, January 1922; Adam S. Bennion, "Graces That Make for a Happy Married Life," *Young Woman's Journal*, August 1927; *Young Woman's Journal*, January 1928; B. Roberts, "Complete Marriage—Righteousness: Mutilated Marriage—Sin," *Improvement Era*, January 1, 1928, 181–91; E. Cecil McGavin, "The Mutual and the Adolescent," *Improvement Era*, August 1, 1929, 830–34; and Adam S. Bennion, "Companionship," *Improvement Era*, September 1, 1937, 536–38.

100. Bederman, *Manliness and Civilization*, 12.

101. J. H. Ward, "The Tide of Life. A Plea for 'Mormon' Civilization. III.," *Improvement Era*, October 1, 1899, 925–26.

102. Reeve, *Religion of a Different Color*, 249.

103. Reeve, 249; and O. Davis, *Latest Word on Mormonism*, 6.

104. Teddy Roosevelt, "Mr. Roosevelt to the 'Mormons,'" *Improvement Era*, June 1, 1911, 712–18, repr. from *Collier's*, April 15, 1911.

105. David O. McKay, "As Youth Contemplates an Eternal Partnership," *Improvement Era*, March 1, 1938, 138.

106. Carter, *Heart of Whiteness*.

107. David O. McKay, "As Youth Contemplates An Eternal Partnership," *Improvement Era*, March 1, 1938, 138. McKay exercised extreme influence on Church doctrine, serving in either the Quorum of the Twelve Apostles or the First Presidency between 1906 and 1951, the year he became president of the Church. His tenure as president ended upon his death in 1971, after he had presided over many major changes and unprecedented expansion to the institution. His anti-Black racism is discussed in detail

in the next chapter and is well-documented in Prince and Wright, *David O. McKay and the Rise of Modern Mormonism,* chap. 4.

108. J. Reuben Clark Jr., "Chastity," *Improvement Era,* December 1, 1938, 714. Clark served as the Undersecretary of State between 1928 and 1929 under President Calvin Coolidge and as the U.S. ambassador to Mexico from 1930 to 1933 under President Herbert Hoover. He was called to serve in the Quorum of the Twelve Apostles in 1934 and served in the First Presidency, in various roles under various presidents, between 1933 and 1945 and from 1951 until his death in 1961. During the tenures of Church presidents Heber J. Grant and George Albert Smith, he virtually acted as Church president himself when those two men were sick and incapacitated at the end of their presidencies. As will be discussed in the next chapter, Clark's anti-Black racist views are well-documented.

109. Carter, *Heart of Whiteness,* 77–78.

110. Bowman, *Mormon People,* 166.

111. The Word of Wisdom requires abstinence from tea, coffee, tobacco, and alcohol, among other products. For a discussion of the Word of Wisdom, see T. Alexander, *Mormonism in Transition,* 265–67.

112. Hansen, "Mormon Sexuality and American Culture," 53.

113. Hansen, "Changing Perspectives on Sexuality and Marriage," 40.

114. For a discussion of the Church's early twentieth-century interest in regulating same-sex sexuality specifically, see Quinn, *Same-Sex Dynamics among Nineteenth-Century Americans.*

115. Francis M. Lyman, "Manhood," *Improvement Era,* January 1, 1904, 175–76.

116. Anthony W. Ivins, "The Greatest Menace to the Church—the Remedy," *Improvement Era,* June 1, 1910, 677–78. Ivins served on the Quorum of the Twelve Apostles from 1907 until 1921 and in the First Presidency from 1921 until his death in 1934.

117. Newel K. Young, "Moral Education of the Adolescent: IX—Love and the Sex-Nature," *Improvement Era,* May 1, 1917, 630–33.

118. Kimball and Kimball, *Spencer W. Kimball,* 271. Callis served on the Quorum between 1933 and his death in 1947.

119. Charles A. Callis, "Self-Conquest," *Improvement Era,* November 1, 1939, 658.

120. John A. Widtsoe, "Woman's Greatest Career: A Consideration of Home, Marriage, Love, and Some Perversions of Love," *Improvement Era,* October 1, 1940, 636.

121. See T. Alexander, *Mormonism in Transition;* Allen and Leonard, *Story of the Latter-day Saints;* Arrington and Bitton, *Mormon Experience;* Mangum and Blumell, *Mormons' War on Poverty;* Bowman, *Mormon People;* Hansen, *Mormonism and the American Experience;* Larson, *"Americanization" of Utah for Statehood;* Lyman, *Political Deliverance;* Mauss, *Angel and the Beehive;* and Neilson, *Exhibiting Mormonism.*

122. Mangum and Blumell, *Mormons' War on Poverty,* 78.

123. Specifically, Arrington explains that that portrayal "appeared to be demonstrated by the activities of the church in stimulating the development of the sugar, salt, and hydroelectric power industries and in promoting grandiose railroad and mining projects." Arrington, *Great Basin Kingdom,* 404.

124. See Walker, *Railroading Religion.*

125. "Editor's Table: President Joseph F. Smith's Opening Address at the Annual Conference," *Improvement Era*, May 1, 1907, 547–48; and Arrington, *Great Basin Kingdom*, 405.

126. T. Alexander, *Mormonism in Transition*, 75.

127. "Editor's Table: President Joseph F. Smith's Opening Address at the Annual Conference," *Improvement Era*, May 1, 1907, 547–48; and Arrington, *Great Basin Kingdom*, 406.

128. See McCormick and Sillito, *History of Utah Radicalism*, esp. chaps. 12 and 13.

129. George Q. Cannon quoted in McCormick and Sillito, *History of Utah Radicalism*, 383–84. Cannon served in either the Quorum of the Twelve Apostles or the First Presidency between 1860 and his death in 1901.

130. "Editorial: Strikes," *Contributor*, August 1, 1883, 439–40.

131. Selections from David O. McKay's speech as quoted in Richard L. Evans, "Editorial: On Unionism," *Improvement Era*, August 1, 1937, 496.

132. Joseph F. Smith to Reed Smoot, August 1, 1911, Joseph F. Smith Letterbooks, typescript in Scott G. Kenney Papers, MS 587, box 6, folder 3, Special Collections, Marriott Library, University of Utah, Salt Lake City (original in Joseph F. Smith Letterbooks, Church History Library), as cited in McCormick and Sillito, *History of Utah Radicalism*, 384.

133. George Q. Cannon quoted in McCormick and Sillito, *History of Utah Radicalism*, 383–84.

134. Bederman, *Manliness and Civilization*, 13–14.

135. See Bender, *American Abyss*.

136. "The Roots of Reform," *Deseret News*, July 31, 1884.

137. "Socialism," March 24, 1900, "A Strange Wedding," May 31, 1901, and April 16, 1914, *Deseret News*.

138. William A. Hyde, "Why I Am a Mormon," *Improvement Era*, April 1913, 538, quoted in McCormick and Sillito, *History of Utah Radicalism*, 419.

139. As quoted in "Comment on Communism," *Improvement Era*, August 1, 1936, 489.

140. "Comment on Communism," *Improvement Era*, August 1, 1936, 489.

141. "Editor's Table: Talks to the Young Men—Learn a Trade," *Improvement Era*, September 1, 1899, 867.

142. Lewis A. Merrill, "Choosing an Occupation," *Improvement Era*, 1902, 216.

143. "Put Yourself into Your Work," *Improvement Era*, March 1, 1903, 361.

144. "Put Yourself into Your Work," 361.

145. "Editor's Table: Talks to the Young Men—Learn a Trade," *Improvement Era*, September 1, 1899, 867.

146. "Editor's Table: Vocations and Industries," *Improvement Era*, April 1, 1913, 635; and "Put Yourself into Your Work," 361.

147. Bederman, "'Women Have Had Charge of the Church Long Enough,'" 441.

148. George H. Brimhall, "Tithing: Temporal Blessings," *Improvement Era*, February 1, 1909, 251–56.

149. Brimhall, "Tithing," 255.

150. Ephraim G. Gowans, "Some Obligations of Citizenship," *Improvement Era,* August 1, 1913, 982–87.

151. "The Editor's Page: The President on Church Security," *Improvement Era,* March 1, 1937, 131.

152. See McCormick and Sillito's discussion of socialism in Utah in *History of Utah Radicalism,* 108.

153. Brimhall, "Tithing," 251–56.

154. Joseph A. Geddes, "The United Order Answers," *Improvement Era,* October 1, 1932, 725–26, 757.

155. General conference is a biannual church gathering held in April and October of each year at which leaders give sermons on a variety of relevant issues.

156. J. Reuben Clark Jr., "Private Ownership . . . under the United Order and the Guarantees of the Constitution," *Improvement Era,* November 1, 1942, 688–752.

157. Clark, "Private Ownership."

158. Section 51 is from the Doctrine and Covenants. William R. Palmer, "United Orders," *Improvement Era,* December 1, 1942, 788–820.

159. Mangum and Blumell, *Mormons' War on Poverty,* 75.

160. Grant as quoted in Harold B. Lee, "Church Security: Retrospect, Introspect, Prospect," *Improvement Era,* April 1, 1937, 205–9. Lee was managing director of the Church Security Program and served on the Priesthood Correlation Committee, wielding considerable influence throughout the 1960s. Lee was on either the Quorum of the Twelve Apostles or in the First Presidency between 1941 and 1972. He was Church president between 1972 and 1973.

161. Lee, "Church Security," 208.

162. Lee, 208.

163. See Lee's reference to the *New York Times* article "The Mormons Show the Way Out," in "Church Security."

164. Clark as quoted in Mangum and Blumell, *Mormons' War on Poverty,* 137.

165. Mangum and Blumell, *Mormons' War on Poverty,* 137.

166. Marba C. Josephsen, "A Challenge to the Church in the News," *Improvement Era,* April 1, 1938, 216.

167. "Front Page News for America: The Catholic Worker, IV. No. 7 November 1936," *Improvement Era,* 1937, 28.

168. Josephsen, "Challenge to the Church in the News," 216.

169. Richard L. Evans, "The Church in the News," *Improvement Era,* April 1, 1937, 212.

170. Mangum and Blumell, *Mormons' War on Poverty,* 155.

171. Arrington and Bitton, *Mormon Experience,* 235.

172. Orval Ellsworth, "What Others Think of the Mormons," *Improvement Era,* October 1, 1942, 625, 665–68.

5. A THOROUGHLY AMERICAN INSTITUTION, 1936–1962

1. Church membership grew exponentially for most of the twentieth century. Membership was 5,165,000 by 1982 and as of the fall of 2020 was 16,565,036. Francis M.

Gibbons, "Statistical Report 1982," The Church of Jesus Christ of Latter-day Saints, https://www.churchofjesuschrist.org/study/ensign/1983/05/statistical-report-1982?lang=eng; "Facts and Statistics," The Church of Jesus Christ of Latter-day Saints, https://newsroom.churchofjesuschrist.org/facts-and-statistics.

2. Shipps, *Sojourner in the Promised Land*, 66–73.

3. Hartzell Spence, "The Story of Religions in America: The Mormons," *Look*, January 21, 1958, 63.

4. For the Johnson–Reed Act, also known as the Immigration Act of 1924, the Asian Exclusion Act, or the National Origins Act, see An Act to Limit the Immigration of Aliens into the United States, and for Other Purposes of 1924, 43 Stat. 153 (1924).

5. Brooks, *Mormonism and White Supremacy*, 59.

6. Brooks, 68, 72.

7. Joseph Fielding Smith, "Editor's Table: The Negro and the Priesthood," *Improvement Era*, April 1, 1924, 564–65. Also see Brooks, *Mormonism and White Supremacy*, 75–78.

8. Brooks, 78.

9. Brooks, 59.

10. At Bob Jones University, Black students were not allowed to attend until 1971, until 1975 only married Black people were allowed to attend so as to discourage interracial dating and marriage, and it was not until 2000 that the school's ban on interracial dating was dropped. Beyond the seminal work of Cone, *Black Theology of Liberation*, see Norris, *Witnessing Whiteness*; Tisby, *Color of Compromise*; Laats, *Fundamentalist U*; and Gorman, Childers, and Hamilton, *Slavery's Long Shadow*.

11. Pascoe, *What Comes Naturally*.

12. See Mason, "Prohibition of Interracial Marriage in Utah," 126.

13. Fortunately, the petition was denied as a result of Black antiracist activism; however, racially restrictive housing covenants remained in place. Oral histories recounting activism against Brewster's proposal, including those of Lucille Bankhead and Albert Fritz, head of the Salt Lake chapter of the NAACP, can be found in Kelen and Stone, *Missing Stories*, 73–77, 101–6.

14. J. Reuben Clark, "Plain Talk to Girls," *Improvement Era*, August 1, 1946, 492; quoted in Bringhurst, *Saints, Slaves, and Blacks*, 159.

15. See Brooks, *Mormonism and White Supremacy*, 49; and Young's original speech reproduced in Harris and Bringhurst, *Mormon Church & Blacks*, 43.

16. J. Reuben Clark Jr. Office Diary, August 30, 1944; and George Albert Smith diary, June 16, 1945; both quoted in Prince and Wright, *David O. McKay*, 63.

17. Brooks, *Mormonism and White Supremacy*, 80.

18. Suzuki, "Important or Impotent?"

19. Despite this report, no civil rights legislation was forthcoming. See Report of Senate Committee to Investigate Discrimination against Minorities in Utah, 26th Legislature of Utah (1947), quoted in W. Bennett, "Negro in Utah," 343.

20. Exec. Order No. 9980 (July 26, 1948); and Exec. Order No. 9981 (July 26, 1948).

21. S. Johnson, *African American Religions*, 327.

22. For fundamentalism's influence on Cold War–era politics and international relations, see Herzog, *Spiritual-Industrial Complex*, and S. Johnson, *African American*

Religions, chap. 7. For Christian fundamentalism's influence on Cold War–era adolescent and sexual cultures, see Moslener, *Virgin Nation,* esp. chap. 2.

23. S. Johnson, *African American Religions,* 332.

24. Moslener, *Virgin Nation,* 63.

25. *Deseret News,* April 28, 1948, quoted in Bringhurst, *Saints, Slaves, and Blacks,* 160.

26. Prince and Wright, *David O. McKay,* 81–82.

27. The Church's Brazilian mission was founded in 1935 and mainly targeted white German immigrants. It was around the late 1930s or early 1940s that missionary efforts began to focus on mixed-race populations who showed interest in the Church. This shift prompted a 1947 investigation by the Church's First Presidency that uncovered what they considered a "serious [racial] problem." See Bringhurst, *Saints, Slaves, and Blacks,* 183. The decision to continue missionizing in Brazil but not to start missions in Nigeria or Cuba can be partially explained by the fact that the mission in Brazil was already well-established with a core group of white priesthood holders, making it possible to convert mixed-race people without worrying about having sufficient white priesthood-holding leaders to run the mission. Thus, the easing of policies related to race and missions was usually only done in the context of a strong white priesthood base or to make it easier for white members to gain the priesthood. For example, it was in 1954 while on a world tour that President McKay developed a special interest in resolving an issue at the South African mission related to white men being denied the priesthood because they could not definitely prove they did not have any Black ancestry. Sympathetic to the problem of these white men, McKay eased genealogical requirements for priesthood. See Prince and Wright, *David O. McKay,* 77–79.

28. Prince and Wright, *David O. McKay,* 74–75.

29. Petrey, *Tabernacles of Clay,* 23.

30. Formalizing the bans in the 1949 statement also had the effect of eliciting internal and sometimes public dissent from a small group of members. For example, Nelson publicly condemned the Church's position five years later in an article for the left-leaning magazine the *Nation.*

31. This statement is reproduced in full in Bringhurst, *Saints, Slaves, and Blacks,* 226.

32. The United States Supreme Court would come to the same conclusion nineteen years later in Loving v. Virginia, 388 U.S. 1 (1967). See Shelley v. Kraemer, 334 U.S. 1 (1948); and Perez v. Sharp, 32 Cal.2d 711 (1948).

33. This failure would be repeated in 1951. See W. Bennett, "Negro in Utah," 343. Beyond Utah, while serving in the First Presidency, Apostle David O. McKay had discussed and supported the defeat of civil rights legislation in Arizona, advising a local Church leader to "use our influence quietly," as quoted in Prince and Wright, *David O. McKay,* 62.

34. Petersen, "Race Problems," 14.

35. Petersen, "Race Problems," 9–10.

36. For illustrative examples, see Carey Daniel, "God, the Original Segregationist," 1955, sermon, Digital Collections at the University of Southern Mississippi, M393

McCain (William D.) Pamphlet Collection, box 4, folder 2, https://usm.access.pre
servica.com/uncategorized/IO_92ab5478-69b5-4763-ade2-a6a016b5d70c; Jones, "Is Segregation Scriptural?"; and J. Harold Smith, "God's Plan for the Races: America's Number One Problem, Segregation," ca. 1950, Del Rio, Texas, radio sermon on XERF,
Land of (Unequal) Opportunity: Documenting the Civil Rights Struggle in Arkansas
Collection, University of Central Arkansas Archives and Special Collections, University of Arkansas Libraries, https://digitalcollections.uark.edu/digital/collection/
Civilrights/id/1572.

37. Petersen, "Race Problems," 14.

38. For an example, see "Post Series: LDS Church Offers Reply," *Denver Post,* January 30, 1966, 31–32.

39. Petersen, "Race Problems," 16.

40. The text was later revised to reflect the 1978 revelation.

41. *Mormon Doctrine* was sold by Church-run Deseret Book until 2010. Brooks,
Mormonism and White Supremacy, 80–81.

42. It is likely that this policy would have continued if not for the Civil Rights Act
of 1964, 78 Stat. 241 (1964).

43. Quoted in Prince and Wright, *David O. McKay,* 64. This was the same year that
John J. Stewart, a BYU professor, published *Mormonism and the Negro* defending and
justifying the Church's bans. The book would be cited repeatedly by media in coverage of the Church's ban in the 1960s.

44. Brooks, *Mormonism and White Supremacy,* 81; and Prince and Wright, *David O.
McKay,* 64, 65.

45. "Extremism Is Never the Answer," *Deseret News,* April 3, 1956.

46. Utah schools had not been formally segregated because there was such a
small population of Black people in the state. Prince and Wright, *David O. McKay,* 67.

47. Prince and Wright, 67, 63.

48. Prince and Wright, 63.

49. "Kill Rights Bill," *Call and Post* (Cleveland), April 11, 1959, 6; and "Utah Kills
Civil Rights Measure," *Daily Defender,* April 8, 1959, 6.

50. Examples include Vern L. Bullough, "Mormon Writ and Modern Ethics,"
Nation, April 6, 1963, 291–92; and Glen W. Davidson, "Mormon Missionaries and the
Race Question," *Christian Century,* September 29, 1965, 1,183.

51. Petrey, *Tabernacles of Clay,* 58. Also see Moslener, *Virgin Nation.*

52. See Fischer, *Spider Web,* and Moslener, *Virgin Nation.*

53. For examples, see D'Emilio and Freedman, *Intimate Matters*; and Murphy, Ruiz,
and Serlin, *Routledge History of American Sexuality.*

54. Petrey, *Tabernacles of Clay,* 59.

55. Moslener, *Virgin Nation,* 5.

56. Orval Ellsworth, "What Others Think of the Mormons," *Improvement Era,*
October 1, 1942, 625; and "The Destiny of 747,000 Mormons Is Shaped in These Hallowed Temple Rooms," *Life,* January 3, 1938, 22.

57. Greer Williams, "Good Mormons Don't Go Broke," *Saturday Evening Post,*
June 10, 1950, 158, 48, 158, 48.

58. Shipps, *Sojourner in the Promised Land*, 98.

59. Andrew Hamilton, "Those Amazing Mormons," *Coronet*, April 1952, 26, 27.

60. Hamilton, "Those Amazing Mormons," 28, 29.

61. Hamilton, 29–30.

62. Hamilton, 30.

63. Shipps, *Sojourner in the Promised Land*, 116n1.

64. Dorothea Lange and Ansel Adams, "Three Mormon Towns: Here Can Be Found the Land of Zion's Past and Present," *Life*, September 6, 1954, 91–100.

65. "Letters to the Editors," *Life*, September 27, 1954, 8.

66. John H. Fenton, "Educated Having Larger Families," *New York Times*, June 6, 1955, 29.

67. Lowry Nelson, "Around the U.S.A.: Mormons and the Negro," *Nation*, May 24, 1952.

68. M. Taylor, "Letters to the Editors: Is Salt Lake City Like Atlanta, Georgia?," *Nation*, January 3, 1953, 20; and Roy W. Doxey, "Letters to the Editor: The Mormons and the Negro," *Nation*, August 16, 1952.

69. While no official Church statement had declared, "Negroes . . . must do menial work and will never go to heaven," as reported in the article, it is entirely possible that such an anti-Black understanding of the justifications for the Church's bans was operating among lay members. Gladwin Hill, "Marked Decline in Racial Bias in Far West Revealed by Survey," *New York Times*, May 29, 1955, 1, 19. For discrimination at Hotel Utah and other Salt Lake City hotels, which regularly discriminated against Black people, including Nobel laureate Ralph Bunche in 1951, opera star Marian Anderson in 1954, and pastor and politician Adam Clayton Powell, among many others, see Peterson, "'Blindside,'" 5.

70. W. Bennett, "Negro in Utah."

71. See Bringhurst, *Saints, Slaves, and Blacks*, 159.

72. Brown v. Board of Education, 347 U.S. 483 (1954).

73. Haws, *Mormon Image in the American Mind*, 25.

74. Frank Ross, "The Face of America: Mormon Temple," *Saturday Evening Post*, April 7, 1956; and Oliver Edwards, "Talking of Books: Intolerance," *Times*, June 27, 1957, 13.

75. Haws, *Mormon Image in the American Mind*, 26.

76. Hartzell Spence, "The Story of Religions in America: The Mormons," *Look*, January 21, 1958, 58.

77. Spence, "Story of Religions in America," 63, 64, 67–68.

78. Spence, 68, 57.

79. Spence, 69.

80. Frank J. Taylor, "The Saints Roll Up Their Sleeves," *Saturday Evening Post*, October 11, 1958, 35.

81. Carl Cramer, "The 'Peculiar People' Prosper: 'Peculiar People,'" *New York Times*, April 15, 1962, 19.

82. "Mormons & Civil Rights," *Time*, April 13, 1959, 96.

83. This success would continue with the Church's Peabody Award–winning, one-hour television special *Let Freedom Ring*, which featured both the choir and its rendition of "Battle Hymn." See Brooks, *Mormonism and White Supremacy*, 90.

84. Metcalf, "'Which Side of the Line?,'" 228.

85. Rifkin, *When Did Indians Become Straight?*, 5, 6.

86. Petersen, "Race Problems."

87. See Kimball and Kimball, *Spencer W. Kimball*, 271.

88. After 1897, same-sex sexuality was not mentioned publicly by any Church official until 1952 when Clark discussed "homosexuals" at a Relief Society meeting.

89. See D. Johnson, *Lavender Scare*.

90. "Idaho Underworld," *Time*, December 12, 1955, http://content.time.com/time/subscriber/article/0,33009,711877,00.html. Also see "Innocence Claimed at Boise," *Denver Post*, January 7, 1956, 16; and "Sex Case Trials to Be Slated," *Denver Post*, January 9, 1956, 40.

91. Skousen would serve in that role until 1960.

92. Skousen quoted in "Alum Chief Talks to S.L. Ad Club," *Salt Lake Tribune*, February 12, 1953, 18; and Winkler, "Lavender Sons of Zion," 77.

93. See Winkler, "Lavender Sons of Zion," esp. chap. 2.

94. Given Skousen's previous employment at BYU and his prominent position in the city, it is likely he was in direct contact with Wilkinson and that they discussed these tactics.

95. For a discussion of this framework, see Petrey, *Tabernacles of Clay*, 54. In 1959, McKay assigned Petersen to help Kimball "develop a scripturally based solution to 'homosexual problems,'" a working relationship that would produce a wealth of knowledge, materials, and programs targeting homosexuality among Church members over the course of the 1960s and 1970s. Petrey, 64.

96. See O'Donovan, "Private Pain, Public Purges"; Petrey, *Tabernacles of Clay*, 84; Prince, *Gay Rights and the Mormon Church*, esp. chap. 10; and Winkler, "Lavender Sons of Zion."

97. Ernest Wilkinson diary, September 12, 1962, quoted in Petrey, *Tabernacles of Clay*, 64.

98. In the 1970s, BYU campus security worked with SLPD to cross-check license plates parked outside gay bars with those registered on campus in order to identify and expel gay students. See "Brigham Young University Police Wrote a Phony Solicitation Letter," Associated Press, September 27, 1979; "Brigham Young U. Admits Stakeouts on Homosexuals," *New York Times*, September 27, 1979, A16; and Ron Barker, "Today's Topic: Ruckus over Powers of the 'Mormon Militia,'" Associated Press, October 22, 1979.

99. Preminger, *Advise and Consent*.

100. Interestingly, as part of his pattern of defiance against the weakening Hays Code, director Otto Preminger featured a gay bar scene in the film in which the Anderson character appeared. It was the first mainstream, postwar movie to feature such a scene.

101. Petrey, *Tabernacles of Clay*, 19.

102. Lee quoted in Prince and Wright, *David O. McKay*, 64; and Petrey, *Tabernacles of Clay*, 37.

103. See Petrey, *Tabernacles of Clay*, esp. chap. 1.

104. See Alvin R. Dyer, "For What Purpose?" Mission Conference, Oslo, Norway, March 18, 1962, Church History Library and First Presidency minutes in David O. McKay Journal, September 26, 1961, box 48, folder 5, David O. McKay Papers, Marriott Library Special Collections, University of Utah, quoted in Petrey, *Tabernacles of Clay*, 26–27; and Prince and Wright, *David O. McKay*, 65.

105. Although not an official Church program, the Intermountain Indian School in Brigham City, Utah, had strong ties with the Church and much of the staff were themselves Saints. For a discussion of BYU's programs directed at Indigenous peoples, see Metcalf, "'Which Side of the Line?,'" 225–45.

106. These are the comments of Golden Buchanan (the de facto head of the ISPP program whom Kimball informally directed as a result of the program's illegality between 1947 and 1954, and head of the family that housed the first Native student, Helen John), quoted in Boxer, "'Lamanites Shall Blossom as the Rose,'" 162.

107. Myrtle Hatch quoted in Boxer, "'Lamanites Shall Blossom as the Rose,'" 170.

108. For a discussion of how these attitudes were related to long-festering resentment around violent interactions between Mormon settlers and Indigenous groups during the nineteenth century, see Boxer, 149–50.

109. Metcalf, "'Which Side of the Line?,'" 227. For an overview of how the Church's programs actively forwarded termination and relocation policy, see O'Neill, "Testing the Limits of Colonial Parenting." Ute Partition Act of 1954, 68 Stat. 868 (1954).

110. Metcalf, "'Which Side of the Line?,'" 228.

111. Kimball expressed this view in his October 1960 general conference talk. However, as Church president, Kimball oversaw the change to the Book of Mormon's reference to "white and delightsome" to "pure and delightsome" in 1981, four years after the Church had lifted its bans on Black priesthood ordination and temple participation. It was not until 2010 that references to Lamanites being "dark" and "with a skin of blackness" were dropped from the text.

112. Stanton, "Indian Student Placement Program and Native Direction," 213.

113. Between 1954 and 1956, at least sixty-six children were baptized without their parents' permission, and such baptisms would continue at least into the early 1960s. See Stanton, 213–14.

114. The age of baptism in the Church is eight years old. It is likely that criticism of the performance of mass baptisms prompted the change in the minimum age for participation. See Boxer, "'Lamanites Shall Blossom as the Rose,'" 153. In response to concerns about this and several similar programs, the Navajo Nation passed a resolution in 1960 preventing non-Navajo people from removing any Navajo minor from the reservation without prior approval.

115. "Hagoth's Children," *Time*, May 26, 1958.

116. Rifkin, *When Did Indians Become Straight?*, 6.

117. After the ISPP was formalized in 1954, it was brought under the direction of the Church's women's organization, the Relief Society, during the same period that

the Relief Society's independence was being corroded, mirroring the gendering of nineteenth-century Mormon colonization projects.

118. "Red & Delightsome," *Time*, September 7, 1959.

119. Hamilton, "Their Indian Guests: Several Hundred Mormon Families Provide Homes and Schooling for Indian Children Who Never before Lived in Houses or Ate at Tables," *Saturday Evening Post*, September 17, 1960, 86.

120. Hamilton, "Their Indian Guests," 84, 85.

121. Stanton, "Indian Student Placement Program and Native Direction," 215; and Boxer, "'Lamanites Shall Blossom as the Rose,'" 154.

122. Hamilton, "Their Indian Guests," 84, 85.

123. Hamilton, "Their Indian Guests," 84, 85. There are some examples of foster parents encouraging students to retain their cultural background; however, these examples are unusual compared to the majority of evidence that students were generally discouraged from doing so. See Stanton, "Indian Student Placement Program and Native Direction," 211–24. On the discouragement of Native cultural practices, see Boxer, "'Lamanites Shall Blossom as the Rose,'" and O'Neill, "Testing the Limits of Colonial Parenting."

124. James Molley, social worker, LDS Church, to "[Navajo] parents," December 10, 1969, box 282, folder 12, Association on American Indian Affairs Papers, quoted in Jacobs, *Generation Removed*, 87.

6. MAKING MORMON PECULIARITY COLORBLIND, 1960–1982

1. See Burke, *Colorblind Racism*, esp. chap. 2; Kendi, *Stamped from the Beginning*; Bonilla-Silva, *White Supremacy and Racism in the Post–Civil Rights Era*; and de Leon, "More Things Change."

2. About these strategies see Crespino, *In Search of Another Country*; Kruse, *White Flight*; and Lassiter, *The Silent Majority*.

3. Brooks, *Mormonism and White Supremacy*, 89.

4. For examples of such scholarship, see Mauss, *Angel and the Beehive*, esp. chap. 4; Bunker, Coffey, and Johnson, "Mormons and Social Distance"; and Haws, *Mormon Image in the American Mind*, esp. chap. 3.

5. For scholarship on the ongoing centrality of race to the U.S. nation-state, more specifically on its commitment to biopolitical forms of governance, see Cacho, *Social Death*; Puar, *Terrorist Assemblages*; Reddy, *Freedom with Violence*; and Weheliye, *Habeas Viscus*.

6. Examples of this kind of continued press coverage in the 1960s include: A. H. Raskin, "A Maverick Starts a New 'Crusade: George Romney Feels That He Has Put across the Compact Car. Now He Is Turning His Missionary Fervor to a Campaign to Reshape American Political Institutions,'" *New York Times*, February 28, 1960, 41; Robert W. Fenwick, "Mormons Often Misunderstood, Regarded as Curiosities," *Denver Post*, April 8, 1960, 41; Robert Cahn, "The New Utah: Change Comes to Zion," *Saturday Evening Post*, April 1, 1961, 32–33, 42–46; Carl Carmer, "The 'Peculiar People' Prosper: 'Peculiar People,'" *New York Times*, April 15, 1962, 19; Stewart Alsop, "George Romney: The G.O.P.'s Fast Corner," *Saturday Evening Post*, May 26, 1962,

15–21; "Do-It-Thyself," *Time,* July 20, 1962; Neil Morgan, "Utah: How Much Money Hath the Mormon Church?," *Esquire,* August 1962, 86–91; "Gov. George Romney," *Daily Defender,* January 23, 1963, 12; "Negro Question," *Time,* October 18, 1963, 83; "Post Series: LDS Church Offers Reply," *Denver Post,* January 30, 1966, 31–32; "Hard Work and Sharing . . . A Church in the News: Story of Mormon Success," *U.S. News and World Report,* September 26, 1966, 90–92, 94; Richard B. Stolley, "A World of Energy, Some Ad-Lib Bumbles," *Life,* March 3, 1967, 74; "No Flag-Burning at Brigham Young: A University without Trouble," *U.S. News and World Report,* January 20, 1969, 58–59; and Robert Kuesterman, "Sports Mill: Protests toward BYU 'Seem So Unjustified,'" *Denver Post,* November 2, 1969, 56.

7. Carl Carmer, "The 'Peculiar People' Prosper: 'Peculiar People,'" *New York Times,* April 15, 1962, 64.

8. "Negro Question," *Time,* October 18, 1963, 83; and "Hard Work and Sharing . . . A Church in the News: Story of Mormon Success," *U.S. News and World Report,* September 26, 1966, 90.

9. "The Dinosaur Hunter," *Time,* April 6, 1959, 84–89; and Stewart Alsop, "George Romney: The G.O.P.'s Fast Corner," *Saturday Evening Post,* May 26, 1962, 16. For coverage of the civil rights situation in Utah, see "Civil Rights Bill Pressed in Utah: 'Full and Equal Treatment' Is Sought, but Chances of Passage Are Held Poor," *New York Times,* February 19, 1961, 71.

10. Francis Miller, "Politics Beckons George Romney: Here Comes the Rambler Man," *Life,* February 2, 1962, 36.

11. Miller, "Politics Beckons George Romney," 39.

12. "Mormon Issue," *Time,* March 2, 1962.

13. Stewart Alsop, "George Romney: The G.O.P.'s Fast Corner," *Saturday Evening Post,* May 26, 1962, 20.

14. "Mormon Issue," *Time,* March 2, 1962.

15. Romney was certainly more liberal than Nixon on race, and their differences did indeed result in Romney's dismissal from his position as Secretary of Housing and Urban Development in 1973. And while Romney did oppose Nixon's segregationist approach to housing policy, he still maintained a racist assimilationist approach and defended Nixon's racial policies publicly. See, for instance, "Guest Privilege: George Romney: A Reply of *Life*'s Editorial on Nixon," *Life,* February 5, 1971, 62A. See Kendi, *Stamped from the Beginning*; Kendi, *How to Be an Antiracist*; and Taylor's analysis of Nixon and Romney's assimilationist, colorblind racism in *From #BlackLivesMatter to Black Liberation,* chap. 2.

16. "Book of Mormon Enters Politics," *Christian Century,* March 28, 1962, 382.

17. "Book of Mormon Enters Politics," 382.

18. Richard B. Stolley, "A World of Energy, Some Ad-Lib Bumbles," *Life,* March 3, 1967, 74. This statement is refuted by Church leaders' castigation of Romney's racial policies in private letters where the First Presidency warned him against taking a stance in favor of civil rights.

19. For example, see Frank Owens, "Expect Mormon Race Stand Change," *Daily Defender,* August 9, 1962, 10.

20. Schuyler was certainly critical of the Church's explicitly racist policies but still found room to praise the institution's welfare program in "Views and Reviews," *New Pittsburgh Courier,* June 4, 1960.

21. "Salt Lake City Lawyer Tells How Mormon Philosophy Hurts Negroes," *Call and Post,* June 9, 1962, 12.

22. Frank Owens, "Mormon's Race Beliefs in Public Eye in Wake of Romney's Political Bid," *Daily Defender,* August 7, 1962, 4.

23. Smith was not wrong about segregation in U.S. Christian churches, whether he was referring to the de facto segregation of Catholic parishes and mainline Protestant denominations or the mandatory segregation of certain evangelical fundamentalist groups. Brooks, *Mormonism and White Supremacy,* 90; and *Church News* and *Deseret News,* July 14, 1962, quoted in Bringhurst, *Saints, Slaves, and Blacks,* 162.

24. "Do-It-Thyself," *Time,* July 20, 1962.

25. "Do-It-Thyself," *Time,* July 20, 1962.

26. Shipps, *Sojourner in the Promised Land,* 100.

27. Brooks, *Mormonism and White Supremacy,* 89.

28. See Brooks's analysis of the booklet that accompanied the choir's *Mormon Pioneers 1965* album in which Columbia executive Goddard Lieberson lauds the Saints' family values and compared the nineteenth-century religious persecution they faced to the genocide of Indigenous peoples. Brooks, *Mormonism and White Supremacy,* 94.

29. Brooks, *Mormonism and White Supremacy,* 94.

30. See Prince and Wright, who also explain that Brown's demotion was highly unusual since it "was the first time since the death of Brigham Young in 1877 that a counselor in the First Presidency had not been retained by a succeeding church president." Prince and Wright, *David O. McKay,* 96, 103.

31. Brown's decision to give the interview may have been, at least in part, motivated by McKay's decision to advance the establishment of a mission in Nigeria following consistent interest in the Church there. This plan would be postponed as a result of Nigerian student activism, precipitating in the denial of visas for Mormon missionaries, which was covered in the press. The plans were indefinitely cancelled in November 1965. See "Black Saints of Nigeria," *Time,* June 18, 1965, 56.

32. David O. McKay Diary, June 5, 1963, quoted in Prince and Wright, *David O. McKay,* 88. Later that month, McKay would also turn down an invitation from President Kennedy to join a White House meeting of religious leaders to discuss the president's proposed civil rights legislation.

33. David O. McKay Diary, June 19, 1963, quoted in Prince and Wright, *David O. McKay,* 68.

34. Wallace Turner, "Mormons Consider Ending Bar on Full Membership for Negro: Present Rules Exclude Colored Persons from Priesthood—Decision by Leader of Sect Is Awaited," *New York Times,* June 7, 1963, 17.

35. "Gov. Romney Leads March against Detroit Segregation," *Denver Post,* June 30, 1963, 1.

36. Jeff Nye, "Memo from a Mormon: In Which a Troubled Young Man Raises the Question of His Church's Attitude toward Negroes," *Look,* October 1963.

37. Nye, "Memo from a Mormon."

38. Three separate civil rights bills failed in Utah's legislature in 1963, but that governing body did repeal the state's antimiscegenation law that year—one of the last states to repeal such a law.

39. McKay was unaware that McMurrin had written the statement.

40. "Position of the LDS Church on Civil Rights," October 6, 1963, included in Bringhurst, *Saints, Slaves, and Blacks*, 227.

41. For another example, see Church leaders' response to Wallace Turner's December 1965 series, submitted by the Church Information Service, in which they deny that the Church's racial policies implied Black inferiority: "Turner has done a great disservice to a highly moral, patriotic, industrious, distinguished and respected segment of American society. . . . [His] assertion that Mormon restrictions and prohibitions against Negroes holding the priesthood are 'an assumption of physical inferiority that runs like hot oil through the Mormon society' is false. The church holds no such doctrine about Negro inferiority." "Post Series: LDS Church Offers Reply," *Denver Post*, January 30, 1966, 31–32.

42. "Negro Question," *Time*, October 18, 1963, 83.

43. "Negro Question," 83.

44. *Deseret News*, December 14, 1963, quoted in Prince and Wright, *David O. McKay*, 64; and Bringhurst, *Saints, Slaves, and Blacks*, 160.

45. Drew Pearson, "Church Transfers a Noisy Benson," *Denver Post*, January 4, 1964, 8.

46. Wallace Turner, "Romney Supports Civil Rights Bill: In Utah, He Tells Party to Shun 'White Horse,'" *New York Times*, January 18, 1964, 10. See also Greg Nokes, "Romney 'Out' of GOP Race," *Denver Post*, January 17, 1964, 6.

47. The NAACP was able to keep the Church's racial politics in the news by considering a resolution at its 1965 summer convention, called for by the organization's Utah chapters, asking foreign countries to deny the Church's missionaries visas until the Black bans were dropped and the institution took a positive stand on civil rights. The resolution was voted down. In May 1966, the Salt Lake chapter of the NAACP issued another statement charging that the Church "has maintained a rigid and continuous segregation stand" and that it has "made no effort to counteract the widespread discriminatory practices in education, in housing, in employment, and in other areas of life." For examples of these incidents, see, "Mormon Meeting Reveals Sharp Civil Rights Split," *Denver Post*, April 17, 1965, 23; "Curbs on Mormons Proposed to NAACP," *Denver Post*, July 1, 1965, 3; "Mormon Ban Sought," *New York Times*, July 2, 1965, 32; "NAACP Resolution: Mormon Resolution Rejected," *Denver Post*, July 4, 1965, 66; "NAACP Asks Ban on Mormon Missionaries" *Daily Defender*, July 7, 1965, 26; "Head of Mormons Calls Racial Bias 'Barrier to Peace,'" *New York Times*, April 11, 1966, 30; "Is Mormonism Reformable on Race?," *Christian Century*, May 4, 1966, 576; "NAACP Resolution Accuses Mormons," *Denver Post*, May 7, 1966, 31; and "Salt Lake Negroes Condemn Mormons,'" *New York Times*, May 8, 1966, 55.

48. Wallace Turner, "Head of Mormons Firm on Negroes: McKay, on Coast, Sees No Easing of Church Views," *New York Times*, November 17, 1964, 34.

49. A public accommodations bill had passed and was signed into law in February and a fair employment measure was passed while the protest continued. The employment bill included a clause exempting religious institutions, including the Church. See "NAACP Presses Protests in Utah: Negro Football Star Leads Pickets at Mormon Offices," *New York Times*, March 10, 1965, 24.

50. Then Apostle David O. McKay advised a local Arizona Church leader to "use our [the Church's] influence quietly" to defeat civil rights legislation in that state. Quoted in Prince and Wright, *David O. McKay*, 62.

51. Glen W. Davidson, "Mormon Missionaries and the Race Question," *Christian Century*, September 29, 1965, 1,183–86.

52. Bringhurst, *Saints, Slaves, and Blacks*, 160; and Prince and Wright, *David O. McKay*, 71.

53. Benson's remarks were so incendiary that they were deleted from the official conference report. Quoted in Prince and Wright, *David O. McKay*, 71.

54. Davidson, "Mormon Missionaries and the Race Question," 1,184.

55. Davidson, 1,184.

56. "Hard Work and Sharing . . . A Church in the News: Story of Mormon Success," *U.S. News and World Report*, September 26, 1966, 90–92, 94.

57. Louis Cassels, "What's the Difference: Seven Religions Born on American Soil," *Denver Post*, March 11, 1966, 15.

58. Haws, *Mormon Image in the American Mind*, 60.

59. Haws, 60. Also see Brooks, *Mormonism and White Supremacy*.

60. Ezra Taft Benson, "Trust Not the Arm of Flesh," *Improvement Era*, December 1, 1967, 58, quoted in Bringhurst, *Saints, Slaves, and Blacks*, 161.

61. See "Ezra Taft Benson Mentioned as Running Mate for Wallace," *Denver Post*, March 7, 1968, 22; and Wallace Turner, "Rightists Strong in Wallace Drive: Birchers and Others Play Key Roles in the West," *New York Times*, September 29, 1968, 75.

62. Indeed, Romney received an ever-higher number of Black voters' support in each of his three successive elections. See "Race Issue May Rise: Religion Could Hamper Romney," *Pittsburgh Courier*, January 8, 1966, 8A; "Holy George," *New Republic*, 1966; Warren Weaver Jr., "Four Hearties of the Good Ship G.O.P.," *New York Times*, November 27, 1966, SM26, 51, 150–53; Jackie Robinson, "Jackie Robinson on George Romney and the Mormons," *Daily Defender*, March 25, 1967, 10; "Romney of Michigan," *Daily Defender*, April 29, 1967, 10; "Romney Urges Fair Treatment to Help Combat Negro Frustration," *Daily Defender*, April 29, 1967, 16; Brock Bower, "Puzzling Front Runner," *Life*, May 5, 1967, 84–88, 90, 92–94; "Romney Defends His Religion," *Daily Defender*, May 9, 1967, 19; "Judge Romney on Rights, Not His Religion—McKissick," *Daily Defender*, May 15, 1967, 6; and Donald Janson, "Romney Opens Wisconsin Campaign," *New York Times*, January 21, 1968, 1, 29. For the few examples of the critical press he (and his wife) received, see "Mrs. Romney's Quandary," *Christian Century*, February 8, 1967, 165; "Mormons Can't, Drop Racial Bias without 'Revelation,' Says Romney," *Daily Defender*, February 25, 1967, 1; and "Politics: Romney Rubs Noses with Voters," *Life*, March 3, 1967, 69–73.

63. Stewart Alsop, "Affairs of State: It's Like Running against God," *Saturday Evening Post*, October 22, 1966, 20.

64. Alsop, "Affairs of State," 20.

65. John Cogley, "Where the Saints Have Trod," *New York Times*, October 23, 1966, BR3, 22. On the denial of these charges of racism, see "Mrs. Romney's Quandary," *Christian Century*, February 8, 1967, 165.

66. Tom Wicker, "Impact of Romney Move: His Withdrawal Could Prove to Be One of Decisive Actions of Election," *New York Times*, February 29, 1968, 22. See also Haws, *Mormon Image in the American Mind*, 44–46.

67. Hartmann, "Olympic 'Revolt' of 1968."

68. Hartmann, "Olympic 'Revolt' of 1968." For specific coverage of the protests of college athletes, see "Negro Athletes Threaten Boycott at Major Colleges," *New York Times*, May 19, 1968, S16; Jack Olsen, "Part 3: The Black Athlete: In an Alien World," *Sports Illustrated*, July 16, 1968, 29–43; Anthony Ripley, "Irate Black Athletes Stir Campus Tension," *New York Times*, November 16, 1969, 1, 35; William Patterson, "Black Athlete and Democracy USA," *Sun Reporter*, December 20, 1969, 4; "Black Athletes 'Get Involved' in 1969," *Daily Defender*, December 23, 1969, 26; and Stu Camen, "More Athletes Stand-Up for Fair Play," *Afro-American*, December 27, 1969, 8.

69. Hartmann, "Olympic 'Revolt' of 1968."

70. Haws, *Mormon Image in the American Mind*, 58.

71. "Herrerias Resigns as Cal Cage Coach," *Denver Post*, April 12, 1968, 59. Also see "Negro Trackmen Shun Utah Meet: 8 on El Paso Squad Won't Compete at Brigham Young?," *New York Times*, April 13, 1968, 31; "Mormon Leaders Deny Having Negro Bias," *Denver Post*, April 14, 1968, 51; and "BYU Wins Triangular Track Meet," *El Paso Times*, April 14, 1968.

72. "Beamon Returns to Texas-El Paso: Citizens Help Trackmen Who Lost Scholarships for Stand," *New York Times*, October 8, 1968, 56.

73. "Mormon Leaders Deny Having Negro Bias," *Denver Post*, April 14, 1968, 51.

74. The school's admittance of Black students was a result of the necessity to comply with the Civil Rights Act of 1964. See Haws, *Mormon Image in the American Mind*, 52–55.

75. Samuel J. Skinner Jr., "San Jose State Black Footballers to Boycott BYU Game," *Sun Reporter*, November 23, 1968, 41; "Negroes Back BYU Boycott," *Denver Post*, November 26, 1968, 48; Samuel J. Skinner Jr., "Moral Issue at San Jose State: Black Gridsters Sacrifice Scholarships," *Sun Reporter*, November 30, 1968, 25; "BYU Tilt Boycott Looms, Seven Face Scholarship Loss," *Daily Defender*, November 30, 1968, 16; "San Jose State Triumphs, 25–21: Brigham Young Is Defeated—7 Negroes in Boycott," *New York Times*, December 1, 1968, S5; and "San Jose Tips BYU Despite Boycott by 7," *Denver Post*, December 1, 1968, 36.

76. "No Flag-Burning at Brigham Young: A University without Trouble," *U.S. News and World Report*, January 20, 1969, 58–59.

77. "No Flag-Burning at Brigham Young," 58–59.

78. "N. Mexico Warns Black Athletes," *Daily Defender*, March 26, 1969, 35; "Blacks Warned about BYU Boycott at New Mexico," *Sun Reporter*, March 29, 1969, 37; and "No Racial Probe Planned at BYU," *Denver Post*, April 4, 1969, 65.

79. Haws, *Mormon Image in the American Mind*, 56.

80. See Haws, *Mormon Image in the American Mind*, chap. 3.

81. See "Wyo. U Grid Team Drops 14 Negroes," *Denver Post*, October 18, 1969, 1; "Wyoming Takes 4th in Row, Sinks Brigham Young, 40–7," *New York Times*, October 19, 1969, S17; Irv Moss, "Reconciliation Chances Fade in Wyo. Dispute," *Denver Post*, October 20, 1969, 53; "Black Players Hit WU Coach for Ousting Them," *Daily Defender*, October 20, 1969, 25; "Wyoming Grid Row 'Dismays' Hathaway," *Denver Post*, October 21, 1969, 43; "School Faculty Senate Backs Black Athletes," *Daily Defender*, October 21, 1969, 26; "The Open Forum: Athletes at Wyoming U.," *Denver Post*, October 22, 1969, 25; "Wyoming Coach Says He'll Not Quit Because of Furor," *Daily Defender*, October 22, 1969, 34; "Black Student Rebellion within WAC Conference," *Daily Defender*, October 23, 1969, 40; "San Jose State Athletes Are 'Standing Up to Be Counted,'" *Daily Defender*, October 23, 1969, 41; "Eaton Facing Legal Action; Rules Relaxed," *Denver Post*, October 24, 1969, 65; "Wyoming Injunction Is Sought," *Denver Post*, October 25, 1969, 6; "After Mormon Bias Protest: Wyoming Fires 14 Black Gridders," *Call and Post*, October 25, 1969, 11B; "Wyoming U Still Tense," *Daily Defender*, October 25, 1969, 34; Irv Moss, "Wyo. Grid Crisis Not Foreshadowed," *Denver Post*, October 26, 1969, 25, 29; "Suit Due in Wyo. Dispute," *Denver Post*, October 29, 1969, 37; "Athletes Reinstatement Sought; Suit Is Filed," *Daily Defender*, October 29, 1969, 28; "Irked by Race Issue, S. Jose Rocks Wyoming," *Afro-American*, November 1, 1969, 8; Anthony Ripley, "Negro Athletes Spark Uproar at U. of Wyoming," *New York Times*, November 1, 1969, 15; "Blacks Threaten Suit: Wyoming U. Off Base," *Call and Post*, November 1, 1969, 13B; Carl Skiff, "Exclusive: The Inside Story of the University of Wyoming Football Confrontation: Showdown at Laramie," *Denver Post*, November 2, 1969, 261; "Black Athletes Seek BYU Ban," *Daily Defender*, November 5, 1969, 40; "Black Athletes Having Their Day in Court," *Daily Defender*, November 11, 1969, 26; "Black Athletes Lawsuit Ruling Due Next Week," *Daily Defender*, November 12, 1969, 34; "Judge Denies Legal Action," *Daily Defender*, November 18, 1969, 27; "Barrett Asks Court to Dismiss Lawsuit," *Daily Defender*, November 24, 1969, 24; "'Ridiculed' Trackman Quits Wyoming Team," *Denver Post*, December 17, 1969, 93, 96; "'Ridiculed' Trackman Quits Wyoming Team," *Denver Post*, December 19, 1969, 43; "White Wyo. Sprinter Quits to Back Protest by Blacks," *Afro-American*, December 27, 1969, 8; and "White Star Joins Black Protest," *New York Amsterdam News*, December 27, 1969, 33.

82. See articles cited in note 81.

83. Haws recounts how Mel Hamilton, a Black Wyoming player who was a part of the Black 14, had been kicked off the team two years earlier when Eaton found out he was going to marry his white girlfriend. Eaton later reinstated his scholarship and allowed him back on the team. See Haws, *Mormon Image in the American Mind*, 53. For one example among many, see the following articles about a white track member who quit Wyoming's team after being ridiculed by his coach and teammates for "associating with Blacks" after he supported the terminated Black football players. "'Ridiculed' Trackman Quits Wyoming Team," *Denver Post*, December 17, 1969, 93, 96; and "'Ridiculed' Trackman Quits Wyoming Team," *Denver Post*, December 19, 1969, 43.

84. For example, see Jim Graham, "Keeping POSTed: Eaton Took Right Stand," *Denver Post*, October 22, 1969, 86; "Mormon Religious Rights," *Denver Post*, October 25,

1969, 12; Bick Lucas, "Emotion, Not Logic, Prevailing in Laramie," *Denver Post*, October 26, 1969, 35; A. S. "Doc" Young, "Good Morning Sports! More on Wyoming Mess,'" *Daily Defender*, October 27, 1969, 24; "The Open Forum: Mail Heavy on Wyoming U Issue," *Denver Post*, October 28, 1969, 17; A. S. "Doc" Young, "Good Morning Sports: The Wyoming Mess," *Daily Defender*, October 30, 1969, 40; Robert Kuesterman, "Sports Mill: Protests toward BYU 'Seem So Unjustified,'" *Denver Post*, November 2, 1969, 56; and "The Open Forum: 'There Is No Hope for the Satisfied Man': Case of Black 14," *Denver Post*, November 21, 1969, 24.

85. Jim Graham, "Keeping POSTed: Eaton Took Right Stand," *Denver Post*, October 22, 1969, 86.

86. "Mormon Religious Rights," *Denver Post*, October 25, 1969, 12.

87. Bick Lucas, "Emotion, Not Logic, Prevailing in Laramie," *Denver Post*, October 26, 1969, 35.

88. "The Open Forum: Mail Heavy on Wyoming U Issue," *Denver Post*, October 28, 1969, 17.

89. Robert Kuesterman, "Sports Mill: Protests toward BYU 'Seem So Unjustified,'" *Denver Post*, November 2, 1969, 56.

90. "BYU Will Seek Black Athletes," *Denver Post*, November 26, 1969, 29.

91. Robert Kuesterman, "Sports Mill: Protests toward BYU 'Seem So Unjustified,'" *Denver Post*, November 2, 1969, 56. Also see D. C. Summers, "The Open Forum: Mormon Reply to Protesters," *Denver Post*, February 9, 1970, 19.

92. See Metcalf, "'Which Side of the Line?,'" 228.

93. G. L. Douglas, "Epistle to the Editor: Mormon Stand," *Denver Post*, November 22, 1969, 33.

94. "BYU Students May Retaliate," *Denver Post*, November 7, 1969, 75.

95. Metcalf, "'Which Side of the Line?,'" 234.

96. Metcalf, 226.

97. Metcalf, 231.

98. James E. Cowart, "Mormonism and the Negro," *Greeley Daily Tribune*, March 14, 1970, 4.

99. "Stanford Drops Brigham Young," *Daily Defender*, November 13, 1969, 41. Also see "Stanford to Bar Contests with Mormon Institutions," *New York Times*, November 13, 1969, 35; "Stanford Breaks with Brigham Young University," *Call and Post*, November 22, 1969, 8B; and Michael Knipe, "Mormons Face Race Conflict," *Times*, December 17, 1969, 7.

100. Haws, *Mormon Image in the American Mind*, 62.

101. "Red Carpet Welcome Given Negro at BYU," *Denver Post*, November 15, 1969, 26.

102. "BYU Confirms Negro Gridder Signed to Squad," *Denver Post*, February 3, 1970, 53.

103. Anthony Ripley, "Irate Black Athletes Stir Campus Tension," *New York Times*, November 16, 1969, 1.

104. See Gary S. Edmonds, "The Open Forum: Threat to Religious Freedom," *Denver Post*, January 20, 1970, 21; D. C. Summers, "The Open Forum: Mormon Reply

to Protesters," *Denver Post*, February 9, 1970, 19; and "NCAA Paper Lays Trouble to Outsiders," *Denver Post*, December 17, 1969, 95.

105. John Bowen, "Board to Consider BYU Ban amidst Latest Alumni Protest," *Stanford Daily*, January 12, 1970, 1.

106. See, for example, "The Open Forum: 'There Is No Hope for the Satisfied Man': Case of Black 14,'" *Denver Post*, November 21, 1969, 24.

107. Edward B. Fiske, "Mormons: Still No Place in the Pulpit for Blacks," *New York Times*, November 23, 1969, E9.

108. Fiske, "Mormons," E9.

109. For a similar example, see John Dart's statement that BYU's "lack of protest demonstrations, beards, mini-skirts, cigarettes or stimulants plus evidence of patriotism and reverence have brought glowing praise from persons who view most other large campuses as havens for the immoral and politically radical." John Dart, "President's View: BYU to Excel Likes of Harvard, Yale," *Denver Post*, March 26, 1970, 12.

110. See William Patterson, "Black Athlete and Democracy USA," *Sun Reporter*, December 20, 1969, 4; "Black Athletes 'Get Involved' in 1969," *Daily Defender*, December 23, 1969, 26; Stu Camen, "More Athletes Stand-Up for Fair Play," *Afro-American*, December 27, 1969, 8; and "Grid Boycott," *Daily Defender*, September 15, 1970, 13; James S. Tinney, "New Mormon Temple Erected a Symbol of 'Ultra Whiteness,'" *Afro-American*, September 21, 1974, 5; and "Latter-Day Saints' Racism," *Daily Defender*, September 14, 1974, 10.

111. See "Mormons Re-emphasize Rule Barring Negroes as Priests," *San Antonio Express*, January 9, 1970, 14-A; "Mormons Repeat Negro Priesthood Ban," *Denver Post*, January 9, 1970, 6; "Statement by Mormons on Role of Negro," *New York Times*, January 9, 1970, 14; Wallace Turner, "Mormons Reaffirm Curb on Negroes," *New York Times*, January 9, 1970, 1, 14; and "Priesthood Denied: Mormons Affirm Ban on Negroes," *Post Herald and Register*, January 11, 1970, 9.

112. See "Second-Class Mormons," *Newsweek*, January 19, 1970, 84; "Mormons and the Mark of Cain: Charges of Racism," *Time*, January 19, 1970, 46; Wallace Turner, "Mormon Rule Shift Hinted," *New York Times*, April 29, 1970, 6; and William F. Reed, "The Other Side of 'The Y': Mormon Policy Is One Thing, the Views of BYU's Team Are Another, and the Differences Are Quite Surprising," *Sports Illustrated*, January 26, 1970, 38–39. While the *Newsweek*, *Time*, and *New York Times* pieces are quite critical of the Church's teachings about race, and the *Sports Illustrated* article provides interviews with BYU students, some of whom identify the Church's bans and U.S. society generally as racist, this criticism still primarily framed the bans as "peculiar" and "anachronistic," ignoring the larger context in which several other evangelical fundamentalist groups maintained explicitly segregationist views and policies, not to mention the widespread acceptance of colorblind, assimilationist (i.e., still racist) views and policies. One *Christian Century* piece, a left-leaning religious publication, did explicitly label the Church's leaders as "white supremacist." "Pigskin Justice and Mormon Theology," *Christian Century*, January 21, 1970.

113. Haws, *Mormon Image in the American Mind*, 49.

114. "Mood Changes toward BYU," *Tucson Daily Citizen*, October 8, 1970, 30.

115. Brooks, *Mormonism and White Supremacy,* 98.

116. "The Marriott Story," *Forbes,* February 1, 1971, 20–24.

117. "The Marriott Story," *Forbes.*

118. Frye Gaillard, "School Days: Indian Youth Sue BIA School," *Akwesasne Notes,* September 1971, 32. Also see Stella Montoya, "BIA Teachers Shave Students' Heads at Utah School for Navajos," *El Grito del Norte,* August 20, 1971, 15; "LDS Negro Unfazed by Priesthood Block," *Denver Post,* June 19, 1971, 34; Ralph H. Jones, "Black Singer Denies Mormon Church Is Racist; Performs for World-Famous Tabernacle Choir," *Philadelphia Tribune,* July 3, 1971, 3; and "Y. Student Officer: Black Student Likes LDS 'Way of Life,'" *Salt Lake Tribune,* March 17, 1976, 30.

119. "Mormons and Blacks," *Christianity Today,* January 30, 1970, 22.

120. "Mormons and Blacks," 22.

121. Petrey, *Tabernacles of Clay,* 105.

122. See Dowland, *Family Values and the Rise of the Christian Right;* Cooper, *Family Values;* and West, "Policing of Poor Black Women's Reproduction."

123. "Mrs. America Cautions Women against Losing Femininity?," *Daily Defender,* March 21, 1966, 18.

124. "Homosexual acts" was officially added as an excommunicable offense to the Church's *General Handbook of Instructions* in 1968. Petrey, *Tabernacles of Clay,* 68.

125. See Jacobson, *Whiteness of a Different Color.*

126. N. Young, "Fascinating and Happy," 193, 194. In 1969, 1970, and 1971, Spencer W. Kimball published *The Miracle of Forgiveness, Hope for Transgressors,* and *New Horizons for Homosexuals* (retitled *A Letter to a Friend* in 1978), respectively. Homosexuality was removed from the *Diagnostic and Statistical Manual* in 1973, the same year the Church first published *Homosexuality: Welfare Services Packet* to help local leaders deal with the issue among members.

127. In fact, Andelin's book was inspired by a series of booklets she read from the 1920s called *The Secret of Fascinating Womanhood.* See N. Young, "Fascinating and Happy"; Petrey, *Tabernacles of Clay;* and Carter, *Heart of Whiteness.*

128. N. Young, "Fascinating and Happy," 193.

129. In 1970, Stephen G. Taggart published *Mormonism's Negro Policy: Social and Historical Origins* and Black Mormon Alan Gerald Cherry published *It's You and Me Lord!* defending the Church. In 1972, Black Mormon Wynetta Willis Martin published *Black Mormon Tells Her Story,* also defending the Church.

130. John Keahey, "Full Mormon Status for Negro 'Will Come,'" *Denver Post,* September 23, 1972, 39.

131. Eleanor Blau, "New Mormon Head: Spencer Woolley Kimball," *New York Times,* January 1, 1974, 15.

132. These controversies included press coverage of each successive Church president's views on race (McKay, Smith, Lee, and Kimball); a 1971 dispute over the Church's construction project near Lincoln Center; a 1974 lawsuit brought by the NAACP against the Church for using its racist priesthood ban to structure Boy Scout troop leadership, which was eventually dismissed when the Church changed its policies for organizing troops; the dedication of a temple in Washington, D.C., in 1974; professional

basketball player Willie Wise quitting the Utah Stars, citing the Church's racial bans in 1975; and a series of public protests against the bans by Church members between 1976 and 1978. The majority of this coverage was actually a result of antiracist activism meant to catch journalists' interest. In contrast, issues like the Church's treatment of and attitude toward Indigenous peoples, which did not benefit from the same level of public activism (although the Red Power movement did take some steps to call out the Church's anti-Native racism), barely registered in the national press. See, for example, Garry J. Moes, "Missionary View Changing," *Denver Post*, May 18, 1973, 5HH.

133. Judy Klemesrud, "Strengthening Family Solidarity with a Home Evening Program," *New York Times*, June 4, 1973, 47.

134. Brooks, *Mormonism and White Supremacy*, 101.

135. "Kings of Bubble Gum," *Newsweek*, September 3, 1973, 89.

136. See Haws, *Mormon Image in the American Mind*, 80. In 1976, the Church would build on its success with the *Homefront* series by producing an hour-long TV special in the same vein called *The Family . . . and Other Living Things*.

137. "Women's 2d Class Role in Religion," *Daily Defender*, October 27, 1973, 24. Also see "Attacks Women's Lib," *Daily Defender*, October 9, 1973, 5.

138. "Smooth Succession?," *Time*, January 14, 1974.

139. Petrey, *Tabernacles of Clay*, 122.

140. Kay Mills, "ERA Facing Strong Mormon Opposition," *Denver Post*, October 21, 1977, 76.

141. Mills, "ERA Facing Strong Mormon Opposition," 76.

142. Sandra Haggerty, "Blacks and the Mormon Church," *Los Angeles Times*, July 5, 1974, B5.

143. "Mormons Pressed on Scouts Policy: Change in Rules on Blacks Fails to Satisfy N.A.A.C.P.," *New York Times*, August 3, 1974, 26.

144. Harvey Duston, "Mormon Leader Wages Sexual Revolution Counterattack," *Brownsville Herald*, December 23, 1974, 8B.

145. Since the 1890s, the Church had refused to openly involve itself in political issues in order to combat accusations of theocracy in Utah and undue political influence over its members.

146. See "Mormon Opposition Factor: Equal-Rights Amendment Faces Utah Battle," *Denver Post*, January 19, 1975, 15; "Utah Rejects ERA Proposal; 4 States Still Needed for Okay," *Denver Post*, February 19, 1975, 36; and "New Blow to Equal Rights," *Times*, February 20, 1975, 6.

147. "Equal Rights for Women—Doomed?," *U.S. News and World Report*, April 28, 1975, 45.

148. Petrey, *Tabernacles of Clay*, 115.

149. Grace Lichtenstein, "Feminism in the Wild West—So Far It's Been Pretty Tame," *New York Times*, May 3, 1975, 22.

150. A Mormon feminist consciousness-raising group had been founded in 1970 in Boston, which was instrumental in publishing the 1971 "Pink" issue of *Dialogue*, a journal focused on providing a more open space for discussing issues related to

Mormonism founded in 1966 and which had been the venue for much dissent against
the Church's Black priesthood and temple bans throughout the 1960s and 1970s. Also
see Grace Lichtenstein, "Paradox in Women's Movement: Feminists Who Are Mormons," *New York Times*, October 28, 1975, 39.

151. See Grace Lichtenstein, "Paradox in Women's Movement," 39; John M.
Crewdson, "Mormon Turnout Overwhelms Women's Conference in Utah," *New
York Times*, July 25, 1977, 27; Judy Klemesrud, "Are Mormons against Feminism? Not
Exactly," *New York Times*, May 5, 1978, A16; and Richard Cohen, "What's at Stake
Here Is More Than Liturgy," *Washington Post*, January 1, 1980, C1.

152. Petrey, *Tabernacles of Clay*, 81.

153. Petrey, 83.

154. This was the same year that Apostle Boyd K. Packer encouraged young men
to assault men who they perceived to show sexual interest in them in his talk "To
Young Men Only" and that the *General Handbook of Instructions* dropped "homosexual acts" and added "homosexuality" to the list of excommunicable sins. A year later,
the Utah legislature would pass its first bill, one of the first in the country, to ban
same-sex marriage. See also "LDS Urges Anti-ERA Letters to Senators," *Denver Post*,
September 1, 1978, 2BB, 67; "Newsnames," *Denver Post*, December 17, 1979, 15; "Newsnames," *Denver Post*, January 2, 1980, 7; Virginia Culver, "Mormons Predict Recovery
from ERA Battle," *Denver Post*, February 8, 1980, 65, 67; and "Mormon Officials Derate
Homosexuality, Welfare," *Denver Post*, April 10, 1981, 73.

155. Petrey, *Tabernacles of Clay*, 105.

156. Kenneth L. Woodward and John Barnes, "Born Again!," *Newsweek*, October 25, 1976, 68.

157. "After a Long, Bitter Debate, the Idaho Legislature Completed Action Tues-
day," Associated Press, February 8, 1977.

158. "After a Long, Bitter Debate." Idaho, Kentucky, Nebraska, Tennessee, and
South Dakota all eventually rescinded ratification of the ERA.

159. For examples, see "Women at Utah Meeting Oppose Rights Proposal," *New
York Times*, June 26, 1977, 32; Lisa Cronin Wohl, "A Mormon Connection? The Defeat
of the ERA in Nevada," *Ms.*, July 6, 1977, 68–70, 80, 83–85; "Backlash Hits ERA at
Women's Meets," *Denver Post*, July 11, 1977, 19; "Mormons Battle Stands of IWY,"
Denver Post, July 12, 1977, 42; and "Obstacle of Tradition Face the Proponents of ERA
Initiative on Ballot," *Washington Post*, October 12, 1978, A2.

160. Judy Klemesrud, "Equal Rights Plan and Abortion Are Opposed by 15,000 at
Rally," *New York Times*, November 20, 1977, 32.

161. For typical examples, see "Equal Rights: Why the Amendment Appears
Doomed," *U.S. News and World Report*, March 28, 1977, 53; "Anita Bryant Commended
by Mormons," *Denver Post*, June 17, 1977, 76; Grace Lichtenstein, "Homosexuals Are
Moving toward Open Way of Life as Tolerance Rises among the General Popula-
tion," *New York Times*, July 17, 1977, 34; Grace Lichtenstein, "Poll Finds Public Split on
Legalizing Homosexual Acts," *New York Times*, July 19, 1977, 17; and Susan Fraker, Lucy
Howard, Elaine Sciolino, and Deborah W. Beers, "Women vs. Women," *Newsweek*,
July 25, 1977, 34.

162. "Mormon Utah; Where a Church Shapes the Life of a State," *U.S. News and World Report,* December 19, 1977, 59. For a similar example, also see Lou Cannon, "Mondale, Touring West, Told of Coal Boom Towns' Social and Economic Problems," *Washington Post,* January 12, 1978, A20.

163. For coverage of these events, see "Around the Nation: A Black Is Ordained to Mormon Priesthood," *New York Times,* June 12, 1978, A16; "Around the Nation: Black Mormon Elevated," Associated Press, June 12, 1978, A5; and Twila Van Leer, "Black LDS Priesthood Holder Says, 'It's a Beautiful Day,'" *Deseret News,* June 12, 1978, B-1, B-2.

164. Donny Osmond quoted in Brooks, *Mormonism and White Supremacy,* 103.

165. For typical examples, see David Briscoe, "Monroe Fleming Says a Policy Change Admitting Blacks to the Priesthood," Associated Press, June 9, 1978; and Kenneth A. Briggs, "Mormon Church Strikes Down Ban against Blacks in Priesthood: Change in 148-Year-Old Policy Was a Result of a 'Revelation,' Letter to Leaders Says," *New York Times,* June 10, 1978, 1, 24.

166. "Mormon Revelation Solves Black Problem," *Denver Post,* July 7, 1978, 7BB.

167. "Blacks and the Mormon Church," *New York Amsterdam News,* June 17, 1978, 4.

168. For instance, see "First in More Than Century: Mormons Ordain Black to the Priesthood," *Denver Post,* June 12, 1978, 28.

169. Petrey, *Tabernacles of Clay,* 47. And see "Now Blacks Can Become Full-Fledged Mormons," *Time,* June 19, 1978, 55; and "Mormonism Enters a New Era but America's Biggest Native Faith Remains a Kingdom Apart," *Time,* August 7, 1978, 54–56.

170. W. Dale Nelson, "A Senator Who Is a Mormon," Associated Press, August 4, 1978.

171. See Judy Mann, "A Mormon for ERA Fearful of Ostracism," *Washington Post,* August 10, 1979, B1; David Briscoe, "A Mormon Woman Who Has Split with Her Church Leadership," Associated Press, November 15, 1979; Michael J. Weiss, "Irked by Sonia Johnson's E.R.A. Crusade, Church Elders Throw the Book of Mormon at Her," *People,* December 3, 1979, 44; and Ben A. Franklin, "Mormon Church Excommunicates a Supporter of Rights Amendment," *New York Times,* December 6, 1979, A26.

172. MERA chartered airplanes with pro-ERA banners to fly over Temple Square during general conference and the Church's Hill Cumorah pageant in upstate New York (a yearly reenactment, open to the public, of Joseph Smith's discovery of the tablets from which he transcribed the Book of Mormon and some of the events therein). MERA activists, including Johnson, also chained themselves to the temple gates during a protest in Seattle, Washington.

173. In response to these attacks, it was during this period that the Church added "Another Testament of Jesus Christ" as the subtitle to the Book of Mormon.

174. Haws, *Mormon Image in the American Mind,* 101.

175. Kenneth A. Briggs, "Mormon Church at 150: Thriving on Traditionalism," *New York Times,* March 30, 1980, 1, 46.

176. Ronald Reagan quoted in Haws, *Mormon Image in the American Mind,* 107. Also see William Rees-Mogg, "William Rees-Mogg in Utah, the Centre of American Conservatism: Why the Mormons Find a Magic in Governor Reagan," *Times,* March 15, 1980, 14.

7. POLYGAMY, OR THE RACIAL POLITICS OF
MARRIAGE AS FREEDOM

1. Technically, Utah had four bans against same-sex marriage: three statutes and one amendment to the state's constitution. The first ban was a statute enacted in 1977 that prohibited marriage between persons of the same sex. See Utah Code Ann. § 30-1-2 (July 15, 1977). In 1995 the state passed a bill banning the recognition of out-of-state same-sex marriages, designed to circumvent the Full Faith and Credit Clause of the U.S. Constitution. See Utah Code Ann. § 30-1-4 (May 1, 1995). Another bill was passed in 2004 banning same-sex marriages and equivalents, such as civil unions. See Utah Code Ann. § 30-1-4.1 (March 23, 2004). The state also passed an amendment to the state constitution in 2004 that banned same-sex marriage and any other type of same-sex domestic union. See Utah Const. art. I, § 29 (2004).

2. Like similar test cases around the country, *Kitchen* was designed to move through the federal court, rather than the state court system, for two reasons: first, this would allow the case to move more quickly through the system, potentially to the Supreme Court, and second, it allowed the plaintiffs to draw primarily on the more expansive interpretations available in the U.S. Constitution while avoiding the limitations of Utah's more restrictive state constitution. While the case may have eventually (certainly much more slowly) made its way to the Supreme Court had it been litigated through the state court system, the plaintiffs almost positively would have lost their case originally because of the more conservative nature of Utah's constitution and the local judicial system. For an overview of how the case was started and litigated, see Tuckett and Wilcox, *Church & State.* See Kitchen v. Herbert, 961 F.Supp.2d 1181 (D. Utah 2013); Hollingsworth v. Perry 570 U.S. 693; United States v. Windsor 570 U.S. 744; California's Proposition 8, California Const. art. I § 7.5 (November 5, 2008); and Defense of Marriage Act, 110 Stat. 2419 (1996).

3. Legally speaking, *Kitchen* is unique for a few reasons. This is the case not only because the District Court's ruling was the first federal level decision to legalize gay marriage and because *Kitchen* was also the first decision that was based on the precedent set in *Windsor,* but it was also unique because the case was instigated by local grassroots efforts rather than professional legal activism, a fact discussed more fully below. Followed by several parallel circuit court decisions, *Kitchen* stood as precedent until the Sixth Circuit Court issued a contradictory ruling upholding the ban on gay marriage in Ohio, Michigan, Kentucky, and Tennessee. Appealed to the Supreme Court, that case, *Obergefell v. Hodges,* was decided in June 2015 and found that the Fourteenth Amendment requires states to license a marriage between two people of the same sex and that states must recognize same-sex marriages licensed and performed in other states. See Obergefell v. Hodges, 576 U.S. 644.

4. *The Rachel Maddow Show,* aired December 20, 2013, on MSNBC, transcript available at http://www.nbcnews.com/id/53994311/ns/msnbc-rachel_maddow_show/.

5. Brown v. Buhman, 947 F.Supp.2d 1170 (D. Utah 2013).

6. Cohabitation was first criminalized by federal legislation in the nineteenth century as a strategy to more easily prosecute Utah's Mormon polygamists, as described

in chapter 3. Because Mormon marriages were common law, federal prosecutors needed the marriage certificate (records that were kept privately by the Church) or they needed wives to testify they were polygamously married (wives were generally unwilling to testify), making it incredibly difficult to get an indictment, let alone a conviction. Proving cohabitation, that a man lived with more than one woman as his wife, facilitated prosecution by sidestepping the need to prove a legal marriage had taken place. Cohabitation is still illegal in Utah and was up until March 2020 used to prosecute Mormon polygamy but not other types of cohabitation, adultery, or religious plural marriage.

Brown was appealed to the Tenth Circuit Court of Appeals in September 2014. In April 2016, the Tenth Circuit ordered dismissal of the case (and, by extension, the findings of the previous court) on the grounds that the Utah County Attorney Office's policy of limiting polygamy prosecutions to those involving child abuse, bigamy, fraud, or violence meant that the Browns had no credible fear of prosecution. While the Browns appealed the Tenth Circuit Court's decision to the Supreme Court in September 2016, the Supreme Court denied certiorari in January 2017, finalizing the Tenth Circuit's decision and leaving Utah's criminalization of cohabitation intact.

Following the Tenth Circuit's decision in *Brown*, the Utah legislature sought to revise the state's bigamy statute to avoid future legal challenges. The proposed bill, HB 99, was narrowly passed in March 2017, altering the wording of the state's definition of bigamy, specifically cohabitation's place in that definition. The law also made bigamy a second-degree felony if the accused was simultaneously convicted of inducing marriage or bigamy under false pretenses, fraud, domestic abuse, child abuse, sexual abuse, human trafficking, or human smuggling. See Utah Code Ann. § 76-7-101 (May 9, 2017). Most recently, however, in March 2020, the Utah legislature completely revised its antipolygamy law with S.B. 102 to significantly reduce the penalty for cohabitation to a $750 fine and community service, making it an infraction rather than a felony. See Utah Code Ann. § 76-7-101 (May 12, 2020).

7. Both before and after *Obergefell v. Hodges* legalized gay marriage nationwide, media, pundits, politicians, and even courts warned that such a decision would lead to the legalization of polygamy. See, for example, Supreme Court Justice Antonin Scalia's dissent in *Lawrence v. Texas* (2003): "State laws against bigamy, same-sex marriage, adult incest, prostitution, masturbation, adultery, fornication, bestiality, and obscenity are likewise sustainable only in light of *Bowers'* validation of laws based on moral choices. Every single one of these laws is called into question by today's decision." See Lawrence v. Texas 539 U.S. 558 (2003). James Oliphant, "Rick Santorum Jeered after Comparing Gay Marriage to Polygamy," *Los Angeles Times*, January 6, 2012, http://articles.latimes.com/2012/jan/06/news/la-pn-santorum-jeered-after-comparing-gay-marriage-to-polygamy-20120106; *The O'Reilly Factor*, aired April 4, 2013, on Fox News; *The O'Reilly Factor*, aired December 16, 2013, on Fox News; Michael Brendan Dougherty, "How Gay Marriage Paves the Way for Legal Polygamy," *The Week*, July 6, 2015, http://theweek.com/articles/564178/how-gay-marriage-paves-way-legal-polygamy; Jane C. Timm, "Ben Carson: Gay Marriage Leads to Polygamy and 'on from There,'" *MSNBC*, October 13, 2015, http://www.msnbc.com/msnbc/carson-gay

-marriage-leads-polygamy; as well as Supreme Court Chief Justice Roberts's dissent in *Obergefell*: "If '[t]here is dignity in the bond between two men or two women who seek to marry and in their autonomy to make such profound choices,' . . . why would there be any less dignity in the bond between three people who, in exercising their autonomy, seek to make the profound choice to marry?" (20). See Obergefell v. Hodges 576 U.S. 644 (2015).

8. See Obergefell v. Hodges 576 U.S. 644 (2015). For an analysis of this trend in representations of Mormon polygamy on television, see Bailey and Zahren, "Post-Homophobia Comes Out."

9. Strictly speaking, if the Supreme Court had granted certiorari, then Utah's criminalization of cohabitation, not bigamy, would have been under review in *Brown*.

10. Here it is important to reiterate my theoretical framing of colonialism and imperialism: I conceptualize race as a colonial governing structure. More specifically, colonialism is "the political order that dominating polities"—in this case the U.S. nation-state—"administer over subjugated peoples" through "military, economic, political, and psychological," as well as ideological, modes, tactics, and practices. As an empire, the United States both occupies and exerts control over various locales, while race as biopolitics serves as the primary matrix of creating populations, justifying the power differentials between those populations and, therefore, the exercise of control by one population over another (or, in the case of the United States, others). See S. Johnson, *African American Religions*, 2, and Foucault's discussion of biopolitics in *"Society Must Be Defended."*

11. Loving v. Virginia, 388 U.S. 1 (1967); and Lawrence v. Texas, 539 U.S. 558 (2003).

12. Reynolds v. United States, 98 U.S. 145 (1879).

13. Puar, *Terrorist Assemblages*.

14. John Iadarola, "Judge DESTROYS Utah Same-Sex Marriage Opponents in Epic Ruling!," December 23, 2013, YouTube video, 6:15, https://www.youtube.com/watch?v=DSqgh9aof88.

15. Holly Tuckett and Kendall Wilcox's documentary *Church & State* (2018) documents Lawrence's role in starting the case and his eventual falling out with the plaintiffs and attorneys after they accepted legal and financial help from the National Center for Lesbian Rights in fighting the appeal.

16. Sbeity does not mention his religious background in his affidavit to the court.

17. Kitchen v. Herbert, 961 F.Supp.2d 1181 (D. Utah 2013), 3.

18. For comprehensive examinations of how racist, Islamophobic representations of Arabs and Muslims persisted through colorblind narratives in the post-9/11 United States, as well as the role of gender exceptionalism in those representations, see Alsultany, *Arabs and Muslims in the Media*, and "Arabs and Muslims in the Media after 9/11." For an overview of how Muslims were deployed as foils in U.S. sexual exceptionalist discourse in the post-9/11 era, see Puar, *Terrorist Assemblages*. For a discussion of how Muslim became a racial category and for a comparative analysis of how the category Muslim was constructed in the pre- and post-9/11 eras, see Rana, *Terrifying Muslims*.

19. Brady McCombs, "Derek Kitchen and Moudi Sbeity, Utah Gay Couple, on the State's Same-Sex Marriage Fight," *Huffington Post*, June 7, 2014.

20. This gendered narrative of exceptionalism is one that scholars of feminism and postcolonialism—particularly Lila Abu-Lughod, Inderpal Grewal, Caren Kaplan, Valentine Moghadam, Chandra Mohanty, Saba Mahmood, and Gayatri Spivak—have analyzed as an imperialist discourse that frames Muslim women as "helpless" and in need of rescuing.

21. *Kitchen*, 4.

22. Examples of Mormon repression of LGBTQ people during this period included encouraging them to marry someone of the opposite sex, the official promotion of homophobic violence, religious and state authorities working together to identify and track BYU students who visited gay bars, and the use of conversion therapy, including electric shock therapy, for BYU students who were either identified as having or who were caught expressing same-sex attraction. For more, see Prince, *Gay Rights and the Mormon Church*; Petrey, *Tabernacles of Clay*; and O'Donovan, "Private Pain, Public Purges."

23. The documentary *Church & State* even participates in a kind of updated version of this type of nineteenth-century Mormon peculiarity discourse—as have many texts since the 1980s—which emphasizes the Church's religious and political dominance in Utah as fundamentally undemocratic and backward compared to other state governments.

24. Bailey and Zahren, "Post-Homophobia Comes Out," 161–62.

25. Despite the fact that The Church of Jesus Christ of Latter-day Saints abandoned polygamy in 1890, the general public still confuses the FLDS, one of the most widely known splinter groups that broke away as a result of the 1890 manifesto, with the mainstream Church—a mistake that the mainstream Church has worked hard, but often in vain, to correct. See Daphne Bramham, "The Taliban among Us," *National Post*, March 22, 2008; and Dorothy Allred Solomon, "American Taliban?," *Marie Claire*, July 14, 2008, http://www.marieclaire.com/politics/a1788/american-taliban.

26. Bailey and Zahren, "Post-Homophobia Comes Out," 172.

27. See, for example, *Time* magazine's profile of Mitt Romney. Jon Meacham, "The Mormon in Mitt," October 8, 2012, *Time*.

28. *Kitchen*, 49.

29. Gordon, *Mormon Question*, 130.

30. *Brown*, 31.

31. The Brown family are members of the Apostolic United Brethren Church, a fundamentalist, Mormon polygamist faith that is part of the Latter-day Saint tradition and is distinct from the mainstream Mormon Church.

32. *Brown*, 6.

33. *Sister Wives*, season 2, episode 10, "Gambling on the Future," aired May 22, 2011, on TLC.

34. In addition, Utah was granted statehood on the condition that "polygamist or plural marriages are forever prohibited" in the Enabling Act and the Irrevocable Ordinance, which were included in Utah's Constitution.

35. Edmunds Act, 22 Stat. 30 (1882). *Brown*, 82.

36. The full statute read as follows: "A person is guilty of bigamy when, knowing he has a husband or wife or knowing the other person has a husband or wife, the person purports to marry another person or cohabits with another person." Utah Code Ann. § 76-7-101(1). This statute has since been revised by Utah's legislature. For those revisions, see note 6 in this chapter.

37. *Brown*, 2.

38. *Brown*, 10.

39. *Brown*, 10.

40. *Brown*, 10–11.

41. *Brown*, 11, 20.

42. Ertman, "Race Treason," 287.

43. As did nineteenth-century anti-Mormons, modern commentators claim that polygamy inevitably leads to a power imbalance in which a small group of wealthy and powerful men control their society's governance. For examples, please refer to note 7. Also see Nadje Al-Ali and Nicola Pratt's analysis of the U.S. government's deployment of gender exceptionalism in justifying the invasion of Iraq in 2003 in *What Kind of Liberation?*

44. Boutilier v. Immigration and Naturalization Service, 387 U.S. 118 (1967).

45. Somerville, "Queer *Loving*."

46. Pace v. Alabama, 106 U.S. 583 (1883); and Plessy v. Ferguson, 163 U.S. 537 (1896).

47. See Oman, "Natural Law and the Rhetoric of Empire."

48. Late Corp. of The Church of Jesus Christ of Latter-day Saints v. United States, 136 U.S. 1 (1890), cited in *Brown*, 18.

49. *Brown*, 20–21.

50. See Johnson's argument that "the political experiment of the United States in democratic freedom . . . has been anchored in and enabled by colonialism." S. Johnson, *African American Religions*, 3.

51. Even if the Tenth Circuit had upheld Waddoups's ruling and the Supreme Court had granted certiorari and found in the Browns' favor, the decision would not have overturned *Reynolds* because the two cases dealt with different constitutional questions.

52. *Brown*, 22.

53. *Brown*, 21.

54. Bailey and Zahren, "Post-Homophobia Comes Out."

55. *Sister Wives*, season 1, episode 1, "Meet Kody and the Wives," aired September 26, 2010, on TLC.

56. Bailey and Zahren, "Post-Homophobia Comes Out," 169.

57. Bailey and Zahren, 169.

58. *Brown*, 33.

59. *Brown*, 33n44.

60. See Denike, "What's Queer about Polygamy?"

61. This is also one of the major assertions and issues addressed by critical race theory. For more on this, see Crenshaw et al., *Critical Race Theory*; Delgado and Stefancic, *Critical Race Theory*; and Holland, *Erotic Life of Racism*.

62. *Brown,* 67–68.

63. The purported objectives of the state were "responsible procreation" and "optimal child rearing," what is referred to as the "gold standard" in the decision. I discuss the gold standard more thoroughly below. *Kitchen,* 48.

64. On heteronormativity (versus heterosexuality), see Berlant and Warner, "Sex in Public"; and Cohen, "Punks, Bulldaggers, and Welfare Queens." For homonormativity, see Stryker, "Transgender History, Homonormativity, and Disciplinarity"; and Duggan, *Twilight of Equality.*

65. For example, see Puar's discussion of Sikh masculinity and South Asian diasporic subjects in chapter 4 of *Terrorist Assemblages.*

66. The conditional nature of this acceptance was made abundantly clear after the death of Supreme Court Justice Ruth Bader Ginsburg opened up an opportunity for the appointment of another justice who would potentially support a reversal of the court's decision in *Obergefell v. Hodges* (among other decisions). The desire to reverse *Obergefell* was articulated by Justices Clarence Thomas and Samuel Alito in the court's denial of certiorari to the case of Kentucky clerk Kim Davis on October 5, 2020. See Alison Durkee, "Thomas, Alito Urge Supreme Court to 'Fix' Decision Legalizing Marriage Equality," *Forbes,* October 5, 2020, https://www.forbes.com/sites/alison durkee/2020/10/05/thomas-alito-urge-supreme-court-to-fix-decision-legalizing-mar riage-equality/#7cf02986342a.

67. For examples of how white supremacy has been administered and upheld through the institution of marriage in the late twentieth and early twenty-first centuries, see Denetdalem, "Carving Navajo National Boundaries"; Eng, *Feeling of Kinship*; Franke, *Wedlocked*; Somerville, "Queer *Loving*"; and Spade, "Under the Cover of Gay Rights."

68. While the decision would affect the ability of all LGBTQ people to marry in Utah, Shelby consistently and exclusively referred to "gays and lesbians" throughout the decision. I purposefully use his language to analyze the limits and problems with the assumptions and reasoning of the decision.

69. *Kitchen,* 41.

70. *Kitchen,* 42.

71. *Kitchen,* 44.

72. On the state's racialized investment in heteronormativity and the unequal application of state support, see Cohen, "Punks, Bulldaggers, and Welfare Queens"; Ferguson, *Aberrations in Black*; Josephson, *Rethinking Sexual Citizenship*; Moller "Supporting Single Mothers"; Moynihan, *Negro Family*; and Rose, "Gender, Race, and the Welfare State."

73. *Kitchen,* 45.

74. *Kitchen,* 46.

75. Hunter, "Sexual Orientation and the Paradox of Heightened Scrutiny."

76. *Kitchen,* 24–25.

77. *Kitchen,* 51.

78. Puar, *Terrorist Assemblages,* 29–30.

79. Puar, 118. See also Eng, *Feeling of Kinship*; Franke, "Domesticated Liberty of *Lawrence v. Texas*"; Franke, *Wedlocked*; and Somerville, "Queer *Loving*."

80. Somerville, "Queer *Loving*," 343–44.

81. See note 61.

82. Eng, *Feeling of Kinship*, 41.

83. Somerville, "Queer *Loving*," 347.

84. Somerville, 357.

85. Eng, *Feeling of Kinship*, 10.

86. Somerville, "Queer *Loving*," 346.

87. See Cacho, *Social Death*.

88. Puar, *Terrorist Assemblages*, 117.

89. There is debate as to which cases constitute the *Insular* decisions. At a minimum, six cases are included: De Lima v. Bidwell, 182 U.S. 1 (1901); Goetze v. United States, 182 U.S. 221 (1901); Dooley v. United States, 182 U.S. 222 (1901); Armstrong v. United States, 182 U.S. 243 (1901); Downes v. Bidwell, 182 U.S. 244 (1901); and Huus v. New York and Porto Rico Steamship Co., 182 U.S. 392 (1901). Other scholars argue that the following cases should also be considered part of the *Insular* decision block: Fourteen Diamond Rings v. United States, 183 U.S. 176 (1901); Hawaii v. Mankichi, 190 U.S. 197 (1903); Gonzales v. Williams, 192 U.S. 1 (1904); Kepner v. United States, 195 U.S. 100 (1904); Dorr v. United States, 195 U.S. 138 (1904); Mendozana v. United States, 195 U.S. 158 (1904); Rasmussen v. United States, 197 U.S. 516 (1905); Trono v. United States, 199 U.S. 521 (1905); Grafton v. United States, 206 U.S. 333 (1907); Kent v. Porto Rico, 207 U.S. 113 (1907); Kopel v. Bingham, 211 U.S. 468 (1909); Dowdell v. United States, 221 U.S. 325 (1911); Ochoa v. Hernández, 230 U.S. 139 (1913); and Ocampo v. United States, 234 U.S. 91 (1914).

90. Crenshaw, "Demarginalizing the Intersection of Race and Sex." Also see Wing, *Critical Race Feminism*.

91. Unenumerated rights refer to unspecified rights that are inferred but not explicitly articulated in law.

92. See the following Supreme Court decisions: Griswold v. Connecticut, 381 U.S. 479 (1965); Loving v. Virginia, 388 U.S. 1 (1967); Eisenhardt v. Baird, 405 U.S. 438 (1972); Goodridge v. Department of Public Health, 440 Mass. 309, 798 N.E.2d 941 (Mass. 2003); and Obergefell v. Hodges, 576 U.S. 644 (2015).

93. Franke, "Domesticated Liberty of *Lawrence v. Texas*," 1,400; and Puar, *Terrorist Assemblages*, chap. 3.

94. See, for example, Shah's discussion of the state's regulation of marriage among and between nonwhite people in the United States in *Stranger Intimacy*, chap. 5. Also see Franke's discussion of former slaves' experiences gaining marital rights during and after the Civil War in *Wedlocked*.

95. Eng, *Feeling of Kinship*, 10. For examinations of how Indigenous people were prevented from maintaining supposedly traditional families through U.S. colonialism, see Jacobs, *Generation Removed*, and *White Mother to a Dark Race*.

96. Puar, *Terrorist Assemblages*, 124.

97. Franke, *Wedlocked*, 9.

98. Eng, *Feeling of Kinship*, 35.

99. See M. Alexander, *New Jim Crow*; Cacho, *Social Death*; A. Davis, *Are Prisons Obsolete?*; Franke, *Wedlocked*; Jacobs, *Generation Removed*, and *White Mother to a Dark Race*; Shah, *Stranger Intimacy*; and Spade, *Normal Life*.

100. Hunter, "Sexual Orientation and the Paradox of Heightened Scrutiny," 1,528.

101. Franke, *Wedlocked*.

102. *Kitchen*, 52.

103. Seegmiller v. LaVerkin City, 528 F3d 762 (10th Cir. 2008).

104. *Seegmiller* as cited by Shelby in *Brown*, 42.

105. *Brown*, 45.

106. *Brown*, 48.

107. *Brown*, 63. It is important to note here that the Tenth Circuit rejected this as grounds for the Browns having a credible fear of prosecution on appeal. See Brown v. Buhman, 822 F.3d 1151 (10th Cir. 2016).

108. *Brown*, 67–68.

109. *The O'Reilly Factor*, aired December 16, 2013, on Fox.

110. Eng, *Feeling of Kinship*, 47.

111. *Brown*, 71.

112. *Brown*, 76.

113. *Kitchen*, 28.

114. *Kitchen*, 28.

115. Eng, *Feeling of Kinship*, 45.

116. S. Johnson, *African American Religions*, 392.

CODA

1. Cohen, "Punks, Bulldaggers, and Welfare Queens," 438.

2. Cohen, "Radical Potential of Queer?," 141.

3. Cohen, 142.

4. Puar, *Terrorist Assemblages*, xiii.

5. Coviello, *Make Yourselves Gods*, 215, 216.

6. "The Family: A Proclamation to the World," The Church of Jesus Christ of Latter-day Saints, accessed October 25, 2020, https://www.churchofjesuschrist.org/study/scriptures/the-family-a-proclamation-to-the-world/the-family-a-proclamation-to-the-world?lang=eng.

7. As quoted in Coviello, *Make Yourselves Gods*, 215.

8. Coviello, 216.

9. Coviello, 217.

10. Coviello, 5.

11. Hesse, "Racialized Modernity," 659.

12. Russell M. Nelson, "We join with many throughout this nation and around the world who are deeply saddened at recent evidences of racism and a blatant disregard for human life," Facebook, June 1, 2020, https://www.facebook.com/permalink.php?story_fbid=3015443371856412&id=501224873278287.

13. Nelson repeated much of his Facebook statement at the October 2020 General Conference meeting. For examples of commentary on his statements, see Peggy

Fletcher Stack, "Racists Need to Repent, Says LDS Church President as Utah Faith Leaders Call for End to Prejudice, Violence," *Salt Lake Tribune*, June 2, 2020, https:// www.sltrib.com/religion/2020/06/01/racists-need-repent-says/; Ted Walch, "President Nelson: 'Deeply Saddened at Recent Evidences of Racism and a Blatant Disregard for Human Life,'" *Deseret News*, June 1, 2020, https://www.deseret.com/faith/2020/6/1/21277362/president-nelson-facebook-post-social-media-racism-vio lence-latter-day-saints-naacp; and Peggy Fletcher Stack, Scott D. Pierce, and David Noyce, "In Blunt Language, Nelson Denounces Racism, Urges Latter-day Saints to 'Lead Out' against Prejudice," *Salt Lake Tribune*, October 4, 2020, https://www.sltrib .com/religion/2020/10/04/blunt-language-nelson/. At least one Mormon commentator pointed out Nelson's failure to discuss the Church's racist history in his statement. See Jana Riess, "The White Privilege of U.S. Mormons," *Religion News Service*, June 3, 2020, https://religionnews.com/2020/06/03/the-white-privilege-of-u-s-mormons/.

14. Brooks, *Mormonism and White Supremacy*, 5.

15. Brooks, 5.

16. Nelson, "We join with many throughout this nation," Facebook, June 1, 2020.

17. See S. Johnson, *African American Religions*, 124–28. Also see Lipsitz, *Possessive Investment in Whiteness*.

18. Ferguson, *Aberrations in Black*, 6.

19. Cohen, "Punks, Bulldaggers, and Welfare Queens," 453.

20. Cohen, "Radical Potential of Queer?," 142.

21. Puar, *Terrorist Assemblages*, 221.

22. Puar, 205.

Bibliography

NEWSPAPERS AND MAGAZINES

Afro-American (Baltimore)
Akwesasne Notes (New York)
American Affairs
American Medical Times
Associated Press
Boston Medical and Surgical Journal
British Medical Journal
Brownsville Herald (Texas)
Call and Post (Cleveland)
Catholic Worker
Christian Century
Christianity Today
Church News (Salt Lake City)
Cincinnati Lancet and Observer
Collier's (New York)
Contributor
Coronet
Daily Defender (Chicago)
Daily Graphic (New York)
DeBow's Review (New Orleans)
Denver Post
Deseret News (Salt Lake City)
Dialogue: A Journal of Mormon Thought
El Grito del Norte (Española, New Mexico)
Esquire
Forbes
Frank Leslie's Illustrated Newspaper (New York)
Greeley Daily Tribune (Colorado)

Harper's Weekly (New York)
Huffington Post
Improvement Era (Salt Lake City)
Journal of Discourses (Salt Lake City)
Judge
Juvenile Instructor (Salt Lake City)
Liahona
Life
Look
Los Angeles Times
Medical Times and Gazette
Ms.
Nation
National Collegiate Athletic Association News
National Era
New Pittsburgh Courier
New Republic
News Journal
Newsweek
New York Amsterdam News
New York Times
Nick Nax
Old Soldier
People
Philadelphia Tribune
(New) Pittsburgh Courier
Post Herald and Register
Puck
Religion News Service
Salt Lake Herald
Salt Lake Tribune
San Antonio Express
San Francisco Medical Press
Saturday Evening Post
Sports Illustrated
Stanford Daily
Sun Reporter (San Francisco)
Time
Times (London)
Tip Top Weekly
Tucson Daily Citizen
U.S. News and World Report
Utah Magazine
Vanity Fair

Washington Post
Wasp
Woman's Exponent (Salt Lake City)
Week
Yankee Notions
Young Woman's Journal (Salt Lake City)

COURT CASES

Armstrong v. United States (1901)
Boutilier v. Immigration and Naturalization Service (1967)
Brown v. Board of Education (1954)
Brown v. Buhman (2013)
Brown v. Buhman (2016)
De Lima v. Bidwell (1901)
Dooley v. United States (1901)
Dorr v. United States (1904)
Dowdell v. United States (1911)
Downes v. Bidwell (1901)
Eisenhardt v. Baird (1972)
Fourteen Diamond Rings v. United States (1901)
Goetze v. United States (1901)
Gonzales v. Williams (1904)
Goodridge v. Department of Public Health (2003)
Grafton v. United States (1907)
Griswold v. Connecticut (1965)
Hawaii v. Mankichi (1903)
Hollingsworth v. Perry (2013)
Huus v. New York and Porto Rico Steamship Co. (1901)
Kent v. Porto Rico (1907)
Kepner v. United States (1904)
Kitchen v. Herbert (2013)
Kopel v. Bingham (1909)
Late Corporation of The Church of Jesus Christ of Latter-day Saints v. United States (1890)
Lawrence v. Texas (2003)
Loving v. Virginia (1967)
Mendozana v. United States (1904)
Obergefell v. Hodges (2015)
Ocampo v. United States (1914)
Ochoa v. Hernández (1913)
Pace v. Alabama (1883)
Perez v. Sharp (1948)
Plessy v. Ferguson (1896)
Rasmussen v. United States (1905)
Reynolds v. United States (1879)

Seegmiller v. LaVerkin City (2008)
Shelley v. Kraemer (1948)
Trono v. United States (1905)
United States v. Windsor (2013)

OTHER PUBLISHED SOURCES

Abu-Lughod, Lila. *Do Muslim Women Need Saving?* Cambridge, Mass.: Harvard University Press, 2013.

Adas, Michael. "From Settler Colony to Global Hegemon: Integrating the Exceptionalist Narrative of the American Experience into World History." *American Historical Review* 106, no. 5 (2001): 1,692–720.

Aikau, Hōkūlani K. *A Chosen People, a Promised Land: Mormonism and Race in Hawai'i.* Minneapolis: University of Minnesota Press, 2012.

Al-Ali, Nadje, and Nicole Pratt. *What Kind of Liberation? Women and the Occupation of Iraq.* Berkeley: University of California Press, 2009.

Alexander, Michelle. *The New Jim Crow: Mass Incarceration in the Age of Colorblindness.* New York: New Press, 2010.

Alexander, Thomas G. "An Experiment in Progressive Legislation: The Granting of Woman Suffrage in Utah in 1870." *Utah Historical Quarterly* 38 (Winter 1970): 20–30.

Alexander, Thomas G. *Mormonism in Transition: A History of the Latter-day Saints 1890–1930.* Chicago: University of Illinois Press, 1996.

Allen, James B., and Glen M. Leonard. *The Story of the Latter-day Saints.* Salt Lake City: Deseret Book, 1979.

Allen, Theodore W. *The Invention of the White Race.* 2 vols. New York: Verso, 1994.

Alsultany, Evelyn. *Arabs and Muslims in the Media: Race and Representation after 9/11.* New York: New York University Press, 2012.

Alsultany, Evelyn. "Arabs and Muslims in the Media after 9/11: Representational Strategies for a 'Postrace' Era," *American Quarterly* 65, no. 1 (March 2013): 161–69.

Appleby, Joyce. "Recovering America's Historic Diversity: Beyond Exceptionalism." *Journal of American History* 79, no. 2 (1992): 419–31.

Arrington, Leonard J. *Great Basin Kingdom: An Economic History of the Latter-day Saints, 1830–1900.* Chicago: University of Illinois Press, 1958.

Arrington, Leonard J., and Davis Bitton. *The Mormon Experience: A History of the Latter-day Saints.* Chicago: University of Illinois Press, 1992.

Arrington, Leonard J., Ferzmorz Y. Fox, and Dean L. May. *Building the City of God: Community and Cooperation among the Mormons.* Urbana: University of Illinois Press, 1992.

Arrington, Leonard J., and Jon Haupt. "Intolerable Zion: The Image of Mormonism in Nineteenth-Century Literature." *Western Humanities Review* 22, no. 3 (Summer 1968): 243–60.

Arvin, Maile. *Possessing Polynesians: The Science of Settler Colonial Whiteness in Hawai'i and Oceania.* Durham, N.C.: Duke University Press, 2019.

Bailey, Courtney W., and Adam James Zahren. "Post-Homophobia Comes Out: The Rise of Mormon Polygamy in US Popular Culture." *Queer Studies in Media & Popular Culture* 1, no. 2 (2016): 159–81.

Baym, Nina. *Woman's Fiction: A Guide to Novels by and about Women in America, 1820–1870*. Ithaca, N.Y.: Cornell University Press, 1978.

Bayoumi, Moustafa. "Racing Religion." *CR: The New Centennial Review* 6, no. 2 (Fall 2006): 267–93.

Bederman, Gail. *Manliness and Civilization: A Cultural History of Gender and Race in the United States, 1880–1917*. Chicago: University of Chicago Press, 1995.

Bederman, Gail. "'The Women Have Had Charge of the Church Long Enough': The Men and Religion Forward Movement of 1911–1912 and the Masculinization of Middle-Class Protestantism." *American Quarterly* 43, no. 3 (September 1989): 432–65.

Beecher, Maureen Ursenbach, Carol Cornwall Madsen, and Jill Mulvay Derr. "The Latter-day Saints and Women's Rights, 1870–1920: A Brief Survey." In *Battle for the Ballot: Essays on Woman Suffrage in Utah, 1870–1896*, edited by Carol Cornwall Madsen, 91–104. Logan: Utah State University, 1997.

Bellah, Robert N. "Civil Religion in America." *Daedalus* 96 (Winter 1967): 1–21.

Bender, Daniel E. *American Abyss: Savagery and Civilization in the Age of Industry*. Ithaca, N.Y.: Cornell University Press, 2012.

Bennett, Herman L. *Africans in Colonial Mexico: Absolutism, Christianity and Afro-Creole Consciousness, 1570–1650*. Bloomington: Indiana University Press, 2003.

Bennett, James B. "'Until This Curse of Polygamy Is Wiped Out': Black Methodists, White Mormons, and Constructions of Racial Identity in the Late Nineteenth Century." *Religion and American Culture: A Journal of Interpretation* 21, no. 2 (Summer 2011): 167–94.

Bennett, John C. *History of the Saints: An Exposé of Joe Smith and Mormonism*. Boston: Leland & Whiting, 1842.

Bennett, Wallace R. "The Negro in Utah." *Utah Law Review* 3, no. 3 (Spring 1953): 340–48.

Bentley, Nancy. "Marriage as Treason: Polygamy, Nation, and the Novel." In *The Futures of American Studies*, edited by Donald E. Pease and Robyn Wiegman, 341–70. Durham, N.C.: Duke University Press, 2002.

Berlant, Lauren, and Michael Warner. "Sex in Public." *Critical Inquiry* 24, no. 2 (Winter 1998): 547–66.

Bigler, David L. *Forgotten Kingdom: The Mormon Theocracy in the American West, 1847–1896*. Spokane, Wash.: Arthur H. Clark, 1998.

Bitton, Davis, and Gary L. Bunker. "Phrenology among the Mormons." *Dialogue: A Journal of Mormon Thought* 9 (Spring 1974): 42–61.

Blackhawk, Ned. *Violence over the Land: Indians and Empires in the Early American West*. Cambridge, Mass.: Harvard University Press, 2006.

Blum, Edward J. *Reforging the White Republic: Race, Religion, and American Nationalism, 1865–1898*. Baton Rouge: Louisiana University State Press, 2005.

Blythe, Christopher James. *Terrible Revolution: Latter-day Saints and the American Apocalypse*. New York: Oxford University Press, 2020.

Bonilla-Silva, Eduardo. *White Supremacy and Racism in the Post-Civil Rights Era*. Boulder, Colo.: Lynne Rienner Publishers, 2001.

Bowman, Matthew. *The Mormon People: The Making of an American Faith*. New York: Random House, 2012.

Boxer, Elise. "'The Lamanites Shall Blossom as the Rose': The Indian Student Placement Program, Mormon Whiteness, and Indigenous Identity." *Journal of Mormon History* 41, no. 4 (October 2015): 132–76.

Briggs, Laura. *Reproducing Empire: Race, Sex, Science, and U.S. Imperialism in Puerto Rico*. Berkeley: University of California Press, 2002.

Bringhurst, Newell G. *Saints, Slaves, and Blacks: The Changing Place of Black People within Mormonism*. 2nd ed. Salt Lake City: Greg Kofford Books, 2018.

Brodie, Fawn M. *No Man Knows My History: The Life of Joseph Smith*. New York: Vintage Books, 1945.

Brodkin, Karen. *How Jews Became White Folks and What That Says about Race in America*. New Brunswick, N.J.: Rutgers University Press, 1994.

Brooks, Joanna. *Mormonism and White Supremacy: American Religion and the Problem of Racial Innocence*. Oxford: Oxford University Press, 2020.

Brown, Gillian. *Domestic Individualism: Imagining Self in Nineteenth-Century America*. Berkeley: University of California Press, 1990.

Bunker, Gary L., and Davis Bitton. *The Mormon Graphic Image, 1834–1914: Cartoons, Caricatures, and Illustrations*. Salt Lake City: University of Utah Press, 1983.

Bunker, Gary L., Harry Coffey, and Martha A. Johnson. "Mormons and Social Distance: A Multidimensional Analysis." *Ethnicity* 4 (1977): 352–69.

Burgett, Bruce. "On the Mormon Question: Race, Sex, and Polygamy in the 1850s and the 1990s." *American Quarterly* 57, no. 1 (March 2005): 75–102.

Burke, Meghan. *Colorblind Racism*. Cambridge: Polity Press, 2019.

Bush, Lester E. "Mormonism's Negro Doctrine: An Historical Overview." *Dialogue: A Journal of Mormon Thought* 8, no. 1 (1973): 11–68.

Bush, Lester E. "A Peculiar People: 'The Physiological Aspects of Mormonism 1850–1975.'" *Dialogue: A Journal of Mormon Thought* 12, no. 3 (Fall 1979): 61–83.

Bushman, Richard L. *Joseph Smith and the Beginnings of Mormonism*. Urbana: University of Illinois Press, 1984.

Byrd, Jodi A. *The Transit of Empire: Indigenous Critiques of Colonialism*. Minneapolis: University of Minnesota Press, 2015.

Cacho, Lisa Marie. *Social Death: Racialized Rightlessness and the Criminalization of the Unprotected*. New York: New York University Press, 2012.

Cady, Linell E., and Tracey Fessenden, eds. *Religion, the Secular, and the Politics of Sexual Difference*. New York: Columbia University Press, 2003.

Cannon, Charles A. "The Awesome Power of Sex: The Polemical Campaign against Mormon Polygamy." *Pacific Historical Review* 43 (1974): 61–82.

Cannon, George Q. "Stirring Times—The Latter-Day Work." In *Journal of Discourses*, vol. 14 (January 8, 1871).

Caplow, Theodore. "Contrasting Trends in European and American Religion." *Sociological Analysis* 46 (Summer 1985): 101–8.

Carter, Julian B. *The Heart of Whiteness: Normal Sexuality and Race in America, 1880–1940*. Durham, N.C.: Duke University Press, 2007.

Chang, David. *The Color of the Land: Race, Nation, and the Politics of Land Ownership in Oklahoma, 1832–1939.* Chapel Hill: University of North Carolina Press, 2010.

Chauncey, George. *Gay New York: Gender, Urban Culture, and the Making of the Gay Male World, 1890–1945.* New York: Basic Books, 1994.

Cobb, Michael. "Pioneer, Polygamy, Probate, and You." *Journal of Law and Family Studies* 11, no. 3 (2009): 275–302.

Cohen, Andy, Lori Gordon, Dan Peirson, and Lisa Shannon. *The Real Housewives of Salt Lake City.* Aired November 11, 2020–present, on Bravo.

Cohen, Cathy J. "Punks, Bulldaggers, and Welfare Queens: The Radical Potential of Queer Politics." *GLQ* 3 (1997): 437–65.

Cohen, Cathy. "The Radical Potential of Queer? Twenty Years Later." *GLQ* 25, no. 1 (January 2019): 140–44.

Cone, James H. *A Black Theology of Liberation.* Maryknoll, N.Y.: Orbis Press, 2010.

Cooper, Melinda. *Family Values: Between Neoliberalism and the New Social Conservatism.* Cambridge, Mass.: MIT Press, 2017.

Cott, Nancy. *The Bonds of Womanhood: "Woman's Sphere" in New England, 1780–1835.* New Haven, Conn.: Yale University Press, 1977.

Coviello, Peter. *Make Yourselves Gods: Mormons and the Unfinished Business of American Secularism.* Chicago: University of Chicago Press, 2019.

Coviello, Peter. "Plural: Mormon Polygamy and the Biopolitics of Secularism." *History of the Present* 7, no. 2 (Fall 2017): 219–41.

Coviello, Peter. *Tomorrow's Parties: Sex and the Untimely in Nineteenth-Century America.* New York: New York University Press, 2013.

Crenshaw, Kimberlé. "Demarginalizing the Intersection of Race and Sex: A Black Feminist Critique of Antidiscrimination Doctrine, Feminist Theory, and Antiracist Politics." In *Feminist Legal Theory: Readings in Law and Gender,* edited by Katherine Bartlett and Rosanne Kennedy, 57–80. Boulder, Colo.: Westview, 1991.

Crenshaw, Kimberlé, Neil Gotanda, Gary Peller, and Kendall Thomas, eds. *Critical Race Theory: The Key Writings That Formed the Movement.* New York: New Press, 1995.

Crespino, Joseph. *In Search of Another Country: Mississippi and the Conservative Counterrevolution.* Princeton, N.J.: Princeton University Press, 2007.

Davis, Angela. *Are Prisons Obsolete?* New York: Seven Stories Press, 2003.

Davis, Oscar Franklyn. *Latest Word on Mormonism: A Survey of "The Mormon Kingdom."* Pittsburgh: National Reform Association, 1913.

Davis, William L. *Visions in a Seer Stone: Joseph Smith and the Making of the Book of Mormon.* Chapel Hill: University of North Carolina Press, 2020.

Daynes, Kathryn M. "Celestial Marriage (Eternal and Plural)." In *The Oxford Handbook of Mormonism,* edited by Terryl L. Givens and Philip L. Barlow, 334–48. New York: Oxford University Press, 2015.

de Leon, Cedric. "The More Things Change: A Gramscian Genealogy of Barack Obama's 'Post-Racial' Politics, 1932–2008." *Political Power and Social Theory* 22 (November 2011): 75–104.

Delgado, Richard, and Jean Stefancic, eds. *Critical Race Theory: The Cutting Edge.* Philadelphia: Temple University Press, 2013.

Deloria, Philip J. *Playing Indian*. New Haven, Conn.: Yale University Press, 1998.

Demerath, N. J., III. "Excepting Exceptionalism: American Religion in Comparative Relief." In "Americans and Religions in the Twenty-First Century," special issue, *Annals of the American Academy of Political and Social Science* 558 (July 1998): 28–39.

D'Emilio, John. "Capitalism and Gay Identity." In *The Gay and Lesbian Studies Reader*, edited by Henry Abelove, Aina Michele Barale, and David M. Halperin, 467–78. New York: Routledge, 1993.

D'Emilio, John, and Estelle B. Freedman. *Intimate Matters: A History of Sexuality in America*. New York: Harper & Row, 1988.

Denetdalem, Jennifer. "Carving Navajo National Boundaries: Patriotism, Tradition, and the Diné Marriage Act of 2005." *American Quarterly* 60, no. 2 (June 2008): 289–94.

Denike, Margaret. "What's Queer about Polygamy?" In *Queer Theory, Law, Culture, and Empire*, edited by Robert Leckey and Kim Brooks, 137–53. New York: Routledge, 2010.

Derr, Jill Mulvay. "Eliza R. Snow and the Woman Question." In *Battle for the Ballot: Essays on Woman Suffrage in Utah, 1870–1896*, edited by Carol Cornwall Madsen, 75–90. Logan: Utah State University, 1997.

Donovan, Brian. *White Slave Crusades: Race, Gender, and Anti-vice Activism, 1887–1917*. Chicago: University of Illinois Press, 2006.

Douglas, Ann. *The Feminization of American Culture*. New York: Knopf, 1977.

Dowland, Seth. *Family Values and the Rise of the Christian Right*. Philadelphia: University of Pennsylvania Press, 2015.

Drury, Allen. *Advise and Consent*. Garden City, N.Y.: Doubleday, 1959.

Duggan, Lisa. *Sapphic Slashers: Sex, Violence, and American Modernity*. Durham, N.C.: Duke University Press, 2000.

Duggan, Lisa. *The Twilight of Equality: Neoliberalism, Cultural Politics, and the Attack on Democracy*. Boston: Beacon Press, 2003.

Dunbar-Ortiz, Roxanne. *An Indigenous Peoples' History of the United States*. Boston: Beacon Press, 2014.

Dunbar-Ortiz, Roxanne. *Not a Nation of Immigrants: Settler Colonialism, White Supremacy, and a History of Erasure and Exclusion*. Boston: Beacon Press, 2021.

Eng, David L. *The Feeling of Kinship: Queer Liberalism and the Racialization of Intimacy*. Durham, N.C.: Duke University Press, 2010.

Epstein, Barbara Leslie. *The Politics of Domesticity: Women, Evangelism, and Temperance in Nineteenth-Century America*. Middletown, Conn.: Wesleyan University Press, 1986.

Ertman, Martha M. "Race Treason: The Untold Story of America's Ban on Polygamy." *Columbia Journal of Gender and Law* 19, no. 2 (2010): 287–366.

Ferguson, Roderick A. *Aberrations in Black: Toward a Queer of Color Critique*. Minneapolis: University of Minnesota Press, 2004.

Firmage, Edwin Brown, and Richard Collin Mangrum. *Zion in the Courts: A Legal History of the Church of Jesus Christ of Latter-day Saints, 1830–1900*. Chicago: University of Illinois Press, 1988.

Fischer, Nick. *Spider Web: The Birth of American Anti-Communism*. Urbana: University of Illinois Press, 2016.

Flake, Kathleen, *The Politics of American Religious Identity: The Seating of Senator Reed Smoot, Mormon Apostle.* Chapel Hill: University of North Carolina Press, 2004.

Fluhman, J. Spencer. *"A Peculiar People": Anti-Mormonism and the Making of Religion in Nineteenth Century America.* Chapel Hill: University of North Carolina Press, 2012.

Foner, Philip S. *The History of the Labor Movement in the United States.* New York: International Publishers, 1947.

Forshey, C. G. Comment on Roberts Bartholow's "Hereditary Descent; or Depravity of the Offspring of Polygamy among the Mormons." *DeBow's Review,* February 1861, 211–12.

Foster, Lawrence. *Religion and Sexuality: Three American Communal Experiments of the Nineteenth Century.* Urbana: University of Illinois Press, 1981.

Foster, Lawrence. *Women, Family, and Utopia: Communal Experiments of the Shakers, the Oneida Community, and the Mormons.* New York: Syracuse University Press, 1991.

Foucault, Michel. *"Society Must Be Defended": Lectures at the Collège de France, 1975–1976.* Translated by David Macey. New York: Picador, 2003.

Franchot, Jenny. *Roads to Rome: The Antebellum Protestant Encounter with Catholicism.* Berkeley: University of California Press, 1994.

Franke, Katherine. "The Domesticated Liberty of *Lawrence v. Texas.*" *Columbia Law Review* 104, no. 5 (June 2004): 1,399–426.

Franke, Katherine. *Wedlocked: The Perils of Marriage Equality: How African Americans and Gays Mistakenly Thought the Right to Marry Would Set Them Free.* New York: New York University Press, 2015.

GhaneaBassiri, Kambiz. *The History of Islam in America.* Cambridge: Cambridge University Press, 2010.

Gibbons, Timothy, Bill Hayes, Christopher Poole, and Kirk Streb. *Sister Wives.* Aired September 26, 2010–present, on TLC.

Gingrich, Newt. *A Nation Like No Other: Why American Exceptionalism Matters.* Washington, D.C.: Regnery Publishing, 2011.

Ginzberg, Lori D. *Women and the Work of Benevolence: Morality, Politics, and Class in the Nineteenth-Century United States.* New Haven, Conn.: Yale University Press, 1990.

Givens, Terryl L. *The Viper on the Hearth: Mormons, Myths, and the Construction of Heresy.* New York: Oxford University Press, 1997.

Godbeer, Richard. *Sexual Revolution in Early America.* Baltimore: Johns Hopkins University Press, 2002.

Goetz, Rebecca Anne. *The Baptism of Early Virginia: How Christianity Created Race.* Baltimore: Johns Hopkins University Press, 2012.

Goldstein, Alyosha, ed. *Formations of United States Colonialism.* Durham, N.C.: Duke University Press, 2014.

Gordon, Sarah Barringer. "The Liberty of Self-Degradation: Polygamy, Woman Suffrage, and Consent in Nineteenth-Century America." *Journal of American History* 83, no. 3 (December 1996): 815–47.

Gordon, Sarah Barringer. *The Mormon Question: Polygamy and Constitutional Conflict in Nineteenth Century America.* Chapel Hill: University of North Carolina Press, 2002.

Gordon, Sarah Barringer. "'Our National Hearthstone': Anti-polygamy Fiction and the Sentimental Campaign against Moral Diversity in Antebellum America." *Yale Journal of Law and the Humanities* 8 (1996): 295–350.

Gorman, James L., Jeff W. Childers, and Mark W. Hamilton, eds. *Slavery's Long Shadow: Race and Reconciliation in American Christianity.* Grand Rapids, Mich.: William B. Eerdmans, 2019.

Greeley, Andrew M. "American Exceptionalism: The Religious Phenomenon." In *Is America Different? A New Look at American Exceptionalism,* edited by Byron E. Shafer. Oxford: Oxford University Press, 1991.

Grewal, Inderpal. *Home and Harem: Nation, Gender, Empire, and the Cultures of Travel.* Durham, N.C.: Duke University Press, 1996.

Hansen, Klaus J. "Changing Perspectives on Sexuality and Marriage." *Multiply and Replenish: Mormon Essays on Sex and Family,* edited by Brent Corcoran, 19–46. Salt Lake City: Signature Books, 1994.

Hansen, Klaus J. *Mormonism and the American Experience.* Chicago: University of Chicago Press, 1981.

Hansen, Klaus J. "Mormon Sexuality and American Culture." *Dialogue: A Journal of Mormon Thought* (Autumn 1976): 45–56.

Hardy, B. Carmon. *Solemn Covenant: The Mormon Polygamous Passage.* Chicago: University of Illinois Press, 1992.

Hardy, B. Carmon, and Dan Erickson. "'Regeneration; Now and Evermore!': Mormon Polygamy and the Physical Rehabilitation of Humankind." *Journal of the History of Sexuality* 10, no. 1 (January 2001): 40–61.

Harris, Matthew L., and Newel G. Bringhurst, editors. *The Mormon Church & Blacks: A Documentary History.* Urbana: University of Illinois Press, 2015.

Hartigan-O'Connor, Ellen. "Gender's Value in the History of Capitalism." *Journal of the Early Republic* 36, no. 4 (Winter 2016): 613–35.

Hartmann, Douglas. "The Olympic 'Revolt' of 1968 and Its Lessons for Contemporary African American Athletic Activism." *European Journal of American Studies* 14, no. 1 (2019): https://doi.org/10.4000/ejas.14335.

Hartog, Hendrik. *Man and Wife in America: A History.* Cambridge, Mass.: Harvard University Press, 2000.

Haskell, Thomas L. "Taking Exception to Exceptionalism." *Reviews in American History* 28, no. 1 (2000): 151–66.

Haslam, Dee Bagwell, and Rob Lundgren. *Escaping Polygamy.* Aired December 30, 2014–present, on Lifetime.

Haws, J. B. *The Mormon Image in the American Mind: Fifty Years of Public Perception.* Oxford: Oxford University Press, 2011.

Heng, Geraldine. *The Invention of Race in the European Middle Ages.* Cambridge: Cambridge University Press, 2018.

Herzog, Jonathan P. *The Spiritual-Industrial Complex: America's Religious Battle against Communism in the Early Cold War.* Oxford: Oxford University Press, 2011.

Hesse, Barnor. "Racialized Modernity: An Analytics of White Mythologies." *Ethnic and Racial Studies* 30, no. 4 (2007): 643–63.

Hixson, Walter L. *American Settler Colonialism: A History.* New York: Palgrave Mac-Millan, 2013.

Holland, Sharon Patricia. *The Erotic Life of Racism.* Durham, N.C.: Duke University Press, 2012.

Horsman, Reginald. *Race and Manifest Destiny: The Origins of American Racial Anglo-Saxonism.* Cambridge, Mass.: Harvard University Press, 1981.

Hoyt, Amy, and Sara M. Patterson. "Mormon Masculinity: Changing Gender Expectations in the Era of Transition from Polygamy to Monogamy, 1890–1920." *Gender and History* 23, no. 1 (April 2011): 72–91.

Hunter, Nan. "Sexual Orientation and the Paradox of Heightened Scrutiny." *Michigan Law Review* 102, no. 7 (June 2004): 1,528–54.

Ignatiev, Noel. *How the Irish Became White.* New York: Routledge Classics, 1995.

Iversen, Joan Smith. *The Anti-polygamy Controversy in U.S. Women's Movements, 1880–1925: A Debate on the American Home.* New York: Garland, 1997.

Jacobs, Margaret D. *A Generation Removed: The Fostering and Adoption of Indigenous Children in the Post-War World.* Lincoln: University of Nebraska, 2014.

Jacobs, Margaret D. *White Mother to a Dark Race: Settler Colonialism, Maternalism, and the Removal of Indigenous Children in the American West and Australia, 1880–1940.* Lincoln: University of Nebraska Press, 2009.

Jacobson, Matthew Frye. *Barbarian Virtues: The United States Encounters Foreign Peoples at Home and Abroad, 1876–1917.* New York: Hill and Wang, 2000.

Jacobson, Matthew Frye. *Whiteness of a Different Color: European Immigrants and the Alchemy of Race.* Cambridge, Mass.: Harvard University Press, 1998.

Jay, Gregory. "White Out: Race and Nationalism in American Studies." Review of *Death of a Nation: American Culture and the End of Exceptionalism,* by David W. Noble. *American Quarterly* 55, no. 4 (December 2003): 781–95.

Johnson, David K. *The Lavender Scare: The Cold War Persecution of Gays and Lesbians in Federal Government.* Chicago: University of Chicago Press, 2004.

Johnson, Donald H., and Kirk H. Porter. *National Party Platforms: 1840–1972.* Chicago: University of Illinois Press, 1956.

Johnson, Sylvester A. *African American Religions, 1500–2000: Colonialism, Democracy, and Freedom.* Cambridge: Cambridge University Press, 2015.

Johnson, Walter. *Soul by Soul: Life Inside the Antebellum Slave Market.* Cambridge, Mass.: Harvard University Press, 1999.

Jones, Bob, Sr. "Is Segregation Scriptural?" Radio sermon on WMUU Bob Jones University, April 17, 1960.

Josephson, Jyl J. *Rethinking Sexual Citizenship.* Albany: SUNY Press, 2016.

Joshi, Khyati Y. "The Racialization of Hinduism, Islam, and Sikhism in the United States." *Equity & Excellence in Education* 39, no. 3 (2006): 211–26.

Justice, Daniel Heath, Mark Rifkin, and Bethany Schneider. "Introduction." *GLQ* 16, no. 1–2 (2010): 5–39.

Kammen, Michael. "The Problem of American Exceptionalism: A Reconsideration." *American Quarterly* 45, no. 1 (March 1993): 1–43.

Kandaswamy, Priya. "Gender and Racial Formation." In *Racial Formation in the Twenty-First Century*, edited by Daniel Martinez Hosang, Oneka LaBennett, and Laura Pulido, 23–43. Berkeley: University of California Press, 2012.

Kaplan, Amy. "Black and Blue on San Juan Hill." In *Cultures of United States Imperialism*, edited by Amy Kaplan and Donald E. Pease, 219–36. Durham, N.C.: Duke University Press, 1993.

Kaplan, Amy. "Manifest Domesticity." In *The Futures of American Studies*, edited by Donald E. Pease and Robyn Wiegman, 111–34. Durham, N.C.: Duke University Press, 2002.

Kauanui, J. Kēhaulani. *Hawaiian Blood: Colonialism and the Politics of Sovereignty and Indigeneity*. Durham, N.C.: Duke University Press, 2008.

Kauanui, J. Kēhaulani. *Paradoxes of Hawaiian Sovereignty: Land, Sex, and the Colonial Politics of State Nationalism*. Durham, N.C.: Duke University Press, 2018.

Kauanui, J. Kēhaulani. "'A Structure, Not an Event': Settler Colonialism and Enduring Indigeneity." *Lateral: Journal of the Cultural Studies Association* 5, no. 1 (Spring 2016): https://csalateral.org/issue/5-1/forum-alt-humanities-settler-colonialism-enduring-indigeneity-kauanui/#fn-351-6.

Kelen, Leslie G., and Eileen Hallet Stone, eds. *Missing Stories: An Oral History of Ethnic and Minority Groups in Utah*. Salt Lake City: University of Utah Press, 1996.

Kelley, Mary. *Private Woman, Public Stage: Literary Domesticity in Nineteenth-Century America*. New York: Oxford University Press, 1984.

Kendi, Ibram X. *How to Be an Antiracist*. New York: One World, 2019.

Kendi, Ibram X. *Stamped from the Beginning: The Definitive History of Racist Ideas in America*. New York: Bold Type Books, 2016.

Kern, Louis J. *An Ordered Love: Sex Roles and Sexuality in Victorian Utopias—The Shakers, the Mormons, and the Oneida Community*. Chapel Hill: University of North Carolina Press, 1981.

Kidd, Colin. *The Forging of Races: Race and Scripture in the Protestant Atlantic World, 1600–2000*. Cambridge: Cambridge University Press, 2006.

Kimball, Edward L., and Andrew E. Kimball Jr. *Spencer W. Kimball: Twelfth President of The Church of Jesus Christ of Latter-day Saints*. Salt Lake City: Bookcraft, 1977.

Kitch, Sally L. *The Specter of Sex: Gendered Foundations of Racial Formation in the United States*. Albany: SUNY Press, 2009.

Kopelson, Heather Miyano. *Faithful Bodies: Performing Religion and Race in the Puritan Atlantic*. New York: New York University Press, 2014.

Kruse, Kevin M. *White Flight: Atlanta and the Making of Modern Conservatism*. Princeton, N.J.: Princeton University Press, 2005.

Kushner, Tony. *Angels in America: A Gay Fantasia on National Themes*. Rev. ed. New York: Theatre Communications Group, 2003.

Laats, Adam. *Fundamentalist U: Keeping the Faith in American Higher Education*. Oxford: Oxford University Press, 2018.

Langum, David J. *Crossing over the Line: Legislating Morality and the Mann Act*. Chicago: University of Chicago Press, 1994.

Larson, Gustive O. *The "Americanization" of Utah for Statehood*. San Marino, Calif.: Huntington Library, 1971.

Lassiter, Matthew D. *The Silent Majority: Suburban Politics in the Sunbelt South*. Princeton, N.J.: Princeton University Press, 2006.

Leavelle, Tracy Neal. *The Catholic Calumet: Colonial Conversions in French and Indian North America*. Philadelphia: University of Pennsylvania Press, 2012.

Limerick, Patricia Nelson. *The Legacy of Conquest: The Unbroken Past of the American West*. New York: W. W. Norton, 1987.

Lipset, Seymour Martin. *American Exceptionalism: A Double-Edged Sword*. New York: W. W. Norton, 1996.

Lipsitz, George. *The Possessive Investment in Whiteness: How White People Profit from Identity Politics*. 20th anniversary ed. Philadelphia: Temple University Press, 2018.

Lowe, Lisa. *The Intimacies of Four Continents*. Durham, N.C.: Duke University Press, 2015.

Lum, D. D. *Social Problems of To-day; or, The Mormon Question in Its Economic Aspects. A Study of Co-operation and Arbitration in Mormondom, from the Standpoint of a Wage-Worker*. Port Jervis, N.Y.: D. D. Lum, 1886.

Lunceford, Brett. "'One Nation under God': Mormon Theology and the American Continent." In *The Rhetoric of American Exceptionalism: Critical Essays,* edited by Jason A. Edwards and David Weiss, 48–62. Jefferson, N.C.: McFarland, 2011.

Lyman, Edward Leo. *Political Deliverance: The Mormon Quest for Utah Statehood*. Chicago: University of Illinois Press, 1986.

Lynn, Karen. "Sensational Virtue: Nineteenth-Century Mormon Fiction and American Popular Taste." *Dialogue: A Journal of Mormon Thought* 14 (1981): 101–11.

Lystra, Karen. *Searching the Heart: Women, Men, and Romantic Love in Nineteenth-Century America*. New York: Oxford University Press, 1989.

Madsen, Carol Cornwall, ed. *Battle for the Ballot: Essays on Woman Suffrage in Utah, 1870–1896*. Logan: Utah State University, 1997.

Madsen, Deborah L. *American Exceptionalism*. Jackson: University of Mississippi, 1998.

Mamdani, Mahmood. *Neither Settler nor Native: The Making and Unmaking of Permanent Minorities*. Cambridge, Mass.: Harvard University Press, 2020.

Mamdani, Mahmood. "Settler Colonialism: Then and Now." *Critical Inquiry* 41, no. 3 (2015): 596–619.

Mangum, Garth L., and Bruce D. Blumell. *The Mormons' War on Poverty: A History of LDS Welfare, 1830–1990*. Salt Lake City: University of Utah Press, 1993.

Marchmont, John. *An Appeal to the American Congress: The Bible Law of Marriage against Mormonism*. Philadelphia: 1873.

Martínez, María Elena. *Genealogical Fictions: Limpieza de Sangre, Religion, and Gender in Colonial Mexico*. Stanford, Calif.: Stanford University Press, 2008.

Mason, Patrick Q. *The Mormon Menace: Violence and Anti-Mormonism in the Post-bellum South*. Oxford: Oxford University Press, 2011.

Mason, Patrick Q. "Opposition to Polygamy in the Postbellum South." *Journal of Southern History* 76, no. 3 (August 2010): 541–78.

Mason, Patrick Q. "The Prohibition of Interracial Marriage in Utah, 1888–1963." *Utah Historical Quarterly* 76, no. 2 (Spring 2008): 108–31.

Mauss, Armand L. *All Abraham's Children: Changing Mormon Conceptions of Race and Lineage.* Urbana: University of Illinois Press, 2003.

Mauss, Armand L. *The Angel and the Beehive: The Mormon Struggle with Assimilation.* Chicago: University of Illinois Press, 1994.

McConkie, Bruce R. *Mormon Doctrine: A Compendium of the Gospel.* Salt Lake City: Bookcraft, 1958.

McCormick, John, and John R. Sillito. *A History of Utah Radicalism: Startling, Socialistic, and Decidedly Revolutionary.* Logan: Utah State University Press, 2011.

McGovern, James R. "The American Woman's Pre-World War I Freedom in Manners and Morals." *Journal of American History* 55, no. 2 (September 1968): 315–33.

McLoughlin, William G. *Revivals, Awakenings, and Reform.* Chicago: University of Chicago Press, 1978.

Mepschen, Paul, Jan Willem Duyvendak, and Evelien H. Tonkens. "Sexual Politics, Orientalism, and Multicultural Citizenship in the Netherlands." *Sociology* 44, no. 5 (2010): 962–79.

Metcalf, R. Warren. "'Which Side of the Line?': American Indian Students and Programs at Brigham Young University, 1960–1983." In *Essays on American Indian and Mormon History,* edited by P. Jane Hafen and Brendan W. Resink, 225–45. Salt Lake City: University of Utah Press, 2019.

Miranda, Deborah A. "Extermination of the Joyas: Gendercide in Spanish California." *GLQ* 16, no. 1–2 (2010): 253–84.

Mitchell, Hildi J. "Good, Evil, and Godhood: Mormon Morality in the Material World." In *Powers of Good and Evil: Social Transformation and Popular Belief,* edited by Paul Clough and Jon P. Mitchell, 161–84. New York: Berghahn Books, 2001.

Mohanty, Chandra Talpade. "Under Western Eyes: Feminist Scholarship and Colonial Discourses." *Feminist Review* 30 (Fall 1988): 61–88.

Mohrman, K. "Polygamy." In *The Routledge Handbook of American Sexuality,* edited by Jason Ruiz and Kevin Murphy, 264–75. New York: Routledge, 2020.

Moller, Stephanie. "Supporting Single Mothers: Gender and Race in the U.S. Welfare State." *Gender and Society* 16, no. 4 (August 2004): 465–84.

Moore, Laurence R. *Religious Outsiders and the Making of Americans.* New York: Oxford University Press, 1986.

Morgensen, Scott Lauria. "The Biopolitics of Settler Colonialism: Right Here, Right Now." *Settler Colonial Studies* 1, no. 1 (February 28, 2013): 52–76.

Morgensen, Scott Lauria. *Spaces between Us: Queer Settler Colonialism and Decolonization.* Minneapolis: University of Minnesota Press, 2011.

Moslener, Sara. *Virgin Nation: Sexual Purity and American Adolescence.* Oxford: Oxford University Press, 2015.

Moynihan, Daniel Patrick. *The Negro Family: The Case for National Action.* Office of Policy Planning and Research, United States Department of Labor, 1965.

Mueller, Max Perry. *Race and the Making of the Mormon People.* Chapel Hill: University of North Carolina Press, 2017.

Murphy, Kevin P., Jason Ruiz, and David Serlin, eds. *Routledge History of American Sexuality*. New York: Routledge, 2020.

Neilson, Reid L. *Exhibiting Mormonism: The Latter-day Saints and the 1893 Chicago World's Fair.* Oxford: Oxford University Press, 2011.

Newman, Brooke N. "Gender, Sexuality, and the Formation of Racial Identities in the Eighteenth-Century Anglo-Caribbean World." *Gender & History* 22, no. 3 (November 2010): 582–602.

Nibley, Charles W. "'Mormonism' Makes for Good Citizenship." *Improvement Era*, June 1, 1916, 741–43.

Norris, Kristopher. *Witnessing Whiteness: Confronting White Supremacy in the American Church*. Oxford: Oxford University Press, 2020.

Nussbaum, Felicity. "The Other Woman: Polygamy, Pamela, and the Prerogative of Empire." In *Women, "Race," and Writing in the Early Modern Period,* edited by Margo Hendricks and Patricia Parker, 138–59. New York: Routledge, 1994.

O'Brien, Jean M. *Firsting and Lasting: Writing Indians Out of Existence in New England*. Minneapolis: University of Minnesota Press, 2010.

O'Donovan, Connell. "'The Abominable and Detestable Crime against Nature': A Brief History of Homosexuality and Mormonism, 1840–1980." In *Multiply and Replenish: Mormon Essays on Sex and Family,* edited by Brent Corcoran, 123–70. Salt Lake City: Signature Books, 1994.

O'Donovan, Connell. "Private Pain, Public Purges: A History of Homosexuality at Brigham Young University." Lecture given at University of California–Santa Cruz, April 28, 1997. Available at Recovery from Mormonism, https://exmormon.org/d6/drupal/byuhis.

Olsen, Mark V., and Will Scheffer. *Big Love*. Aired March 12, 2006–March 20, 2011, on HBO.

Oman, Nathan B. "Natural Law and the Rhetoric of Empire: *Reynolds v. United States,* Polygamy, and Imperialism." *Washington University Law Review* 88, no. 66 (2010–2011): 661–706.

Omi, Michael, and Howard Winant. *Racial Formation in the United States*. New York: Routledge, 2015.

O'Neill, Colleen. "Testing the Limits of Colonial Parenting: Navajo Domestic Workers, the Intermountain Indian School, and the Urban Relocation Program, 1950–1962." *Ethnohistory* 66, no. 3 (July 2019): 565–92.

Orsi, R. A. "The Religious Boundaries of an In-Between People: Street Feste and the Problem of the Dark-Skinned 'Other' in Italian Harlem, 1920–1990." *American Quarterly* 44, no. 3 (1992): 313–47.

Packer, Boyd K. "To Young Men Only: An Address Given at the Priesthood Session of General Conference." October 2, 1976. Pamphlet.

Parker, Trey, dir. *South Park*. Season 7, episode 12, "All about Mormons." Aired November 19, 2003, on Comedy Central.

Parker, Trey, Robert Lopez, and Matt Stone. *The Book of Mormon: Original Broadway Cast Recording*. Ghostlight Records, 2011.

Pascoe, Peggy. *What Comes Naturally: Miscegenation Law and the Making of Race in America*. Oxford: Oxford University Press, 2009.

Pearsall, Sarah. "'Having Many Wives' in Two American Rebellions: The Politics of Households and the Radically Conservative." *American Historical Review* 118, no. 4 (October 2013): 1,001–28.

Pearsall, Sarah. "Native American Men—and Women—at Home in Plural Marriages in Seventeenth-Century New France." In "Men at Home," edited by Raffaella Sarti, special issue of *Gender & History* 27, no. 3 (November 2015): 591–610.

Pease, Donald E. "New Perspectives on U.S. Culture and Imperialism." In *Cultures of United States Imperialism*, edited by Amy Kaplan and Donald E. Pease, 22–38. Durham, N.C.: Duke University Press, 1993.

Pérez, Hiram. "The Rough Trade of U.S. Imperialism." *Journal of Homosexuality* 59, no. 7 (2012): 1,081–86.

Pérez, Hiram. *A Taste for Brown Bodies: Gay Modernity and Cosmopolitan Desire*. New York: New York University Press, 2015.

Perry, Diane. "Race Bias Bans Blacks from Heaven." *Pittsburgh Courier*, March 21, 1970.

Petersen, Mark E. "Race Problems—As They Affect the Church." Speech given at the Convention of Teachers of Religion on the College Level, Brigham Young University, August 27, 1954.

Peterson, F. Ross. "'Blindside': Utah on the Eve of *Brown v. Board of Education*." *Utah Historical Quarterly* 73, no. 1 (Winter 2005): 4–20.

Petrey, Taylor M. *Tabernacles of Clay: Sexuality and Gender in Modern Mormonism*. Chapel Hill: University of North Carolina Press, 2020.

Pivar, David J. *Purity Crusade: Sexuality Morality and Social Control, 1868–1900*. Westport, Conn.: Greenwood Press, 1973.

Porter, Glen. *The Rise of Big Business, 1860–1920*. West Sussex, U.K.: Wiley-Blackwell, 1973.

Preminger, Otto, dir. *Advise and Consent*. 1962.

Prince, Gregory A. *Gay Rights and the Mormon Church: Intended Actions, Unintended Consequences*. Salt Lake City: University of Utah Press, 2019.

Prince, Gregory A., and W. M. Robert Wright. *David O. McKay and the Rise of Modern Mormonism*. Salt Lake City: University of Utah Press, 2005.

Puar, Jasbir. *Terrorist Assemblages: Homonationalism in Queer Times*. Durham, N.C.: Duke University Press, 2007.

Quinn, D. Michael. *Early Mormonism and the Magic World View*. Salt Lake City: Signature Books, 1998.

Quinn, D. Michael. "LDS Church Authority and New Plural Marriages, 1890–1904." *Dialogue: A Journal of Mormon Thought* 18, no. 1 (Spring 1985): 9–105.

Quinn, D. Michael. *The Mormon Hierarchy: Origins of Power*. Salt Lake City: Signature Books, 1994.

Quinn, D. Michael. *Same-Sex Dynamics among Nineteenth-Century Americans: A Mormon Example*. Chicago: University of Illinois Press, 1996.

Rana, Junaid. *Terrifying Muslims: Race and Labor in the South Asian Diaspora*. Durham, N.C.: Duke University Press, 2011.

Rauchway, Eric. "More Means Different: Quantifying American Exceptionalism." Review of *The Age of Mass Migration: Causes and Economic Impact*, by Timothy J. Hatton and Jeffrey G. Williamson; and *Globalization and History: The Evolution of a Nineteenth-Century Atlantic Economy*, by Kevin H. O'Rourke and Jeffrey G. Williamson. *Reviews in American History* 30, no. 3 (September 2002): 504–16.

Reagan, Ronald. "Election Eve Address: A Vision for America." Speech delivered November 3, 1980. https://www.reaganlibrary.gov/archives/speech/election-eve-address-vision-america.

Reddy, Chandan. *Freedom with Violence: Race, Sexuality, and the US State*. Durham, N.C.: Duke University Press, 2011.

Reeve, W. Paul. *Religion of a Different Color: Race and the Mormon Struggle for Whiteness*. Oxford: Oxford University Press, 2015.

Rich, Christopher B., Jr. "The True Policy for Utah: Servitude, Slavery, and 'An Act in Relation to Service.'" *Utah Historical Quarterly* 80, no. 1 (Winter 2012): 54–74.

Rifkin, Mark. *When Did Indians Become Straight? Kinship, the History of Sexuality, and Native Sovereignty*. Oxford: Oxford University Press, 2011.

Robertson, Lindsay G. *Conquest by Law: How the Discovery of America Dispossessed Indigenous Peoples of Their Land*. New York: Oxford University Press, 2005.

Roediger, David R. *The Wages of Whiteness: Race and the Making of the American Working Class*. New York: Verso, 2007.

Roediger, David R. *Working toward Whiteness: How America's Immigrants Became White: The Strange Journey from Ellis Island to the Suburbs*. New York: Basic Books, 2005.

Rose, Nancy E. "Gender, Race, and the Welfare State: Government Work Programs from the 1930s to the Present." *Feminist Studies* 19, no. 2 (Summer 1993): 318–42.

Ruether, Rosemary Radford. *America, Amerikkka: Elect Nation and Imperial Violence*. New York: Routledge, 2014.

Ryan, Mary P. *Cradle of the Middle Class: The Family in Oneida County, New York, 1790–1865*. Cambridge: Cambridge University Press, 1981.

Ryan, Mary P. *Empire of the Mother: American Writing about Domesticity, 1830–1860*. New York: Institute for Research in History and Haworth Press, 1982.

Samuels, Shirley, ed. *The Culture of Sentiment: Race, Gender, and Sentimentality in Nineteenth-Century America*. New York: Oxford University Press, 1992.

Schuller, Kyla. *The Biopolitics of Feeling: Race, Sex, and Science in the Nineteenth Century*. Durham, N.C.: Duke University Press, 2018.

Sellers, Charles. *The Market Revolution: Jacksonian America, 1815–1846*. New York: Oxford University Press, 1991.

Shafer, Byron E., ed. *Is America Different? A New Look at American Exceptionalism*. Oxford: Oxford University Press, 1991.

Shah, Nayan. *Stranger Intimacy: Contesting Race, Sexuality, and the Law in the North American West*. Los Angeles: University of California Press, 2011.

Shipps, Jan. "Difference and Otherness: Mormonism and the American Religious Mainstream." In *Minority Faiths and the American Protestant Mainstream*, edited by Jonathan D. Sarna, 81–109. Chicago: University of Illinois Press, 1998.

Shipps, Jan. *Sojourner in the Promised Land: Forty Years among the Mormons.* Urbana: University of Illinois Press, 2000.

Sklar, Kathryn Kish. *Catherine Beecher: A Study in American Domesticity.* New Haven, Conn.: Yale University Press, 1973.

Slotkin, Richard. *The Fatal Environment: The Myth of the Frontier in the Age of Industrialization, 1800–1890.* Norman: University of Oklahoma Press, 1985.

Slotkin, Richard. *Gunfighter Nation: The Myth of the Frontier in Twentieth-Century America.* Norman: University of Oklahoma Press, 1992.

Slotkin, Richard. *Regeneration through Violence: The Mythology of the American Frontier, 1600–1860.* Norman: University of Oklahoma Press, 1973.

Smith, Henry Nash. *Virgin Land: The American West as Symbol and Myth.* Cambridge, Mass.: Harvard University Press, 1950.

Smith, Joseph Fielding. *The Way to Perfection: Short Discourses on Gospel Themes; Dedicated to All Who Are Interested in the Redemption of the Living and the Dead.* Salt Lake City: Genealogical Society of Utah, 1931.

Smithers, Gregory D. "The 'Pursuits of the Civilized Man': Race and the Meaning of Civilization in the United States and Australia, 1790s–1850s." *Journal of World History* 20, no. 2 (2009): 255–56.

Snorton, C. Riley. *Black on Both Sides: A Racial History of Trans Identity.* Minneapolis: University of Minnesota Press, 2017.

Somerville, Siobhan. "Queer." In *Keywords for American Cultural Studies,* 2nd ed., edited by Bruce Burgett and Glenn Hendler, 203–7. New York: New York University Press, 2014.

Somerville, Siobhan. *Queering the Color Line: Race and the Invention of Homosexuality in American Culture.* Durham, N.C.: Duke University Press, 2008.

Somerville, Siobhan. "Queer Loving." *GLQ* 1, no. 3 (2005): 335–70.

Spade, Dean. *Normal Life: Administrative Violence, Critical Trans Politics, and the Limits of Law.* Brooklyn, N.Y.: South End Press, 2011.

Spade, Dean. "Under the Cover of Gay Rights." *New York University Review of Law and Social Change* 37, no. 79 (2013): 79–100.

Spear, Jennifer. *Race, Sex, and Social Order in Early New Orleans.* Baltimore: Johns Hopkins University Press, 2010.

Spence, Hartzell. "The Story of Religions in America: The Mormons." *Look,* January 21, 1958, 56–69.

Spivak, Gayatri Chakravorty. "Can the Subaltern Speak?" In *Marxism and the Interpretation of Behavior,* edited by Cary Nelson and Lawrence Grossberg, 271–316. Urbana: University of Illinois Press, 1988.

Stanton, Megan. "The Indian Student Placement Program and Native Direction." In *Essays on American Indian and Mormon History,* edited by P. Jane Hafen and Brendan W. Resink, 211–24. Salt Lake City: University of Utah Press, 2019.

Stenhouse, Mrs. T. B. H. (Fanny). *Tell It All: The Story of a Life's Experience in Mormonism.* Hartford, Conn.: A. D. Worthington, 1875.

Stewart, John J. *Mormonism and the Negro.* Orem, Utah: Bookmark, 1960.

Stoler, Ann Laura. *Carnal Knowledge and Imperial Power: Race and the Intimate in Colonial Rule.* Berkeley: University of California Press, 2002.

Strong, Josiah. *Our Country: Its Possible Future and Its Present Crisis.* New York: Baker & Taylor, 1885.

Stryker, Susan. "Transgender History, Homonormativity, and Disciplinarity." *Radical History Review* 2008, no. 100 (2008): 145–57.

Suzuki, Masao. "Important or Impotent? Taking Another Look at the 1920 California Alien Land Law." *Journal of Economic History* 64, no. 1 (March 2004): 130–31.

Takaki, Ronald. *Strangers from a Different Shore: A History of Asians in America.* Boston: Little Brown, 1989.

Talbot, Christine. *A Foreign Kingdom: Mormons and Polygamy in American Political Culture, 1852–1890.* Chicago: University of Illinois Press, 2013.

Talbot, Christine. "'Turkey Is in Our Midst': Orientalism and Contagion in Nineteenth Century Anti-Mormonism." *Journal of Law and Family Studies* 8 (2006): 363–88.

Tallie, T. J. *Queering Colonial Natal: Indigeneity and the Violence of Belonging in Southern Africa.* Minneapolis: University of Minnesota Press, 2019.

Talmage, T. De Witt. *The Brooklyn Tabernacle: A Collection of 104 Sermons.* New York: Funk & Wagnalls, 1884.

Taylor, Keeanga-Yamahtta. *From #BlackLivesMatter to Black Liberation.* Chicago: Haymarket Books, 2016.

Thornton, Russell. *American Indian Holocaust and Survival: A Population History since 1492.* Norman: University of Oklahoma Press, 1987.

Tiryakian, Edward A. "American Religious Exceptionalism: A Reconsideration." In "Religion in the Nineties," special issue of *Annals of American Academy of Political and Social Science* 527 (May 1993): 40–54.

Tisby, Jemar. *The Color of Compromise: The Truth about the American Church's Complicity in Racism.* Grand Rapids, Mich.: Zondervan, 2018.

Tompkins, Jane. *Sensational Designs: The Cultural Work of American Fiction, 1790–1860.* New York: Oxford University Press, 1985.

Tuckett, Holly, and Kendall Wilcox, dirs. *Church & State.* Blue Fox Entertainment and Quadrille Film Production, 2018.

Turner, Frederick Jackson. "The Significance of the Frontier in American History." Address delivered at the 41st Annual Meeting of the State Historical Society of Wisconsin, December 14, 1893. https://babel.hathitrust.org/cgi/pt?id=wu.89069486553&view=1up&seq=1&skin=2021.

Tuttle, Leslie. *Conceiving the Old Regime: Pronatalism and the Politics of Reproduction in Early Modern France.* Oxford: Oxford University Press, 2010.

Tyrrell, Ian. "American Exceptionalism in an Age of International History." *American Historical Review* 96 (October 1991): 1,031–71.

Ulrich, Laurel Thatcher. *A House Full of Females: Plural Marriage and Women's Rights in Early Mormonism, 1835–1870.* New York: Vintage Books, 2017.

Umbach, Greg (Fritz). "Learning to Shop in Zion: The Consumer Revolution in Great Basin Mormon Culture, 1847–1910." *Journal of Social History* 38, no. 1 (Autumn 2004): 24–61.

U.S. News and World Report. "No Flag-Burning at Brigham Young: A University without Trouble." January 20, 1969, 58–59.

Van Wagenen, Lola. "In Their Own Behalf: The Politicization of Mormon Women and the 1870 Franchise." *Dialogue: A Journal of Mormon Thought* 24 (Winter 1991): 31–43.

Wald, Kenneth D., and Allison Calhoun-Brown. *Religion and Politics in the United States.* Lanham, Md.: Rowman & Littlefield, 2011.

Walker, David. *Railroading Religion: Mormons, Tourists, and the Corporate Spirit of the West.* Chapel Hill: University of North Carolina Press, 2019.

Watson, Blake A. *Buying America from the Indians: "Johnson v. McIntosh" and the History of Native Land Rights.* Norman: University of Oklahoma Press, 2012.

Weber, Brenda R. *Latter-day Screens: Gender, Sexuality, and Mediated Mormonism.* Durham, N.C.: Duke University Press, 2019.

Weheliye, Alexander G. *Habeas Viscus: Racializing Assemblages, Biopolitics, and Black Feminist Theories of the Human.* Durham, N.C.: Duke University Press, 2014.

Welke, Barbara. *Law and the Borders of Belonging in the Long Nineteenth-Century United States.* New York: Cambridge University Press, 2010.

Welter, Barbara. "The Cult of True Womanhood: 1820–1860." *American Quarterly* 18, no. 2, part 1 (Summer 1966): 151–74.

Wenger, Tisa. *Religious Freedom: The Contested History of an American Ideal.* Chapel Hill: University of North Carolina Press, 2017.

Werner, Maggie. "Reaping the Bloody Harvest: 'Don't Ask, Don't Tell' and the US Imperial Project." *Feminist Formations* 26, no. 1 (Spring 2014): 93–114.

West, Traci C. "The Policing of Poor Black Women's Reproduction." In *Religion and Sex in American Public Life,* edited by Kathleen M. Sands, 135–54. Oxford: Oxford University Press, 2000.

White, Jean Brickmore. "Women's Place Is in the Constitution: The Struggle for Equal Rights in Utah in 1895." *Utah Historical Quarterly* 42, no. 4 (Fall 1974): 34–59.

White, Richard. *"It's Your Misfortune and None of My Own": A New History of the American West.* Norman: University of Oklahoma Press, 1991.

White, Richard. *The Middle Ground: Indians, Empires, and Republics in the Great Lake Region, 1650–1815.* Cambridge: Cambridge University Press, 1991.

Whitney, Orson F. *History of Utah.* Salt Lake City: George Q. Cannon & Sons, 1893. https://www.google.com/books/edition/_/Gi5IAQAAMAAJ?hl=en&gbpv=0.

Widstoe, John A. "Evidences and Reconciliations: IV. Why Are the Latter-day Saints a Peculiar People?" *Improvement Era,* September 1, 1942, 577.

Wilcox, Melissa A. "Outlaws or In-Laws? Queer Theory, LGBT Studies, and Religious Studies." In *LGBT Studies and Queer Theory: New Conflicts, Collaborations, and Contested Terrain,* edited by Karen E. Lovaas, John P. Elia, and Gust A. Yep, 73–100. Binghamton, N.Y.: Harrington Park Press, 2006.

Wing, Adrien Katherine, ed. *Critical Race Feminism: A Reader.* 2nd ed. New York: New York University Press, 2003.

Winkler, Douglas A. "Lavender Sons of Zion: A History of Gay Men in Salt Lake City, 1950–1979." PhD diss., University of Utah, May 2008.

Witgen, Michael. "A Nation of Settlers: The Early American Republic and the Colonization of the Northwest Territory." *William and Mary Quarterly* 76, no. 3 (July 2019): 391–98.

Wolfe, Patrick. "Settler Colonialism and the Elimination of the Native." *Journal of Genocide Research* 8, no. 4 (2006): 387–409.

Wood, Gordon. "Evangelical America and Early Mormonism." *New York History* 61, no. 4 (October 1980): 359–86.

Young, Ann Eliza. *Wife No. 19, or The Story of a Life in Bondage, Being a Complete Exposé of Mormonism, and Revealing the Sorrows, Sacrifices, and Sufferings of Women in Polygamy.* Hartford, Conn.: Dustin, Gilman, & Co., 1875.

Young, Neil J. "Fascinating and Happy: Mormon Women, the LDS Church, and the Politics of Sexual Conservatism." In *Devotions and Desires: Histories of Sexuality and Religion in the Twentieth-Century United States,* edited by Gillian Frank, Bethany Moreton, and Heather R. White, 193–213. Chapel Hill: University of North Carolina Press, 2018.

Zakim, Michael, and Gary J. Kornblith. *Capitalism Takes Command: The Social Transformation of Nineteenth-Century America.* Chicago: University of Chicago Press, 2011.

Index

Dalton, Clyde, 246
Dart, John, 363n109
Davidson, Glen W., 244–45
Davis, Kim, 373n66
Davison, Jacquie, 259
Dawes Act (General Allotment/Dawes
   Severalty Act) (1887), 137, 141, 337n106
DeBow's Review, 69
Defense of Marriage Act, 271
degeneration, 31, 99, 173, 182, 203; racial,
   4, 31, 33–34, 35, 36, 68, 71, 100, 117–18,
   139, 154, 167, 282
*Delusions: An Analysis of the Book of
   Mormon* (Campbell), 27
democracy, 88, 109, 110, 112, 141, 174,
   307–8, 318n34, 333n38; fostering, 91,
   334n41; free enterprise and, 188;
   multicultural, 15
Denver Post, 213, 245, 251, 254, 261, 266
desegregation, 212–13, 219, 307
Deseret: State of, 51; term, 327n12
Deseret News, 191, 208, 212–13, 239, 244,
   262
*Desperate Attempt to Solve the Mormon
   Question, A* (Keppler), 132
despotism, 4, 77, 85, 98, 122–23, 138, 139,
   276, 282
Devens, Charles, 120
Diagnostic and Statistical Manual,
   364n126
Dialogue, "Pink" issue of, 365n150
discrimination, 230, 243, 285, 288, 292,
   298; racist, 90, 159, 161, 207, 211, 219,
   220, 222, 229, 233, 237–38, 241, 242, 252,
   253, 255, 257, 307, 265, 352n69; religious, 274–79; sexual, 291
divorce, 182, 184, 260, 295, 334n48
Dixon, Hepworth, 81, 82
Doctrine and Covenants, 321n9, 338n135;
   Section 132 of, 38–41
domesticity, 42, 55, 60, 66; cult of, 37, 39,
   58–59, 61–62, 74, 169, 329n34
Doxey, Roy W., 219
Drury, Allen, 225

Due Process Clause, 275, 280, 281, 284,
   296, 299

Easter Islanders, 120
Eaton, Lloyd W., 250, 251, 361n83
economic conditions, 77, 189, 190, 283
economic development, 42, 178
economic planning, 156, 188
economic policy, 77, 189, 337n115
economic system, 7–8, 82, 83, 136, 138,
   140, 190; cooperative, 24, 74, 195
economy, 11, 73, 74, 75, 76, 81, 82, 181,
   202, 217, 268; barter, 189; capitalist,
   18, 85, 138, 188; communal, 189;
   industrial, 100; national, 78, 83, 90,
   136, 164, 188; political, 25, 42–44, 141
Edmunds, George, 133, 142
Edmunds Act (Edmunds Anti-Polygamy
   Act) (1882), 133, 134, 135, 137, 140, 141,
   142, 160, 337n95
Edmunds–Tucker Act (1887), 141, 142,
   144, 160, 342n49
education, 169, 170, 243, 247; Indigenous,
   226–27, 229; interracial, 229; sex, 259;
   women and, 175, 176
Edwards, Harry, 247, 251
Elder Northfield's Home (Bartlett), 102
electric shock therapy, 225, 371n22
Elizabeth I, 6
Emery, George W., 115
empire, 11, 115, 293, 327n17; Black
   religion and, 318n34; era of, 83–84;
   Reynolds and, 117–21, 123, 125–26,
   132–37; U.S., 7, 46, 50, 53, 85, 86, 87,
   89, 108, 116, 139, 161, 202–3, 283–84,
   301, 306, 308, 370n10; theology and,
   208
Enabling Act (1894), 148, 371n34
Eng, David, 291, 292, 298
Epstein, Barbara, 41
equality, 112, 169, 234, 241, 301;
   economic, 42; gender, 174, 175–66,
   177, 178, 179, 194, 197, 258, 259; racial,
   213, 278

K . M O H R M A N is clinical teaching track assistant professor of ethnic studies at the University of Colorado Denver.